THE CASUALTY GAP

THE CASUALTY GAP

The Causes and Consequences of American Wartime Inequalities

Douglas L. Kriner
Francis X. Shen

UNIVERSITY PRESS
2010

OXFORD
UNIVERSITY PRESS

Oxford University Press, Inc., publishes works that further
Oxford University's objective of excellence
in research, scholarship, and education.

Oxford New York
Auckland Cape Town Dar es Salaam Hong Kong Karachi
Kuala Lumpur Madrid Melbourne Mexico City Nairobi
New Delhi Shanghai Taipei Toronto

With offices in
Argentina Austria Brazil Chile Czech Republic France Greece
Guatemala Hungary Italy Japan Poland Portugal Singapore
South Korea Switzerland Thailand Turkey Ukraine Vietnam

Copyright © 2010 by Oxford University Press, Inc.

Published by Oxford University Press, Inc.
198 Madison Avenue, New York, New York 10016

www.oup.com

Oxford is a registered trademark of Oxford University Press

Library of Congress Cataloging-in-Publication Data
Kriner, Douglas L.
The casualty gap : the causes and consequences of American
wartime inequalities / Douglas L. Kriner, Francis X. Shen.
    p. cm.
Includes bibliographical references and index.
ISBN: 978-0-19-539096-4
1. War and society—United States.   2. War casualties—United States.
3. Battle casualties—United States.   I. Shen, Francis X.   II. Title.
HM554.K77 2010
303.6'608694097309045—dc22   2009028230

9 8 7 6 5 4 3 2 1

Printed in the United States of America
on acid-free paper

To all those who have given their lives in defense of our nation.

Preface

This book argues that when we calculate the human costs of war, we must think about both the number of soldiers killed *and* the distribution of American combat deaths. We should acknowledge the possibility of a "casualty gap"—a disparity in the concentration of wartime casualties among communities at different points on the socioeconomic ladder.

Introducing the casualty gap into our discussions of U.S. military policy will serve to reinvigorate debate over the nation's long-held norm of equal sacrifice in war. Moreover, the potential policy implications of open recognition and honest discussion of the casualty gap are both significant and widespread. As seen in original survey experiments, which are discussed in the book, when Americans are explicitly made aware of the potential inequality implications of military policy, they drastically change their military policy preferences. The results suggest that if Americans know that soldiers who die come disproportionately from poorer parts of the country, they are much less willing to accept large numbers of casualties in future military endeavors.

While knowledge of the casualty gap is one way in which the gap affects public opinion, we show in this book that there is also an alternative pathway. When a soldier dies, it is not only the soldier's family but also the soldier's community that suffers. Because of the casualty gap, some Americans see clearly the full human toll of combat, while others from communities that suffer fewer casualties are relatively insulated from battle deaths. Such disparities in local casualty rates can significantly influence citizens' military policy preferences and political behaviors. Moreover, the concentration of war casualties in poor communities has significant consequences for politics, policy, and the vibrancy of the American democratic system.

Over the course of nine chapters, we support our claims with extensive empirical analysis. In chapters 2 and 3 we probe whether a casualty gap actually exists and, if so, why. We analyze the home of record for virtually every soldier killed in World War II, Korea, Vietnam, and Iraq. Using this database and integrating it with demographic data from multiple years of the U.S. census, we conduct empirical analysis at the county and place levels to uncover inequalities in the geographic distribution of combat casualties across America. While modest casualty gaps emerged in World War II, beginning with the Korean War we find strong evidence of substantial casualty gaps emerging along socioeconomic lines.

We then identify and discuss two mechanisms most likely to have produced the casualty gaps observed in each of the four wars. First, the process through which some young men and women enter military service while others do not is clearly an important factor that could produce casualty gaps. Military and independent analysts alike have long recognized that among the many factors that influence an individual's decision to enlist, economic incentives are particularly important. Once enlisted, a second process to note is that of occupational assignment within the military itself. If, on average, individuals from counties that are worse off socioeconomically bring to the military fewer *ex ante* educational and occupational skills, then it is more likely that these soldiers may find themselves in roles that increase their proximity to combat. These mechanisms suggest that an individual-level casualty gap underlies those observed between socioeconomically advantaged and disadvantaged communities. Although data limitations prevent us from testing this claim directly, through a series of original analyses using newly integrated data sets we amass considerable indirect empirical evidence that the most plausible explanation for differences in community casualty rates—and the one most consistent with the data—is that a parallel gap exists between rich and poor individuals.

The argument that America's wars are fought disproportionately by those from communities at the lower end of the socioeconomic spectrum is, of course, not a new one. In 1862 Confederate soldier Stephen W. Rutledge lamented, "What is gained anyway? It is a rich man's war and a poor man's fight."[1] Protesters in 1863 popularized Rutledge's phrase, "Rich man's war, poor man's fight," as they objected to the commutation clause in the Enrollment Act of 1863, which allowed drafted men to buy their way out of service for $300.[2] Similar rhetoric is still seen in the popular press. In August of 2005 *New York Times* columnist Bob Herbert, reflecting on a new round of U.S. military deaths in Iraq, wrote: "For the most part, the only people sacrificing for this war are the troops and their families, and very few of them are coming from the privileged economic classes."[3]

What is new in our book is not the *claim* that inequality is tied to wartime death but the *evidence* we present to support it. As empirically grounded political scientists, we were surprised to note that Herbert, writing in 2005, had only a handful more studies available to cite on inequalities in combat casualties than did Rutledge, when he wrote his war diaries more than a century earlier. Despite a proliferation of literature on inequality, political scientists have largely failed to address this fundamental question about the distribution of casualties across socioeconomic classes, racial divides, and other social cleavages.

After documenting the casualty gap and exploring its causes, we next investigate its immediate ramifications for American politics. The existence of a casualty gap concentrates the costs of war in some communities while insulating many others from direct local experience of the consequences of the nation's military policies. We thus explore how the opinions, policy preferences, and electoral behaviors of residents of high-casualty communities diverge significantly from those of their fellow citizens from low-casualty communities.

We also show for the first time that wartime deaths may have lasting consequences for civic engagement and political participation. It is striking that, despite the large amount of scholarship on civic engagement in the United States—even on war and civic engagement—specific links between battle casualties and levels of political and civic participation have not been established. Our book covers new ground as it provides strong empirical evidence from multiple sources that, years after the last gun falls silent, the casualty gap continues to affect the richness of democracy in America by depressing political engagement and participation in communities that sacrificed disproportionately in service to the nation on foreign battlefields.

When we started this project as graduate students in 2004, we thought we were setting out to spend a summer writing a short article. We expected to find much written on the topic of inequalities and war casualties. As we soon learned, however, the issue of casualties and inequality has only rarely been studied quantitatively. A small collection of studies focusing primarily on Vietnam casualties comprises most of the empirical scholarship. These studies generally failed to compare across wars, and the empirical methods they employed were not consistent. A parallel lacuna in the extant literature that we encountered was a dearth of theoretical research into the forces that cause casualty inequalities to emerge and that produce changes in them over time.

As political scientists, we were also concerned that inequalities in the distribution of wartime casualties might have both immediate and lingering consequences for American political and civic life. Again, we found serious limitations in existing theory and empirical scholarship. Too often, analysts and scholars alike have conceptualized wartime "casualties" as a monolithic event that affects all Americans in the same way. As the second half of our book shows, this approach to casualties is severely misleading. Treating casualties as such misses the significant variance in citizens' exposure to the costs of war from community to community. Indeed, this variance is critical to understanding the more nuanced ways in which wartime casualties affect the public's evaluation of its leaders, military policy preferences, and electoral decisions. Moreover, we show that the parts of America that bore the greatest war casualty burdens in Korea and Vietnam have experienced depressed political engagement and participation in both the short and long term. The effects of wartime casualties are much greater and more varied than previously thought.

Our hope is that this book will provide an objective, empirical basis for engaging in new discussion and debate about inequality and casualties. Our goal is to provide readers with the most comprehensive empirical analysis of the casualty gap to date—its scope, causes, and consequences. To implement our research plan, we draw on a large number of data sets, statistical analyses, and illustrative examples. For readers who wish to examine the details of the statistical models, we include a series of technical appendices. For the general readership, we have attempted to translate the statistical results into easily understood figures and summary tables.

We recognize that the ensuing debate will necessarily intersect with partisan and political positions. We hope, however, that these debates will be grounded in fact, not rhetoric. Regardless of the controversy that a frank recognition and discussion of the casualty gap will inevitably engender, it is time for America to enter the casualty gap debate. We hope that our analysis is a starting point for further discussion among citizens, scholars, and politicians alike. At our website, www.casualtygap.com, we invite readers to join in this dialogue and debate. In order to have an informed debate about specific policy responses, however, we must first come to a consensus about the contours of the casualty gap and its consequences. We hope the empirical analysis in this book moves us closer to that consensus.

Acknowledgments

We are indebted to a large number of individuals and institutions who made this project possible.

For instructive comments, reviews, and feedback we thank Jamie Druckman, Benjamin Fordham, John Gerring, Dan Hopkins, Mike Horowitz, Will Howell, Mark Jeunnette, Michael Koch, Cathie Martin, Ryan Moore, Andrew Reeves, Christine Rossell, Theda Skocpol, and Graham Wilson; seminar participants at the University of Chicago, Harvard University, the American Political Science Association and Midwest Political Science Association; and our anonymous reviewers.

For assistance in fielding our survey experiments, we thank Janet Ulrich at Opinion Research Corporation. For help with obtaining casualty data, we thank Janice Ramseur of the Office of the Assistant Secretary of Defense for Public Affairs.

We thank everyone at Oxford University Press for their support of this project. We are especially grateful to our editor, Dave McBride, for his guidance from the start, and to Alexandra Dauler, Paul Hobson, and Carol Hoke for their help in seeing the manuscript through the production process.

Doug wishes to thank both Boston University and the Center for American Political Studies at Harvard University for their generous financial support of this project. Francis recognizes that his research has been supported by the NSF-IGERT program "Multidisciplinary Program in Inequality & Social Policy" at Harvard University (Grant No. 9870661). Francis would also like to thank John Paul Shen for constant support and insightful comments, and Kenneth Wong and Jennifer Hochschild for their support and mentoring. Both authors note that this work is *Ad Maiorem Dei Gloriam*.

We owe special debts to several individuals who have given generously of their time. We thank Liam Schwartz for dutifully reading drafts and listening to us talk about this project amidst baseball and breakfast. We thank our parents, Gary and Debbie Kriner and Jerome Shen and Bridget Brennan, for their many years of love and support. Their investment in our education and encouragement for our academic endeavors have made this book possible.

Finally, we thank Jillian Goldfarb and Sophia Beal. They read every draft, heard every idea, and offered insightful feedback, which greatly improved the manuscript. Even more importantly, we could not have completed this book were it not for Jill and Sophie's tireless love and cheerful support amidst the many hours we devoted to the project. They have our love and deepest gratitude.

Contents

THE CASUALTY GAP

1

The Casualty Gap

When we contemplate the costs of war, we instinctively focus on the human element. In the Gettysburg Address, Abraham Lincoln famously described the sacrifice of fallen soldiers as "the last full measure of devotion" as he sought to reassure a war-ravaged nation that the principles for which its men fought and died justified their sacrifice. Other politicians before and since have similarly kept the human toll of war foremost in their minds when guiding the ship of state in wartime.[1] This emphasis on war's human costs by political elites is further reinforced by the mass media. Contemporary coverage of the war in Iraq continues to report the names of the fallen, just as newspapers did during the Civil War almost 150 years ago. Recognizing this critical importance of wartime casualties, scholars in various disciplines have long endeavored to understand how combat deaths shape public opinion, political outcomes, and policymaking. However, when attempting to measure these costs of war, academics, politicians, and the media alike all too often do so in the same way: by simply adding up the numbers. The analysis in this book challenges the conventional view that the human costs of war can be understood as a single, aggregate total.[2]

To account fully for the costs of war we must consider not only the overall number of casualties but also how this sacrifice has been shared.[3] Consider South Carolina's experience with the war in Iraq. As of

December 2008 the Palmetto State had lost sixty-five of its citizens in Iraq. Three of these sixty-five were from Orangeburg, a small town of 13,000, in which almost a quarter of the population lives below the poverty line, more than double the state average. By contrast, the resort town of Hilton Head, which has a population almost triple that of Orangeburg and a median family income more than double, had suffered no casualties. Charleston, South Carolina's second largest city, with a population of just under 100,000, had suffered only one casualty.[4] Certainly, South Carolina's war experience is suggestive of significant inequalities in sacrifice among rich and poor communities.

Yet, simple examples such as this are incomplete. In this book we move beyond anecdotes and engage in rigorous empirical investigation of the casualty gap—the unequal distribution of wartime casualties across America's communities—in four wars: World War II, Korea, Vietnam, and Iraq. Drawing on publicly available military records for almost every fallen soldier, we document empirically that, when Americans fight and die for our nation, a casualty gap of some sort has always emerged. Although the contours of this gap have changed significantly over time, beginning with the Korean War casualty gaps have consistently emerged along socioeconomic lines. Communities with lower levels of income, educational attainment, and economic opportunities have paid a disproportionate share of the human costs of war.[5]

The existence of a casualty gap stands in direct contradiction to long-standing democratic norms of equality in military sacrifice. Reaching back to antiquity, there was a presumption that in a democracy military sacrifice should be shared by all of the citizenry. For example, in his funeral oration during the Peloponnesian War, the great Athenian Pericles exhorted his fellow citizens to have more children, in part because he believed that only those with a direct stake in the outcome of military affairs can craft the wisest policy course: "Never can a fair or just policy be expected of the citizen who does not, like his fellows, bring to the decision the interests and apprehensions of a father."[6] This principle of shared sacrifice was openly embraced by George Washington, who proclaimed the ideal that every citizen who enjoys the rights and privileges of citizenship "owes not only a portion of his property, but even of his personal service to the defense of it."[7] More generally, Alexis de Tocqueville, in the classic 1840 treatise, *Democracy in America*, warned that the U.S. government must appeal "to the whole community at once: it is the unequal distribution of the weight, not the weight itself, which commonly occasions resistance."[8] Whether America's experience in recent wars has matched this ideal is intrinsically of great importance.

It is also important to examine the often overlooked ramifications of the casualty gap for politics and policymaking. Since the Vietnam War, a burgeoning literature at the nexus of American politics and international relations has examined the influence of combat casualties on a diverse range of political phenomena. Political scientists typically view war casualties, or the anticipation of them, as an independent variable to explain outcomes such as: presidential approval; popular assessments of military campaigns more generally; electoral results; and even the propensity of democracies to go to war.[9] However, most of these analyses focus only on the raw *number* of casualties and pay little attention to their *distribution*.[10] This is problematic because inequality in sacrifice also has the potential to influence dramatically politics, policymaking, and the fabric of American democracy itself.

After documenting the casualty gap and investigating the forces that create it, in chapters 4 through 8 we explore two pathways through which the casualty gap has important political ramifications. First, because inequality in combat deaths conflicts with the dominant national norm of shared sacrifice, knowledge of a casualty gap can affect all Americans' support for military endeavors. Whether the nation's wartime sacrifices meet this norm of equality can critically shape Americans' opinions and political behaviors. In this way, the casualty gap is a cost of war every bit as concrete as the actual number of casualties in a given conflict. As a result, we argue that existing scholarship presents an incomplete picture of how combat casualties may influence American politics.

The second pathway explores the political consequences that follow from some Americans experiencing death more directly and acutely in their communities than others. Most prior analyses implicitly assume that war and combat casualties are monolithic events that affect all segments of society equally. However, as our analysis in chapter 2 unambiguously demonstrates, war casualties are neither uniformly nor randomly distributed across society. This uneven exposure of citizens to the costs of war through the lens of their local communities raises the distinct possibility that battle deaths affect some Americans differently than others. As a result, the relationships between war deaths and various political phenomena are considerably more complex and contingent than acknowledged by most prior research.[11] Once inequalities are acknowledged, the dominant paradigm linking casualties, domestic political pressures, and democratic constraints on military policymakers requires some amendment. To understand fully the nexus between casualties and political outcomes and democratic constraints on military policymakers, we must explicitly recognize the fact that not all segments of society experience casualties equally.

Toward this end, we must explore the fault lines along which these inequalities routinely emerge.

To assess the first pathway—the effects of learning about the casualty gap on Americans' beliefs and policy preferences—we conducted two experiments, as detailed in chapter 4. In fall 2007 we asked a nationally representative sample of more than 1,000 Americans to evaluate a possible future American invasion of Iran. We randomly assigned individuals to one of three groups. Each group was first told the number of American casualties to date suffered in Iraq. But at this point we varied the interpretive frame for understanding this number. The first group was not given any additional information. The second was told that this wartime sacrifice has been shared by rich and poor communities alike. Finally, the third group was told that America's poor communities have suffered significantly higher casualty rates than the nation's rich communities. The subjects were then asked how many casualties they would be willing to accept in a future military mission to halt Iran's nuclear program and stop the infiltration of Iranian-backed forces into Iraq.[12]

The results of this experiment, confirmed by a similar follow-up experiment in spring 2009, were clear and resounding: when Americans learn about the casualty gap, they are much more cautious in supporting costly conflicts. In our fall 2007 experiment, the average reported number of acceptable casualties in the Iran scenario was *40 percent* lower among individuals who were told about inequality in the Iraq War than among their peers who were merely informed of the number of casualties suffered thus far in Iraq. Conversely, individuals who were assured that the ideal of equality was being met were actually willing to accept a higher number of deaths than respondents in the control group. The evidence is clear: Americans cherish the norm of shared sacrifice, and they factor the casualty gap into their support for war efforts.

To assess the second pathway—the effects of differential exposure to the costs of war through local community lenses on Americans' opinions and political behaviors—we conducted multiple empirical analyses with data from the Korean, Vietnam, and Iraq wars. Across analyses we find that those who live in communities with higher casualty rates hold systematically different opinions and exhibit different political behaviors than their peers from communities more shielded from the human costs of war. The emergence of such cleavages has significant implications for public opinion formation and for the political pressures brought to bear on military policymakers. Finally, we find strong evidence that the casualty gap may have lingering negative consequences for the vibrancy of American democracy. Extensive empirical evidence shows that citizens from high-casualty communities are disproportionately likely to sour on their government and withdraw from political life. As a result, levels of civic and political engagement are depressed, and a feedback loop emerges: the populations with the most to lose in war become those communities with the least to say to their elected officials.

THE POLITICS OF CASUALTIES

Given the casualty gap's normative and political importance, the dearth of attention it has received from scholars is perhaps surprising. A small number of prior studies have sought to analyze whether American war deaths are disproportionately borne by socioeconomically disadvantaged communities.[13] However, existing studies on casualty inequalities have been limited in scope with mixed results.

The media, too, has largely avoided engaging in detailed and sustained discussion of the casualty gap. In some cases, isolated journalists and news outlets have tackled the question of casualty inequality. For example, in October of 2003 the *Austin American-Statesman* conducted an independent analysis of 300 casualties from the war in Iraq. These soldiers, the article reported, disproportionately came from small, rural communities with below-average levels of income and educational attainment.[14] However, *Lexis Nexis* searches of hundreds of major U.S. newspapers and television news transcripts reveal that such stories are the exception to the rule of Iraq War coverage by both the print and the broadcast media.[15]

Moreover, even when the popular press does engage the inequality issue, the conventional wisdom it offers is often mistaken. For example, when the *American-Statesman* asked whether similar disparities in combat deaths existed in the Vietnam War the associate director of the Vietnam Center at Texas Tech University, Steven Maxner, replied, "I don't think so. During the war in Southeast Asia, you had the draft."[16] As we show in the empirical analyses in the next chapter, this speculation is not correct. A significant socioeconomic casualty gap emerged in both the Korean and the Vietnam wars. Others argue that changes in military manpower policies in the 1960s made Vietnam the first "working-class war."[17] For example, in their book *AWOL: The Unexcused Absence of America's Upper Classes from Military Service and How It Hurts Our Country*, Kathy Roth-Douquet and Frank Schaeffer argue that the change in service patterns "has everything to do with the Vietnam war."[18] Our analysis shows that this claim, too, is mistaken, as significant casualty gaps also emerged in the Korean War. In short, the dearth of scholarly research on the casualty gap has led to misperceptions about the nature of inequality and military sacrifice.

Finally, with but a few exceptions—such as Representative Charles Rangel's (D-NY) repeated calls for the reinstatement of a draft—politicians have also been reluctant to raise the specter of a casualty gap, directly or indirectly. Even hinting at a casualty gap in public discourse remains taboo. Anecdotal evidence of this taboo comes from a botched joke told by Senator John Kerry (D-MA). Speaking to students at Pasadena City College in October 2006, Kerry said, "You know, education—if you make the most of it, you study hard, and you do your homework, and you make an effort to be smart, you can do well. If you don't, you get stuck in Iraq."[19] The ensuing chorus of criticism of Kerry's comments came from both Democrats and Republicans. Fellow Democrat Harold Ford, who was running for the U.S. Senate in Tennessee, commented that "Whatever the intent, Senator Kerry was wrong to say what he said."[20] White House spokesman Tony Snow called Kerry's statement "an absolute insult" and said that "Senator Kerry not only owes an apology to those who are serving but also to the families of those who've given their lives in this."[21] Lost amid the verbal firestorm was the empirical question, is there a real, not just rhetorical, relationship between socioeconomics and casualty rates? Was Senator Kerry's joke simply a tasteless faux pas with no grounding in reality, or did the reaction to his comments reveal a more fundamental hesitance to face up to inequality in military sacrifice? Rather than engage in a public debate grounded in data, most policymakers and media pundits alike were happy to let the story slide.

Why are questions of the casualty gap so often relegated to the periphery of public, political, and academic discourse? Part of the answer is that casualties and information concerning them are inherently political. The politics of casualties has a long history that extends back to the world's earliest conflicts. Since ancient times, governments have seen benefits in withholding casualty data from the public. For the Spartans in ancient Greece, information about force sizes and casualties sustained were tightly-held state secrets.[22] A similar politics of casualties has characterized more recent conflicts with the result that even official histories have sometimes consciously blotted casualties out of the story.[23]

An important consideration in the politics of casualties is that the release, or withholding, of casualty data involves strategic calculations about what message the data may send to both one's own nation and to the enemy. As historian Alfred Vagts states, "While a war is on, publication of one's own casualties, with indications about time and place, which *per se* would be at the disposal of the ministries of war or similar statistical agencies, might be of considerable aid and comfort to the enemy and might help him to judge the other side's remaining and available strength."[24] Casualties may also influence domestic political debates, which in turn can send important signals to foreign actors about the government's willingness to stay the course.[25] This has further encouraged politicians to mask casualty data; for example, when losses started to mount for the Germans after 1942 in World War II, the Nazi government simply stopped releasing its casualty figures.

The United States has long been a leader in the timely dissemination of casualty data to the public.[26] For example, in World War I, the Senate Committee on Military Affairs called to task the Secretary of War and urged him to release full casualty information to the public as expeditiously as possible.[27] This dedication to providing accurate, timely casualty information continued throughout World War II and later conflicts, and technological developments over the course of the twentieth century have made possible rapid and accurate dissemination of such data.

However, recent history makes clear that a revised politics of casualties continues to exist. Confronted with a widespread belief that the American public will not tolerate large numbers of American casualties, contemporary policymakers have gone to considerable lengths to manage carefully the way in which casualty information is presented to the public.[28] Government reporting about the extent of non-fatal casualties, as well as mental illness resulting from combat service, has not been wholly transparent. Members of Congress, recognizing the need for a more complete accounting of the human costs of war, challenged the George W. Bush administration to release more information. On December 7, 2005, seven members of Congress wrote to President Bush to request that his administration "provide the American people with a full accounting of the American casualties in Iraq since the March 19, 2003, invasion, including a full accounting of the fatalities, the wounded, those who have contracted illnesses during their time overseas, and those suffering from mental afflictions as a result of their service in Operation Iraqi Freedom and Operation Enduring Freedom." The Congressmen were concerned that existing data, which was incomplete with regards to the breadth of the human costs, did "not accurately represent the true toll that this war has taken on the American people."[29]

Government control of the visibility of U.S. casualties in the mass media has also sparked political debate. The George W. Bush administration enforced a policy that prohibited media coverage of deceased military personnel returning to the Ramstein, Germany, or Dover, Delaware, bases.[30] Reaction to the decision was mixed, but public opinion favored media coverage of the coffins. When a national poll asked, "Should the public be allowed to see pictures of the coffins arriving in the United States?" it found that 62 percent responded "yes," whereas only 27 percent responded "no."[31] The administration argued that this change in policy was not a strategic choice but a recognition of the intensely personal and private dimension of a soldier's death. White House spokesman Trent Duffy stated that "We must pay attention to the privacy and to the sensitivity of the families of the fallen, and that's what the policy is based on and that has to be the utmost concern." However, in response, Navy veteran and U.S. Representative Jim McDermott (D-WA) argued, "This is not about privacy. This is about trying to keep the country from facing the reality of war."[32]

In February 2009, the Obama administration announced a change in this policy. Secretary of Defense Robert Gates explained that "media coverage of the dignified transfer process at Dover should be made by those most directly affected: on an individual basis by the families of the fallen. We ought not presume to make that decision in their place."[33] When asked about the political motivations of the original ban, Secretary Gates declined to speculate.

The multifaceted politics of casualties thus goes a long way toward explaining the relative lack of public, political, and academic discourse on the casualty gap. Many in government have a keen interest in reducing the visibility of casualties for fear that greater public exposure will minimize their freedom of action. And any who wade into the debate run the risk of a swift and strong political backlash. Nevertheless, only by examining the casualty gap can we truly assess the full costs of war.

PLAN OF THE BOOK

In the following eight chapters we explore the causes and consequences of the casualty gap from World War II through Iraq.[34] The statistical analyses in these chapters provide convincing proof that casualty inequalities are real and persistent and that these gaps have significant effects on public support for war and political behavior. While the statistical reality we uncover does not lead directly to neatly packaged policy responses, we should recognize that communities with less are sacrificing more.

In chapter 2 we marshal an extensive array of quantitative data to document the existence of casualty gaps in each of the four wars. However, the contours of these gaps have changed dramatically over time. Although we do find evidence of several modest casualty gaps in World War II, it is in Korea that the data show a dramatic change: strong, significant, socioeconomic casualty gaps begin to emerge. The data continue to show strong evidence of casualty gaps between high- and low-income and education communities in Vietnam and Iraq, and, on some metrics, these gaps appear to have widened over time.

Why do these casualty gaps exist? In chapter 3 we explore the capacity of two mechanisms to explain the casualty gaps that emerged in each of the four wars: selection into the armed forces and occupational assignment within the military. Selection mechanisms capture the complex mix of volunteering, active military recruitment, and conscription policies that shape the composition of the military. Occupational assignment mechanisms capture the process through which the military assigns some recruits to positions with high risks of combat exposure and others to occupations with considerably lower combat risks. Changes in these selection and assignment policies over time help explain both variance in the nature of the casualty gaps observed across wars and even, in the case of Vietnam, temporal changes in the casualty gap within a single conflict.

Our emphasis on selection and assignment mechanisms and their critical role in casualty gap formation stands in marked contrast to polemics contending that the casualty gap is the result of generational differences in patriotism, Vietnam, or the rise of individualism. Rather, changes in the operation of these policy mechanisms, not in individual citizens' willingness to serve, best explain the variance in casualty gaps we observe.

The prominence of the socioeconomic casualty gaps observed in chapters 2 and 3 raises questions about the ways in which a casualty gap might influence public opinion and policymaking. In chapters 4 and 5 we identify two pathways by which the casualty gap affects opinion and political behavior. The first pathway posits that mere awareness of the casualty gap may cause Americans to reevaluate and adjust their military policy preferences. The second recognizes the ability of Americans' uneven exposure to the human costs of war through the lenses of their local communities—a direct result of the casualty gap—to create significant cleavages in political opinions and behaviors.

A priori it is not theoretically clear that the first pathway should produce significant effects. If Americans expect and accept that the burden of military sacrifice is not shared equally across the country when the nation goes to war, then their judgments about war efforts should not be affected by information that confirms their expectations. If, however, Americans embrace the norm of shared sacrifice, then information about the empirical reality of casualty inequality should significantly affect their military policy preferences and judgments. In chapter 4 we find that, when confronted with evidence of the casualty gap, Americans are more unlikely to support the war in Iraq and less willing to tolerate casualties in future martial endeavors.

While these experimental results are telling, they leave open questions about what happens outside of an experimental setting. Moreover, the experiments offer little insight into the ramifications of another real-world consequence of the casualty gap—that some communities experience the costs of war more acutely than others. Accordingly, in chapters 5 through 8 we investigate the second pathway: the effects of variance in local casualty rates across the country on citizens' real-life social and political behaviors.

We begin in chapter 5 with the recognition that a soldier's death marks the beginning of family and community grieving, remembrance, and response. Politicians and community leaders also take notice when one of their own falls on the battlefield. Through social networks and media coverage, the death of even a single soldier can be "experienced" by many citizens beyond just the soldier's immediate family. Accordingly, we propose and investigate three mechanisms through which local casualties may influence public opinion and political behaviors: (1) personal contact, (2) elite cues, and (3) local media. Through each of these mechanisms, Americans from high-casualty communities may form very different judgments about a war and accordingly exhibit political behaviors that differ from those of their fellow citizens from low-casualty communities.

Chapters 6, 7, and 8 test this theory by exploring both the short-term and long-term consequences of higher local casualty rates. In chapter 6 we examine variance in support for Vietnam between residents of high- and low-casualty communities. In chapter 7 we perform similar analyses in the context of Iraq. Consistent with expectations, we find that Americans who experienced the human costs of war most intensely through the lens of their local community were more likely to oppose the war, favor the withdrawal of U.S. forces, and vote against the party in power than were their peers from low-casualty communities. As a result, our empirical models suggest that if all Americans experienced the Vietnam and Iraq conflicts in the same way that residents of the hardest hit communities did, both past and recent politics could have unfolded quite differently.

In chapter 8 we extend the time horizon of our analysis to examine the lingering consequences of the casualty gap for civic engagement and political participation in the United States. Using multiple data sources at both the individual and aggregate levels, we find that citizens from communities that suffered high casualty rates in Vietnam were significantly less likely to engage in politics for years and even decades after the war than were their peers from low-casualty communities.

We conclude in chapter 9 by speculating about the future of the casualty gap. We argue that, due to advances in medical technology and the likely small scale of future conflicts, a "wounded gap" will become an increasingly important dimension of inequality that policymakers must consider. Given existing disparities in health care for veterans, a wounded gap may pose a particularly vexing challenge. Finally, whether it is deaths

or wounds, we argue that raising awareness of the gap is critically important. Because Americans factor in the inequality consequences of conflicts when they evaluate the costs of war and forge their military policy
preferences, fostering public recognition and discussion of the casualty
gap should have significant consequences for the formulation of military
policy.

It is imperative that scholars, politicians, and the media alike demys-
tify and acknowledge the empirical reality that not all parts of the country
share the burdens of war equally. The words of President John F. Kennedy
ring true when we think about the casualty gap:

> We must move on from the reassuring repetition of stale phrases
> to a new, difficult, but essential confrontation with reality. For the
> great enemy of truth is very often not the lie—deliberate, con-
> trived, and dishonest—but the myth—persistent, persuasive, and
> unrealistic. Too often we hold fast to the clichés of our forebears.
> We subject all facts to a prefabricated set of interpretations. We
> enjoy the comfort of opinion without the discomfort of thought.[35]

Our fundamental goal in this book is to challenge the myth of shared
sacrifice by looking carefully at the facts of the casualty gap and its effects
on our polity.

2

Inequality and U.S. Casualties from WWII to Iraq

On September 21, 2006, Sgt. Allan Bevington, a twenty-two-year-old combat engineer, made the ultimate sacrifice for his country when an improvised explosive device (IED) detonated in Ar Ramadi, Iraq. Sgt. Bevington hailed from Beaver Falls, a small town in western Pennsylvania. Years ago Beaver Falls was "known for its cold-drawn steel." But in recent years, "like much of the Steel Belt, it's had a decline in population and jobs."[1] The 2000 census reported that the percentage of Beaver Falls residents with a college degree was a little less than 10 percent, less than half of the national average of 25 percent. The local unemployment rate, which soared into double digits, far exceeded the average in other parts of the country, and the median household income was more than $20,000 a year less than the national average.[2] In an article published by the *Beaver County Times*, U.S. Army recruiter Sgt. 1st Class Edward G. Landry, who had recruited Bevington in high school, reflected on the reason the young soldier had enlisted. Landry recalled that for Bevington, "It was something to do with his life...There were not a lot of options there...It was a way out of Beaver Falls."[3]

How typical is Sgt. Bevington's story? How many other soldiers who have died in Iraq came from economically depressed parts of the country? Are the patterns that link community demographics and local casualty rates the same as those that emerged in previous wars? Or is the

14

contemporary conflict in Iraq different from previous American armed conflicts?

Clearly, such questions are politically explosive. They are of obvious normative importance, and they threaten a key tenet of what the great American political sociologist Seymour Martin Lipset termed the "American Creed": equality of opportunity for all citizens.[4] If citizens from socioeconomically disadvantaged communities are systematically paying a disproportionate share of the nation's wartime costs, the norm of equality of opportunity would appear illusory. As a result, when such questions rise to the fore of the national debate, they often provoke polarizing claims that are not well grounded in empirical evidence.[5]

Questions about equality in military sacrifice are almost as difficult to answer definitively as they are intrinsically important. However, by drawing on a number of databases maintained by the National Archives and the U.S. Department of Defense (DOD), we can obtain information on almost every soldier who died in World War II, Korea, Vietnam, and the current hostilities in Iraq. For each casualty, the military provides information on the soldier's home of record before entering the Armed Services. By merging this casualty information with population and other demographic data from the U.S. census, we can systematically investigate what types of communities have suffered the highest casualty rates in each of America's last four major wars. Utilizing these data, we explore the question of whether communities like Beaver Falls, which lag behind the rest of the country in terms of socioeconomic opportunity, bear a disproportionate share of the nation's sacrifice on foreign battlefields. Equally importantly, we also investigate alternate possibilities, including whether more rural communities or communities with greater percentages of racial minorities bear a disproportionate share of combat casualties. Finally, we test all of these hypotheses against the null hypothesis that there is no systematic casualty gap.

The data we present in this chapter provide strong evidence that U.S. combat casualties are not distributed uniformly across society. Beginning with the Korean War, we find that some communities, particularly those like Beaver Falls, have borne a disproportionate share of America's wartime sacrifice. The size of the differences in casualty rates between rich and poor communities may not be as great as some of the rhetoric from the Left suggests. While socioeconomically disadvantaged communities do bear disproportionately large shares of the casualty burden, some wealthy and highly educated communities have also suffered significant numbers of casualties. However, contra the protestations of some on the Right, the casualty gap is real, and, perhaps equally significantly, the data suggest that this gap may have widened over time.

STUDYING CASUALTIES AND INEQUALITY

Ours is not the first analysis to explore the question of whether U.S. combat casualties have hailed disproportionately from socioeconomically disadvantaged communities. More than sixty years ago, under the direction of sociologist Jessie Bernard, Janet Schaefer and Marjorie Allen examined the distribution of World War II casualties from St. Louis, Missouri, and searched for correlations between the number of casualties in a census tract and that tract's median rent and education levels. Perhaps surprisingly, Schaefer and Allen found little evidence of any socioeconomic casualty gap in World War II; instead, they concluded that: "No one class, as measured by economic status or by education, contributed more than its share to the war in terms of fatal casualties."[6]

In the intervening six decades, a number of studies conducted by scholars from a host of disciplinary backgrounds, including history, political science, economics, sociology, and demography, have looked for evidence of a socioeconomic casualty gap. Some have found strong evidence that socioeconomically disadvantaged communities have borne a disproportionate share of the nation's casualties. Others have yielded mixed results and uneven empirical support for assertions of a casualty gap. Still others, like Schaefer and Allen's study, have produced no systematic evidence of a socioeconomic casualty gap.[7]

Reviewing this motley state of affairs, sociologist Thomas C. Wilson argues that the variance may be "due in large part to the cumulative effect of methodological inconsistencies across studies and methodological flaws within them."[8] Some previous studies analyze casualties from only a single state or region of the country. Other researchers focus more narrowly on a specific age cohort or restrict their analyses to short periods of time. Moreover, the measures used for socioeconomic status change from study to study, and many analyses examine only one potential explanation for inequalities in casualties, while failing to control for other possibilities. Finally, only a handful of analyses examine more than one conflict at a time.[9] Without the comparative perspective afforded by empirical analyses of multiple wars, it is difficult to discern trends in inequalities and changes in the relationships between community demographics and variance in local casualty rates over time.

Our analysis in this chapter builds on this previous research and introduces major advances. What distinguishes our work most from earlier scholarship is the breadth of our investigation. We marshal all available casualty data from each of our nation's four major wars over the past seventy years. Then, using the military home-of-record information and the best available demographic data from the U.S. census, we paint the most accurate picture possible of the sacrifice experienced by every community in the United States in each conflict, and we investigate which community demographic characteristics—if any—correlate with higher or lower local casualty rates. Not only does this research design free us from concerns raised by analyzing only a subset of the population, but it also allows us to engage in cross-conflict comparisons of casualty gaps.

After constructing these integrated databases, our analysis employs a two-step approach. We begin by examining simple bivariate correlations between community demographics and local casualty rates. For example, what is the median family income of communities that suffered high battlefield casualty rates in World War II, Korea, Vietnam, and Iraq? By contrast, what is the same figure for communities that suffered substantially lower casualty rates? Is there a significant difference between them, or do high- and low-casualty communities look roughly the same on this dimension? Such basic comparisons provide perhaps the simplest and clearest tests of whether casualty gaps exist along socioeconomic lines. Then we supplement these simple analyses with multivariate statistical models that allow us to test the effects of multiple potential factors that might drive local casualty rates simultaneously. For example, across all four conflicts we can examine the effect of a community's racial composition on its casualty rate after controlling for its median income or level of educational attainment. Together, these two sweeps of analysis offer powerful insights into the nature of military casualty gaps and changes in them over time.

DEFINING AND MEASURING THE CASUALTY GAP

In the analysis that follows, we assess the evidence for a casualty gap in each of the United States' last four major wars. We use the term *casualty gap* to describe a systematic, significant difference in local casualty rates between communities that differ on a demographic dimension. For example, if we find evidence that communities with lower median incomes or lower levels of educational attainment suffer systematically higher casualty rates on average than communities with higher levels of income and education, we conclude that the data reveal evidence of a casualty gap between socioeconomically advantaged and disadvantaged communities. Casualty gaps may also exist along other dimensions; for example, we could find that rural communities suffer higher casualty rates on average than more urban or suburban communities or that communities with greater concentrations of minorities have endured higher casualty rates than those with fewer racial and ethnic minorities. A casualty gap, then, refers to a significant difference in community-level casualty rates along some salient dimension.[10]

To determine whether casualty gaps exist, we first must compile local casualty rates for every community in the United States for each of the four wars. To investigate evidence of casualty gaps we want to examine the differences in local casualty rates at the lowest level of aggregation. The larger the community, the more heterogeneous it can be. For example, if we found that states with higher unemployment rates suffered higher casualty rates on average than those with lower unemployment, this would be evidence that suggests the existence of a socioeconomic casualty gap. However, because there is considerable variance in local economic conditions across communities within each state, it is more informative to see whether high casualty rates are concentrated even more narrowly among individual communities facing tough economic times. The smaller the geographic unit in which we observe relationships between casualty rates and socioeconomic status, the more confident we can be that the relationship is real. Thus, for each war we analyze local casualty rates at the lowest level of aggregation possible given the available data. For World War II, Korea, and the complete Vietnam casualty records, this is the county level. For the war in Iraq and for a large subset of our Vietnam data, we are able to analyze local casualty rates at the place level.[11] Throughout the book, when we use the term "place" we are referring to Census Designated Place.

To construct local casualty rates for every community across the United States, we first determined from available U.S. Department of Defense records the total number of casualties in each county/place for each war by using reported information on each casualty's "home of record" before entering the Armed Services.[12] Then, using census data we divided these totals by the relevant county or place populations to obtain a per-capita casualty rate. To ease interpretation, for all four wars we report the casualty rate per 10,000 male residents.[13] For a more detailed discussion of the data sources used in each case, we refer interested readers to the technical appendix that accompanies this chapter.

Geographic Variance in Local Casualty Rates

A necessary but not sufficient condition for a casualty gap is significant variance in local casualty rates across the country. Perhaps the simplest way to determine whether war sacrifice is shared equally by communities across the country is to plot the variance in local casualty rates using a histogram. Accordingly, figure 2.1 plots the distribution of local casualty rates suffered by each of the more than 3,000 U.S. counties in the war in Vietnam. The graph demonstrates that there is considerable variance in county-level casualty rates across the country. In Vietnam, the average county casualty rate was about six per 10,000 male residents, but the stan-

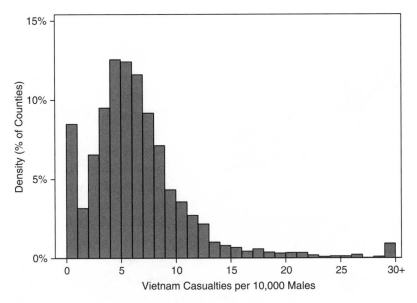

Figure 2.1. County-level Vietnam casualty rates.

dard deviation about that mean is also quite high.[14] More than 300 counties suffered casualty rates that were more than twice as high as that of the median county, while a large number of counties also suffered casualty rates significantly lower than the mean or median county. Histograms for the other conflicts, which are presented in the online appendix, also demonstrate considerable variation in community casualty rates.

Figures 2.2 and 2.3 illustrate this variance in local casualty rates geographically. Figure 2.2 presents data from the war in Iraq showing that casualty rates have varied substantially across states. Each state in figure 2.2 is shaded according to its casualty rate; the darker the shading, the greater the per-capita casualty rate that state has suffered in Iraq. Variation, however, is not just across but also *within* states. Figure 2.3 presents county-level Vietnam casualty rates. Each county on the map is shaded according to its casualty rate; the darker the shading, the higher the per-capita price that county paid on the battlefields of Southeast Asia. Some of the highest casualty rates in the darkest regions on the map are sparsely populated western counties that suffered only one or two casualties; because of their small populations, however, even this small number translates into a very high casualty rate. Nevertheless, even after putting these cases aside, figure 2.3 shows considerable variance in the spatial distribution of casualties across the country and even within individual states.

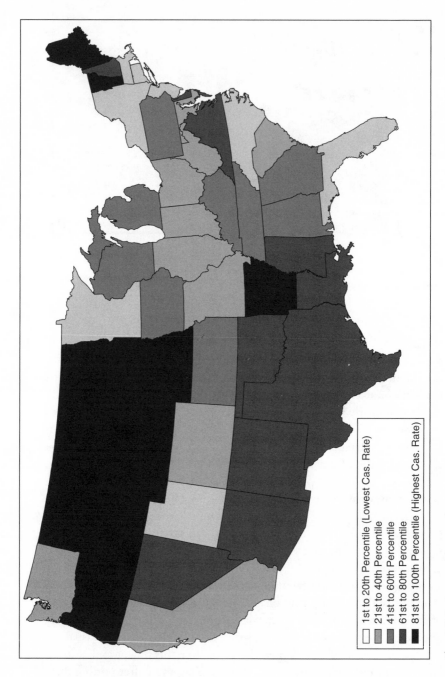

Figure 2.2. Iraq casualty rates by state.

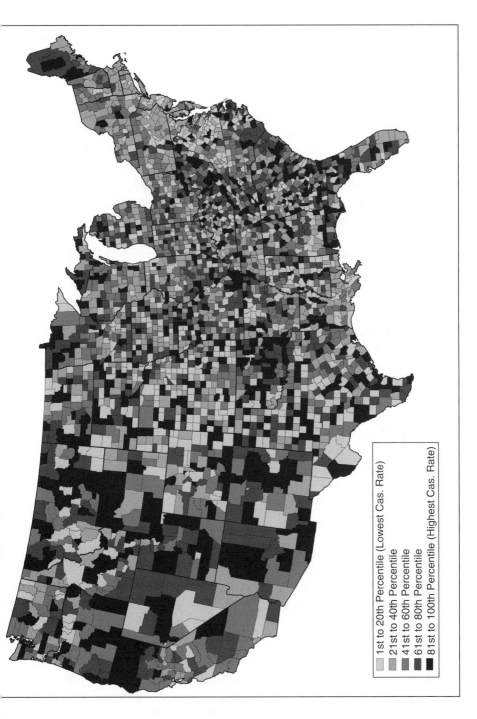

Figure 2.3. Vietnam casualty rates by county.

Having confirmed that there is significant geographic variation in local casualty rates, we explain in the remainder of this chapter why some parts of the country bear a greater burden than others.

EXPLAINING THE CASUALTY GAP

We earlier defined the casualty gap as a significant difference in community-level casualty rates along some salient dimension. What dimensions are likely to be most salient in explaining variance in local casualty rates? Previous research suggests that eight demographic characteristics are the most likely suspects in explaining the pattern of casualty rates across the country: income, education, unemployment, race, rural farm population, partisanship, geographic region, and age. We consider each of these factors in turn and discuss how we account for them in our statistical models. More detailed descriptions and summary statistics of each variable are offered in the technical appendix.

Income and Education

A number of studies have examined whether economically advantaged communities have paid a lower share of the human costs of war than economically depressed ones. However, the results of this previous scholarship have been surprisingly mixed. To resolve this dispute and investigate the socioeconomic casualty gap hypothesis, our analyses include measures of both a community's median family income and its level of educational attainment derived from U.S. census data.[15] We measure education in World War II, Vietnam, Korea, and Iraq as the percentage of residents with a college degree.[16] To measure income, we use median family income in all but our World War II models. Because the available 1940 census data file does not report county-level income data, for World War II we use the same proxy employed by Schaefer and Allen, median rent per month.[17]

If socioeconomic casualty gaps exist, we should see statistically significant inverse correlations between a community's income and education levels and its casualty rate. If, however, a socioeconomic casualty gap does not exist, then high-casualty communities should be no poorer or less educated on average than communities that have suffered lower wartime casualty rates.

Unemployment

While median income and education may best reflect a community's underlying socioeconomic status, a third factor—its unemployment rate—gives an additional gauge of the state of the local economy. A community must have men and women in the service before it can suffer casualties. In addition, the attractiveness of military service should be inversely related to the health of the local civilian labor market. Conventional wisdom holds that when it comes to the success of military recruiting, the local economy is critically important. Such an assumption is commonplace in popular culture, particularly on the Left, as illustrated in Michael Moore's *Fahrenheit 9/11*. Moore vividly captures on film military recruiters' intense efforts to sign up new enlistees in his hometown, the economically impoverished Flint, Michigan, where in 2003 unemployment stood at 16.5 percent, almost three times the national average. More recently, an August 2009 *Los Angeles Times* headline announced, "With jobs harder to find, work gets easier for Army recruiters." In the article, Staff Sgt. A.J. Calderon of the Los Angeles Recruiting Battalion discussed how the down economy had been a boon for recruiting. "This is definitely a good thing for the Army," said Calderon.[18]

Academic studies of patterns in military recruiting confirm the importance of local economic conditions in generating volunteers. A comprehensive study of military recruiting techniques by the nonpartisan Government Accountability Office (GAO) reported that "the economy has been the single most important factor recently affecting recruiting success." Researchers at the GAO found that "the better the civilian job market, the harder DOD must compete for talent."[19] The extant academic literature also offers at least some support for the hypothesis that casualty rates may be greater in communities with higher levels of local unemployment. In one of the only previous studies to compare casualty gaps in different wars, sociologist John Willis found that, although some socioeconomic factors, such as median income and education, had different effects in World War II and Vietnam, unemployment was a constant. In both wars, Willis found that casualty rates were lower in states with lower unemployment levels.[20]

If communities with tighter labor markets send a disproportionate share of young men and women into the military and these soldiers are eventually exposed to combat, then a community's unemployment rate should be positively correlated with its casualty rate.

Race

Casualty gaps may not fall only or even primarily along socioeconomic lines. For decades, scholars, politicians, and pundits alike have examined potential racial disparities in military service and casualties.[21] For example, during the Vietnam War the question of whether African Americans were suffering a disproportionate share of the costs in Southeast Asia garnered significant attention. In 1966 Gene Grove noted in the *New York Times Magazine* that African Americans accounted for 18.3 percent of the U.S.

Army's fatalities in Vietnam, which was 5 percent higher than the percentage of blacks in the army and 7 percent higher than the overall percentage of blacks in the population.[22] Martin Luther King Jr. also weighed in on the subject and criticized the U.S. government for "sending their [African Americans'] sons and their brothers and their husbands to fight and to die in extraordinarily higher proportions relative to the rest of the population."[23] The military took note of these arguments and took affirmative steps in an effort to reduce racial imbalances in sacrifice.

A number of previous analyses have found evidence of a racial casualty gap between communities with greater concentrations of racial minorities and those with smaller minority populations.[24] However, analyses of casualty patterns in the post-Vietnam era suggest that racial casualty gaps have dissipated. In their comprehensive study of U.S. casualties from 1975 to 1993, *All That We Can Be*, sociologists Charles Moskos and John Sibley Butler found little evidence of a racial casualty gap. Comparing the proportion of casualties that are African American to the national population and the percentage of African Americans in military service, Moskos and Butler argue that "no serious case can be made that blacks suffer undue casualties in America's wars and military interventions."[25] In a similar vein, a 2005 study of the Iraq War carried out by sociologist Brian Gifford examined the possibility of racial disparities in the first twelve months of fighting in Operation Iraqi Freedom. Comparing the percentage of minority deaths in this period to a national average and the overall racial distribution in the military, Gifford's results "conditionally support Moskos and Butler's (1996) position that African-Americans do not disproportionately bear the ultimate burden of U.S. military operations, nor do other racial or ethnic minorities."[26]

Given these sometimes contradictory findings and the evidence that suggests a general diminishing of the racial casualty gap over time, for each of the four wars we include in our regression models census measures for the size of each community's African American population.[27] If a racial casualty gap exists, then we should see counties and census places with larger minority populations suffering systematically higher casualty rates than communities with smaller minority populations. If a racial casualty gap did characterize earlier wars but not more recent conflicts in the wake of changes in military recruitment and other policies, then we should find that this disparity between high- and low-minority population communities decreased and eventually disappeared over time.

Rural Farm Population

Although the urban-rural divide does not often receive much consideration in social-scientific investigations of casualties, there are strong reasons to believe that a casualty gap may exist along this dimension and that the nature of this gap, too, may have changed over time. Accordingly, in each of our models we include a variable measuring each community's rural farm population. As we discuss in more detail in chapter 3, rural political and demographic dynamics played an important role in the history of military manpower policy. Farm interests heavily influenced the origins of the draft. In crafting the draft law that supplied manpower for World War II, the farm lobby was able to secure the "first and most successful exception to universal service... [and] when farmers did leave the farm, twice as many left for higher paying industrial jobs as for the armed forces."[28] Such policies may have resulted in rural communities bearing a disproportionately small share of the casualty burden.

However, by the 2000s this situation and the burden facing rural communities may have fundamentally changed. In 2007 experts on rural policy at the University of New Hampshire's Carsey Institute speculated that there was a " 'basic unfairness' about the number of troops dying in Iraq who are from rural areas."[29] The Carsey Institute's analysis argues that "diminished opportunities are one factor in higher military enlistment rates in rural areas," and, in addition, it suggests that individuals from rural farm communities may bring lower levels of skills to the military. This, in turn, might increase rural soldiers' exposure to high-risk military occupations and combat duty. As a consequence, in the Iraq War it may be the case that "rural communities are 'being asked to pay a bigger price.' "[30]

Our expectations for the relationship between casualties and rural farm population are thus historically contingent. In earlier conflicts, military manpower policies that granted exemptions to more rural areas may have produced a casualty gap between rural and urban areas. Yet, in the contemporary conflict in Iraq, the dynamic may well have changed, and rural areas may now be bearing a disproportionate share of the nation's casualties.

Partisanship

Another possibility is that casualty gaps may emerge along partisan lines. Belief in the military's mission is a possible contributing factor that might affect both military enlistment patterns and casualty rates.[31] Partisanship may be an important predictor of a community's baseline support for a military endeavor in two ways. First, particularly since the demise of isolationism as a political force with the advent of the Cold War, Republicans at both the elite and mass levels have tended to hold more hawkish foreign policy preferences than Democrats.[32] If so, then the more a community leans toward the Republican Party in national elections, the more likely its citizens may be to enlist in the military and seek combat roles. Alternatively, a wealth of political science scholarship has shown that support for wars is heavily correlated with support for the commander-in-chief.[33] Accordingly, it is plausible that in areas of the country where the sitting president enjoys staunch support, there is greater interest in serving in that president's military campaign.

To test between these possibilities, we included in each model a measure of the Republican presidential candidate's share of the two-party vote in the election immediately prior to the war.[34] If the first hypothesis is correct, then the resulting coefficient should be positive and significant across conflicts. If the latter hypothesis holds, then the sign of the coefficient should vary according to whether the incumbent president is a Democrat or a Republican.[35]

Geographic Region and Age

Citing the particularly deep roots of military tradition in the states of the former Confederacy, scholars have also raised the possibility that casualty rates may vary significantly along regional lines. In its 2006 annual report on the social composition of the military, the DOD specifically highlighted the geographic dimension and noted that "the South region has the greatest ratio of enlistees."[36] To account for the possibility that the South may be providing a greater proportion of enlistees and, similarly, that those enlistees may subsequently be more likely to find themselves in combat situations, we include in every model a regional control variable for the South.

A final demographic dimension that may contribute to casualty rate variance is community age. Although it rarely triggers political debate, basic realities of military service suggest that a casualty gap may emerge between older and younger communities.[37] Because combat soldiers are mostly young, we expect communities with lower median ages to shoulder a larger share of the fighting burden than communities dominated by older cohorts. Thus, as a final control variable, all of our multivariate analyses include a measure of age for each county or census place. For all but the World War II models, where the data availability is more limited, we use median age as our age variable. For World War II, we use instead the percentage of county residents who are males age 15–19 in the 1940 census, the demographic group most likely to be called into service.[38]

ASSESSING THE CASUALTY GAP ACROSS FOUR WARS

To determine whether we see evidence of casualty gaps along any of these eight dimensions, we adopt two different analytic approaches. First, to investigate the most important question motivating our analysis—whether combat casualties are concentrated in socioeconomically disadvantaged communities—we examine the bivariate relationships between a community's casualty rate and its median family income and level of educational attainment. Then, to ensure that any observed relationships between casualty rates and these socioeconomic demographics are not spurious and to investigate the relationships between local casualty rates and the other six demographic characteristics, we conduct a multivariate statistical analysis. This multivariate analysis allows us to examine the influence of each demographic characteristic on a community's casualty rate controlling for other dimensions of that community's demographics. As a result, we can ascertain what the effect of a shift in one specific variable—for example, an increase in median income—is on a community's casualty rate while holding all other factors, such as that community's minority composition or partisanship, constant.

To examine the relationship between a community's socioeconomic situation and its casualty rate in each of the four wars, we first divide all American communities into deciles for both of our key socioeconomic measures—median income and education. By definition, after weighting by population, 10 percent of Americans live in communities in the lowest income decile, 10 percent live in communities in the highest decile, and 10 percent live in each decile in between.[39] If there is no casualty gap along income or educational lines, then the percentage of casualties that falls in each decile should equal 10 percent. To visualize whether each decile falls above or below this 10 percent line, we present a series of graphs that shows the percentage of casualties from communities in each decile. If each decile shared the costs of war equally, then we should see a perfectly horizontal line. However, if there is a casualty gap between communities with high and low levels of income and education, then we should see the casualty percentages change systematically as we move from low to high income and education deciles. If poorer and less-educated communities are bearing a greater proportion of deaths, then the decile bars on the lower end of the socioeconomic spectrum (farther left) will rise above the 10 percent line, and the decile bars on the higher end (farther right) will fall below the 10 percent benchmark.

Figure 2.4 charts the relationships between local casualty rates and a community's median family income from World War II to the war in Iraq. Figure 2.4 presents clear and consistent evidence of an inverse relationship between casualty rates and income in every war except World War II. Every other war exhibits a general pattern in which wealthier portions of the country bear less of the casualty burden than poorer communities. The consistency of the patterns in the three post–World War II

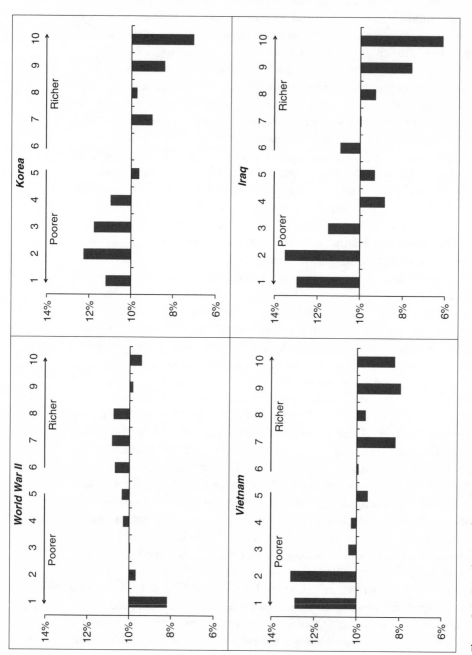

Figure 2.4. Distribution of casualties by income decile, WWII through Iraq.

Note: Each gray bar indicates the percentage of casualties (above and below 10 percent) in each decile. World War II deciles are based on median county rent.

conflicts is notable. In Korea, Vietnam, and Iraq, the lowest three income deciles took on 35 percent, 36 percent, and 38 percent of the casualties, respectively. At the same time, in these wars the top three deciles by income suffered only 25 percent, 26 percent, and 23 percent of the casualties, respectively. Thus, when we compare the top and bottom ends of the income distribution of casualties, we see in Korea a difference of 10 percent, in Vietnam of 10 percent, and in Iraq of 15 percent.

Figure 2.5 constructs a parallel analysis that examines the concentration of combat casualties among education deciles. The education data pattern largely mirrors that observed with community income levels. In World War II we find no evidence that communities with lower levels of education bore a disproportionate share of the nation's casualties. In fact, the bottom 30 percent of the country in terms of educational attainment suffered less than 30 percent of the nation's casualties in World War II. However, in each subsequent war we observe the opposite relationship. In Korea, Vietnam, and Iraq, the lowest three deciles bore 35 percent, 36 percent, and 41 percent of total casualties, respectively, while the top three deciles in terms of educational attainment accounted for only 26 percent, 23 percent, and 23 percent of casualties, respectively. Thus, we see a difference of 9 percent in Korea, 13 percent in Vietnam, and fully 18 percent in Iraq. In concert with our income analysis, the data not only strongly support the contention that a significant socioeconomic casualty gap exists but also suggest a trend of rising casualty inequality over time.[40]

Another way to see the magnitude of the socioeconomic casualty gap is to examine the difference along each dimension between communities that suffered high casualty rates and those that did not. In this analysis, we divide all of the communities into two groups: the first includes all communities whose casualty rates place them in the top quarter of the casualty distribution; the second group comprises all other communities.[41] From census data, we can then calculate the average median family income and the average percentage of residents with a college degree for both groups. To provide a constant metric, we adjust the income data from previous periods to reflect their value in year 2000 dollars.[42] The results for median income presented in figure 2.6 show that, while sacrifice is shared equally in World War II, beginning with the war in Korea significant income gaps emerged. In raw dollar terms, this income casualty gap increased over time from conflict to conflict: a $5,500 gap in Korea, an $8,200 gap in Vietnam, and a $13,200 gap in Iraq.

A similar pattern emerges when we examine the percentage of respondents with a college degree in high- and low-casualty communities. These numbers are presented in figure 2.7. Again in World War II we

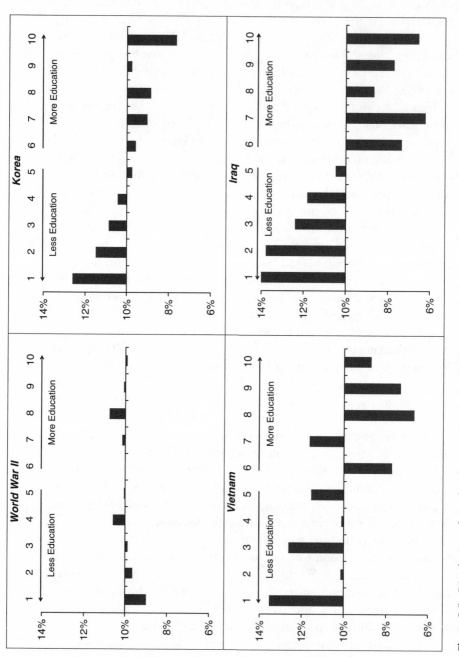

Figure 2.5. Distribution of casualties by education decile, WWII through Iraq.

Note: Each gray bar indicates the percentage of casualties (above and below 10 percent) in each decile.

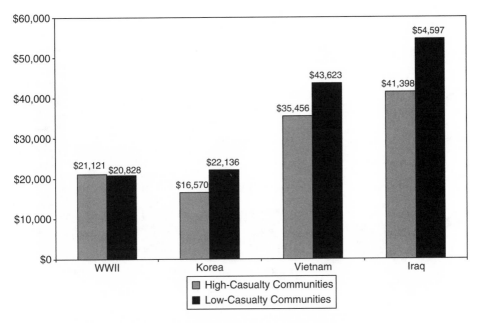

Figure 2.6. Median family income in high- and low-casualty communities.

find no evidence that casualties were concentrated disproportionately in low education communities. In the Korean, Vietnam, and Iraq wars, by contrast, we see a significant difference in college rates between high- and low-casualty communities. In Korea the percentage of residents with four or more years of college drops from 6.2 percent in low-casualty communities to 4.1 percent in high-casualty communities, a 34 percent decrease. In Vietnam, 11 percent of residents of low-casualty communities had completed four or more years of college versus just 8.3 percent of residents in high-casualty communities, a 25 percent difference. In Iraq, 25.1 percent of residents in communities with no casualties had a college degree, compared to only 15.2 percent of residents in the highest casualty communities. Put another way, the communities that have suffered the highest casualty rates in Iraq possess levels of college educational attainment that are almost 40 percent lower, on average, than those of communities that have not yet suffered a casualty in the Iraq War.

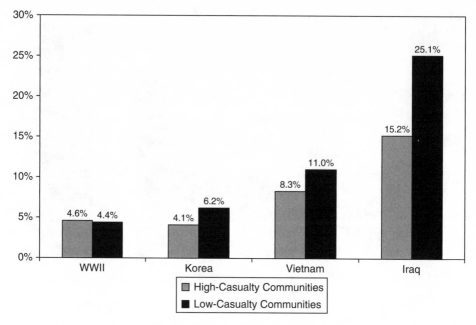

Figure 2.7. Percentage of residents with a college degree in high- and low-casualty communities.

A final way to illustrate the significant inverse relationships between a community's socioeconomic status and its local casualty rate is to examine the covariance among different communities' values on both dimensions geographically. To illustrate this negative correlation, figure 2.8 presents two maps of the state of Pennsylvania that show data from the Korean War, in which the socioeconomic casualty gap began to emerge. The first map shades each county by its level of educational attainment. In this map, we use the percentage of each county that holds a high school diploma.[43] The second map shades each county by its casualty rate suffered in Korea per 10,000 male residents. Darker shading in the maps indicates higher educational attainment and higher casualty rates, respectively. As we can see, the two are not perfectly correlated. Not all counties with strong levels of education suffered low casualties, and not all counties with low education levels suffered high casualties. However, the two are strongly negatively correlated. For example, Centre County in the middle of Pennsylvania is one of the darkest regions in the education map, which indicates its high level of educational attainment. In the bottom casualty map, by contrast, it is one of the lightest counties in the state, which indicates that Centre County was among the bottom

20 percent of Pennsylvania counties in terms of the casualty rate it sustained in the Korean War. We see a similar pattern in the Philadelphia suburbs (in the lower right-hand corner of the state). Chester, Delaware, and Montgomery counties were all in the highest education category (top 20 percent). In terms of casualty rates, by contrast, Delaware and Montgomery counties were in the lowest quintile, and Chester was in the second lowest.

Finally, consider the group of counties beginning in the southwestern region of the state along the Maryland border and then extending up through Johnstown and central western Pennsylvania to include Cambria and Clearfield counties. Six of the seven counties in this contiguous group fell into the lowest education bracket (bottom 20 percent) with less than 26 percent of residents having completed high school. In sharp contrast, three of these counties were in the top 20 percent of counties in terms of their Korean War costs with casualty rates exceeding 6 per 10,000 male residents; three more were in the second highest casualty bracket. Looking at the state as a whole, we find that more than 80 percent of the counties in the top education quintile were in the bottom two casualty rate quintiles. By contrast, 65 percent of counties in the bottom quintile in terms of educational attainment fell within the top two quintiles in terms of casualty rates. Thus, across the state, we see strong evidence that communities with lower levels of educational attainment suffered systematically higher casualty rates on average than did other counties in Pennsylvania with higher levels of educational attainment.

Each of the preceding analyses offers strong evidence of the emergence of a socioeconomic casualty gap beginning in the Korean War; moreover, most of the evidence suggests that the magnitude of this gap may have increased over time, particularly in the ongoing conflict in Iraq. These bivariate analyses provide the most straightforward way of examining the relationships between community casualty rates and socioeconomic demographics. Yet, they cannot tell us much about the relative influence of all of the demographic factors that might affect a community's casualty rate. For example, might casualty rates be higher on average in low-income areas because these areas tend to have larger percentages of racial minorities? Might it be because they tend to be more rural than wealthier communities? To answer questions such as these, we need to examine the effect of a community's socioeconomic status after controlling for other factors that could also influence its casualty rate. Toward this end, we now employ multiple regression models to assess the relative influence of all eight community demographics in determining the casualty rate of a county or census place in each of the four wars.

A.

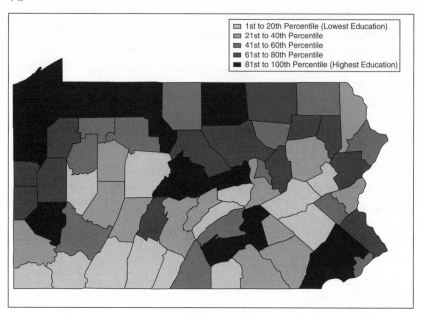

B.

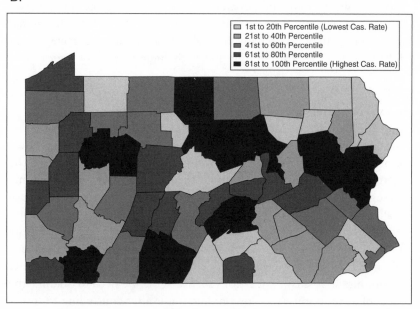

Figure 2.8. (A) Pennsylvania counties by percentage with a high school degree in the Korean War; (B) Pennsylvania counties by casualty rate in the Korean War.

Table 2.1 summarizes the results of this multivariate analysis by reporting the magnitudes of all statistically significant effects from the regression model.[44] When we use the term *statistically significant* in this section, we mean that we can say with at least 95 percent confidence that the relationship we find is statistically different from zero. While there is still a chance that a statistically significant relationship we observe is due to random error, our models suggest that this is exceedingly unlikely.[45] For

Table 2.1. First Differences, Expressed as Percentage Change in Local Casualty Rate, for Statistically Significant Casualty Gaps

	WWII	Korea	Vietnam	Iraq
Income		–27.4%	–8.6%	–17.6%
25th–75th percentile change				
10th–90th percentile change		–41.9%	–15.6%	–36.9%
Education (% College)				
25th–75th percentile change	+5.9%		–5.1%	–19.8%
10th–90th percentile change	+11.7%		–10.0%	–46.5%
Unemployment				
25th–75th percentile change	+3.2%	+8.6%		
10th–90th percentile change	+6.4%	+16.8%		
% African American Residents				
25th–75th percentile change	–11.6%	–10.1%	–6.6%	–3.2%
10th–90th percentile change	–34.5%	–29.6%	–19.1%	–20.9%
Southern State				
Non-South to South change		+7.4%	+11.1%	+44.6%
Age				
25th–75th percentile change	–4.0%			
10th–90th percentile change	–7.4%			

Note: Blank cells indicate that no statistically significant effect exists in either the income (table 2A.3) or the education (table 2A.4) models. Effects are considered statistically significant if the relevant regression coefficient is p <.10. All significance tests are two-tailed. See technical appendix for full details of statistical methodology. Partisanship and rural farm population were not significant predictors in any of our models and thus are excluded from this table.

a full discussion of the data and the statistical models we used to generate the results presented in table 2.1, we refer readers to the technical appendix that accompanies this chapter.

Even after controlling for a host of additional demographic characteristics of each community, our multiple regression analysis finds strong evidence of significant socioeconomic casualty gaps in Korea, Vietnam, and Iraq. Consistent with our bivariate analyses summarized in figures 2.4 and 2.6, the regression models find strong evidence of an inverse relationship between a community's median family income and its casualty rate for the Korean, Vietnam, and Iraq wars. Moreover, the size of this estimated income effect in all three conflicts is substantial. Table 2.1 presents a series of first differences that illustrate the estimated effect of a shift in each independent variable while holding all other variables constant at their means or medians. From table 2.1, we see that in Korea a move from the 25th to the 75th percentile in income produces a 27 percent decrease in the local casualty rate, while in Vietnam, a similar shift produces a decrease of 9 percent.[46] In Iraq, moving from the 25th to the 75th percentile produces a decrease of 18 percent in the local casualty rate. The casualty gap is even larger at the tails of the income distribution. In Korea, a shift in a community's median income from the 10th to the 90th percentile decreases its predicted casualty rate by 42 percent; in Vietnam, this shift produces a 16 percent drop; and in Iraq it decreases the estimated place-level casualty rate by 37 percent.

The regression analyses also find evidence of significant relationships between a community's average level of educational attainment and its casualty rate. As in the earlier bivariate analyses, for World War II the regression model finds an unexpected and statistically significant positive relationship between community education levels and casualty rates. However, the nature of this relationship has changed in subsequent wars. In Korea the regression model finds a negative relationship between a community's educational attainment and its casualty rate, and by the Vietnam era this negative relationship was statistically significant. While the variable measuring the percentage of residents who have completed four or more years of college yielded a statistically insignificant coefficient in the Korean models, replicating the model with a measure of the percentage of residents twenty-five and older with a high school diploma yielded a strong, statistically significant negative coefficient. Thus, consistent with our bivariate analyses, alternate multivariate models also show strong evidence of an education gap emerging during the Korean conflict.

Finally, the regression analysis suggests that the size of this casualty gap between communities with high and low levels of education is considerably larger in the context of the contemporary war in Iraq than it was in Vietnam. First differences, again holding all other variables constant at their means or medians, show that a move from the 25th to the 75th education percentile in Vietnam is associated with a 5 percent decrease in a community's casualty rate, whereas a similar move in Iraq is associated with a 20 percent drop in the local casualty rate. Again, at the tails of the distribution the size of the casualty gap is even more extreme, particularly in Iraq. A move from the 10th to the 90th education percentile in Iraq is associated with a 47 percent decrease in the local casualty rate.

Finally, the multiple regression analyses allow us to examine the relationship between a third socioeconomic variable, local unemployment rates, and local casualty rates after controlling for other community-level characteristics. On the unemployment dimension we see the first modest piece of evidence for a socioeconomic casualty gap in World War II. For both World War II and Korea, the regression models find a positive and statistically significant relationship between local unemployment and local casualty rates. In World War II, the estimated size of the unemployment casualty gap is rather modest. Increasing a county's unemployment rate from the 10th to the 90th percentile boosted its predicted casualty rate by 6 percent. In Korea, by contrast, the unemployment gap was significantly larger as a similar increase in local unemployment increased a county's predicted casualty rate by 17 percent. In the Vietnam and Iraq wars, the regression models find no evidence of a statistically significant relationship between community unemployment and casualty rates.[47]

The preceding bivariate and multivariate analyses provide strong support for the hypothesis that a significant socioeconomic casualty gap has emerged during recent U.S. military engagements. However, they call into question an argument frequently made in the existing literature that Vietnam was the critical juncture at which this casualty gap came into existence. Previous scholarship has argued that Vietnam marked a turning point in our nation's military manpower policies and moved the country away from an era of more or less uniform military service across the social classes that had held in the 1940s and 1950s.[48] As a 2003 article in the *New York Times* put it, "The Vietnam War stands as the defining epoch in the creation of what has become today's professional, blue-collar military."[49] This alleged transformation of the composition of the U.S. military, in turn, is sometimes assumed to have concentrated casualties among poor communities. Yet, all of our empirical analyses suggest that the socioeconomic casualty gap emerged very quickly after World War II. While many cuts of the data suggest that the nature of this gap may have widened over time, particularly in Iraq, Vietnam was not the genesis of the socioeconomic casualty gap. Instead, a casualty gap between socioeconomically disadvantaged and better-off communities has characterized every major U.S. military conflict since the Korean War.

Having established the existence of significant casualty gaps between high- and low-income and education communities in Korea, Vietnam, and Iraq, as well as a gap between high and low unemployment communities in World War II and Korea, we next examine whether a similar casualty gap emerged along racial lines. While race and class are undeniably intertwined, once we control for income or education and unemployment, we find no evidence of a racial casualty gap in which communities with larger percentages of minorities are bearing a disproportionately large share of the casualty burden. If anything, our data suggest the reverse case.[50] This is not to say, however, that heavily minority communities did not suffer high casualty rates. Because communities with higher percentages of minorities were also, on average, poorer communities, many heavily minority communities did have casualty rates that were higher than the national average. Thus, our results are consistent with previous analyses finding that blacks comprised a slightly greater percentage of Vietnam dead than their percentage of the general population. Our analysis suggests, however, that this disparity is primarily the result of African Americans' lower socioeconomic status. Indeed, the models show that poor white communities suffered casualty rates even higher than those suffered by communities with larger black populations and identical socioeconomic characteristics.

Investigating the racial casualty gap more closely affords a unique opportunity to assess the capacity of policy reforms to redress perceived inequalities in combat casualties. During Vietnam, critics raised important questions about numerical fairness, and by 1967 debate over a racial casualty gap had firmly emerged on the political agenda. In response to an analysis by the Marshall Commission released in February 1967, the DOD consciously attempted to limit the number of black soldiers on the front lines.[51] In light of this within-war policy change, we estimated a series of separate regressions to assess the relationships between community demographics and Vietnam county casualty rates on a year-by-year basis. These new models suggest that the military's policies had a significant effect on casualty distribution by community racial makeup. For 1966 and 1967 we find no statistically significant relationship between a county's African American population and its casualty rate. For 1968 and 1969, however, we find a strong, statistically significant, negative relationship between the two. Thus, these additional rounds of analysis are at least consistent with the hypothesis that the DOD's policy shift had the intended effect of minimizing African American casualty rates; only in the wake of the reforms did communities with larger concentrations of African Americans begin experiencing casualty rates that were systematically lower than other communities with identical socioeconomic characteristics.[52]

Our multivariate analysis also allows us to investigate whether an urban-rural divide in casualty rates has emerged in America's last four major wars. In World War II, Korea and Vietnam, we observe an inverse relationship between a county's casualty rate and its percentage of rural farm residents. These modest negative relationships may be products of the institutional deferment and exemption system, which favored keeping farm laborers at home during these wars. However, after controlling for other demographic variables, none of the regression coefficients meet conventional levels of statistical significance. In Iraq, by contrast the relationship between a community's percentage rural farm residents and its casualty rate is positive, though the relevant coefficients again fail to reach conventional levels of statistical significance. In Iraq, higher concentrations of rural farm residents are positively associated with casualty rates. Without institutionalized draft protections and in the face of severe downturns in the farming economy, individuals in rural farm communities may be both more likely to join the military and more likely to end up in proximity to combat. Yet, the size of any urban-rural casualty gap after controlling for socioeconomic factors is quite modest.

Turning to our partisanship variable, we find little evidence in our multivariate analyses of any significant relationships between local casualty rates and support for the Republican presidential candidate in the preceding election. While there are significant bivariate state-level correlations in Iraq, with greater support for Bush in 2000 associated with higher state casualty rates, this relationship does not hold when we utilize state-level partisanship as an explanatory variable in our place-level models. In a similar vein, additional county-level Iraq models fail to find any significant relationship between support for Bush and county casualty rates.

While partisanship does not provide a compelling explanation, the multivariate analyses do offer some evidence for systematic regional differences in casualty rates. In every model, the coefficient for the southern regional variable was positive, and in the Korea, Vietnam, and Iraq models it was statistically significant. This finding is consistent with research that finds the South more hawkish and steeped in military ethos than other regions. Finally, our multivariate models offer little evidence of a systematic relationship between a community's age characteristics and its casualty rate. In World War II we find evidence that counties with older populations suffered lower casualty rates on average than counties with younger populations.

Taken as a whole, our empirical analysis finds strong evidence of significant socioeconomic casualty gaps between rich and poor communities in the United States, even after controlling for a number of additional demographic variables. In each major U.S. military conflict since Korea, median family income and/or levels of college education were significantly related to local casualty rates. Counties and places with lower incomes and levels of educational attainment suffered systematically larger casualty rates than other communities with higher incomes and higher percentages of college graduates. In addition, local unemployment rates were significant predictors of casualty rates in World War II and Korea.

For those expecting to see racial differentials in casualty rates, the results of our statistical analysis are striking. Not only do we fail to find any evidence of statistically significant racial casualty gaps, but we also find that, after controlling for socioeconomic conditions, a greater percentage of minorities in a community is related to *lower* casualty rates.

Our results also remind us that the contours of the casualty gap have varied over time and across wars. The differences are quite stark between World War II and the wars that have followed in its wake. Korea, not Vietnam, witnessed the emergence of significant casualty gaps along community income and educational lines. Finally, as illustrated most clearly in our bivariate analyses, the size of the socioeconomic casualty gap along both education and income dimensions appears to have grown over time and reached its peak in the current conflict in Iraq. We discuss these differences and the forces driving them in greater detail in the next chapter.

THE INDIVIDUAL-LEVEL CASUALTY GAP AND THE PROBLEM OF ECOLOGICAL INFERENCE

The preceding analyses show strong evidence of a socioeconomic casualty gap between rich and poor and between high- and low-education *communities*. Communities that have lagged behind the rest of the country in generating economic and educational opportunities for their citizens have borne a disproportionate share of America's wartime casualties in the major conflicts since Korea. Still, it is not the case that America's wealthier communities have been completely insulated from wartime death. As our analysis of income and education deciles in figures 2.4 and 2.5 make plain, communities at the upper ends of both distributions *have* experienced casualties and oftentimes in considerable numbers. Rather, our data show that socioeconomically disadvantaged communities have suffered a greater share of wartime casualties per capita than have communities with higher levels of income and educational attainment.

This casualty gap at the community level is normatively troubling. As we show in a series of experiments in chapter 4, when Americans learn of the nature of this community-level casualty gap between rich and poor localities, their military policy preferences change dramatically. Moreover, as we argue in the second half of the book, because Americans view war through the lens of their local communities, the existence of a community-level casualty gap has significant immediate and long-term political ramifications. Some Americans, particularly those from socioeconomically disadvantaged communities, see the costs of war much more directly than do other Americans, and this differential exposure to casualties dramatically influences their political opinions and behaviors.

While this chapter began with the question of whether *communities* like Beaver Falls bear a disproportionate share of the nation's casualty burden, the next logical question is whether *individuals* from socioeconomically disadvantaged backgrounds are dying disproportionately. Indeed, when we think about what forces could cause the casualty gaps that we observe at the community level, the most obvious possibility is that community variance is a result of differential casualty rates between rich and poor individuals. Under this working hypothesis, poorer and less-educated individuals are more likely to enter the military and die in combat than richer and more educated individuals. Moreover, because such individuals logically hail disproportionately from poorer communities with lower levels of educational attainment, this individual-level casualty gap produces those observed at the community level. We elaborate on this hypothesis and examine the indirect evidence for it in considerably more detail in the following chapter.

While we argue that an individual-level casualty gap is the most logical explanation for the patterns in the casualty data we have observed at the aggregate level, we cannot conclude from the community-level casualty data alone that poorer individuals or those with lower levels of education are dying at higher rates than individuals with greater socioeconomic opportunities. To do so would be to commit what social scientists call an error of ecological inference. From aggregate-level data alone, we cannot make inferences about processes at the level of individuals. All that we know from the analyses presented thus far in this chapter is that there is a casualty gap between socioeconomically advantaged and disadvantaged counties and places. While it is highly unlikely, it is possible that the casualties in a community with a low median income and level of educational attainment are predominantly from high-income, high-education backgrounds. For example, it might be that a deceased soldier from a poor county came from the richest neighborhood in that county. If so, then there may not be any socioeconomic casualty gap at the individual level, even though one exists at the county level. Conversely, it could be the case that a deceased soldier from a rich county came from the poorest neighborhood in that county. If casualties from communities with high median incomes and educational attainment are themselves socioeconomically disadvantaged, then the individual-level casualty gap may be significantly larger than that observed at the community level.

In order to explore these possibilities, additional analysis is needed. If there were no obstacles to data access, we would examine the socioeconomic backgrounds of all of the men and women who died in service to our nation on foreign battlefields. We would then compare their background characteristics to those of other men and women who also served in the U.S. military. Finally, we would compare the characteristics of both of these groups to the demographics of all citizens who are eligible for military service in the country as a whole. Understandably, much of this information on individual soldiers' backgrounds is not available for scholarly research. For privacy reasons, the Department of Defense does not make available data on individual soldiers' socioeconomic backgrounds prior to entering the service. Moreover, while we were able to obtain some enlistment data for the Iraq War from the DOD, comprehensive records from previous conflicts are not available, in no small part because of a catastrophic fire in 1973 at the National Personnel Records Center that destroyed the records of more than sixteen million soldiers.

Without these data on individual soldiers' socioeconomic backgrounds, we cannot conclude *definitively* that a casualty gap exists between individuals from socioeconomically advantaged and disadvantaged backgrounds. However, this does not mean that we cannot say *anything* about the likelihood of an individual-level casualty gap. Indeed, by taking advantage of modern electronic databases of public records we can identify precise home addresses for subsamples of our Iraq data. By integrating this information with block group census data we can then compare how the socioeconomic demographics of deceased soldiers' precise neighborhoods stack up against those of their census places. This comparison gives us significant leverage on the ecological inference challenge. To the extent that soldiers are coming from block groups that mirror the socioeconomic status of the larger community, then we can be more assured that our aggregate findings from earlier in the chapter are being driven by individual-level differences. Moreover, if soldiers hail from block groups that are poorer or less educated than their community averages, then our community-level analysis may even understate the true individual-level casualty gap. If, however, soldiers are coming from neighborhoods that are richer or more educated than their communities as a whole, it would cast doubt on the individual-level explanation.

Examining Socioeconomic Variation within the Community

Thus far in the chapter we have argued that looking solely at national casualty totals obscures important variation across localities. However, what about variation *within* those localities? Especially in large, heterogeneous communities such as New York City and Los Angeles, significant socioeconomic variation exists across neighborhoods. As a result, knowing that a fallen soldier was from New York City, for example, tells us very little about the soldier's likely socioeconomic status. However, if we can learn the socioeconomic demographics of that person's home census block group—a much smaller geographic unit of about a thousand residents— then we know much more about the soldier's likely socioeconomic background.[53] Given this variation, it is important to discern whether the neighborhoods of deceased soldiers are higher, lower, or about the same as the community average in terms of socioeconomic status.

In order to carry out this investigation, we first needed to know where deceased soldiers lived before they joined the military. While the Department of Defense does not provide this information directly, it provides enough identifying information to allow for effective searching through public-records databases. Utilizing online databases, we were able to identify the last home address prior to entering military service for a large subsample of Iraq War casualties.[54] Because address searches had to be conducted individually by hand and in consultation with additional public sources for corroboration, the prohibitive time costs limited the scope of our inquiry. We were, however, able to identify home addresses for: (1) every casualty from the nation's five largest cities (New York, Los Angeles, Chicago, Houston, and Philadelphia), (2) a random sample of 100 casualties, (3) the 100 casualties from the poorest places, and (4) the 100 casualties from the richest places. In total, we identified home-of-record addresses for more than 400 soldiers who died in the Iraq War.

For each soldier for whom we identified a home address, we used the Census Bureau's American Fact Finder tool to obtain the demographic characteristics of the soldier's block group, the lowest level of aggregation for which income and educational data are available. We then compared these neighborhood demographics to the characteristics of the census place as a whole. This new round of empirical evidence provides strong, though again not conclusive, support for the hypothesis that an individual-level casualty gap underlies the disparities we have identified at the community level. First, as presented in figure 2.9, in each of the five largest cities in the country, casualties have come overwhelmingly from block groups that have significantly lower college education rates than the city as a whole.[55] In New York, most casualties' block groups had significantly lower college education rates than the citywide average. In the median casualty block group, only 14 percent of residents twenty-five years of age and older had completed four or more years of college; by contrast, for all New Yorkers the relevant figure was 27 percent. Alternatively, when cutting the data in a different way we see that more than three quarters of all casualties from New York lived in block groups with levels of educational attainment lower than the city's overall average. Similarly, in Los Angeles the college completion rate of the median casualty neighborhood was almost 14 percentage points lower than for the city as a whole, and slightly smaller, though still significant, disparities existed in Houston, Chicago, and Philadelphia.[56] While we cannot infer from this data that

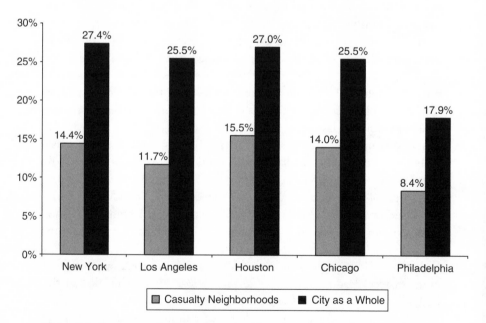

Figure 2.9. Percentage of college-educated residents in each city and in the median Iraq War casualty block group from each city.

Note: The dark bar represents the percentage of residents in each city who hold a college degree. The light bar represents the percentage of residents with a college degree in the median block group that suffered casualties from each city in the Iraq War.

fallen soldiers from these communities themselves came from poorer educational backgrounds than the median resident of their communities, the concentration of casualties in socioeconomically disadvantaged neighborhoods of these cities is strongly consistent with our hypothesis of an individual-level casualty gap.

We turn next to a similar analysis of our three additional samples: a randomly drawn sample of 100 casualties, the 100 casualties from the richest places, and the 100 casualties from the poorest places. For each group, we compared the income and education levels of the median casualty block group with the relevant statistics for the median census place. Figures 2.10 and 2.11 present the results of this analysis. On the education dimension, in all three of our samples we find that the median block group had a lower college completion rate than the median city or town (figure 2.10). With respect to income, figure 2.11 shows that in our sample of casualties from the wealthiest places, the income level of the median block group was significantly lower than for the median place in the sample (by almost $6,000). Cutting the data another way, we find that a full two-thirds of the casualties from these communities came from block groups with median incomes lower than that of their city or town as a whole. In both the random sample and the sample of casualties from the

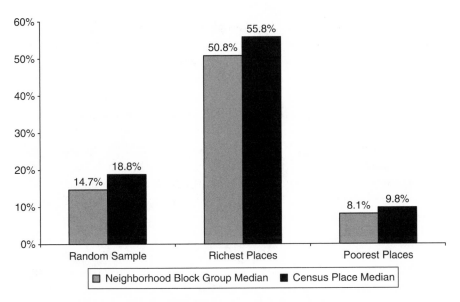

Figure 2.10. Percentage of college-educated residents for subsets of Iraq War casualties at the census-place and block-group levels.

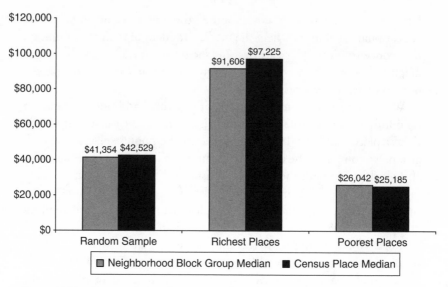

Figure 2.11. Community median income for subsets of Iraq War casualties at the census-place and block-group levels.

poorest places, the incomes of the median block group almost exactly mirrored those of the median census place.

While our additional block group–level analysis cannot fully assuage ecological fallacy concerns, they strongly suggest that the soldiers who are dying in Iraq are coming disproportionately from lower socioeconomic backgrounds. For each of our subsamples, we found that soldiers who died in Iraq came disproportionately from block groups with lower levels of educational attainment than the larger community as a whole; these differences were particularly acute among urban casualties. With respect to income, we found that casualties from poor communities also came from poor neighborhoods within those communities. By contrast, casualties from rich communities came disproportionately from block groups with lower levels of income than those of the community overall. Finally, in our random sample we found that the deceased soldiers' specific block groups were, if anything, slightly poorer and less educated than their communities as a whole.

We readily recognize that even this data is not conclusive evidence of an individual-level casualty gap. Although the average census block group contains only about 1,000 residents, there is still heterogeneity in terms of individual incomes or levels of educational attainment within each block group. Thus, even though we show that most of the casualties in our samples came from neighborhoods with levels of income and education that are the same as (or even lower than) those of their community as a whole, we cannot say with certainty that the soldiers who died in Iraq came from more socioeconomically disadvantaged backgrounds, on average, than their peers in the civilian population. Although it is not conclusive, this additional evidence nevertheless is strongly consistent with the contention that when America goes to war, it is the poorer and less educated in society who are more likely to die in combat.

EXPLAINING THE CASUALTY GAP

The empirical analyses we have presented in this chapter show that since the conclusion of World War II, socioeconomically disadvantaged communities have borne a disproportionate share of America's war casualties. However, this finding immediately leads to questions about mechanisms: *why* and *how* do casualty gaps develop?

In the following chapter we argue that two mechanisms—selection into the military and occupational assignment within it—combine to powerfully shape casualty distributions. Selection pressures drive more men and women with lower *ex ante* socioeconomic opportunities into the military; strategic priorities then serve to sort these individuals into occupations with greater exposure to combat. We argue that these two interrelated mechanisms, as well as changes in them over time, produce both the casualty gaps we observe between socioeconomically advantaged and disadvantaged communities and a parallel casualty gap between advantaged and disadvantaged individuals. While we cannot prove absolutely that this is the precise causal chain that generates the casualty gaps identified in this chapter, through additional rounds of analysis we endeavor to convince readers that this is both the most *plausible* causal chain and the one that best fits more subtle patterns in the empirical data.

Technical Appendix to Chapter 2

In this technical appendix we present the details of our analytic strategy to examine the relationship between a community's socioeconomic status and its share of U.S. war casualties in World War II, Korea, Vietnam, and Iraq. We elaborate on the data and present the full results of the statistical models we used to generate the various figures and tables presented in the chapter text. We also conduct an additional round of analyses that model Vietnam casualty rates at the place level as a robustness check on our results at the county level.

A. DATA

To determine whether casualty gaps emerged in each of our nation's last four major wars, we first had to construct measures of community casualty rates across the country.[1] We obtained raw casualty data on individuals killed in World War II, Korea, and Vietnam from a series of casualty databases maintained by the U.S. National Archives.[2] For Iraq, we used data made publicly available by the Statistical Information Analysis Division (SIAD) of the Department of Defense.[3] Our casualty data for Operation Iraqi Freedom include all soldiers killed through December 31, 2008. All of these data files provided individual casualty records with information on the deceased soldier's home of record prior to entering the armed forces.[4] We then tallied these individual casualties by the smallest possible geographic unit for which both casualty and complete census data were available. This was the county level for World War II, Korea, and Vietnam, though in Vietnam we also had a subnational sample of place-level data to use for limited analyses. We were able to use national, comprehensive place-level data for our Iraq analyses.[5]

Once we determined the total number of casualties per locale, we calculated the casualty rate by dividing by a male population denominator to control for the significant variation in size across counties and places in the country. To make the casualty rate more accessible, we then multiplied the per-capita rate by 10,000.[6]

Armed with these measures, we were able to examine the relationships between a community's local casualty rate and its demographic characteristics, including its unemployment rate, median income, level of educational attainment, racial composition, rural farm population, median age, partisan composition, and geography. To operationalize these community demographics, we turned to various years of data publications by the U.S. Census Bureau.[7] The data collected in the decennial censuses are well timed to capture the demographic characteristics of the counties in which individuals lived before entering military service. We were able to match 1940 census data with WWII casualties, 1950 census data with Korean casualties, 1970 census data with Vietnam casualties, and 2000 census data with casualties from the present Iraq conflict.[8]

To measure income, we used median family income in all but our World War II models. For World War II, where the measure was unavailable in the data set, we used the very similar measure of median rent per month.[9] Education measures for all years were highly correlated with measures of income; as a result, we estimated separate income and education models. To measure partisanship, we included a measure of the percentage of county residents who voted for the Republican presidential candidate in the election immediately preceding each war: Wendell Willkie in 1940, Thomas Dewey in 1948, Barry Goldwater in 1964, and George W. Bush in 2000.[10] Because we do not have this partisanship variable measured at the place level, in the Iraq place-level models we included the state percentage for Bush in 2000. The coefficients and significance for the socioeconomic variables, however, were not sensitive to the inclusion of this state-level partisanship measure. To capture regional variation, we include a South regional dummy variable.[11] Table 2A.1 provides, for each conflict, the definition of each demographic measure included in the statistical analyses. Table 2A.2 provides summary statistics for all of the variables considered in our models.

Table 2A.1. Definition and Source of Demographic Variables Used in Analyses

	WWII	Korea	Vietnam	Iraq
Census Year	1940	1950	1970	2000
Census Geography Level[a]	County	County	County	Place
Unemployment	% of civilian work force 14+ who are not employed	% of civilian work force 14+ who are not employed	% of civilian work force 16+ who are not employed	% of civilian work force 16+ who are not employed
Income	median rent/month[b]	median family income	median family income	median family income
Education	% of residents age 25+ with at least 4 years of college	% of residents age 25+ with at least 4 years of college	% of residents age 25+ with at least 4 years of college	% of residents age 25+ with at least a BA degree
Race[c]	% of residents who are black	% of residents who are black	% of residents who are black	% of residents who are black
Rural Farm	% rural farm residents	% rural farm residents	% rural farm residents	% rural farm residents
Age	% males age 15–19	median age	median age	median age
Partisanship	% GOP in 1940 pres. election	% GOP in 1948 pres. election	% GOP in 1964 pres. election	% GOP in 2000 pres. election (state level)
Regional	South dummy variable	South dummy variable	South dummy variable	South dummy variable

[a.] See discussion in text for more details on these different units of analysis. [b.] Median family income for 1940 was not available in our data set, so we used median rent per month in tenant dwellings as a proxy. See discussion in appendix for further explanation. [c.] We also ran models with the percentage of nonwhite residents. Due to the strong correlation between percent nonwhite and percent African American, the results were substantively similar.

Table 2A.2. Summary Statistics for Outcome and Explanatory Variables Used in Analyses; Weighted Averages Reported

	Mean	Std. Dev.
World War II		
Casualty rate (per 10,000 males)	45.6	11.7
% Males 14+ not employed	14.4	5.3
Median rent	18.6	9.6
% age 25+ with at least 4 years of college	4.4	2.0
% Black	9.8	14.6
% Rural farm residents	22.9	24.3
% Males age 15–19	4.7	0.7
% Vote for GOP in 1940 pres. elec.	44.8	12.8
Korea		
Casualty rate (per 10,000 males)	4.3	2.1
% Persons 14+ not employed	4.7	2.1
Median family income (in $1,000s)	3.0	0.8
% age 25+ with at least 4 years of college	5.9	2.7
% Black	10.0	13.1
% Rural farm residents	15.3	18.7
Median age	30.2	3.5
% Vote for GOP in 1948 pres. elec.	44.6	13.5
Vietnam		
Casualty rate (per 10,000 males)	5.3	3.7
% Persons 16+ not employed	4.4	1.6
Median family income (in $1,000s)	9.7	2.1
% age 25+ with at least 4 years of college	10.7	4.7
% Black	10.9	11.7
% Rural farm residents	4.1	7.4
Median age	28.7	3.7
% Vote for GOP in 1964 pres. elec.	38.1	10.8
Iraq (place level)		
Casualty rate (per 10,000 males) - Place	0.4	1.7
% Persons 16+ not employed	6.7	3.2
Median family income (in $1,000s)	49.3	16.9
% age 25+ with at least a bachelor's degree	25.0	12.4
% Black	14.7	17.5
% Rural farm residents	0.1	0.4
Median age	34.2	4.4
% Vote for GOP in 2000 pres. elec.	47.9	7.9

The table presents averages weighted by county/place population. For the presidential vote averages, weights are the total number of ballots cast. See text for discussion of calculation of casualty rates and table 2A.1 for definitions of control variables.

B. MODEL SPECIFICATION

Having prepared our casualty and demographic databases, we developed county- and place-level regression models. For each of the four wars, our dependent variable in all of the models is the casualty rate per 10,000 males. Our analysis is truly national, with virtually every county or place included for each war.[12] Our independent variables are the eight demographic measures, including either income or education (but not both simultaneously) in each regression.[13] Because our observations are clustered by state, we also cluster on the state and employ robust standard errors.[14] The general form of our regression model is as follows:

$$Casualty\_Rate_i = \beta_0 + \beta_1 \, Unemployment_i + \beta_2 \, Income \, / \, Education_i +$$
$$\beta_3 \, Afr\_American_i + \beta_4 \, Farm_i + \beta_5 \, Age_i + \beta_6 \, GOP\_Prez_i + \beta_7 \, South_i + \varepsilon_i \qquad [1]$$

Results from empirical analyses of the factors driving casualty inequalities in World War II, Korea, Vietnam, and Iraq, which were used to create the first differences reported in table 2.1, are summarized in tables 2A.3 (education) and 2A.4 (income).

Table 2A.3. OLS Regression Analyses of Factors Influencing Casualty Rates, WWII to Iraq, Models Employing Income Measures

	WWII	Korea	Vietnam	Iraq
Unemployment	10.204	21.178***	−0.292	−0.421
	(7.897)	(4.149)	(7.168)	(2.308)
Income	0.019	−0.820***	−0.242*	−0.015***
	(0.114)	(0.148)	(0.127)	(0.003)
Race	−42.006***	−3.864***	−4.144***	−1.000***
	(6.181)	(0.904)	(1.377)	(0.361)
Rural	−8.651	−0.320	−1.941	3.271
	(5.888)	(0.458)	(1.246)	(2.616)
Age	251.997***	0.006	−0.039	−0.019
	(70.673)	(0.024)	(0.025)	(0.012)
Partisanship	−7.350	0.667	−0.337	−1.847
	(5.002)	(0.775)	(1.389)	(1.125)
South	1.446	0.537	0.716	0.390**
	(1.623)	(0.529)	(0.689)	(0.187)
Constant	40.830***	5.832***	10.186***	3.397***
	(6.595)	(1.369)	(1.627)	(0.720)
Observations	3,023	2,995	3,101	19,413
R^2	0.202	0.054	0.009	0.001

All of the models report robust standard errors clustered on state; all significance tests are two-tailed.
*p < .10, **p < .05, ***p < .01.

Table 2A.4. OLS Regression Analyses of Factors Influencing Casualty Rates, WWII to Iraq, Models Employing Education Measures

	WWII	Korea	Vietnam	Iraq
Unemployment	19.148**	45.263*	2.613	–0.063
	(8.089)	(22.855)	(8.486)	(2.346)
Education	134.392***	–1.780	–8.878*	–2.383***
	(27.036)	(13.619)	(4.441)	(0.422)
Race	–42.535***	–1.543	–3.739**	–0.883**
	(6.563)	(1.522)	(1.512)	(0.354)
Rural	–2.337	1.807	–1.215	2.823
	(4.784)	(1.792)	(1.549)	(2.591)
Age	203.914*	0.087	–0.039	–0.017
	(110.571)	(0.095)	(0.027)	(0.012)
Partisanship	–7.911	2.499	–0.335	–1.676
	(4.979)	(1.638)	(1.387)	(1.133)
South	1.865	1.569**	0.981*	0.427**
	(1.749)	(0.673)	(0.550)	(0.188)
Constant	35.189***	–2.012	8.612***	2.929***
	(6.373)	(6.103)	(1.672)	(0.680)
Observations	3,064	3,053	3,101	19,413
R^2	0.194	0.027	0.009	0.002

All of the models report robust standard errors clustered on state; all significance tests are two-tailed.
$^*p<.10$, $^{**}=p<.05$, $^{***}p<.01$.

C. ADDITIONAL STATISTICAL MODELS

Both the bivariate and multivariate statistical analyses found strong evidence of substantial socioeconomic casualty gaps in Korea, Vietnam, and the war in Iraq. However, one issue that we grappled with at length in the chapter is the level of analysis and the problem of ecological inference. Because we only know the demographic characteristics of fallen soldiers' communities, we cannot draw conclusions about the socioeconomic status of these soldiers themselves. Although it does not eliminate the ecological inference problem, one way that past scholars have sought additional leverage on the question is by examining geographic units even smaller than the county. For example, Barnett, Stanley, and Shore (1992) analyzed the demographics of a stratified sample of Vietnam casualties at the census-tract and block-group levels. In the chapter, we conducted a similar analysis for three subsets of Iraq War casualties, which showed that most of the casualties in our samples came from neighborhoods with lower levels of income and educational attainment than even the relevant figures for their census place as a whole. These analyses suggest that if we could examine all casualties at a smaller geographic unit

Table 2A.5. Place-Level Analyses of Vietnam Casualty Rates

	[1]	[2]	[3]
Unemployment	4.459	5.790	3.659
	(3.915)	(4.858)	(4.230)
Income	–0.144**		
	(0.072)		
College		–3.897***	
		(1.350)	
High school			–3.699***
			(1.103)
South	1.823***	2.075***	1.737***
	(0.615)	(0.530)	(0.566)
Constant	3.622***	2.545***	4.312***
	(0.915)	(0.352)	(0.800)
Observations	7,388	7,388	7,388
R^2	0.075	0.072	0.081

Casualty rate in the Vietnam place-level models is the number of casualties per ten thousand residents. All of the models report robust standard errors clustered on state; all significance tests are two-tailed. $^*p<.10$, $^{**}p<.05$, $^{***}p<.01$.

the results would likely bolster our claims about the presence of a strong socioeconomic casualty gap.

To provide additional leverage on this question, we were also able to replicate our Vietnam analyses for a large subset of casualties at the place level. Although it is not as comprehensive as the 2000 census used to construct place-level models in Iraq, the 1970 State of the Cities Data System (SOCDS) maintained by the Department of Housing and Urban Development (HUD) does provide some demographic data on all places with populations greater than 2,500 (with a few exceptions in which the census reported data on communities with even lower populations). More than 65 percent of the American public lived in one of the census places for which 1970 census data are available, and more than 70 percent of Vietnam casualties came from one of these communities.[15]

Because the SOCDS data set did not contain all of the demographic information available from the census at the county level, we were unable to include all of the variables in the same form that we did in our first round of county-level analysis. In particular, the SOCDS did not include a measure of age or race at the place level. The variables we were able to consider were unemployment, median family income, percentage of residents with four years of college, percentage of high school graduates, and the South regional dummy variable. We also had to use total place population (as opposed to just male population) as the denominator for constructing the casualty rate.

The results from the place-level regressions reported in table 2A.5 confirm our results at the county level. In all three models we find strong, statistically significant inverse relationships between a census place's level of income or educational attainment and its local casualty rate in Vietnam. The consistency of our results across multiple specifications and levels of analysis greatly improves confidence in the robustness of the evidence for socioeconomic casualty gaps observed across wars.

3

Selection, Occupational Assignment, and the Emergence of the Casualty Gap

The analyses presented in the preceding chapter provide compelling evidence that in Korea, Vietnam, and Iraq a significant casualty gap emerged between socioeconomically advantaged and disadvantaged communities. The data also show that on some metrics the gap appears to have widened in the Iraq conflict. We turn now to the nature of the forces that produced these casualty gaps and caused them to vary across wars.

What factors affect which Americans die in war? We discuss in this chapter two possible answers: selection into the armed forces and occupational assignment within the military. We begin by examining the mechanisms through which new soldiers enter the armed forces. The men and women who enter the U.S. military are not a random sample of eligible citizens drawn from the nation as a whole. Rather, some Americans actively seek out military service; others are recruited into it; and, when demand outstrips supply, the federal government, up until 1973, has turned to conscription. If the resulting composition of the military does not mirror that of society as a whole, then selection mechanisms may set the stage for casualty gaps to emerge.

However, even a military whose composition reflects the demographics of the nation as a whole can experience a casualty gap. Not all members of the armed forces face the same risk of dying on a foreign battlefield because the military assigns some soldiers to occupations with high levels of combat exposure, while it assigns other soldiers to occupations with much lower levels of battlefield risk. As Col. Samuel Hays wrote in *Army Magazine* in 1967, "In many ways the differences in sacrifice between those who are called to the service and those who are excused are less drastic than the differences which result from different assignments in the Services . . . no one could find much equity between pounding a type-writer in the Pentagon and carrying the M16 rifle in the jungles of Vietnam."[1] This occupational assignment, too, is far from random. Through a series of tests the military assesses each new soldier's aptitudes and preexisting skill sets. On the basis of this information and additional evaluations, it assigns soldiers to the tasks best suited to their personal skills and to the military's needs. If soldiers assigned to positions with high risks of combat exposure differ systematically from soldiers assigned to occupations with lower levels of combat risk, then occupational assignment, too, has the potential to generate a casualty gap.

Thus, selection and assignment mechanisms may each lead to the emergence of casualty gaps—particularly, as our analysis reveals, along socioeconomic lines. However, for selection and assignment to explain the patterns observed in chapter 2, they must change across wars. More specifically, such changes in selection and assignment mechanisms must logically accord with the observed variance in casualty gaps over time. To understand why selection and assignment processes change, we focus on two interrelated factors: the contours of the social and political environment in which manpower policies are made and the nature and scale of the conflict at hand.

While politicians are reticent to interfere in the military's occupational assignment practices, they frequently weigh in on how the armed forces should be recruited. When the military relies on conscription, national, state, and local officials can dramatically influence the composition of the armed forces by determining what groups of Americans are eligible for military service and how those from the eligible pool are inducted. Alternatively, political forces can dramatically change selection mechanisms if policymakers opt, as they did in 1973, to end conscription altogether and mandate an all-volunteer force. Such changes in manpower policy can fundamentally alter the relationship of the military to society.

Equally important, the nature and scale of the conflict itself critically determine the military's needs for manpower, particularly for the front-line forces. As a result, these strategic needs can affect the operation of both selection and assignment mechanisms. When more soldiers are needed, the military may change the way it recruits, and when a conflict requires more combat infantry, military leaders adjust personnel assignment patterns accordingly.[2] Large-scale conflicts and the resulting intense demand for combat troops circumscribe both the military's and political leaders' flexibility; by contrast, smaller-scale conflicts with less intense demand for combat troops give civilian and military policymakers more flexibility in how they obtain and utilize personnel resources. This can have significant ramifications for the nature of the casualty gap.

To assess the effects that military selection and occupational assignment policies have on the casualty gap, we marshal a broad array of historical and empirical evidence. We review extensive literatures in political science and other disciplines that suggest how selection and assignment might produce casualty gaps, particularly along socioeconomic lines. We also revisit our casualty data to test whether changes in the casualty gap both across and within wars correspond to changes in selection and assignment processes.

By understanding the mechanisms most likely to have produced casualty gaps, we gain additional leverage into the question we ended with in chapter 2: Is there an unobserved casualty gap at the individual level— between citizens with higher and lower levels of socioeconomic opportunity—that underlies the observed casualty gap at the aggregate level between socioeconomically advantaged and disadvantaged communities? Because of the barriers to ecological inference, our aggregate-level casualty data in chapter 2 alone cannot tell us whether a casualty gap also exists at the individual level. However, our analysis in this chapter goes a step further. If the mechanisms most likely to have produced the observed casualty gaps (i.e., the mechanisms that best fit the historical and empirical data) produce casualty gaps at both the individual and the community levels, then the best available evidence is most consistent with the theory that there is both a community- *and* an individual-level casualty gap. The evidence we present in this chapter is still not conclusive; however, it does shift the burden of proof to those who reject an individual-level casualty gap. Those who would deny such a gap must put forward evidence for plausible alternative mechanisms that could produce the observed casualty gaps at the community level without generating a corresponding gap between socioeconomically advantaged and disadvantaged individuals.

MECHANISM #1: SELECTION IN THE MODERN WARS

One of the most straightforward explanations for inequality in wartime death is inequality in who serves in the military. For more than fifty years, an extensive literature at the crossroads of sociology, history, economics, and political science has investigated military manpower policies and changes in them over time.[3] In the online appendix we review this literature in greater depth, but here we focus more narrowly on the extent to which inequality in service can help explain inequality in casualties.

The decision to serve in the military involves a mix of economic and noneconomic factors.[4] While noneconomic motivations, such as the call of patriotic duty or the desire to seek adventure, certainly motivate individuals to enlist, economic factors also play a large role. Military sociologist Charles Moskos categorized these different sets of incentives as the "institutional" and "occupational" motivations for military service.[5] For those who embrace an institutional view, military service "is legitimated in terms of values and norms… [It is] a purpose transcending individual self-interest in favor of a presumed higher good." Military service for these individuals is a calling. By contrast, for those who see the military through a more occupational lens, military service "is legitimated in terms of the marketplace."[6] Both institutional and occupational incentives have clearly played an important role in shaping the decisions of millions of young men and women to serve our nation in the armed forces, and the relative balance of these two incentives has varied across individuals and over time.[7]

However, an extensive literature testifies to the critical importance of economic incentives in spurring enlistments throughout U.S. history.[8] At the aggregate level, a number of studies have demonstrated strong correlations between the health of the economy and patterns in military enlistments. For example in a 1994 RAND study of the factors correlated with the successful recruitment of high-quality enlistments from 1978 to 1993, two of the factors with the greatest influence on the number of such recruits obtained by the army were the youth unemployment rate and the rate of military pay growth relative to the civilian sector.[9]

This linkage continues to the present day. Reflecting on the surge in military enlistments during the economic troubles of 2008, which followed immediately on the heels of two of the most difficult recruiting years in recent memory (2006 and 2007), Undersecretary for Personnel and Readiness David S. C. Chu readily acknowledged the faltering economy's role in boosting volunteering: "We do benefit when things look less positive in civil society."[10] Other analyses of enlistment decisions at the individual level demonstrate, logically, that the young men and women most likely to volunteer are those for whom the occupational and educational benefits that the military affords are more appealing than their options in the civilian labor market.[11] As summarized by military historian Peter Karsten, "most volunteers, today and for the past 200 years, joined the service in order to gain economic rewards, social mobility, or skills needed later in civilian life."[12] To be sure, there is much to applaud in the military's role in promoting social and economic mobility for those whose other options are not as promising.

The evidence for the critical importance of economic incentives in volunteering dynamics is perhaps even stronger when we examine the military's own recruitment policies. The armed forces do not stand by passively waiting for enough men and women to volunteer. Rather, throughout U.S. history the military has aggressively recruited new soldiers into the service.[13] And when the military has experienced difficulty in attracting enough volunteers, it has repeatedly targeted its recruiting efforts on those facing the greatest difficulties in the civilian labor market. For example, in the wake of World War I the chief of the recruiting division of the Adjutant General's Office explained that "our appeal is not to the skilled workman, but to the young man who has been unable to complete his education." In some cases, military recruiting campaigns were even geographically targeted to cities and regions facing the bleakest economic prospects. For example, in the early 1920s the General Recruiting Service identified the youth in places like Aberdeen, South Dakota, as strong prospects for recruiting: after the harvesting season, "many of these young men . . . find themselves many miles from home, out of employment with little or no money and, if properly approached, conclude that the Army offers the best solution to their difficulties." In such conditions, the military can more successfully compete with the civilian labor market.

Similarly, when President Roosevelt ordered a dramatic expansion of the military's size in anticipation of U.S. involvement in World War II, those recently unemployed were among the most attractive targets. One directive stated explicitly, "If a factory has just closed down in some town in the district, at once rush a canvassing party there." This targeted military recruiting dovetailed nicely with the New Deal goal of providing Depression relief. In 1934 General Douglas MacArthur went before the U.S. Senate and, in addition to arguments based on military necessity, used unemployment as one of the reasons the country should expand its armed forces. "There is no method that I know of," said MacArthur, "which has been devised in the efforts the government has made to relieve unemployment that would do it so cheaply." In the analysis of historian Robert Griffith, "the massive unemployment of the Great Depression represented a bonanza to the regular army."[14]

Recruiters' appeals to economic interests continued after World War II. Echoing Moskos's occupational conception of military service, historian Mark Grandstaff's study of the Korean War era found that "the efforts of advertisers, recruiters, and community organizations convinced the public that a modern military career was similar to other middle-class 'careers.'" In the 1950s the "military was promoting itself as a big business which was a good employer providing its personnel 'substantial opportunity for improvement' and 'good working conditions.'"[15]

Economic inducements remain at the forefront of military recruiting efforts to meet the demand for troops in Iraq. While recruiters and advertisers use a wide range of tactics to reach potential enlistees, economic incentives remain a very visible and important tool in their arsenal. Enlistment bonuses of up to $40,000 and money for college are prominently touted in recruiting pamphlets and literature.[16] In addition, on the army's Web site under the heading "It's More than Just Salary" the army places itself in direct competition with civilian careers and shows potential recruits how military pay and benefits can substantially outpace those of similar careers in the civilian sector.[17]

If volunteers throughout U.S. history have been driven to enlist, at least in part, by economic incentives, then selection mechanisms may contribute to the emergence of socioeconomic casualty gaps. Because of data limitations it is difficult to examine their influence directly; however, one observable implication of our proposed logic is that the casualty gap should grow as the military's reliance on volunteers increases. If we return to our data, this is the pattern we see emerging. Volunteers comprised only a third of the military in the early 1940s, whereas 66 percent of the fighting force was filled by draftees. In Korea, the percentage of the military's ranks filled by volunteers rose to roughly 50 percent, and in Vietnam it increased even further to about 60 percent.[18] Thus, one of the most unambiguous trends across these three conflicts is an increasing reliance on volunteers, which correlates strongly with the emergence of the casualty gap between socioeconomically advantaged and disadvantaged communities.

The reason for this dramatic change in the military's volunteer composition from World War II to Korea to Vietnam is almost certainly the vastly different combat manpower requirements of the three conflicts. Table 3.1 presents casualty and military mobilization information for six of America's largest wars. Outside of the Civil War, America's peak mobilization came in World War II, when more than one in ten Americans were in the military, and if we take gender restrictions into account, the percentage of the eligible population in arms was far higher. By contrast, participation levels in Korea and Vietnam were 4 percent, about one-third of the World War II level. When fewer men are needed to fight, the government has less need to supplement volunteering with conscription. Further, with a military increasingly defined as occupation rather than institution, marketplace incentives grew more prominent.

As the military's reliance on volunteers increased, socio-economic casualty gaps also increased. In World War II – a war whose massive manpower needs required a full two-thirds of the armed services to be recruited through conscription – we saw little evidence of a casualty gap between

Table 3.1. Serving and Dying in America's Major Wars

	Civil War	World War I	World War II	Korea	Vietnam	Iraq
[1] Estimated U.S. population	27,489,561	92,228,531	131,669,275	151,325,798	203,212,877	284,796,887
[2] Estimated number serving in military	3,447,363	4,734,991	16,112,566	5,720,000	8,744,000	1,400,000
[3] Estimated casualties	517,808	116,516	405,399	36,574	58,220	4,212
[4] Estimated % of those serving who died	15.02%	2.46%	2.52%	0.64%	0.67%	0.30%

Sources for casualty and service information is the Department of Defense's *Principal Wars in Which the United States Participated, U.S. Military Personnel Serving and Casualties* (updated through December 2008) and Livermore (1901). The Korean War casualty count is for in-theater casualties; the Department of Defense recognizes 54,246 American casualties sustained worldwide during the Korean War. Civil War casualty numbers include those killed in action and those dying from disease, from both the Union and Confederate armies. Source for Iraq War casualty and service information (active duty personnel, excluding the estimated 1.1 million serving in the Reserves) is data through December 31, 2008 provided by the Department of Defense's Statistical Information Analysis Division. Source for estimated U.S. population is the U.S. Census, various years.

high and low income or education communities. Indeed, the only evidence of a socio-economic casualty gap that we observed in World War II was between communities with high and low levels of unemployment. And on this dimension, we cited government reports showing that the military openly targeted its recruiting efforts in communities where factories had closed and unemployment spiked. Moreover, in the years leading up to World War II military officials, including General Douglas MacArthur, bolstered their case for an expanded military by emphasizing its value as a full employment program. Thus, while the relatively lower reliance on economically-influenced volunteers may help explain the lack of an income or education casualty gap in World War II, the military's targeted recruiting policies dovetail nicely with the only observed casualty gap along the unemployment dimension.

In the Korean and Vietnam wars, by contrast, in which more than half of the fighting force comprised volunteers, we saw significant socioeconomic casualty gaps emerge. This correlation between variance in the military's reliance on volunteers and the size of the socioeconomic casualty gaps across these three wars is not conclusive proof of a causal link. However, the evidence is strongly consistent with our hypothesis that economic considerations factor into volunteers' decision to join the military and that those economic decisions in turn contribute to the creation of socioeconomic casualty gaps at the community level.

The War in Iraq and the AVF

In 1973 the United States abolished the draft and instituted the all-volunteer force (AVF).[19] As a result, the Iraq War is unique in our sample because it has been waged entirely by men and women who volunteered for military service. According to our theoretical logic, this dramatic change in selection mechanisms should open the door for significant socioeconomic casualty gaps to emerge. Consistent with this expectation, the empirical analyses of the preceding chapter show that the war in Iraq has generated perhaps the largest casualty gap between socioeconomically advantaged and disadvantaged communities of any of the four wars.

To this point, we have been able to demonstrate a correlation only between the percentage of the military recruited as volunteers and the size of the socioeconomic casualty gap at the community level. However, the rich array of military personnel records available on the modern AVF allows us to go further and determine more directly whether military recruits are truly coming disproportionately from socioeconomically disadvantaged communities.

Ideally, we would like to know whether military recruits themselves come disproportionately from socioeconomically disadvantaged family backgrounds. As discussed before, this claim is widespread in the existing literature. Because the military does not keep data on the preenlistment family incomes of new recruits, the question is difficult to answer directly. However, the military does record the ZIP code for each recruit.[20] Therefore, most analyses follow a path similar to the one we now adopt and examine whether military recruits come disproportionately from low-income and low-education ZIP codes. The technical appendix provides details of the data and analytic techniques.

We begin by examining the distribution of enlistments in different parts of the country. Here we focus on new recruits into the U.S. Army. According to Department of Defense figures, as of January 2009 almost 60 percent of Iraq War casualties served in the army; when the U.S. Army Reserve and Army National Guard are included, this figure rises to almost 75 percent. As a result, trends in army recruitment data offer the best insight into how selection mechanisms may be producing the casualty gaps we observe in chapter 2. In figure 3.1 we present a ZIP code–level analysis of the percentage of army recruits by income quartile from 1999 to 2006 that utilizes demographic ZIP code data from the 2000 census.[21] The recruiting data from earlier years shows an even greater gap along socioeconomic lines. Army recruits have come disproportionately from parts of the country that are lower on the socioeconomic scale. To be sure, this disparity has decreased significantly over time. Nevertheless, while the distribution has flattened somewhat over the period 1999–2006, a substantial gap remains between the top and the lower quartiles.[22]

When subjected to more rigorous statistical analysis, the relationships suggested by these summary statistics continue to hold. To examine the relationships between a ZIP code's median income and level of educational attainment and its per-capita army recruitment rate during the period from 1999 to 2006, we constructed statistical models that parallel those reported in chapter 2. The full regression results are reported and discussed in the technical appendix. Identical models for recruits into all service branches that yield virtually identical results are presented in the online appendix that accompanies this chapter. Even after controlling for other ZIP code demographics, we find strong, statistically significant inverse relationships between a community's army recruitment rate and its median income and percentage of college-educated residents. Figure 3.2 presents a series of first differences derived from our models to illustrate the estimated effect of a shift in each independent variable while holding all other variables constant at their means or medians. These analyses suggest that moving from the bottom to the top quartile on either the college or income metric produces an almost 20

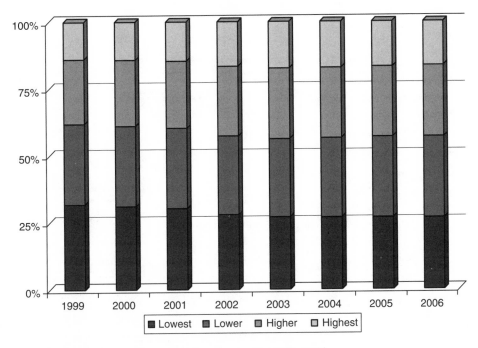

Figure 3.1. Army enlistments by income quartile, 1999–2006.

percent drop in per-capita recruits. Moving from the bottom to top decile suggests an even greater reduction of 40 percent.

The results of our ZIP code–level army recruiting analysis mirror quite well the results from our place-level analysis of casualty rates. Community income and education levels were statistically significant predictors both of a community's casualty rate and of its enlistment rate.

While our ZIP code–level analysis of recruits cannot speak to the personal backgrounds of individual soldiers, additional data from military sources suggest that the army is increasingly drawing on recruits with lower levels of *ex ante* skills and economic opportunities in the civilian realm.[23] As early as 2005, to cope with the decreased supply of willing recruits needed for continued military operations in Iraq and Afghanistan, the army increased the allowable percentage of low-skilled, Category IV recruits from less than 1 percent to 4 percent.[24] In a similar vein, the proportion of recruits in the highest category also dropped precipitously. These and similar personnel recruiting shifts had an almost immediate effect on the individual-level composition of the army. According to the Department of Defense's FY 2006 personnel report, the proportion of recruits deemed "high quality" by the military declined sharply from

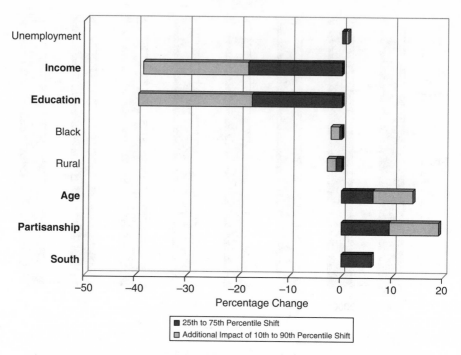

Figure 3.2. The impact of ZIP code demographics on ZIP code per-capita army enlistment rates, 1999–2006.
Note: Statistically significant effects are indicated with boldface.

60 percent in 2003 to 45 percent in 2006.[25] In October of 2007 the army reported its lowest levels of volunteers for basic training in any year since the introduction of the AVF in 1973. This only increased the pressure for further changes to recruitment policies that may have produced even wider enlistment gaps in more recent years.[26]

Whether this trend changes in the wake of the financial crises of 2008 and 2009 and beyond remains to be seen, but certainly for the period we analyze in chapter 2 there is evidence that the military has struggled in some years to meet its enlistment quotas, and as a result it has drawn increasingly on recruits without high school diplomas and with lower standardized test scores. Such selection mechanisms have the potential to create casualty gaps at both the community level and the individual level.

Taken as a whole, the evidence on disparities in military service goes a long way toward explaining the casualty gap that has emerged in Iraq. For example, in chapter 2 we found that communities in the bottom three income deciles have suffered 38 percent of the nation's casualties in Iraq, while those in the top three deciles have suffered 23 percent of the casualty burden. In terms of army enlistments, the bottom three income deciles together comprise 35 percent of army recruits, while the top three income deciles have contributed only 21 percent from 1999 to 2006. Thus, if casualties were simply a random draw from the army as a whole, we would expect to see a casualty gap between the top and the bottom income deciles of approximately 14 percent; the actual figure in chapter 2 is only slightly higher at 15 percent. That these two figures are so similar suggests that variation in enlistment explains in large part variation in casualties. However, there remains additional variation across communities to be explained.

As a more direct test of the relationship between enlistments and casualties, we integrated our casualty and enlistment databases by replicating our chapter 2 models with an additional variable: county per-capita enlistment levels. As described in detail in the technical appendix, we found that enlistments are positively related to local casualty rates, just missing standard significance levels. Consistent with our expectation, communities that have more residents enlisted in the AVF have experienced higher casualty rates in Iraq. However, even after controlling for a community's enlistment rate, we continue to find strong, statistically significant effects for median income and education. Thus, selection mechanisms explain part but not all of the casualty gap story. Accordingly, in the next section we turn our analytic focus to the mechanism of occupational assignment within the military.

MECHANISM #2: OCCUPATIONAL ASSIGNMENT WITHIN THE MILITARY

The vast majority of those who serve do not die in combat, and those who do die are not a random sample of the military population as a whole. Table 3.1 estimates, for each major war, the U.S. population, the number of Americans serving in the military, and the number of casualties as a percentage of those serving in the military. The selection mechanism tells us only how we move from those who live in the country (row 1) to those who serve in the military (row 2). It does not tell us how we move from those who serve (row 2) to those who die (row 3). This move from service to death is important to investigate because combat death is so rare. In World War II, more than 97 percent of those who served in the armed forces did not perish in combat. In Korea, Vietnam, and Iraq this percentage rose to more than 99 percent.

The most significant predictor of a soldier's likelihood of dying in wartime is his or her proximity to combat.[27] The reason that most military personnel do not die during wartime is that they are either not deployed to the theater of war or deployed but not engaged in combat operations. During the Korean War, for instance, only about 25 percent of the army's strength was deployed to South Korea, and of those deployed units, only about 33 percent saw combat in 1953.[28] Once deployed to a war zone, a soldier's exposure to combat is largely a function of his or her occupational assignment within the military. For example, in 1953 the percentage of personnel in army infantry divisions engaged in combat was 62 percent, almost double the average for all units in the theater of war. Given the infantry's prominence in front-line combat, it is not surprising that infantry have traditionally borne the brunt of the casualty burden.

Recognizing the critical importance of differential exposure to combat dangers, we rephrase the subtitle of the 1967 Marshall Commission's report—"Who Serves When Not All Serve?"—and investigate a related, but different question: "Who serves *in front-line combat units* when not all do?" Since World War I, the military has relied on various forms of aptitude testing to optimize its personnel assignment process; these tests, in turn, help determine which soldiers face the greatest exposure to battlefield risk. In World War II, the army and marines used the Army General Classification Test (AGCT) to help assign more than 12 million new recruits to military occupations. The military also attempted to identify those with preexisting occupational skills suited to meet specific military needs. However, in a comprehensive, three-volume study of World War II personnel policy, Columbia economist Eli Ginzberg documented the military's failure to develop a system that took full advantage of its manpower resources:

> Not until the end of the war did the Army finally develop a system whereby it was able to keep men with high ability and skill in a special pool until suitable assignments could be found for them. The pressures to get men into training or duty positions were always very great... This meant that on any one day, unmet requirements determined to what unit a man would be sent. Once it was determined that a recruit could meet the minimum performance standards of the unit he was to join, no further questions were asked. Pressure and speed resulted in frequent errors. Older men, in a flabby condition, were sent for infantry training; young athletes with low intelligence scores were sent to Signal Corps units where men with a flair for numbers or gadgets were needed... It was not until early 1944, too late in the war to affect most recruits, that the Army adopted the system of profiling men which had been instituted much earlier in the Canadian and British armies.[29]

The immediate manpower needs did not allow enough time to develop more efficient occupational assignment procedures, particularly in the early years of the war.

Military leaders learned a great deal from these experiences in World War II, and as a result the instruments they subsequently used for occupational assignment became considerably more complex.[30] In 1950, on the eve of the Korean War, the military adopted a new uniform test for all of the services, the Armed Forces Qualification Test (AFQT). Although modeled on the earlier AGCT, the AFQT was designed to serve only as a general screening mechanism for applicants and new recruits. Each branch then used recruits' AFQT results, as well as their scores on more specialized, service-specific testing batteries, such as the Army Classification Battery, to assign new soldiers to specific occupations.[31] This process lasted through the Vietnam War, and it greatly improved the efficiency of occupational assignment.

After Vietnam, the Department of Defense directed all of the service branches to adopt and utilize a new test for both general screening and occupational assignment: the Armed Services Vocational Aptitude Battery (ASVAB). The stated purpose of the ASVAB is "to determine eligibility for enlistment and to establish qualifications for assignment to specific skills."[32] The military uses this information in conjunction with stated preferences, soldier performance during initial training, and additional background information such as physical capabilities to determine a soldier's primary military occupational specialty (PMOS).[33]

Thus, particularly in Korea, Vietnam, and Iraq, occupational assignment has followed a clear pattern of sorting by ability. For example, in his study of combat infantrymen in Korea, Lieutenant Colonel Roger Little found that "personnel assignment policies introduced an additional screening effect" as "men with civilian skills or education were assigned to rear-echelon duties . . . [whereas] men assigned to the rifle company were most likely to lack highly valued social attributes."[34] Echoing Little's analysis, historian George Flynn, in his study of assignment policies in Korea, observed that "without question military assignment, controlled by the armed forces and not Selective Service, to a combat arm correlated [inversely] with education, which correlated with income status and race."[35] If the soldiers thus singled out for combat occupations are also more likely to hail from socioeconomically disadvantaged communities, then occupational sorting could contribute to the casualty gaps we observe in chapter 2.

Unfortunately, we do not have data on the military occupations, socioeconomic backgrounds, and home communities of all of the members of the armed forces with which to test directly our hypotheses about occupational assignment. However, we can test them indirectly using the data we introduced in chapter 2. If our arguments about occupational assignment and its consequences are correct, then we should see two patterns in the casualty data. First, we should find a larger casualty gap among infantry casualties; that is, infantry casualties should be more heavily concentrated in communities with lower median incomes and levels of educational attainment than noninfantry casualties. Second, we should see divergent patterns between officer casualties and enlisted casualties. Assignment processes suggest that enlisted casualties, on average, should come disproportionately from communities at the lower end of the socioeconomic scale. Officer casualties, by contrast, should come, on average, from communities with substantially higher levels of income and education. We are able to test these two hypotheses with additional rounds of analysis of our casualties datasets.

For each soldier, the Korea, Vietnam, and Iraq casualty data files list his or her PMOS.[36] Using this information, we can create two casualty rates for each community—its number of *infantry casualties* per 10,000 males and its number of *noninfantry casualties* per 10,000 males.[37] We then reestimate the models from chapter 2 to examine how a community's demographic characteristics correlate with both its infantry and noninfantry casualty rates. If the occupational assignment process is random, then we should see no significant differences between the results of the two models. If, however, military occupational assignment results in a disproportionate number of recruits from poorer, less-educated communities entering the infantry, then we should see stronger negative correlations between community income/education and infantry casualty rates than between community income/education and noninfantry casualty rates. In other words, the socioeconomic casualty gap should be larger for infantry casualties than for noninfantry casualties.

Available data also allow us to examine differences between enlisted and officer casualty rates.[38] If officer and enlisted casualties come from similar parts of the country, then we should see no difference in the relationship of the two casualty rates to community demographics. If, however, occupational assignment makes it more likely that recruits from socioeconomically advantaged communities will enter the officer corps than recruits from less advantaged communities, then we should see the community demographic variables having different effects in the enlisted and officer statistical models.[39]

The results, presented in full in the technical appendix and summarized in figures 3.3 and 3.4, indicate that assignment policies contributed to the casualty gaps observed in chapter 2. In Korea, Vietnam, and Iraq, both infantry (figure 3.3) and enlisted (figure 3.4) casualty rates are more closely tied to socioeconomic conditions than noninfantry and officer

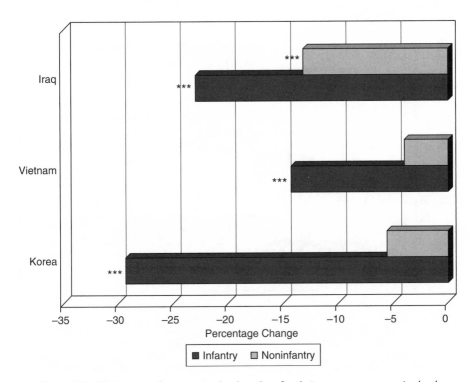

Figure 3.3. The impact of community-level median family income on community-level infantry and noninfantry casualty rates.

Note: Two-tailed significance denoted as: * p<.10, ** p<.05, *** p<.01. Each bar represents the estimated effect of a shift from the 25th to the 75th percentile in community income.

casualty rates, respectively. Our statistical models suggest that moving from the 25th to the 75th percentile in terms of county median income would produce a 29 percent drop in a community's Korean infantry casualty rate but no statistically significant change in its noninfantry casualty rate. In Vietnam the same shift would produce a 14 percent drop in the infantry casualty rate but again no significant change in the noninfantry rate. Finally, in Iraq a similar trend appears: Moving from the poorest quartile to the richest quartile would produce a 23 percent drop in a community's infantry casualty rate versus only a 13 percent drop in its noninfantry casualty rate. The results of our infantry versus noninfantry casualty rate models suggest a casual pathway: Community casualty rates are driven by infantry casualty rates, and poorer parts of the country are contributing disproportionately more soldiers to those infantry occupations.

Turning to the analyses of enlisted and officer casualty rates, we see another important distinction. While there is a significant inverse relationship between community income levels and enlisted casualty rates in each war, in the models of officer casualty rates the income coefficient is

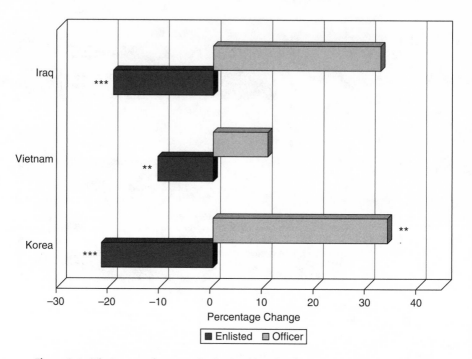

Figure 3.4. The impact of community-level median family income on community-level enlisted and officer casualty rates.

Note: Two-tailed significance denoted as: $^*p<.10$, $^{**}p<.05$, $^{***}p<.01$. Each bar represents the estimated effect of a shift from the 25th to the 75th percentile in community income.

actually positive, albeit statistically insignificant, for Vietnam and Iraq. Casualties from the enlisted ranks are from communities that are, on average, much less affluent than the communities of casualties from the officer corps. Figure 3.4 presents the estimated effect of shifts in community income on both enlisted and officer casualty rates. Moving from the 25th percentile to the 75th percentile of place median income suggests a 23 percent reduction of the enlisted casualty rate in Korea, an 11 percent drop in Vietnam, and a 19 percent decrease in Iraq. By contrast, the same shifts in community income have no statistically significant influence on officer casualty rates in Vietnam and Iraq and have a positive effect on the Korea officer casualty rate.

Revisiting our block-group analyses of Iraq casualties from the 100 richest and poorest census places from chapter 2 affords an additional test of this hypothesis. Previously, we compared the socioeconomic demographics of these casualties' neighborhoods with those of their communities as a whole. We found that most of the soldiers from the richest places lived in block groups with lower levels of median income and educational attainment than their community as a whole; conversely, casualties from poor communities hailed disproportionately from neighborhoods whose socioeconomic demographics are virtually identical to those observed at the place level. Here we revisit this data and compare the proportion of each group that were officers versus enlisted personnel. The results are striking. Whereas 24 percent of the casualties from the 100 richest places were officers, only 2 percent of those from the poorest cities and towns were in the officer corps.

This evidence suggests a further way in which differences in types of service contribute to the casualty gap. Enlisted personnel, who comprise the vast majority of combat casualties, come disproportionately from communities on the lower rungs of the socioeconomic ladder. Officers, by contrast, are less likely to die in combat and come disproportionately from communities at the higher end of the socioeconomic spectrum.

Thus, the evidence for occupational sorting in our casualty data is abundantly clear. Casualty rates for the infantry and the enlisted ranks are more strongly related to community wealth and education than are noninfantry and officer casualty rates. Because lower-skilled recruits are more likely to come from less advantaged communities and because they are subsequently more likely to be assigned to occupations with greater combat risks than recruits with higher skills, the occupational assignment mechanism may produce a casualty gap, even if the military as a whole is representative of the civilian population. Similarly, because the enlisted ranks come disproportionately from lower income/education communities and because they are more likely than officer ranks, on average, to see front-line combat, assignment by rank also explains why a casualty gap can develop even if the military's overall demographics may roughly mirror society.

THE SELECTION MECHANISM REVISITED: THE ROLE OF THE DRAFT

The available data strongly suggest that both selection and assignment mechanisms combined to produce the casualty gaps observed in the preceding chapter. However, for World War II, Korea, and Vietnam, our description of military selection mechanisms is incomplete; in each of these conflicts the military relied to varying degrees on the draft to meet its need for manpower. These drafts were critically important components of military selection policies, and they also affected the operation of occupational assignment. Our goals in this section are threefold. First, we discuss whether changes in draft policies over time correlate with changes in the casualty gap across wars observed in chapter 2. Second, by exploiting a near natural experiment during the Vietnam War—the adoption of the draft lottery in December of 1969—we examine whether a dramatic and sudden shift in draft policies affects the nature of the casualty gaps that emerge within a single conflict. Finally, we consider whether the absence of the draft can provide insight into the widening of the casualty gap in the current war in Iraq.

Changes in the Draft and in the Casualty Gap over Time

Earlier in the chapter we argued that the relative percentages of the military filled by volunteers and draftees can have a significant influence on the nature of the casualty gap. By inducting into military service young men for whom the economic inducements of a military career were insufficient to prompt them to volunteer, the draft should yield a fighting force more representative of the nation as a whole. Yet, the nature of the draft has changed considerably over time in response to the changing scales of the conflicts the military has waged and in response to shifting political dynamics. We now consider whether the specific features of the World War II, Korea, and Vietnam drafts and changes in them over time correlate with the specific casualty gaps observed in chapter 2.

While the military recruited aggressively in the late 1930s by emphasizing the economic benefits of military service and targeting young men with limited opportunities in the civilian sector, volunteerism alone failed to provide enough men for the massive struggle of World War II. In 1940 President Franklin Roosevelt took aggressive steps to bolster the nation's fighting force by signing into law the Selective Training and Service Act, which provided for the nation's first peacetime draft. The sheer scale of the impending conflict forced policymakers to cast a wide net to meet the requisite manpower demand. Even before Pearl Harbor, the draft law conscripted almost a million men into the armed services, and by the end of 1945 that total had soared to more than ten million.

The Selective Training and Service Act did grant some categories of men exemptions from military service.[40] For example, one occupational group that had great success in obtaining protections from the draft was farmers. This element of draft design is consistent with our finding in chapter 2 that rural communities in World War II, Korea and Vietnam suffered lower casualty rates, on average, than urban communities, all else being equal.[41] However, the scale of the demand for manpower limited the ability of both federal policymakers and local draft boards alike to place too many restrictions on the pool of men eligible for induction. Exempting too many able-bodied men from the draft could have seriously jeopardized the military's ability to secure the troops it needed to wage a long, costly, two-front war.[42]

In fact, the World War II medical and mental fitness requirements for draft eligibility may help explain the *positive* relationships previously observed between a community's income and education levels and its casualty rate. For instance, in a two-month period in the summer of 1941 alone, draft boards rejected more than 90,000 registrants in forty-seven states because they failed to meet the fourth-grade-level literacy requirement; ultimately, draft boards rejected more than five million men between the ages of eighteen and thirty-seven as a result of their physical exams.[43] Thus, the World War II draft may help explain our finding that—in stark contrast to Korea and Vietnam—the poorest and most undereducated counties actually suffered lower than average casualty rates in World War II. More men in these communities were simply deemed unfit for induction into the service.[44]

Changes in the draft's design and implementation, which began in the late 1940s and continued after Korea, also offer important insights into the contours of the casualty gaps observed for the Korean and Vietnam wars in chapter 2. What set the Korean draft apart from the World War II draft was its dramatically smaller scale. Whereas the military conscripted more than 10 million men into the armed forces (66 percent of the total force) in World War II, only 1.5 million men (50 percent of the total force) were drafted in Korea.[45] Because the demand for manpower was much smaller, policymakers had more freedom to expand the system of exemptions and deferments. One of the most important changes was the considerable expansion of student deferments, which allowed young men with strong test scores and good academic standing to continue their education.[46] The Selective Service Act of 1948 also opened the door for expanded occupational exemptions on the grounds of providing for "the fullest possible utilization of the nation's technological, scientific, and other critical manpower resources."[47] In the analysis of Peter Kindsvatter, a retired lieutenant colonel and command historian of the U.S. Army Ordnance Center and School, these changes to the draft law, combined with the significantly smaller demand for manpower, afforded local draft boards more flexibility in using exemptions within the law to shield skilled workers in war-related occupations from conscription.[48] The result, in the analysis of sociologists Morris Janowitz and Roger Little, was that "since the outbreak of Korean hostilities, selective service probably operates to procure a relatively larger number of lower class youth for the Army. Although at the time of registration all social classes are represented, by the time of call-up for induction, lower class youths will be less likely to have acquired occupational or educational deferment."[49] Thus, the design of the Korean draft did not lend itself to blunting the emergence of a socioeconomic casualty gap in the same way as the more inclusive World War II draft. This, combined with the greater percentage of volunteers used to wage the considerably smaller conflict, likely contributed significantly to the emergence of the socioeconomic casualty gap.

Finally, during the interwar period between Korea and Vietnam these changes in the draft continued to accelerate. Perhaps foremost among them was the expansion of the deferment and exemption system that shielded a growing number of young men from conscription. The effect of this transformation, according to historian George Flynn, was "the channeling and protection of elites during the 1950s."[50] By 1964, almost 30 percent of men registering for the draft received some type of deferment in contrast to only 9 percent in 1944.[51] Those remaining in the pool had increasingly fewer economic and educational opportunities than those exempted. Although statistics comparing enlisted and drafted military personnel are rare, army data on new recruits in 1964 shows a considerable difference in the average educational attainment of volunteers and draftees. Whereas 40 percent of army volunteers in 1964 had not graduated high school, only 29 percent of drafted men had failed to complete high school, a figure only slightly higher than the number for civilian 19-year old males, 25 percent.[52] These systematic changes to the draft in the 1950s and 1960s, coupled with the increased reliance on volunteers to wage significantly smaller-scale conflicts, likely contributed to the substantial casualty gaps between high- and low-income and education communities observed in the preceding chapter.

The Draft Lottery and Its Ramifications for the Casualty Gap

Specific provisions of the three wartime drafts and changes in them over time correlate strongly with changes in the casualty gap observed across the three wars. However, perhaps the best possible test of whether draft policies influence the casualty gap is afforded by a near natural experiment that occurred in the middle of the Vietnam War—the introduction of a draft lottery in December 1969. As the war in Vietnam dragged on, draft exemptions and deferments generated increasing public outcry. Amid the particularly contentious debate over the draft reauthorization process, President Johnson recognized fundamental inequities in the operation of the draft.[53] To address this politically sensitive issue, Johnson created the National Advisory Commission on Selective Service (NACSS). On December 3, 1966, this commission, headed by Burke Marshall, released the "Marshall Report," which, while arguing that the nation must continue the draft, recognized the need for changes. Although the 1967 reauthorization did not introduce significant legal changes, the push for reform had begun, and on December 1, 1969, a lottery system was implemented for all men between the ages of nineteen and twenty-six. The lottery was in place for the remainder of the draft, which slowed and then expired in 1973.[54]

The adoption of the lottery was clearly designed to make the draft at least appear to be more equitable. To the extent that it exposed a wider swath of young men from a broader range of communities to the real possibility of being drafted, the draft lottery could have served to reduce the casualty gap. However, the advent of the draft lottery did not close all of the outlets available to those seeking to avoid induction. Even with the lottery in place, a number of exemptions and deferments were still available. In particular, because educational deferments were still available through September 1971 and the draft was eliminated in 1973, "individuals enrolled in college could delay their risk of induction through most of the years of the draft lottery."[55] As a result, the shift in draft policy was perhaps not as dramatic as it superficially appeared; yet, if the introduction of the lottery does correlate with a significant reduction in the size of the socioeconomic casualty gap, it would be strong evidence in support of our claims that draft policies—and selection mechanisms more generally—shape the nature of the casualty gaps that emerge in wartime.

To test for the lottery's effect, we revisit our Vietnam data and look for differences in the relationships between a community's socio-economic status and its casualty rate before and after the introduction of the lottery. Toward this end, we first reestimate our multiple regression analysis of Vietnam county casualty rates, but we disaggregate the data into two periods. The first model examines the determinants of county casualty rates through 1969; the second examines the factors that explain county casualty rates after 1969. In the pre-lottery period, we again find strong, negative relationships between a county's median income and educational attainment and its casualty rate; after the introduction of the lottery, however, while the estimated relationships are still negative, the resulting coefficients are smaller in magnitude and statistically insignificant. To examine this relationship further, we also re-examined our place-level casualty data. In a simple bivariate analysis, the negative correlations between a community's income or educational attainment and its casualty rate are almost twice as large in the pre-lottery period as those observed in the post-lottery period. Moreover, when replicating pre- and post-lottery variants of the multiple regression analyses discussed in chapter 2's technical appendix, we find that income and education were statistically significant predictors of a community's casualty rate in both periods; however, consistent with the bivariate results, the size of the effect was considerably larger in the pre-lottery period. Thus, across additional rounds of analysis, the evidence suggests that the socioeconomic casualty gap decreased in magnitude following the introduction of the draft lottery, but it persisted nonetheless.

Our historical examination of changes in draft policy over time strongly suggest that the nature of the draft significantly contributes to the type and scope of casualty gaps, but that even a draft lottery cannot eliminate a gap. The massive scale of World War II and the enormous accompanying demand for manpower forced policymakers to adopt a wide-reaching draft that blunted the emergence of socioeconomic casualty gaps. By contrast, faced with much smaller demands for manpower in the Korean and Vietnamese conflicts, policymakers narrowed the focus of the draft considerably.[56] Finally, in the latter stages of the Vietnam War, policymakers responded to public pressures and instituted a draft lottery to assuage concerns about inequities in conscription. While the lottery did not eliminate the casualty gap between socioeconomically advantaged and disadvantaged communities, our data suggest that the reform did mitigate it considerably.

The Absence of a Draft and the Iraq Casualty Gap

Both selection and occupational assignment mechanisms have likely contributed to the socioeconomic casualty gaps that have arisen in the ongoing war in Iraq. Our army recruiting data demonstrate that communities at the top of the socioeconomic ladder are underrepresented in terms of military recruits. Moreover, as in previous wars, occupational assignment mechanisms have made recruits from socioeconomically disadvantaged communities disproportionately likely to serve in front-line combat units.

However, taken individually, neither selection nor sorting mechanisms seem able to explain why the Iraq War casualty gap is substantively larger than those observed in Korea or Vietnam. Although comparable data on the military's composition do not exist for prior wars, the modern AVF is likely as representative of the country as the fighting forces that waged the Korean and Vietnam wars, if not more so. This is almost certainly true with respect to the volunteer components of those forces. For example, in the first four years of the AVF (from 1973 through 1976), only 35.7 percent of army recruits were deemed "high quality" because they scored at or above the 50th percentile on the AFQT. In the military as a whole, this figure was 43.7 percent.[57] Although recent data suggest that the percentage of army recruits with a high school diploma fell below that of the civilian population in 2006, the disparities today are much smaller.[58] Though significant inequalities remain (figures 3.1 and 3.2), analyses of additional military enlistment data at the ZIP code level show that the military has made tremendous strides in becoming more representative of the nation as a whole during the past three decades.[59] Similarly, we find nothing to suggest that military occupational assignment procedures have changed dramatically since the early conflicts in ways that could create an even larger casualty gap in Iraq. However, by examining the operation of selection and sorting mechanisms together in a conflict that, in terms of scale, is considerably smaller than either the Korean or Vietnam wars, we can speculate about how an even larger casualty gap might emerge.

The most obvious difference between Iraq and the conflicts that preceded it is that Iraq has not required mass mobilization and the reinstatement of the draft. The starkly different scales of Korea and Vietnam on the one hand versus Iraq on the other placed very different demands on the military to recruit replacement soldiers for front-line combat duty. In Korea and Vietnam, when intense fighting and casualties prompted a strong need for the individual replacement of soldiers in front-line units, the military reached disproportionately for draftees. As the Supreme Court noted in a decision evaluating gender and combat assignment, the draft mechanism is "characterized by a need for *combat troops*."[60]

The data make it perfectly clear that draftees went overwhelmingly to the front lines. In Flynn's analysis of draftees in the war in Vietnam, he notes that, while the percentage of the armed forces filled by draftees had declined in Vietnam, the combat role of draftees remained similar: "Draftees went into the infantry and volunteers into support elements."[61] Draftees ended up more frequently in combat for several reasons. Most important, they were used to replace those positions that were open— and combat infantry positions were more likely to become open as soldiers were killed or rotated off duty. As the need to replace soldiers in combat units grew, so did the share of the death toll borne by draftees. Flynn found that the share of battle deaths borne by draftees increased dramatically from 28 percent in 1965 to 34 percent in 1966 and to 57 percent in 1967. By 1969, draftees were 88 percent of the infantry and accounted for 50–70 percent of deaths, even though they constituted a much smaller percentage of the entire armed forces.[62]

The draft mechanism, then, was not just a policy of conscription but of *conscription into combat roles*. To understand the casualty gap, we need to know who was going into the foxholes, and, as Peter Kindsvatter recounts, in World War II and Korea, "just as during the Vietnam War, the foxholes had to be filled with growing numbers of draftees once the volunteers, regulars, and recalled reservists had become casualties or had been rotated home."[63] This understanding of the draft mechanism is consistent with our earlier finding that the introduction of the draft lottery at the end of 1969 served to reduce the casualty gap. If draftees were in fact disproportionately being sent into combat roles and if the lottery broadened the socioeconomic distribution of draftees, then the two policies logically combined to produce a more equitable socioeconomic distribution of soldiers on the front lines of combat.[64]

The draft mechanism of supplying combat troops stands in stark contrast to the processes of selection and occupational assignment operative in Iraq. In the Iraq War, soldiers sent to the front lines are volunteers driven to join the military, at least in part, because of economic incentives as opposed to government conscription. Equally important, these soldiers reach the front lines only after the sophisticated occupational sorting process described earlier.[65] The much smaller scale of the conflict has not compelled the military to make drastic changes in recruitment, such as implementing a wide-ranging draft, to attract replacement soldiers. Indeed, as discussed earlier, the lowering of acceptance standards for new recruits may have actually increased the casualty gap. By contrast, the presence of a draft mechanism in previous wars to meet the large demand for replacement combat soldiers—even if the design of the draft failed to produce complete equity in those conscripted—may have ameliorated the casualty gap by diminishing the influence of occupational assignment.

CASUALTY GAPS AT THE INDIVIDUAL LEVEL

We conclude this chapter with the same question that we discussed at the end of chapter 2: Is the observed casualty gap between socioeconomically advantaged and disadvantaged communities the result of individual Americans with fewer socioeconomic resources and opportunities bearing a disproportionate share of the nation's wartime sacrifice? Or could socioeconomic casualty gaps at the community level arise without a corresponding gap at the individual level? It is *possible* that some mechanism may produce a casualty gap between rich and poor communities while not producing a parallel gap between individuals with high and low levels of socioeconomic opportunity. However, we argue that such an alternative explanation is not very *probable*.

In chapter 2 we showed that casualties were coming not just disproportionately from poor or less-educated *towns* and *cities* but also from less advantaged *neighborhoods* within those census places. This was strongly consistent with, if not conclusive proof of, our hypothesis that a casualty gap exists not only at the community level but also at the individual level. We now revisit the hypothesis in light of our analyses of selection and occupational assignment.

First, our analysis of selection mechanisms suggests that these mechanisms could conceivably create a casualty gap between rich and poor and between high- and low-education communities without generating a corresponding casualty gap at the individual level. The nature of a potential recruit's local civilian labor market, not that person's individual skill level and opportunities, may be the most important factor driving the volunteering dynamic. In tight labor markets, a wide range of young men and women may find that the opportunities afforded by military service exceed those available in the civilian sphere. Moreover (recent developments not withstanding), since the 1970s the military has dramatically increased its recruiting standards. Accordingly, individuals with high levels of education and skills in tight labor markets may be ideal recruiting targets. Thus, economic incentives and military recruiting could conceivably produce a fighting force that comprises a highly skilled and educated cohort of young men and women who hail disproportionately from socioeconomically disadvantaged communities that offer fewer opportunities in the civilian labor market. In this way, volunteering and recruiting dynamics could set the stage for the emergence of a socioeconomic casualty gap at the community but not at the individual level.

However, individuals from wealthier backgrounds with higher levels of education are not only better positioned to compete for the opportunities available in the civilian sector in that community, but they are also better equipped to seek out opportunities in other parts of the country. Thus, the young men and women most likely to find the economic and educational benefits that the military affords attractive are those with fewer skills and socioeconomic opportunities. For these individuals, the military provides greater opportunities for upward mobility than their limited options in the civilian sphere, and consequently they should be more likely to volunteer for military service. Moreover, when the demand for manpower was considerably greater than it is in the contemporary period—as it was in each of our prior conflicts—the military was under increased pressure to admit applicants with fewer *ex ante* skills. Military statistics on volunteers from the 1960s and 1970s support this claim. As documented previously, volunteers in these periods had lower levels of educational attainment, on average, than both their drafted and civilian peers. In this way, selection mechanisms sow the seeds for a casualty gap to emerge between individuals with varying levels of socioeconomic opportunity. And because individuals with fewer skills and opportunities come disproportionately from socioeconomically disadvantaged communities, selection mechanisms should also contribute to a casualty gap at the community level.

Occupational assignment mechanisms also support the hypothesis that an individual-level socioeconomic casualty gap underlies the community-level disparity. By assigning, on average, new soldiers with greater educational and occupational skills to occupations with comparably less exposure to combat risk and those with fewer skills and resources to occupations with higher risks of seeing combat, occupational assignment creates the conditions for a casualty gap to emerge at the individual level.[66] Because soldiers with higher aptitudes and skill are, on average, more likely to come from high-education and high-income home communities and because these soldiers are systematically steered away from high risk occupations, such as combat infantry, assignment should also produce differential casualty rates at the community level.

Taken together, our analysis of selection and occupational assignment mechanisms suggests that a casualty gap also exists at the individual level. Indeed, the only way in which the assignment mechanism can produce a community-level casualty gap (and the likeliest way in which selection mechanisms can do so) is by first producing a casualty gap between individuals with greater and fewer socioeconomic resources and opportunities. As in the preceding chapter, the evidence marshaled in this chapter is not conclusive proof of this hypothesis. However, it strongly supports the contention. For an individual-level casualty gap not to underlie those observed at the community level in chapter 2, a different mechanism would have to exist that could create a casualty gap at the community level without creating a corresponding gap between socioeconomically advantaged and disadvantaged individuals. Moreover, to fit the data as well as the selection and assignment mechanisms proposed here, any alternative mechanism must also explain the observed variance in casualty gaps both across and even within individual wars.[67] Absent compelling evidence for a counterargument, the data are most consistent with the conclusion that poorer and less-educated citizens are more likely to die in America's wars than richer and more educated citizens.

Technical Appendix to Chapter 3

In this technical appendix we present the details of our analytic strategy to examine the selection and occupational assignment mechanisms that contribute to the emergence of casualty gaps. We elaborate on the data analyzed and present the full results of the statistical models used to generate the figures and tables presented in the chapter text.

A. VARIATION IN ENLISTMENT RATES ACROSS COMMUNITIES

A factor that likely explains differentials in community casualty rates is variation in community enlistment rates. If more soldiers are enlisting from poorer and less-educated communities, it might in large part explain why those communities pay a higher cost on the battlefield. To test this relationship in the context of the Iraq War, we conducted several additional analyses.

We first constructed a ZIP code–level database to analyze the relationship between ZIP code demographics and ZIP code recruit figures for the period 1999–2006. Through a Freedom of Information Act (FOIA) request to the Department of Defense, we obtained data on the number of new recruits in each ZIP code from 1999 through 2006. As discussed in the chapter, other analysts, including the Department of Defense, National Priorities Project, and Heritage Foundation, have similarly made use of this ZIP code–level recruit data. However, conflicting conclusions and methodologies in these studies suggest a need for additional examination of the data.

In the text we analyzed the simple bivariate relationship between recruits and ZIP code–level income. Here, to test the relationship between enlistment rates and community demographics more directly, we estimated a multiple regression model with each ZIP code's enlistment rate as the dependent variable. To remain consistent with our casualty rate analysis, we calculated ZIP code community enlistment rates by summing the number of enlistments in each ZIP code for the eight years in our sample and dividing by the total population of the ZIP code.[1] To make the enlistment rate more accessible, we then multiplied the per-capita rate by 10,000. Because army soldiers constitute the bulk of casualties in the Iraq War (approximately 75 percent through December 2008), we focus here specifically on the determinants of community enlistment rates into the army. Alternative models that examine enlistment rates for all of the service branches yield substantively similar results.

To construct our enlistment rate regression model, we paralleled our casualty rate analysis in chapter 2 and integrated the enlistment rate data with a nearly identical set of sociodemographic variables drawn from the 2000 census.[2] The variables in our models were the following: median family income, percentage of residents with a college degree, unemployment rate, percentage of African Americans, percentage of rural farm residents, median age, 2000 GOP presidential vote share, and a dichotomous variable for Southern states. Variables were defined as they were in chapter 2 (table 2A.1).[3] We also cluster on the county and employ robust standard errors. The general form of our regression model is as follows:

$$Enlistment\_Rate_i = \beta_0 + \beta_1 Unemployment_i + \beta_2 Income / Education_i + \beta_3 Afr\_American_i + \beta_4 Farm_i + \beta_5 Age_i + \beta_6 GOP\_Prez_i + \beta_7 South_i + \varepsilon_i \qquad [1]$$

The results of this analysis are presented in table 3A.1.

Looking at the regression results, we find the expected inverse relationship between ZIP code enlistment rates and ZIP code measures of income and education. Rising median family income and greater levels of college completion in a community are associated with a decline in per-capita military recruitments. As discussed in the text (figure 3.2), first differences holding all other variables constant at their means or medians suggest that a move from the 25th to the 75th percentile of income results in a 19 percent drop in a ZIP code's enlistment rate, and a similar move up the education scale results in an 18 percent drop. At the extremes of

Table 3A.1. OLS Regression Analyses of Factors Influencing Army Enlistment Rates at the ZIP code level, 1999–2006

	Income	Education
Unemployment	–7.106	39.733
	(45.992)	(44.371)
Income	–0.644***	—
	(0.096)	
Education	—	–80.215***
		(6.259)
Race	–4.637	–1.859
	(5.390)	(5.540)
Rural	–9.775	2.438
	(11.499)	(7.994)
Age	0.578**	0.420*
	(0.289)	(0.229)
Partisanship	29.900***	26.087***
	(6.742)	(6.513)
South	1.027	3.028*
	(1.926)	(1.584)
Constant	45.506***	34.452***
	(13.556)	(11.298)
Observations	31,601	31,592
R^2	0.015	0.021

All of the models report robust standard errors clustered on county; all significance tests are two-tailed. * p < .10, ** p < .05, *** p < .01.

the distribution, moving from the 10th to the 90th percentile along either the income or the education dimension is associated with a reduction of 40 percent in enlistment rates. There is also geographical variation, as moving from a Southern to a non-Southern state is associated with a 6 percent decrease in the enlistment rate.

Thus, the ZIP code–level recruit models provide strong evidence that socioeconomic inequality in enlistment rates may contribute to the socioeconomic casualty gaps observed in chapter 2. Poorer and less-educated parts of the country are, on average, sending more of their young men and women into the armed forces. This, in turn, could lead to a greater percentage of their residents making the ultimate sacrifice.

To further test this link, we performed a final round of analysis in which we integrated the recruit data with our casualty database employed in chapter 2. By aggregating up from the ZIP code to the county level and then matching places with their corresponding county, we were able to replicate our earlier Iraq models with an additional covariate: military enlistments. In these models we operationalize enlistments as the estimated number of new army recruits, 1999–2006, per one thousand place male residents.[4] We present the results of these new Iraq models in table 3A.2. The first and third columns of the table reproduce for comparison purposes the base model (identical to the last columns in tables 2A.3 and 2A.4). The second and fourth columns present the models with the recruits per capita explanatory variable.

The results in columns 2 and 4 show that selection into the military (i.e., the per-capita number of military recruits in a community) is positively and significantly related to a community's wartime casualty rate. However, even when we include the per-capita recruitment variable, the significant and inverse relationships between family income levels (table 3A.2, col. 2) and college degree levels (table 3A.2, column 4) and place casualty rates remain virtually unchanged. In short, although service rates are a significant factor, "Who serves?" does not fully explain "Who dies?" in Iraq. This is consistent with the theory presented in this chapter that even if the military were to mirror society demographically, other forces— particularly occupational assignment mechanisms within the military— can still produce casualty gaps.

B. VARIATION BY OCCUPATION AND RANK

If the military assigns new recruits with lower *ex ante* skills to occupations with greater exposure to combat, then assignment mechanisms could produce a casualty gap at both the individual and the community levels. To test this hypothesis indirectly, we reestimate our casualty analyses from chapter 2 but disaggregate each community's casualty rate by infantry vs. noninfantry and officer vs. enlisted casualties.[5] If our hypotheses about occupational assignment are correct, then enlisted and infantry casualties should come systematically from poorer, less-educated parts of the country than officer and noninfantry casualties, respectively.

The explanatory variables are identical to those used in the chapter 2 models. As in chapter 2, we ran separate models for education and income. For space purposes, we present only the income results in this appendix, though we note that the education analyses reveal essentially the same patterns. The full results of the income models are reported in tables 3A.3 (infantry vs. noninfantry) and 3A.4 (enlisted vs. officer). These results form the basis for the estimated effects presented in figures 3.3 and 3.4.

The results strongly support our hypotheses about the role of occupational assignment in contributing to the socioeconomic casualty gap.

Table 3A.2. Additional OLS Regression Analyses of Factors Influencing Iraq Place-Level Casualty Rates, Controlling for Military Recruitment Levels

	Income		Education	
	[1]	[2]	[3]	[4]
	Base model	With recruits	Base model	With recruits
Unemployment	−0.421	−0.398	−0.063	−0.143
	(2.308)	(2.329)	(2.346)	(2.374)
Education	—	—	−2.383***	−2.042***
			(0.422)	(0.385)
Income	−0.015***	−0.012***	—	—
	(0.003)	(0.003)		
Race	−1.000***	−0.959***	−0.883**	−0.863**
	(0.361)	(0.334)	(0.354)	(0.324)
Rural	3.271	3.086	2.823	2.685
	(2.616)	(2.530)	(2.591)	(2.513)
Age	−0.019	−0.021*	−0.017	−0.019
	(0.012)	(0.012)	(0.012)	(0.012)
Partisanship	−1.847	−1.791	−1.676	−1.672
	(1.125)	(1.102)	(1.133)	(1.098)
South	0.390**	0.298*	0.427**	0.330*
	(0.187)	(0.190)	(0.188)	(0.191)
Per-capita	—	0.008**	—	0.008**
recruit level		(0.004)		(0.004)
Constant	3.397***	3.131***	2.929***	2.766***
	(0.720)	(0.687)	(0.680)	(0.653)
Observations	19,413	19,413	19,413	19,413
R^2	0.001	0.004	0.002	0.004

All of the models report robust standard errors clustered on state; all significance tests are two-tailed.
*$p < .10$, **$p < .05$, ***$p < .01$.

Looking first at military occupation, we see a marked difference in our infantry vs. noninfantry models. In both Korea and Vietnam, a significant, inverse relationship exists between county median family income and infantry casualty rates. Poorer counties suffered significantly higher infantry casualty rates, on average, than wealthier communities. By contrast, in these conflicts we find no evidence of a statistically significant correlation between a county's median income and its noninfantry casualty rate. In the Iraq models, both infantry and noninfantry casualty rate are significantly and inversely related to place income, but as discussed in the text the magnitude of the effect is greater for the infantry casualty rate.

Table 3A.3. Comparing Infantry and Noninfantry Casualty Rate Regression Models in Korea, Vietnam, and Iraq

	Korea		Vietnam		Iraq	
	Infantry	Noninfantry	Infantry	Noninfantry	Infantry	Noninfantry
Unemployment	10.870***	10.308***	2.748	-3.041	-0.201	-0.220
	3.660	(2.947)	(3.926)	(4.418)	(1.989)	(1.106)
Income	-0.727***	-0.094	-0.176***	-0.066	-0.009***	-0.006***
	(0.122)	(0.090)	(0.059)	(0.080)	(0.002)	(0.002)
Race	-2.731***	-1.133***	-1.479***	-2.666***	-0.670**	-0.330
	(0.758)	(0.317)	(0.543)	(0.944)	(0.251)	(0.336)
Rural	-0.053	-0.266	-0.531	-1.410*	1.781	1.491
	(0.359)	(0.264)	(0.688)	(0.742)	(1.814)	(2.033)
Age	-0.032*	0.038***	-0.027*	-0.012	-0.006	-0.013**
	(0.021)	(0.012)	(0.015)	(0.016)	(0.011)	(0.006)
Partisanship	0.673	-0.006	-0.012	-0.325	-0.798	-1.049*
	(0.697)	(0.215)	(0.529)	(0.916)	(0.920)	(0.619)
South	0.324	0.213*	0.401	0.314	0.064	0.326**
	(0.472)	(0.121)	(0.271)	(0.454)	(0.118)	(0.132)
Constant	4.800***	1.032*	4.918***	5.270***	1.528***	1.869***
	(1.161)	(0.607)	(0.865)	(1.015)	(0.504)	(0.505)
Observations	2,995	2,995	3,101	3,101	19,413	19,413
R^2	0.066	0.027	0.016	0.006	0.001	0.001

All of the models report robust standard errors clustered on state; all significance tests are two-tailed. * $p < .10$, ** $p < .05$, *** $p < .01$.

Table 3A.4. Comparing Enlisted and Officer Casualty Rate Regression Models in Korea, Vietnam, and Iraq

	Korea		Vietnam		Iraq	
	Enlisted	Officer	Enlisted	Officer	Enlisted	Officer
Unemployment	19.915***	1.263*	2.418	-2.919**	-0.399	-0.164
	(4.091)	(0.664)	(6.660)	(1.229)	(2.282)	(0.106)
Income	-0.898***	0.077***	-0.275**	0.025	-0.015***	0.001
	(0.146)	(0.025)	(0.117)	(0.025)	(0.003)	(0.001)
Race	-4.028***	0.165*	-3.595***	-0.380	-0.960**	-0.022
	(0.887)	(0.090)	(1.193)	(0.235)	(0.362)	(0.048)
Rural	-0.150	-0.170*	-1.925*	-0.017	3.540	-0.166
	(0.439)	(0.101)	(1.047)	(0.289)	(2.611)	(0.164)
Age	-0.009	0.015***	-0.049**	0.008	-0.021*	-0.000
	(0.023)	(0.006)	(0.023)	(0.005)	(0.012)	(0.001)
Partisanship	0.646	0.021	-0.301	-0.107	-1.901*	0.018
	(0.757)	(0.067)	(1.302)	(0.167)	(1.053)	(0.193)
South	0.444	0.093**	0.579	0.132	0.362**	0.046
	(0.532)	(0.040)	(0.597)	(0.110)	(0.170)	(0.040)
Constant	6.081***	-0.248	9.830***	0.382	3.414***	0.005
	(1.269)	(0.252)	(1.533)	(0.328)	(0.679)	(0.117)
Observations	2,995	2,995	3,101	3,101	19,413	19,413
R^2	0.065	0.024	0.012	0.008	0.001	0.000

All of the models report robust standard errors clustered on state; all significance tests are two-tailed. * $p<.10$, ** $p<.05$, *** $p<.01$.

With respect to the control variables, the Korean War models show a statistically significant, positive correlation between a county's unemployment rate and its infantry and noninfantry casualty rate. In each model, we find strong negative correlations between the size of a county's black population and its infantry and noninfantry casualty rate; only in the noninfantry Iraq model does the coefficient fail to reach conventional levels of statistical significance. Finally, in Vietnam we find a statistically significant negative relationship between a county's median age and its infantry casualty rate. This is consistent with a pattern of assignment in which younger soldiers end up in the infantry and closer to the front lines of combat. By contrast, in Korea the coefficient for a county's median age and its noninfantry casualty rate is actually positive, whereas in Vietnam the relationship is negative but not statistically significant. However, in the Iraq models the coefficients for median age are negative in both models, and the relationship is statistically significant only in the model of noninfantry casualty rates.

The enlisted and officer casualty rate models provide further evidence that the casualty gap may be driven in part by sorting within the military. In Korea, Vietnam, and Iraq, a consistent pattern emerges: Enlisted casualty rates are significantly and inversely related to community income levels, but officer casualty rates are not. In all three wars, officer casualty rates are *positively* correlated with income, and the relationship rises to statistical significance in Korea. In additional models, we see almost the same patterns with respect to community education levels. Enlisted casualties are concentrated disproportionately in low-income and low-education communities.

With respect to other variables in the model, we find some evidence of significant correlations between unemployment in a community and either its enlisted or officer casualty rate. In Korea, both officer and enlisted casualty rates are positively correlated with a community's level of unemployment. In Vietnam, we continue to see the positive relationship between unemployment and enlisted casualty rates, though the coefficient fails to reach conventional levels of statistical significance. The coefficient for officer casualty rates, by contrast, is negative in the Vietnam model. We also see more evidence of age disparities. The coefficients for median age are negative in all three models of enlisted casualties, and they are statistically significant in the Vietnam and Iraq models. By contrast, in Korea and Vietnam we see a positive relationship between a county's median age and its officer casualty rate, and in Korea this relationship is statistically significant.

Taken together, our analyses of differences across occupation and rank offer considerable insight into the mechanisms that likely produced the socioeconomic casualty gaps we observe in chapter 2. A community's share of the wartime sacrifice is a function not only of how many in that community serve but also of *how* community members serve. Our evidence suggests that poorer and less-educated communities suffer higher casualty rates in part because they send disproportionately more of their community members into the infantry and enlisted ranks, which experience the greatest exposure to combat and consequently comprise the lion's share of the nation's total wartime casualties.

4

Do Casualty Gaps Matter?

The previous two chapters clearly demonstrate that a casualty gap exists. Poorer parts of the United States and most likely poorer individuals suffered a disproportionate share of casualties in Korea and Vietnam, and they continue to do so in the war in Iraq. Starting in this chapter and continuing throughout the rest of the book, we consider the implications of the casualty gap. Political scientists have long studied how combat casualties affect both popular support for war and the course of military policymaking adopted in Washington, D.C. However, existing scholarship has paid almost no attention to *inequality* in military sacrifice. It has failed to consider the possibility that Americans care not only about the size of the military costs of war but also about how this burden is distributed across society.

Precisely how Americans will react to information about inequality in military sacrifice is uncertain. For some, the existence of casualty inequalities may be neither surprising nor cause for concern. Consider, for the purpose of comparison, inequality and another American institution, the fast-food restaurant. It would not be surprising to learn that those working on the front lines of the nation's burger joints are from lower-income neighborhoods.[1] Similarly, few would be shocked to find that those in upper management are more likely to have had better educational opportunities. These market forces, which put low-education, low-skilled workers on the fry griddles and high-education, high-skilled managers into plush corporate offices, produce an outcome that shareholders desire because it maximizes efficiency of operations. Not only are we less inclined to see a moral problem with the fast-food restaurant's operations, but we could also argue that the company provides its entry-level workers with important opportunities for career advancement that they would not obtain otherwise. If this market logic holds in the military service context as well, then Americans should expect a casualty gap, and the gap should not affect their support for war efforts.

Moreover, the military's recruitment of individuals of lower socioeconomic status may provide opportunities for social mobility that would not be otherwise available. By providing occupational and educational resources to citizens who lack them in the civilian sphere, the military may serve as a powerful engine fostering upward mobility along the socioeconomic ladder. There may be society-wide benefits, too, if one agrees with Judge Richard Posner's argument that "the true consequence of the demographics of the armed forces—a consequence that communitarians should applaud—is that the nation's admiration for these scions of the lower middle class helps to bind the different income classes together."[2]

Others, however, may find the casualty gap normatively troubling precisely because they do not see the military as just another employer.[3] This view is grounded in Defense Department Form 4 itself, the form that American soldiers sign when they enlist or reenlist in the armed forces. On the second page of the form, individuals read the following statement: "My enlistment/reenlistment agreement is more than an employment agreement."[4] The language of the form codifies what our civics classes teach us: Military service is more than just a job. It is service to the nation that may place one in harm's way, and because it is public service of the highest order, we might not be satisfied with purely market-based results. As defense analyst Robert Osgood has observed, "A nation's ability to sustain a defense program is not only a matter of the gross national product, per capita income, and the other objective criteria of economic strength but, just as much, a reflection of what the citizenry, its political representatives, and government officials are willing to sacrifice in terms of competing values for the sake of a particular national strategy."[5]

How do Americans balance these competing perspectives when they evaluate the casualty gap? To determine whether knowledge of a casualty gap affects citizens' support for America's war efforts, we conducted a series of controlled experiments. When Americans run their cost-benefit analysis of both real and hypothetical war scenarios, do they think only about how many soldiers may die, or do they also consider the distributional consequences of wartime casualties?

While our experiments explore a theme as old as the Republic—inequality and military sacrifice—they move the casualty gap to center stage in a new way. As we have already mentioned, policymakers, scholars, and the media alike repeatedly discuss and debate the importance of casualties in shaping Americans' military policy judgments and preferences. Yet, typically lost amid the analysis and debate are questions about inequities in the distribution of this sacrifice. All too often the casualty gap is simply not part of our national political dialogue.[6] What would happen if this changed, that is, if the casualty gap were a metric that we, as Americans, were confronted with when making decisions about war and peace?

Based on our experimental results, it appears that explicit discussion of the casualty gap has the power to change substantially public support for the nation's military campaigns. When Americans know that the men and women who are sacrificing their lives on foreign battlefields are coming disproportionately from poorer areas of the country, citizens are much more cautious in their support for both the Iraq War and for preemptive warfare more generally. Our experiments suggest that mere awareness of the casualty gap can significantly reduce the number of casualties Americans are willing to accept in future missions. Moreover, a follow-up experiment conducted in the spring of 2009 suggests that even when replicating our casualty sensitivity experiment under a new president and in a period in which economic concerns, not Iraq, were first and foremost on Americans' minds, the casualty gap continues to influence substantially the public's willingness to tolerate large numbers of casualties in future military endeavors.

THE CASUALTY GAP AND PUBLIC SUPPORT FOR WAR

A growing body of research at the nexus of American politics and international relations asserts the critical importance of public opinion to the military policymaking process, particularly with regard to decisions about the use of force. In a 2002 review of the literature, political scientist Louis Klarevas argues that public support is still the "essential domino" of military policymaking. Strong public support, he contends, is "vital to the successful conduct of military operations" in contemporary American politics.[7] Consistent with this view, a robust literature investigates the factors that drive the American public's support for war. Much of this literature, in turn, focuses on the importance of combat casualties.

One of the most common analytic frames that scholars use to model the opinion-formation process is that of the cost-benefit calculation.[8] From this perspective, citizens rationally assess the likely costs and benefits of a military action, weigh them against each other, and then decide whether to support the use of force accordingly. Many studies focus primarily on the "cost" side of this equation, particularly on U.S. casualties. In the judgment of political scientist Scott Gartner, "casualties represent the primary information individuals use to evaluate war, assess past costs, estimate future costs, and formulate their positions."[9] Political scientist John Aldrich and colleagues echo Gartner's assessment in a recent survey of the wartime opinion literature: "Combat casualties are important because the willingness to pay the costs of war is one of the central mechanisms by which public opinion might affect foreign policy choices."[10] As a result, since John Mueller's pioneering research, which demonstrates that support for the Vietnam War declined precipitously as U.S. casualties mounted, numerous studies have explored the linkages between U.S. combat casualties and wartime support.[11]

Increasingly, political scientists have begun to emphasize the conditional nature of casualties' influence on public opinion. Some scholars argue that Americans do not instinctively recoil in the face of battle deaths; rather, the nature of the military objectives being served affects casualty tolerance. When the military's objectives are closely tied to the national interest or the aim of a military venture is to restrain an adversary that threatens the United States or its allies rather than to produce internal policy change within another country, the public is more willing to accept battlefield casualties.[12] This perspective may help explain why the Bush administration in 2002 and 2003 initially placed greater emphasis on the threat Iraq posed to the United States and our allies in the region—despite the difficulties of precisely ascertaining Saddam's weapons capacities—instead of the more easily substantiated argument that Saddam was a brutal dictator whose removal was justified on humanitarian grounds.[13]

Other scholars focus on the importance of military context in determining the effect of casualties on public support for war. For example, Scott Gartner and Gary Segura show that, during the Vietnam War, short-term spikes in casualties drove popular support for the conflict when the marginal casualty rate was increasing; however, when casualty rates are decreasing, cumulative casualties were a better predictor of wartime support.[14] Alternatively, Peter Feaver, Christopher Gelpi, and Jason Reifler argue that casualties do not erode popular support for war as long as the public perceives that the United States is winning and can succeed in achieving its policy goals.[15] Once public assessments of the prospects for victory fade, however, casualties begin to weaken popular support for war.

Finally, still other scholars emphasize the critical role played by political elites, first in providing the public with information about the state of affairs on the ground and then in helping the public interpret these developments and update their policy preferences accordingly. Elite consensus can sustain popular support for military action even in the face of high casualties. By contrast, elite dissension sows the seeds of popular discord.[16]

While this literature has improved our understanding of the linkages between U.S. casualties and popular support for war, no existing study has explicitly examined the consequences of *inequalities* in the *distribution* of these wartime costs across the country on the public's willingness to support both ongoing and future military interventions.[17] In his seminal analysis of U.S. military policymaking, political scientist Bruce Russett observes that American blood, even more than treasure, is the single most important cost of war in the eyes of the American public.[18] Yet, we know very little about how, precisely, the public measures this cost. Is public opinion only moved by the number of lives lost? Or does the public also respond to information about the types of communities that bear a disproportionate share of this wartime sacrifice?

To explore the effect of a very modest cue concerning the nature of the casualty gap on Americans' beliefs and preferences—including their support for the ongoing war in Iraq and for a future hypothetical military intervention—we crafted three questions for an Opinion Research Corporation CARAVAN omnibus poll administered in late September 2007.[19] CARAVAN is a twice weekly telephone survey that employs a random-digit dialing (RDD) methodology to ensure a nationally representative sample of 1,003 adult Americans.[20]

We began the experiment by randomly assigning respondents to one of three groups. Respondents in all three groups were told the following: "As of September 2007, more than 3,750 American servicemen have been killed in Iraq and thousands more wounded." The first group, the control group, received no additional information. The second group, the "shared sacrifice" treatment group, was told further that "This sacrifice has been shared by rich and poor communities all across America." The third group, the "casualty gap" treatment group, was told the following instead: "Many of these casualties have been from poor communities. In fact, America's poor communities have suffered nearly twice as many casualties as America's rich communities."[21] All three groups were then asked a standard question that Gallup has repeatedly used in the last four years: "In view of developments since we first sent our troops to Iraq, do you think the United States made a mistake in sending troops to Iraq?"

In all, 58 percent of respondents from our survey answered that the Iraq War was a mistake, the exact same percentage that Gallup observed in its September 14–16, 2007 poll.[22] However, as the results presented in table 4.1 illustrate, there was considerable variance in this percentage

Table 4.1. Percentage of Respondents Who Believed the Iraq War was a Mistake, by Inequality Cue

	Control Group	Shared Sacrifice Group	Casualty Inequality Group
% Mistake	56.2%	56.5%	61.6%

across the treatment and control groups. Telling individuals just one additional bit of information about the presence or absence of a casualty gap had a considerable impact on respondents' beliefs about whether the war in Iraq was a mistake. Approximately 56 percent of respondents in both the control group and the shared sacrifice treatment group answered that the war in Iraq was a mistake. By contrast, in the casualty gap treatment group this number rose to 62 percent.[23]

This 6 percentage point increase is of note in its own right; the magnitude of the effect is even more striking when we remember the modest nature of the inequality cue and the large amount of information that most Americans already possessed on Iraq, with which this new cue had to compete. It is quite possible that an even more thorough accounting of the casualty gap, complete with vivid descriptions of individual soldiers and the effects of their deaths on poor communities could produce an even larger effect. Moreover, by September of 2007, four years into the Iraq War—longer than America's involvement in the Second World War—most Americans had already made up their mind on the war. The war had dominated two national elections, and continued wrangling over the war's origins and plans for its future featured prominently in the early stages of the 2008 presidential campaign. If a simple cue about casualty inequality could change popular attitudes on a military venture to this extent in the Iraq context, it is quite possible that the mere acknowledgement of a casualty gap could have even greater effects in other environments in which popular attitudes are more malleable and not so polarized along partisan lines.

While the immediate effect of the casualty inequality cue on opinions about the war in Iraq was quite strong, what was perhaps more surprising was its lingering influence on respondents' answers to two subsequent questions. Without mentioning the casualty gap in Iraq again, we next asked respondents in all three groups a question that probed casualty sensitivity toward a hypothetical military action against Iran. Following a previous study of the determinants of casualty sensitivity by political scientists Peter Feaver and Christopher Gelpi, we first read all of the

Table 4.2. Number of Casualties Acceptable for a Hypothetical U.S. Military Mission to Halt Iran's Nuclear Program, by Inequality Cue

	Control Group		Shared Sacrifice Group		Casualty Inequality Group	
	Mean	75th Percentile	Mean	75th Percentile	Mean	75th Percentile
Acceptable Casualties	28,206	1,000	28,471	4,000	16,923	500

respondents the following prompt: "When American troops are sent overseas, there are almost always casualties. For instance, 43 Americans were killed in Somalia, 383 in the Gulf War, roughly 54,000 in Korea, roughly 58,000 in Vietnam, and roughly 400,000 in World War II."[24] We then asked the respondents to consider the following scenario: "Imagine for a moment that a future president decided to send military troops to halt Iran's nuclear program and stop the infiltration of Iranian-backed forces into Iraq." Finally, we asked all of the respondents: "In your opinion, what would be the highest number of American military deaths that would be acceptable to achieve this goal?"[25]

The results in table 4.2 clearly demonstrate that, even though the inequality cues were not repeated before this second question, respondents who had previously learned of the casualty gap in Iraq exhibited significantly greater levels of casualty sensitivity to this hypothesized military venture than did individuals previously assigned to the control or shared sacrifice treatment groups.[26] For members of the control group, the mean number of acceptable casualties was just over 28,000, while the respondents at the 75th percentile would accept 1,000 casualties. For members of the casualty gap group, however, the mean number of casualties deemed acceptable was *40 percent less.* Instead of upward of 28,000 casualties, after a mere mention of casualty inequality, these respondents on average stated that fewer than 17,000 casualties would be acceptable to achieve America's aims in a military venture against Iran.[27] Moreover, the effect is particularly strong when we examine the relative preferences of those at the 75th percentile of each group's preferences. The respondents at the 75th percentile of the inequality group would accept only 500 casualties in a military engagement with Iran, half of that for the control group and one eighth of the acceptable number of casualties for the 75th percentile respondents in the shared sacrifice treatment condition.

Table 4.3. Percentage of Respondents Who Supported Returning to a Draft, by Inequality Cue

	Control Group	Shared Sacrifice Group	Casualty Inequality Group
% for Draft	20.8%	18.6%	24.0%

The effect of the shared sacrifice treatment is also notable. For respondents in this group, the mean level of acceptable casualties for the Iraq mission is virtually identical to that in the control group. However, the figure for respondents at the 75th percentile was four times higher. By this metric, respondents who were told in the previous question that rich and poor communities were both sharing in the sacrifice in Iraq were considerably *more* accepting of future casualties in an operation against Iran than those who were told nothing about the presence or absence of casualty inequality in Iraq.

We concluded our experiment by asking all of the respondents a final question taken from the 2006 General Social Survey: "Do you think we should return to a military draft at this time, or should we continue to rely on volunteers?"[28] Our analysis in the preceding chapter demonstrates that simply reinstating the draft would almost certainly *not* eliminate the emergence of socioeconomic casualty gaps in current or future wars. The military employed drafts in both Korea and Vietnam, and significant casualty gaps emerged in each. However, our analysis does suggest that, depending on their design, drafts can mitigate the size of the socioeconomic casualty gap. More important, in the rare instances when questions about equity in military service do appear on the national agenda, proposals to reintroduce the draft, such as those sponsored by New York Democrat Charlie Rangel, receive the greatest public attention and scrutiny. Given the issue's salience and the perceived rigidity of popular beliefs on the matter, the draft question represents another important test for the influence of the casualty gap cue. Results for this question broken down by inequality cue are presented in table 4.3.

Of the control group respondents, 21 percent expressed support for returning to a military draft to meet the nation's need for service personnel. For the shared sacrifice treatment group, however, this figure declines somewhat to 19 percent. By contrast, for the casualty gap treatment group, support for the draft increased substantially to 24 percent.[29] It is important to note that, even after priming respondents to consider the existence of a socioeconomic casualty gap, public support for the return of the draft remains meager. However, while the increase in raw numbers is small, this shift represents a 30 percent difference between casualty gap and shared sacrifice treatments in terms of the fraction of the public that supports a return to the draft. Thus, priming the public to think about military personnel policies through the lens of the casualty gap has a significant impact on their policy attitudes, even on a subject as polarizing as whether the nation should return to a compulsory military induction program that it abandoned more than three decades ago.

In the technical appendix we construct additional multivariate statistical analyses to ensure that the effects of inequality cues on respondents' evaluations of the Iraq War, casualty tolerance for future missions, and support for the draft hold even after controlling for their partisanship and other demographic characteristics. Even with the additional controls, in each case we find that inequality cues had statistically significant effects on respondents' military judgments and policy preferences.

THE CASUALTY GAP'S INFLUENCE IN 2009

The results of our September 2007 experiment strongly suggest that Americans change their military judgments and policy preferences when they learn of the casualty gap. However, the circumstances in which this survey experiment was conducted were far from ordinary. In the fall of 2007, the war in Iraq and the effectiveness of the U.S. troop "surge" was perhaps the most salient issue on the national political agenda. The Iraqi insurgency continued to rage, and U.S. casualty rates, while lower than in the summer of 2007, remained high. This unique set of circumstances raises the possibility that information about the casualty gap may not have the same degree of influence on public opinion in less tumultuous times. To check the robustness of our findings, we conducted a second experiment in late March 2009.[30] At the time of our follow-up CARAVAN survey, Barack Obama, not George W. Bush, occupied the Oval Office; the financial crisis and economic concerns had replaced Iraq as the dominant issue on the national political stage; and U.S. casualty rates in Iraq had decreased by more than 80 percent from the fall of 2007. As a result, this second experiment allows us to examine whether information about the casualty gap continues to influence Americans' military policy preferences in a dramatically different political and strategic environment.

In this follow-up study, we asked respondents a slightly modified version of our casualty sensitivity question. They were again assigned randomly to one of three groups. All of the respondents received the following information: "When American troops are sent overseas, there are almost always casualties. For instance, roughly 36,000

Americans were killed in Korea, 58,000 in Vietnam, and over 4,000 in Iraq."[31] The control group received no further information and was then asked this question: "In your opinion, what would be the highest number of American deaths that would be acceptable to halt Iran's nuclear program?" After hearing the same prompt with the casualty tallies in Korea, Vietnam, and Iraq, the second group of respondents received the "shared sacrificed" treatment, which told them that, "This sacrifice has been shared by rich and poor communities all across America." They were then asked: "Knowing that all communities will likely share in the war burden, in your opinion what would be the highest number of American deaths that would be acceptable to achieve the following goals?" Finally, the third group received the "casualty gap" treatment. After hearing the casualty totals from the three wars, this group was told that "Many of these casualties have been from poor communities. In fact, in each of these wars America's poor communities have suffered significantly higher casualty rates than America's rich communities." They were then asked: "In your opinion, knowing that poor communities will likely bear a greater share of the war burden, what would be the highest number of American deaths that would be acceptable to halt Iran's nuclear program?"

Because Americans' responses to casualty sensitivity questions vary widely and are far from normally distributed, political scientists Christopher Gelpi and Peter Feaver have proposed clustering responses into six categories that range from those who will tolerate no casualties in a given operation to those who will tolerate 50,000 or more.[32] This method allows easy comparisons of the percentages of respondents that fall into each group. Here we adopt this metric, but to facilitate comparisons, we focus on three categories: those that would accept between 0 and 50 casualties to halt Iran's nuclear program; those that would accept between 51 and 5,000 casualties; and those that would accept more than 5,000 casualties to achieve the goal. The first category represents a very high degree of casualty sensitivity. Even the first Persian Gulf War entailed more than 50 casualties; thus, respondents in this group are unwilling to support even a similar mission to achieve the stated aim of halting Iran's nuclear program. By contrast, the third category represents a low degree of casualty sensitivity. Respondents in this group are willing to suffer even more casualties than what the United States has thus far (through March 2009) sustained in Iraq to prevent Iran from acquiring nuclear weapons. Table 4.4 summarizes the percentage of respondents in each of these three categories across the three treatments in both the March 2009 and the September 2007 surveys.

Table 4.4. Number of Casualties Acceptable for a Hypothetical U.S. Military Mission to Halt Iran's Nuclear Program, by Inequality Cue

	March 2009			September 2007		
	Control Group	Casualty Inequality Group	Shared Sacrifice Group	Control Group	Casualty Inequality Group	Shared Sacrifice Group
0–50	50.2%	55.1%	45.9%	64.1%	68.8%	57.7%
51–5,000	34.8%	30.9%	37.4%	17.6%	13.3%	21.3%
> 5,000	15.0%	14.0%	16.7%	18.3%	17.9%	21.0%

Strongly consistent with our argument that knowledge of the casualty gap shapes popular preferences, in both surveys the percentage of respondents in the high casualty sensitivity category (those willing to accept fifty or fewer casualties) is greater in the inequality group than in the control group. In the March 2009 survey, 55 percent of respondents who were told of casualty inequalities in the nation's preceding major wars said that they would accept fewer than fifty casualties to halt Iran's nuclear program, versus 50 percent in the control group. By contrast, only 46 percent of respondents who received the "shared sacrifice" treatment expressed the highest level of casualty sensitivity. In the 2007 survey we observed an almost identical pattern.

In the low casualty sensitivity category, we see the reverse pattern. In both surveys, the percentage of residents willing to accept more than 5,000 casualties to achieve U.S. objectives is smaller in the inequality group than in the control group, which was told nothing about the emergence of casualty gaps in prior wars. By contrast, among those in the "shared sacrifice" treatment, the percentage willing to accept large casualty totals to halt Iran's nuclear program is even higher than in the control group in both surveys. In the technical appendix, we construct statistical models to determine whether these relationships between inequality cues and casualty sensitivity hold even after controlling for respondents' partisanship and other demographic characteristics. These results strongly support our contention that information about the casualty gap significantly affects Americans' military policy preferences. Regardless of whether we interviewed respondents when martial concerns were highly salient or when economic troubles had largely driven military matters from the national consciousness, our experiments offer strong evidence that Americans consider not only the number but also the *distribution* of casualties when forging their opinions.

BRINGING THE CASUALTY GAP INTO THE PUBLIC SPHERE

We began this chapter by proposing two alternative frameworks through which Americans might view and assess the casualty gap. Reevaluating these in light of the experimental evidence, it appears that, rather than uncritically accepting the casualty gap as an inevitable result of the labor market, Americans are disturbed by casualty inequalities. The results of our experiments suggest that concerns over equity in military service and sacrifice are as influential now as they were in the early days of the Republic.[33] Strong strands of egalitarian thinking about military affairs are evident throughout American history, and a similar egalitarian instinct continues to shape public opinion today.[34] The idea that poorer segments of the country are bearing a disproportionate share of the nation's sacrifice on the battlefield is antithetical to American democratic norms and political thought. As such, for both policymakers and millions of average Americans alike, the persistence of casualty gaps across American wars and the widening of that gap in recent years are issues of genuine concern. Indeed, given this fundamental conflict between core values and the realities of contemporary military conflict and policy, it is little wonder that most discussions of the casualty gap are deeply submerged and kept far from the mainstream of political debate. When the issue does briefly arise, as in John Kerry's botched joke that implied a gap in front-line military service between high- and low-education communities, an honest accounting and open discussion of the casualty gap and its consequences is replaced instead by a barrage of partisan attacks and distortions before both sides quickly agree once again to move the question far from the political agenda.

Our evidence in chapters 2 and 3 finds conclusively that the casualty gap is real. Our analysis in this chapter finds that the casualty gap matters. Knowledge of the casualty gap affects public support for both the ongoing war in Iraq and for hypothetical future military endeavors. When incorporating casualties into their cost-benefit analyses, Americans do more than simply count the number of war dead. Unlike costs counted in dollars spent or equipment lost, the human costs of war can not be so neatly mesaured. Our experiments show that when assessing the human costs of military action and incorporating them into their retrospective policy judgments and prospective military policy preferences, Americans care both about the size of those costs and how they have been borne across the country.

Technical Appendix to Chapter 4

In this appendix we provide more details about the experimental data, and we estimate multivariate statistical models to ensure that the effects of inequality cues continue to hold after controlling for respondents' partisanship and other demographic characteristics.

Because the respondents were randomly assigned to one of the control or treatment conditions, the difference in means reported in tables 4.1, 4.2, and 4.3 are all unbiased. To be sure that the randomization was successful, we compared the background characteristics of each group and found no systematic differences across control and treatments on any major demographic dimension. However, multivariate statistical analyses allow us to analyze the effect of each treatment experimental cue while also controlling for other factors that might affect respondents' military policy attitudes, such as partisanship, gender, age, race, and educational attainment, as well as respondents' estimate of the number of soldiers killed or wounded from their hometown and neighboring communities. In each case, the regression results in table 4A.1 mirror the simple difference in means results presented in the tables in the text.

As the logistic regression in the first column shows, the inequality cue increased respondents' probability of answering that the war in Iraq was a mistake. Moreover, the inequality cue had a major impact on respondents' casualty sensitivity. In the second column in table 4A.1, we esti-

Table 4A.1. Regression Analyses of Impact of Inequality Cue on Military Policy Attitudes

	Iraq was a mistake	Casualty sensitivity	Ordinal casualty sensitivity	Return to draft
Inequality cue	0.31**	–12.41*	–0.26*	0.29*
	(0.17)	(7.86)	(0.17)	(0.19)
Republican	–1.78***	22.88**	0.89***	0.18
	(0.21)	(13.21)	(0.22)	(0.24)
Democrat	0.87***	–10.72*	–0.37**	0.67***
	(0.20)	(8.04)	(0.20)	(0.22)
Male	0.10	10.67*	0.60***	0.81***
	(0.16)	(7.81)	(0.18)	(0.20)
Age	0.00	–0.86	–0.07***	0.16***
	(0.03)	(1.19)	(0.03)	(0.03)
Black	0.70**	13.40	0.39*	–0.14
	(0.36)	(17.32)	(0.28)	(0.36)
Asian	–1.48**	–8.01	0.71**	–0.28
	(0.78)	(9.00)	(0.44)	(1.29)
Latino	–0.03	10.32	0.32	0.51*
	(0.34)	(20.14)	(0.35)	(0.38)
Education	0.06	–2.66	–0.01	0.04
	(0.05)	(2.55)	(0.06)	(0.06)
Local casualties in Iraq	0.07	2.05	–0.12*	0.07
	(0.07)	(4.29)	(0.08)	(0.08)
Constant	–0.20	37.01***	—	–3.95***
	(0.38)	(18.70)		(0.50)
Log-likelihood	–450.61	—	–706.93	–368.41
Observations	794	525	525	779

All of the models report robust standard errors; all significance tests are one-tailed. $^*p<.10$, $^{**}p<.05$, $^{***}p<.01$.

mate an ordinary least squares (OLS) regression of the factors affecting respondents' raw number of casualties that would be acceptable to prevent Iran from developing weapons of mass destruction and continuing to infiltrate Iraq. Consistent with the simple bivariate results presented in table 4.2, the multiple regression also shows evidence of a strong effect for the inequality cue on casualty sensitivity. According to our model, respondents who were informed about the casualty gap would accept approximately 12,000 fewer casualties on average, all else being equal, than respondents who were not told of the casualty gap in Iraq. However, because of the considerable variance in raw casualty number responses, we also followed Feaver and Gelpi's lead and reparameterized responses on a six-point ordinal index.[1] The first category captures respondents who would accept zero casualties; the second, casualty tolerances between 1 and 50; the third, tolerances between 51 and 500; the fourth, tolerances between 501 and 5,000; the fifth, tolerances between 5,001 and 50,000; and the sixth, tolerances greater than 50,000. The ordered logit model in column three estimates an identical model specification on this transformed dependent variable. Here again, we see a strong negative effect for the inequality cue even after controlling for partisan, gender, race, and other differences. The final column in table 4A.1 presents a logistic regression of support for returning to a draft. Consistent with the bivariate results in table 4.3, the relevant coefficient for the inequality cue is positive and significant, which indicates that exposure to the existence of a casualty gap in Iraq increased a respondent's likelihood of supporting a return to a draft.

As a final robustness check, before giving respondents the inequality cue in the "Was Iraq a mistake?" question, we queried respondents' support for withdrawing U.S. forces from Iraq. The mean difference between respondents who later received the inequality cue and those who did not was only 0.02 on a seven-point scale, which had a standard deviation of 2.42. Thus, there was no difference between these two groups of people in their attitudes toward the Iraq War *before* receiving the inequality cue, while a substantial difference emerged *after* the cue was given. As a result, we are confident that the differences across treatment and control conditions observed in these questions are the result of the various treatments and not of unobserved differences in respondents assigned to each group.

To ensure that our findings for the influence of casualty inequality cues on Americans' military policy preferences were not an artifact of the unique political and military environment of September 2007, we replicated a very similar version of our Iran casualty sensitivity question in late March of 2009. This experiment was also included in an Opinion Research Corporation CARAVAN telephone omnibus survey with a nationally representative sample of 1,003 Americans who were selected using a random-digit dialing methodology. The summary statistics presented in table 4.4 of the text strongly suggest that, even in this dramatically different political and strategic environment, information about casualty inequality continued to have a significant impact on Americans' casualty tolerance for a future military mission to halt Iran's nuclear weapons program.[2] However, to ensure that this result continues to hold even after controlling for respondents' demographic characteristics, we reestimated, with two minor changes, the models in columns two and three of table 4A.1 with data from both surveys. First, because we were unable to ask the question about respondents' estimates of their local community's casualty totals in Iraq, this variable was excluded from the new models. Second, because the new models pool observations from two surveys, they also include a dummy variable to identify observations from the March 2009 survey. The results are presented in table 4A.2.

In both the OLS and the ordered logit models, the inequality cue continues to have a statistically significant, negative influence on the number of casualties a respondent is willing to tolerate to halt Iran's nuclear weapons program. The control variables also continue to behave in largely the same way as they did in the models using only the September 2007 survey. Finally, the coefficient for the March 2009 dummy variable in the ordered logit model was positive and statistically significant, which

Table 4A.2. Regression Analyses of Impact of Inequality Cue on Casualty Sensitivity, September 2007 and March 2009 Surveys

	Casualty sensitivity	Ordinal casualty sensitivity
Inequality cue	–7.01*	–0.20**
	(4.77)	(0.11)
Republican	17.22***	0.76***
	(6.80)	(0.12)
Democrat	–2.43*	–0.38***
	(4.89)	(0.12)
Male	18.67***	0.71***
	(4.46)	(0.10)
Age	–0.09	–0.08***
	(.77)	(0.02)
Black	–1.52	0.53***
	(7.28)	(0.16)
Asian	–8.97*	0.58*
	(6.90)	(0.38)
Latino	11.85	0.22
	(12.40)	(0.22)
Education	–2.52**	–0.01
	(1.39)	(0.03)
March 2009 survey	–2.78	0.30***
	(4.72)	(0.11)
Constant	26.43***	—
	(11.04)	—
Log-likelihood	—	–2012.62
Observations	1,471	1,471

All of the models report robust standard errors; all significance tests are one-tailed. *p < .10, **p < .05, ***p < .01.

suggests that Americans may have been, on average, willing to accept more casualties to disarm Iran in 2009 than they were at the height of the Iraqi insurgency in 2007.[3]

Collectively, these results make an important contribution to the extensive literature within international relations on the determinants of casualty sensitivity.[4] While past work has focused on the civil/military divide, the nature of the proposed mission, perceived prospects for success and other factors that might influence Americans' willingness to tolerate casualties from case to case, the results of our experiment add an important and often-overlooked factor to the mix: open discussion of casualty inequalities.

5

How Local Casualties Shape Politics

We saw in the previous chapter that Americans care deeply about equality in military sacrifice. When presented with even modest informative cues about the existence of a socioeconomic casualty gap, respondents in our nationally representative survey were more critical of the Iraq War and more reluctant to accept casualties in possible future military campaigns. The experimental data strongly suggest that, if recognized and discussed more explicitly, the casualty gap can have significant ramifications for military policymaking. However, the analyses in chapter 4 present only one pathway by which the casualty gap can affect politics and policymaking in the United States.

Starting in this chapter we transition to a second pathway, diagrammed in figure 5.1, by which a casualty gap can affect public opinion and behavior. The first pathway, at the top of figure 5.1, recognizes that Americans may significantly adjust their military policy preferences if they become aware that a socioeconomic casualty gap exists. The second pathway, at the bottom of figure 5.1, traces the most straightforward consequence of the casualty gap: the fact that exposure to the human costs of war is spread unevenly across the country. By exposing some Americans—since Korea, predominantly those from socioeconomically disadvantaged counties and places—to the full weight of the human costs of war through the lens of their local communities while largely

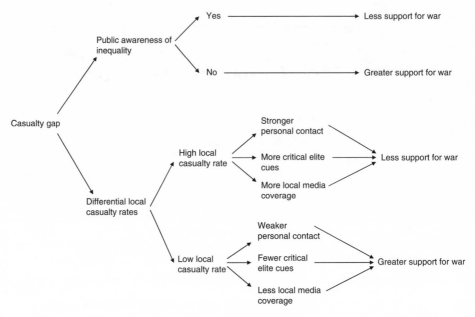

Figure 5.1. Pathways through which the casualty gap influences opinions and behavior.

insulating residents of other communities from these costs, the casualty gap can create significant cleavages in political opinions and behaviors.

The death of a soldier is, of course, an intimately personal and private loss borne most intensely by that soldier's family and loved ones. However, even a cursory perusal of obituaries written for soldiers who have made the ultimate sacrifice in Iraq shows that communities also share in the grieving process. For example, within a two-week span in March 2007, Maine's South Portland High School lost two of its graduates in the deserts of Iraq. In May 2008 it lost a third. The *Portland Press Herald* noted that the latest death "tested the strength of the community." Family members of the fallen soldiers described how the entire community pulled together to face the new tragedy in its midst, and the school's principal, Jeanne Crocker, discussed the widespread soul searching that the latest death had prompted: "There's the struggle to understand why. How could this be?" Regardless of the answers, Crocker concluded, "There's no question that hearts are broken today."[1]

Similarly, in her work with Vietnam-era oral histories, Heather Brandon vividly demonstrated that individual deaths can have ripple effects throughout a community. Joel Brown, the brother of Gordon Brown, who died in Vietnam, remembered that Lackawanna, New York, was "a real close community, about four hundred houses in this one section, and...that's where four kids came from: my brother, this Gary kid, the DiTommaso boy, who's still missing in action, and Mrs. DiTommaso's next-door neighbor, who was hit real bad.... It was tough in the neighborhood then. You get over one, and the next thing you know, somebody else got it."[2] These accounts suggest that the death of a soldier can affect an entire community. Friends and neighbors, politicians and community leaders, and even just readers of the local newspaper join in the grieving, mourning, and healing.

Thus, even though most Americans do not experience the same pain as a devastated widow or fatherless child, it does not necessarily follow that Americans are unaffected when soldiers from their community die in battle. Indeed, soldiers' deaths reverberate throughout society. Moreover, they reverberate loudest for those who experience them most directly through the lens of their local communities.

In this chapter we seek to understand the mechanisms through which local casualties can have these community-wide effects. Specifically, we focus on three possibilities shown at the bottom of figure 5.1. The casualty rate suffered by each American's local community can affect (1) one's sense of personal contact with fallen soldiers, (2) the type of elite cues one receives, and (3) the scope and tenor of war coverage one sees in the local media. Through each of these mechanisms, we argue, the casualty gap can create politically salient cleavages in Americans' wartime opinions and behaviors, and these in turn can fundamentally influence the course of politics and policy.

LOCAL CASUALTIES AND POLITICAL BEHAVIOR

In a single week in August of 2005, the town of Brook Park, Ohio, population 21,000, was devastated by the loss of twenty young men from the nearby 3rd Battalion, 25th Marines base. Many of the fallen Marines hailed from the small, blue-collar town itself, where Ford Motor Company had long been a leading employer. The tragedy prompted an outpouring of grief from the afflicted families and the greater community: visits from politicians offering condolences, public memorial services, and row after row of flags at half-mast. The gravity of the loss, highlighted by repeated stories in the local and national media that emphasized the disproportionate nature of the cost in lives borne by this one small town, prompted a range of emotions spanning the gamut from anguish to anger, from patriotic fervor to a newfound reflection on whether the war in Iraq was worth the cost. A resident from a nearby town admitted that, while he had initially supported Operation Iraqi Freedom, the deaths of his neighbors brought the war home, made it real, and gave him pause: "Seeing their names and there's a lot of connections.

There's a guy from Ohio State, where I graduated from, and there's a guy who played football at Normandy and that's right around the corner, you know, in Parma. And just the connections that, you know, you personally feel when you see different things like that."[3]

As Americans, we are all affected when a fellow citizen dies in service to the nation. Collectively, we venerate the sacrifice of our armed forces; honoring the war dead as the guarantors of our freedom is a tradition strongly rooted in American culture.[4] However, particularly in the smaller-scale conflicts that the nation has waged since World War II, a war's human costs hit closer to home for some Americans than they do for many others. Political scientists Peter Feaver and Chris Gelpi rightly remind us that for many if not most Americans war deaths may be considerably removed from their everyday experience.[5] The residents of Brook Park and other communities like it have clearly experienced the war in Iraq in a way that many Americans have not.

Most political science analyses of wartime public opinion and political behaviors have focused on the response of the nation as a whole to U.S. casualties. Many studies have documented how wartime support wanes in the face of mounting war dead, while others have examined how trends in casualty rates and short-term spikes in battle deaths track changes in public support for a war and its leaders.[6] Yet, comparatively little scholarship has examined the implications of the fact that not all Americans experience this war death equally. For example, does it matter that when some citizens think about the human costs of the Iraq War their first thought may be of the funeral of a young man or woman from their home community, whereas for others it may be only the number of reported casualties scrolling across the bottom of a cable news ticker?

As we review in the coming chapters, a handful of recent studies have begun to explore this question by demonstrating correlations between local casualties and citizens' political beliefs and behaviors.[7] We seek to build on this foundation in a number of respects. However, before turning to our own analyses of the political consequences of local casualties in the Vietnam and Iraq wars, we must first explore the causal mechanisms through which local casualties might influence individuals' political preferences and decisions.

Prior scholarship is largely silent on the precise mechanisms through which local casualties shape residents' opinion and voting calculus. Indeed, this problem has plagued scholarship on the political consequences of casualties in general; this includes the voluminous literature arguing that national casualty trends can explain significant shifts in public opinion. Political scientist Adam Berinsky has discovered that the average American in most wars probably has only a faint idea of how many casualties the country has sustained. In a survey experiment conducted during the Iraq conflict, Berinsky found tremendous variance in respondents' estimations of the number of U.S. casualties suffered in the Middle East. Moreover, respondents' estimates were in large part determined by their partisan predispositions, as Democrats gave systematically higher casualty estimates than the actual figure, while Republican estimates were considerably lower than the correct casualty total.[8] If the public does not know how many casualties there are, how can casualty counts influence their attitudes and behaviors?

It is possible that most citizens are more aware of the number of casualties suffered by their local community than by the nation as a whole; however, there is little hard data suggesting that this is the case. Given that, at least since World War II, most Americans have not lost an immediate family member on a foreign battlefield, how might local communities' wartime experiences shape the way in which citizens form their evaluations of policies and politicians? To answer this question, we need better theory than existing scholarship provides.

A NEW THEORY OF LOCAL CASUALTY INFLUENCE

To develop our theory we draw on multiple literatures within political science to identify three possible mechanisms by which local casualties may influence the opinions and political behaviors of citizens. After discussing these mechanisms in the remainder of this chapter, we test the theory in the following three chapters by collecting and presenting a large amount of empirical evidence that local casualty rates have significantly influenced citizens' opinions and voting propensities during both the Vietnam and Iraq wars.

Mechanism #1: Personal Contact with Local Casualties

The first mechanism by which citizens in high-casualty communities may develop different political attitudes and behaviors than citizens in low-casualty communities is their increased likelihood of personal contact with relatives, friends, and neighbors of deceased soldiers. At first glance, the ability of the personal contact mechanism to explain the reactions of most Americans may seem limited. Even in wars with tens of thousands of casualties, the number of war dead constitutes only an infinitesimal percentage of the American public. For the vast majority of Americans, the probability of losing an immediate family member is extremely low. Combat casualties, in the words of Peter Feaver and Christopher Gelpi, "are not a concrete reality to the vast majority of American citizens."[9] If we accept narrow conceptions of "concrete reality" and personal contact, then Feaver and Gelpi are correct that casualties should not directly affect the vast majority of American citizens. If, however, we examine both the events subsequent to a soldier's death and the capacity of Americans' myriad of formal and informal networks to intensify a sense of connection with casualties of war, then there is good reason to reconceptualize the notion of personal contact.

When an American soldier dies, whether in combat or noncombat operations, uniformed military service representatives are sent to notify the soldier's next of kin.[10] Today the military employs and trains casualty assistance officers to handle these difficult situations.[11] After receiving the tragic news, family members must begin to make funeral plans while they wait for their loved one's remains to arrive. After next of kin are notified, the office of the assistant secretary of defense for public affairs makes an official confirmation of the death. As we discuss shortly, this is when local news media become important actors. Once the casket arrives, most families choose to have some sort of funeral or remembrance service.

It is during the funeral and remembrance rituals that a private death most clearly becomes a community loss. Funerals for soldiers killed in Iraq, for example, have drawn large numbers of mourners. At army Cpl. Nathan Hubbard's funeral in 2007, St. Anthony of Padua Catholic Church "held so many mourners...it was filled beyond its 1,400-seat capacity."[12] The community was not just lining up inside the church, either: "Afterward, the funeral procession to Clovis District Cemetery passed through miles of residential streets decorated with red, white and blue ribbons and lined with people waving American flags."[13]

Similar outpourings of support are seen in the community responses to many other Iraq War deaths. As Holli VanWert of Madras, Oregon, described it after local soldier Thomas Tucker's death, "Madras is a 6,000-person family. You can fight amongst yourselves, but if anyone gets hurt, gets sick or dies, the community pours out like you've never seen, and I know the Tuckers feel this."[14] The residents of Camden, Arkansas, "lined up about 10 yards apart along the four-mile [funeral procession] route...each with hand on heart and clutching an American flag" for army Spc. Jonathan Cheatham after his death in July 2003.[15] When army Sgt. Kurtis Arcala of Palmer, Alaska, died in Iraq in 2005, his community all chipped in for the funeral expenses. Anticipating large crowds, the Arcala family decided to use Raven Hall on the Alaska state fairgrowwunds. The family, however, could not afford the $500 rental fee. On hearing the news, the town of Palmer pulled together. Mayor John Combs and his wife, Linda, contributed the first $100. "This is one of our sons," they said, and "[money] should not be an issue." Townspeople, former classmates, and others also contributed, and the employer of Sgt. Arcala's aunt, Weldin Construction, made up the rest. The support for Sgt. Arcala's family reminds us that a single casualty can have an enormous impact on community members even when, as Sgt. Arcala's aunt noted, "there's no blood shared."[16] When community members lose a son or daughter of their hometown, they respond not because they are related by blood but because they are related by the ties of community.

Once we account for the public nature of Americans' mourning rituals and widespread community support for fallen soldiers, we can see the need to broaden the definition of "personal contact" beyond simply being an immediate friend or family member of the deceased. From the hundreds or thousands who pay their respects or see the funeral procession, to the hundreds or thousands more in schools and workplaces who hear the news, a soldier's death can become a concrete reality for many in a community.

Moreover, once we embrace a more expansive definition of "personal contact," we must consider the ability of Americans' vast networks of family, coworkers, and friends to expand considerably the number of lives touched by a single death. Social network theorists provide us with theoretical and empirical tools to understand the ripple effects of each casualty. In a 2006 study, Duke University sociologist James Moody employed quantitative network analysis to estimate the number of Americans who know someone killed or wounded in Iraq through formal and informal social networks. Extending his analysis with casualty data as of December 2008 yields some startling figures. Moody's empirical model suggests that more than 200,000 Americans may have lost a direct family member in Iraq, while another 1.7 million have had a direct relative wounded in the Middle East. The magnitude of the ripple effects is even greater when we move beyond family ties and examine contact with the human costs of war through broader social networks. According to Moody's algorithm, more than a million Americans may know the name of a soldier killed in Iraq while 10 million Americans may know the name of a wounded soldier.[17]

While Americans' social networks can stretch across the country and even the globe, most networks are densest in individuals' local communities. As a result, citizens from communities that have suffered disproportionately high casualty rates should be more likely to feel a sense of personal contact with the human costs of war than Americans from low-casualty communities. Indeed, two Gallup surveys conducted in 2006 provide a unique opportunity to test this hypothesis. Each survey asked respondents the following question: "Do you personally have any close friends, family members, or coworkers who have served in Iraq in the U.S. military since the war began, or not?" For those who responded in the affirmative, Gallup asked this follow-up question: "Were any of them wounded or killed while serving in Iraq?" Across the two polls, 54 percent of Americans said that they knew someone who had served in Iraq, and 10 percent replied that they knew a soldier who had been killed or wounded in the Middle East.

The reported figure from the Gallup poll—that almost 10 percent of Americans claim to know someone killed or wounded in Iraq—requires explanation because it is considerably higher than the estimate generated by Moody's social network algorithm. One possibility is that this inflated number is the result of overreporting, a result analogous to the very strong majorities of Americans who self-report voting in public opinion surveys despite considerably lower actual turnout rates. Alternatively, the much higher figure may be an indication that the standard conception of "personal contact" is simply too narrow. Many citizens may feel that they "know" a casualty of war even if the fallen soldier is not within their immediate network of family and friends. For example, it would be unsurprising to us if the Brook Park resident quoted earlier would respond that he "knew" an Iraq War casualty even if he and the fallen soldiers had no direct interpersonal contact. Many Americans may not even be able to remember a fallen soldier's name, but because of some shared connection—because they went to the same high school or college or lived in the same community or in neighboring towns—they may feel that they "know" a casualty of war when prompted by an interviewer. Americans who live in communities that have suffered disproportionately large casualty rates should be more likely to have such shared connections with fallen soldiers.

Unfortunately, Gallup does not provide precise geographic data on each respondent's home community to test this hypothesis. However, because each poll reported every respondent's state of residence, we are able to test empirically whether residents of states that suffered high casualty rates are more likely to report knowing a killed or wounded soldier than their peers from low-casualty states. The relationship between a respondent's home state casualty rate and his or her probability of personally "knowing" a casualty is strong, positive, and statistically significant. Respondents from states that were in the top quarter of states in terms of casualty rates suffered in Iraq were almost twice as likely to respond that they personally knew a casualty of war than were respondents from states in the bottom quarter of the casualty rate distribution. Whereas only 8 percent of respondents from states in the bottom casualty quartile answered that they knew a killed or wounded soldier, 16 percent of respondents from the upper quartile of the state casualty distribution reported knowing a casualty.[18]

Moreover, this relationship remains strong even after statistically controlling for an individual's partisanship, educational attainment, gender, age, marital status, and race. Indeed, of these controls the only other statistically significant predictor of personal contact with a casualty is the respondent's age. Older Americans logically have less direct contact with the young cohort of service members fighting in the Middle East. Full results from the logistic regression are reported in the chapter's technical appendix.

Thus, there is compelling quantitative evidence to support the anecdotal evidence that personal contact with combat casualties—broadly defined—is not limited to an infinitesimally thin slice of U.S. society, even in the case of the Iraq War, one of the nation's smallest wars in terms of the number of lives lost. Millions of Americans feel that they have personally been touched by the human costs of war, and the people most likely to feel this direct personal contact with fallen service members are those who live in communities that have experienced a disproportionate share of the casualty burden. Because of the war's closer proximity to these citizens, they might exhibit policy preferences and political behaviors that differ from those of citizens who experience the war's costs less directly.

Mechanism #2: Elite Cues

The cues of political elites are a second mechanism through which local casualties might influence citizens' opinions and behaviors.[19] For example, political scientists John Zaller and Adam Berinsky both emphasize the importance of elite cues to explain why public opinion in some circumstances remains steadfast in support of a military action in the face of high casualties and, in other cases, quickly wanes as combat deaths mount. Rather than instinctively recoiling and withdrawing support for military measures when confronted with casualties, Zaller, Berinksy, and others argue that the mass public looks to political elites for signals on how to process battlefield developments. When there is bipartisan elite consensus behind a military action the public rallies around the president and his military policies. However, support for war begins to erode in the face of open dissension in Washington.

Yet, the rhetoric and public maneuverings of political elites may do more than just explain shifts in wartime support among the American public as a whole. Indeed, elite cues may help explain variance in support for military action around the country. Individual politicians, like the voters they represent, may logically view the war first and foremost through the lens of their own constituency's experience with it.[20] As a result, politicians from high-casualty communities may be more likely to speak out against the war and send negative cues to their constituents than politicians and other elites from communities that have suffered lower casualty rates.

There is extensive anecdotal evidence to believe that this is so. For example, the first House Republican to break ranks with the Bush administration's united front on Iraq was North Carolina's Walter Jones. At first blush, Jones would appear to be one of the most unlikely House Republicans to abandon the party line and the White House. Although his father served in the House as a Democrat until 1990, Walter Jones first won his seat under the GOP banner in the Republican "revolution" of 1994. Roll-call analyses of Jones's voting behavior suggest that he is one of the most conservative members of the House of Representatives, and before the Iraq War he earned strong marks from the John Birch Society, as well as a perfect rating from the Christian Coalition. Jones was also an early supporter of President Bush's decision to invade Iraq and remove Saddam Hussein from power. Indeed, perhaps Congressman Jones's first major splash on the national stage was accomplished by his move, with Congressman Robert Ney on the Committee on House Administration, to rename French fries "freedom fries" in the House cafeteria to protest France's refusal to support the American-led invasion. Despite this pedigree, in June of 2005 Walter Jones became one of the first Republicans to join Dennis Kucinich (D-OH) on a stage before the cameras to declare publicly his support for legislation that would end the war in Iraq.

What led to the congressman's transformation? In Jones's own words, the trigger that caused his reevaluation of the war was a funeral he attended for a fallen U.S. Marine in his home district in North Carolina. While he watched with tears in his eyes as a young widow with twins received a crisply folded American flag and read aloud a final letter sent home from her husband, one of the little boys dropped a toy, which a marine in the honor guard retrieved for him. In that poignant moment, according to Jones, "It hit me: This little boy would never know his daddy." A devout Christian, Jones describes his first personal contact with the human costs of the war in Iraq as a "spiritual happening" and acknowledges that "at that point I fully understood the loss that a family feels. The whole way [home], 72 miles, I was thinking about what I [had] just witnessed. I think God intended for me to be there."[21] That day, Jones resolved to write personally to the family of every American soldier killed in Iraq, and he posts pictures of every casualty outside of his House office.

In a similar vein, one of the most prominent early critics of the administration's policies in Iraq in the upper chamber was Nebraska Republican Chuck Hagel, whose home state as of December 2008 had suffered the fifth highest casualty rate of any state in the Union. Commensurate with his state's sacrifice was Hagel's emphasis on casualties and the human costs of war, which were a constant feature of the antiwar rhetorical cues that Hagel sent to his constituents until his retirement at the end of the 110th Congress.

A speech by Pennsylvania Democratic Senator Robert Casey in July of 2007 brings the importance of local casualties into perhaps even sharper relief. In defending his resolve to continue voting for a change in course in Iraq, the moderate Democrat read on the Senate floor the names and hometowns of all 169 Pennsylvanians who had given their lives in the Middle East, and he emphasized that this represented the third highest total of any state. Casey reminded his peers and, perhaps more importantly, his constituents: "Those numbers surely don't tell the whole story. Especially when we consider the traumatic effect the war has had on individual families. These fighting men and women were born into families, not into divisions and brigades. They are sons and daughters, husbands and wives, fathers and mothers."[22] By explicitly reminding Pennsylvanians of the sacrifice they have borne, Casey's rhetoric may contribute toward gaps in opinion and behavior that mirror the geographic contours of the casualty gap.

The elite cues mechanism is also supported by more rigorous empirical testing reported in full in this chapter's technical appendix. Systematically analyzing Douglas Kriner and William Howell's database of more than 5,000 speeches given in the House of Representatives and Senate on the war in Iraq between March 2003 and May 2006, we find clear evidence that the number of speeches a member of Congress made against the Iraq War is positively and significantly related to the casualty rate of that member's home state.[23] Our results suggest that, all else being equal, members of Congress from states with casualty rates at the 75th percentile gave 32 percent more speeches in Congress critical of the war than did their peers with otherwise identical partisan and constituency characteristics but whose states had suffered casualty rates at the 25th percentile. At the extremes of the casualty distribution, the effects are even larger. For example, a shift in home state casualty rate from the 10th percentile to the 90th percentile doubles the expected number of antiwar speeches a member will give on the floor.

Our statistical analysis provides compelling evidence that the anecdotal observations about the importance of local casualties in fueling the antiwar rhetoric of Congressman Walter Jones, Senator Chuck Hagel, and Senator Robert Casey are part of a more general phenomenon affecting members of Congress. Members routinely cite their personal contact with the families of deceased soldiers as a reason for their war positions and rhetoric, and our statistical analysis strongly suggests that home state casualties are an important force in driving the signals they send to their constituents.

Although we have focused our analysis on members of Congress, state and local politicians are also affected. For example, following the previously mentioned death of Sergeant Arcala in Iraq, Alaska governor Frank Murkowski issued a public statement and flew a flag over the state capitol at half-mast.[24] Similarly, when army Cpl. Blake Stephens was killed by a roadside bomb in May of 2007, the mayor of Pocatello, Idaho, Roger Chase, expressed the entire community's condolences to the family, ordered the city hall flags flown at half-mast, and called on all residents to do the same. Following his lead, a number of volunteers planted American flags along the road for the entire route from Stephens's former high school to his parents' home.[25] If higher local casualty rates cause elites to pay more attention publicly to the human costs of war—and, as shown in many cases at the congressional level, to be more critical of the war or at least to be more wary of staying the course militarily—elites may in turn affect local public beliefs and behaviors related to the war.

Mechanism #3: The Local Media

A final mechanism through which local casualties may affect opinions on the war and patterns of political behavior is through differential coverage by local media outlets. For most Americans, perhaps the only way they will be exposed to the human costs of a foreign war is through the news media. Even as the spectrum of media outlets has expanded dramatically in recent years, most Americans continue to get their news from local sources.[26]

Some existing research suggests that local media coverage of a foreign conflict is dramatically shaped by the sacrifices that a local community endures. For example, research by political scientist Scott Gartner into media coverage of the 2000 terrorist attack on the USS *Cole* found that local newspapers from communities that lost a sailor in the attack were considerably more likely to give significant media attention to the incident than were papers from areas with little local connection.[27] This variance in local media coverage, in turn, can create cleavages in public opinion across the country. For example, in their study of variation in popular support for the invasion of Iraq, political scientists William Howell and Jon Pevehouse found that popular attitudes were heavily influenced by the balance of elite discourse individuals observed on local television news broadcasts.[28] Survey respondents exposed to more reports of congressional opposition to the Bush administration's war plans were less likely to support a preemptive strike against Saddam Hussein than were their peers with similar demographic characteristics who hailed from regions that received more pro-war coverage in their local media outlets.

Comparable studies of the Vietnam era are lacking, but anecdotal evidence from interviews with families suggests that many had experiences similar to that of Jeanene Forrest, who lost her brother Donald in Vietnam. Talking about watching the local news over dinner, Jeanene remembered that "At every meal, you had to have dead silence, so you could hear names. I always listened for names and different places that I recognized."[29] Although the first "television war" drew national media attention, it was local connections made prominent in local media coverage that resonated most.

While a comprehensive analysis of local media coverage of the war in Iraq is beyond the scope of this chapter, a cursory examination of reporting on several soldiers killed in the war illustrates that local media outlets routinely devote considerable attention to casualties from their own communities, including poignant details and sobering discussions of the fallen soldier's connections to the community. For example, in August of 2007, Spc. Michael Anthony Hook of Altoona, Pennsylvania, died in a helicopter crash in northern Iraq. The citizens of Altoona were no strangers to the horrors of war. The town of 50,000 had lost a soldier just two months earlier, while a third soldier had died in 2004. Moreover, less than ten miles away the small town of Hollidaysburg had lost four soldiers out of a total population of less than 6,000. The *Altoona Mirror* ran several full stories honoring Spc. Hook's sacrifice. Local reporters interviewed family and friends, including the Altoona Area High School football coach, who remembered Hook's dedication above all else: "He was a young man who gave everything he had."[30] Even the sports page reminded readers of the loss of one of their own when it referenced the moment of silence that was held for Specialist Hook and his family before the local high school baseball game.[31] Five weeks later, the *Mirror* ran an article that discussed a group of local soldiers' mothers who had banded together to provide mutual support, baked goods, and other gifts for soldiers overseas. In the interview, group member Lou Ann Leamer discussed how the group responds to reports of casualties in Iraq:

> When Leamer hears bad news, she wonders whether Blair County lost a local son or daughter. When there is a local viewing and/or funeral, Leamer attends. "We support the kids, the families, the community and each other," she said. The most recent need for support came in August when Altoona Army Spc. Michael Hook was one of 14 U.S. soldiers killed in Iraq in a helicopter crash. "It's very hard," Leamer said. "His mother just joined last year, so we didn't know him, but we knew her." Leamer's first thought was how Hook's mother felt when she opened the door to find

someone from the military. "If I was faced with that, I don't know what I would've done," she said. "It's just heartbreaking. I spend a lot of time thinking about these kids. We have a picture board of the kids, and I look at that and think, God, they're babies."[32]

Turning to a different region of the country, we see another example of local media covering a local casualty in great depth. In November 2003 Staff Sgt. Paul Neff II of Fort Mill, South Carolina, died in Iraq when a shoulder-mounted missile struck his Black Hawk helicopter. The *Fort Mill Times* ran a series of articles that celebrated Neff's life and remembered his deep ties with many in the community. The *Times* interviewed teachers and friends from Fort Mill High School, where Neff had graduated in 1991, and even quoted from his senior yearbook. It humanized the costs of war further by relaying a story about his engagement. As Staff Sgt. Neff waited for an opportune moment with a ring in his pocket, his girlfriend beat him to the punch and asked him to marry her before he had a chance to pop the question.[33] A week later, the *Times* memorialized Neff again and reprinted in full the eulogy that his sister delivered at his funeral in Michigan.[34]

The *Rock Hill Herald*, the main newspaper from the next town down I-77 South from Fort Mill, also honored Neff in a series of articles. Two other larger regional papers, the *Charlotte Observer* of Charlotte, North Carolina, and *The State*, of Columbia, South Carolina, also memorialized Neff. However, apart from two brief synopses on the AP wire, searches of *Lexis Nexis* and *NewsLibrary* newspaper archives suggest that most other media outlets even in the Southeast gave Neff's death only superficial coverage, usually including the information only in an updated list of U.S. casualties to date in Iraq.

An extensive literature in political science suggests that such intense local media coverage of war casualties has the capacity to shape public opinion. By constructing various frames for the war, the media may have a considerable impact on how the public evaluates the war.[35] Alternatively, the media need not necessarily present news from Iraq or any other war in a positive or negative frame to influence public opinion. Instead, the media's conscious decision to emphasize some aspects of the war rather than others may prime the public to weigh heavily that aspect when judging the war and its progress.[36]

When local media outlets pay considerable attention to local casualties, humanize the costs of war, and make plain the connections of far-away events to local communities, they may affect the opinions of their readers through both framing and priming. Presenting news from Iraq through the frame of its local costs may temper popular support for a conflict and raise questions about the conduct of an increasingly costly overseas conflict. Alternatively, significant attention to local casualties may merely prime individuals to keep these local consequences of the war firmly in mind when evaluating the war and its leaders. Neither framing nor priming will necessarily cause media consumers to turn against the president or his policies. Indeed, some may well rally around the flag and the commander-in-chief with resolve that their friends and neighbors will not have died in vain. Nonetheless, because of its capacity to connect even a remote war with readers' everyday lives and communities, the local media provides a powerful third mechanism by which variance in local casualty rates can produce variance in political attitudes and behaviors across the country.

CONCLUSION

Varying levels of personal contact with the human costs of war, differential cues sent by political elites, and local media coverage that connects developments on faraway battlefields with the fabric of community life are all ways in which local casualties might affect Americans' political opinions and behaviors. Through the transmission lines of social networks, political discourse, and local media coverage, private mourning and remembrance enter the public sphere. In this way, each casualty sends ripple effects throughout the fallen soldier's community. Because of the casualty gap, these ripple effects are much stronger in some communities—particularly socioeconomically disadvantaged ones—than in others.

  In the next three chapters we investigate the effects of variance in local casualty rates on both aggregate- and individual-level political outcomes. Specifically, we examine whether Americans from communities that suffered the highest casualty rates in recent wars are more likely to support bringing the conflict to an end, to vote against incumbent politicians affiliated with the war, and to exhibit lower levels of political engagement in a war's aftermath than their peers. Toward this end, we use the same casualty variables created in our analysis in chapter 2—casualty rates for a particular community or state—but we use them in a new way. In social science parlance, casualty inequality was used in chapters 2 and 3 as a "dependent variable"—something to be explained. In the analyses ahead, we employ local casualty rates as an "independent variable"—something to do the explaining. We try to understand whether variance in local casualty rates has affected Americans' policy opinions, voting behaviors and levels of political engagement. In doing so, we begin to uncover the full implications of the casualty gap.

Technical Appendix to Chapter 5

STATISTICAL SUPPORT FOR THE PERSONAL CONTACT MECHANISM

To test the relationship between casualty rates and a respondent's probability of reporting that he or she knew a killed or wounded soldier, we conducted additional statistical analysis. The results of a logistic regression that generated the predicted impact of a respondent's home state casualty rate (per 100,000 male residents) on the probability that the respondent will report "knowing" a soldier killed or wounded in the Iraq War are presented in table 5A.1.[1] In addition to a respondent's home state casualty rate, we also included indicator variables for partisanship, educational attainment, age, gender, marital status, and race. The coefficient for home state casualty rate is positive, as expected, and highly statistically significant. The only other statistically significant relationship from the model is that between age and casualty contact; older Americans were significantly less likely to personally know a soldier killed or wounded in the war. This result, too, is consistent with expectations; younger cohorts are predominant in the military ranks in general, and particularly in positions with the greatest exposure to combat. As a result, younger Americans should be more likely to feel a personal connection with a casualty of war than older Americans.

Table 5A.1. Logistic Regression of Factors Influencing Whether a Respondent Knows a Casualty of the War in Iraq

	Knows a casualty
State casualty rate	0.36***
	(0.11)
Democrat	–0.28
	(0.18)
Republican	–0.27
	(0.18)
Education	0.02
	(0.05)
Age (in 10s)	–0.14***
	(0.04)
Male	0.23
	(0.15)
Married	0.03
	(0.07)
Black	0.20
	(0.29)
Constant	–2.29***
	(0.54)
Log-likelihood	–652.26
Observations	1,981

All of the models report robust standard errors; all significance tests are two-tailed. $^*p<.10$, $^{**}p<.05$, $^{***}p<.01$.

STATISTICAL SUPPORT FOR THE ELITE CUES MECHANISM

To determine whether the positions of political elites are shaped by the wartime experiences of their constituents, we used the Kriner and Howell Iraq speeches database to construct a measure of the number of speeches against the war made by every member of the House and Senate between March 2003 and May 2006. For each speech, coders identified every occurrence of 46 specific arguments: 12 each for and against the initial decision to use force in Iraq, and 11 each supporting and opposing the conduct of the the invasion/occupation of the country. Speeches that contained more arguments opposing the administration than supporting it were coded as critical.[2] We then used a negative binomial count model to estimate the effect of each member's home state casualty rate (per 100,000 male residents) on the number of antiwar speeches he or she gave during this period. If local casualties affect the public cues of political elites, then we would expect members from states hardest hit by the war to give more speeches critical of the Iraqi conflict and the Bush administration's conduct of it than their peers from states with low casualty rates.

In addition to state casualty rates, the models also controlled for a variety of other personal and district-level characteristics that might influence a member's rhetoric in Congress. First, we controlled for each member's partisanship and ideology. Logically, Democrats should be considerably more aggressive in challenging President Bush and his policies than Republicans; furthermore, because opinion splits on the war have also largely tracked ideological cleavages, we also expect more liberal members as measured by Common Space scores to criticize the war more aggressively than conservative members of Congress. The statistical model also included dummy variables that identified whether each member was part of the House or the Senate leadership structures and whether each member had a seat on a foreign policy committee.[3] Moreover, to see whether the effect of being in the leadership varied by party, we added an interaction variable that identified Democratic leaders. We also included variables that identified whether each member served in the House or Senate and whether each member served in both the 108th and the 109th Congress or in only one. The model also included a measure of each member's seniority within the relevant chamber.

Finally, we included a series of measures to control for other characteristics of each member's home state. Legislators from states where President Bush performed well in 2004 may be less likely to criticize the administration's conduct of the war than members from states that rejected the Bush platform in the last election. Because economics and casualty rates are strongly correlated, we control for a measure of each state's economic conditions—its unemployment rate in 2006. Finally, we examined whether the military characteristics of each member's constituency—namely the number of active-duty military personnel and veterans in a state—affected his or her propensity to criticize the Iraq war on the floor.

Table 5A.2 presents the full regression results of the negative binomial event count model. However, because the coefficients from negative binomial models are difficult to interpret directly, figure 5A.1 presents a series of first differences that graphically illustrate the effect of each independent variable on the percentage change in the number of speeches critical of the war given by a member of Congress. Specifically, each bar illustrates the effect of a shift in a variable from its 25th to 75th percentile (0 to 1 in the case of dummy variables) on the estimated number of antiwar speeches a member gives while holding all other variables constant at their means or medians.

Table 5A.2. Event Count Model of the Determinants of
Congressional Speeches That Opposed the Bush Administration's
Conduct of the War in Iraq

	Antiwar Speeches
State casualty rate	0.42***
	(0.17)
Democrat	2.88***
	(0.87)
Common space score	−0.26
	(1.29)
Party leader	−0.58
	(0.50)
Party leader * Democrat	1.02*
	(0.57)
Foreign policy committee	0.57***
	(0.21)
Senate	0.16
	(0.26)
Seniority in chamber	0.05***
	(0.01)
Served in both terms	1.34***
	(0.26)
% Bush 2004	−0.67
	(1.41)
State unemployment 2006	0.10
	(0.10)
Total in military (in 10Ks)	−0.02
	(0.03)
Total veterans (in 100Ks)	0.05***
	(0.02)
Constant	−3.82
	(1.08)
Log-likelihood	−1114.44
Observations	583

All of the models report robust standard errors; all significance tests are two-tailed. $^*p < .10$, $^{**}p < .05$, $^{***}p < .01$.

To preserve the scale, the effects of two variables are not included in figure 5A.1. Most important, the single greatest predictor of the number of speeches given by a member of Congress opposing the war was the member's partisanship. The average Republican gave a little more than 0.5 speeches that criticized the war and the president's conduct of it from March 2003 to June 2006, whereas the average Democrat gave more

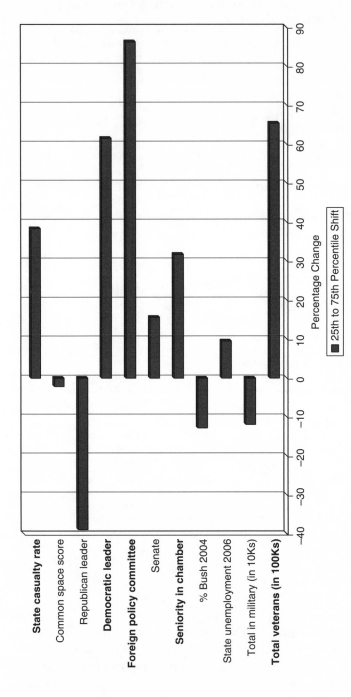

Figure 5A.1. The impact of state casualty rate and other factors on number of antiwar speeches given by members of Congress between March 2003 and May 2006.

Note: Statistically significant effects are indicated with boldface.

than 11 during the same period. As a result, all of our first differences are estimated with the Democratic dummy variable set equal to one.[4] Similarly, first differences show that whether or not a member served in both the 108th and the 109th Congresses had a very strong impact on the number of speeches that member gave; indeed, those who served in only one Congress gave more than 70 percent fewer antiwar speeches than did their colleagues who served in both.

As discussed in the chapter, figure 5A.1 begins by showing unambiguously that the experience of a member's home state during the Iraq War was indeed a strong, systematic predictor of that member's rhetoric on the war. The resulting coefficient in the statistical model is strongly positive and highly statistically significant. First differences suggest that, all else being equal, members from states with casualty rates of 2.3 deaths per 100,000 male residents gave almost 40 percent more speeches in Congress critical of the war than did their peers with otherwise identical partisan and constituency characteristics but whose states had suffered casualty rates of 1.6 deaths per 100,000 male residents. At the extremes of the casualty distribution, the effects are even larger. For example, a shift in home state casualty rate from the 10th percentile to the 90th percentile more than doubles the expected number of antiwar speeches a member will give on the floor. Members of Congress routinely cite their personal contact with the war as a reason for their war positions and rhetoric, and our statistical analysis strongly suggests that home state casualties are an important force driving their rhetoric and the signals they send to their constituents.

After controlling for partisanship, a member's ideological Common Space score had no additional statistically significant impact on his or her war rhetoric. However, a member's position within the two chambers' party leadership structures did have an important impact on the member's level of criticism of the war in Iraq. Republican Party leaders almost never publicly criticized the war or the Bush administration's handling of it. Conversely, Democratic leaders were substantially more likely to criticize the president and his policies than were the party rank and file. Indeed, Democratic leaders' expected volume of antiwar rhetoric was 60 percent higher on average than that of other Democrats not in the party leadership. Moreover, the model suggests that members with strong substantive interests in and positions of internal institutional power over foreign policy were also more critical of the war than their peers. Members of both chambers' foreign policy committees made about 80 percent more antiwar speeches on average than their peers with identical demographic and constituency characteristics who did not serve on a foreign policy committee. Senators were no more or less likely to make a large number of statements opposing the war than their counterparts in the House. However, more senior members of both chambers were considerably more active in speaking out against the conflict than junior members.

Finally, the model found some evidence that other constituency characteristics besides home state casualty rate influenced the volume and tone of congressional rhetoric. Legislators from states where Bush polled well in 2004 may have given slightly fewer speeches that criticized the war than their peers, yet the estimated effect is statistically insignificant. Similarly, the model found little evidence that state economic conditions or numbers of active duty military personnel had any influence on the volume of antiwar rhetoric. However, the analysis does suggest that members from areas with strong contingents of military veterans were more active in condemning the war and the Bush administration's conduct of it than their peers with fewer veterans in their home states. This result foreshadows the finding in chapter 7 that Republican Senatorial incumbents in 2006 paid a particularly steep electoral price in counties with high veteran populations.

6

Political Ramifications of the Vietnam Casualty Gap

As a result of the casualty gap, some American communities—particularly socioeconomically disadvantaged ones—suffer disproportionately high local casualty rates, while others escape with significantly lower casualty rates. Residents of high-casualty communities are much more likely to feel a greater sense of personal contact with the human costs of war than residents of low-casualty communities. They receive different types of elite cues concerning the war, and they experience the war in a fundamentally different way through coverage of the war in local media outlets. Through each of these mechanisms, the casualty gap ensures that some Americans see strong local connections to foreign events, while others are more insulated from an overseas conflict and its immediate human costs.

However, the effect of war casualties almost certainly varies widely across individuals. Heightened exposure to a war's human costs may cause some in high-casualty communities to oppose the war, while reinforcing others' support for it. As an example, consider the following story from Heather Brandon's study of how families of fallen soldiers responded to the Vietnam War. Reflecting on the death of their brother Joel in Vietnam and the possibility of their own children being drafted into military service, Kenneth and Gordon Brown expressed starkly contrasting views. Gordon said, "I have two boys now. If they get drafted, they better get their asses into the army." Kenneth, on the other hand, exclaimed, "If there's any way at all I can keep my son out of the military, I'm going to."[1] A similar split is readily apparent in stories from the current context of the war in Iraq. Some Americans who have experienced losses in Iraq—in their families, communities, or constituencies—reaffirm their resolve to continue supporting the war so that the dead will not have died in vain. Others, by contrast, confess that being confronted with the human costs of war has shaken their support for the military endeavor and increased their desire to end the U.S. commitment in Iraq.

Because these divergent individual reactions to casualties occur, it is possible that greater exposure to war casualties could weaken or strengthen war support among residents of high-casualty communities. In figure 5.1 of the preceding chapter, we theorized that the net effect of this greater local exposure to casualties is to *increase* opposition to the war and the political leaders waging it. However, because both responses are possible at the individual level, additional empirical data are needed to test this hypothesis. Accordingly, we adopt a large-N statistical approach to assess the *average* effects of local community casualty rates on residents' opinions and behaviors. Our approach complements newspaper accounts and qualitative studies; such studies use in-depth interviews to offer vivid images and details about the ways in which particular families handle the death of a loved one or neighbor, but they cannot answer questions about larger patterns. Our statistical analyses allow us to estimate the net effect of the casualty gap on citizens' opinion formation and political behaviors. All else being equal, do high local casualty rates erode residents' support for war and increase their willingness to vote against incumbent politicians, as we have theorized they might? Or, do citizens from high-casualty communities, on average, rally behind a military operation and its political leaders?

To answer these questions, our analysis proceeds in two parts. Beginning with the Vietnam War, the chapter first examines the effect of casualties on changes in public evaluations of the war over time. Specifically, it examines the influence of local casualties on respondents' judgment of whether the United States should ever have entered the Vietnam War at all and on their support for withdrawing U.S. forces from the fight. Having established a strong link between local casualty rates and policy attitudes, the analysis next investigates whether these differential opinions on the war manifested themselves in different voting patterns. This additional line of analysis is critically important to establishing the consequences of the casualty gap for military policymaking; what matters is not just if people's opinions change but also if those opinion shifts are transformed into concrete political pressure at the ballot box.[2]

CASUALTIES, PUBLIC OPINION, AND THE VIETNAM WAR

Although Gallup, Roper, and other polling organizations have conducted systematic surveys of public opinion since the 1930s, the Vietnam War sparked a revolution in scholarly understanding of the dynamics that underlie support for major military conflicts within the United States.[3] The flowering of the behavioral revolution in political science, coupled with the development of modern sampling and polling techniques and an abundance of hard data, spurred a number of contemporary efforts to understand the mix of demographic, group, and societal factors that drove opinion formation on the war. Writing before the Tet offensive violently shook the foundations of popular support for U.S. policy in Southeast Asia, political scientist Sidney Verba and colleagues found that, while the majority of Americans supported President Johnson and his conduct of the war, there was also considerable support for negotiations with Hanoi and other measures short of withdrawal that would hasten an end to the conflict. Perhaps most surprisingly, Verba et al. found that many of the standard dimensions on which opinion cleavages routinely arise—partisan identification, class, occupation, and region—were not significant predictors of opinion on Vietnam, at least not at this early stage of the war.[4] Subsequent analyses would find some evidence of demographic cleavages by the later stages of the conflict and modest evidence that self-interest—either knowing someone involved in the war or serving in it oneself—had some significant effects on opinion dynamics.[5]

Against this rich backdrop of analyses of the individual-level determinants of support for the war, political scientist John Mueller's path-breaking study explored not individual respondents' opinions at a given moment in time but rather aggregate-level fluctuations in support for war over its course.[6] At the heart of Mueller's theory is the proposition that national casualties—specifically logged cumulative casualties—drove changing levels of support for U.S. military involvement in Southeast Asia. The rapid accumulation of casualties in 1967 and 1968 eroded the strong bipartisan support President Johnson had enjoyed for his prosecution of the war. When President Nixon moved into the Oval Office, support for the war did not vanish as American battle deaths continued to mount—but it continued a slow decline from a greatly reduced mean level.

Since Mueller's pioneering research, a number of scholars have examined the relationship between war casualties and changes in public opinion. For example, RAND analyst Eric Larson's comprehensive analysis of opinion dynamics in conflicts since Vietnam found strong evidence that logged cumulative casualties are an important predictor of trends in support for most military actions in the contemporary period regardless of scale, including Panama, Somalia, and the first Persian Gulf War.[7] Other scholars have examined "marginal casualties"—the more recent casualties experienced in the last quarter or month—to explain short-term shifts in support for war. For example, Scott Gartner and Gary Segura found that, when marginal casualties in Vietnam were increasing, the number of casualties sustained by U.S. forces in the last quarter was the strongest predictor of shifts in support for the war. However, when marginal casualty rates began to decrease, logged cumulative casualties instead became the best predictor of war opinion.[8]

Thus, American public opinion does indeed seem to respond to changes in conditions on the ground in the theater of war. As the human toll of a conflict rises, support for a military venture wanes. However, an important question remains. While the relationships between logged cumulative and marginal casualties and opinion change appear robust, particularly for Vietnam, does focusing solely on the experience of the nation as a whole mask considerable variation in support among residents of different communities? When seeing the latest casualty tally on the evening news, do all Americans react in the same way? Do they all decrease their support for the war by the same amount? Or, does the wide variance from community to community in individual citizens' direct experience with casualties manifest itself in different judgments about the war and its leaders?

Scott Gartner, Gary Segura, and Michael Wilkening's study is the most significant research to date on the importance of local casualties in understanding opinion formation in Vietnam.[9] Using a series of nine surveys of Californians from 1965 to 1972, which asked respondents whether they approved or disapproved of the president's handling of the situation in Vietnam, Gartner and his colleagues probed the effects of both logged cumulative national casualties and of local casualties sustained by a respondent's county on his or her probability of supporting the administration and its war policies. Their analysis finds that both national and local casualties had a significant impact on support for the president's handling of the war in Vietnam.[10]

The next section builds upon existing research in three ways. First, whereas the Gartner, Segura, and Wilkening study examined only the effect of local casualties on evaluations of the administration's handling of the war (a factor that Verba et al. suggested in the pre-Tet years could be tapping support for President Johnson more generally), we examine the effect of local Vietnam casualty rates on both respondents' *retrospective* judgment of the decision to go to war and on their *prospective* policy preferences. Specifically, we investigate the effects of local Vietnam casualties on each respondent's overall judgment of whether the U.S. was right to get involved militarily in Vietnam and on each respondent's preferred policy course for the future: withdrawing U.S. forces, maintaining the status quo, or escalating the U.S. presence.

Expanding the scope of analysis is important because support for initial involvement is correlated but not perfectly predictive of subsequent preferences on withdrawal. For example, National Election Study (NES) data from the Vietnam era show that believing that the United States should have stayed out of Vietnam and support for withdrawal are correlated but not remarkably so.[11] At the end of the Bush presidency, opinion dynamics regarding the war in Iraq showed a similar pattern. A number of Americans continued to support the initial decision to invade Iraq while insisting that the time had come to reduce the footprint of U.S. forces there. Conversely, other Americans continued to denounce the Bush administration's decision to engage Saddam Hussein militarily but contended that, once committed, the nation simply could not leave the job unfinished. Thus, it is theoretically important to evaluate casualties' effects on both components of opinion.

Second, our analysis expands upon Gartner, Segura, and Wilkening's research by investigating the influence of local casualties on the opinions of a nationally representative sample, not just on the opinions of Californians. National Election Study data from 1964 to 1972 afford the necessary geographic locators for each respondent, as well as relevant war-related questions and demographic information to examine the impact of local casualties on opinion dynamics for a wider swath of the American public.

Third, and perhaps most important, we keep the socioeconomic casualty gap firmly in mind when discussing and interpreting the effects of local casualty rates on opinion formation. Too often in previous research on the political consequences of geographic variance in the distribution of casualties across the country, these socioeconomic inequalities are either ignored or mentioned only in passing. As we discuss in the conclusion, if local casualties produce opinion and behavioral cleavages, it matters considerably that high casualty rates are not randomly distributed across the country but rather are concentrated in specific types of communities, particularly socioeconomically disadvantaged ones. For if the concentration of a war's costs among socioeconomically disadvantaged communities diminishes the scope of political pressure brought to bear on politicians to end a military conflict, the democratic checks on military policies may not be as strong as previously envisioned.

LOCAL CASUALTY RATES AND SUPPORT FOR THE VIETNAM WAR

To examine the influence of local casualties on public support for the Vietnam War, we analyze two survey questions from the National Elections Studies Cumulative File. The first question, included in every survey from 1964 to 1972, asked respondents the following: "Do you think we did the right thing in getting into the fighting in Vietnam, or should we have stayed out?" Supplementing this query, which measured popular support for the initial decision to intervene in Southeast Asia, was a second question included in all surveys from 1964 to 1970: "Which of the following do you think we should do now in Vietnam?" Respondents could indicate their support for one of three options: "Pull out entirely"; "keep our soldiers in Vietnam but try to end the fighting"; or "take a stronger stand even if it means invading North Vietnam." In the chapter's technical appendix, we report ordinal regression models that examine the influence of casualties on the range of possible policy preferences from escalation to withdrawal. To ease the substantive interpretation of the results, in the text we transform this ordinal variable into a binary one and focus on the effect of casualties on a respondent's propensity to favor withdrawing forces from Vietnam. Both sets of models, however, produced nearly identical results.

Casualties

To examine the influence of combat casualties on wartime opinion along these two dimensions, we created two casualty measures. Following Mueller, the first measure is simply the logged number of cumulative casualties sustained by U.S. forces in Southeast Asia at the time of each survey.[12] The value of this variable is identical for all respondents in a given year, and its inclusion allows us to track the well-documented decreasing willingness of Americans to support the war and its continuation.[13]

However, we argue that individuals react both to the overall conditions on the ground, as measured by national casualties, and also to their own unique window into the war afforded by the experience of soldiers from their local communities. To examine the influence of local casualty rates on war support, we include the casualty rate suffered by each respondent's home county at that point in the war measured in deaths per 10,000 male residents.[14] By including both national casualties and local casualties in our statistical models, we seek to demonstrate that local casualties shape an individual's opinions, even after controlling for the effect of the mounting number of cumulative American casualties suffered in the war.

Demographic Control Variables

Despite considerable scholarly debate on their relative importance, previous research has suggested a host of demographic characteristics that may be correlated with a respondent's preferences on Vietnam policy. First, even though many early analyses of Vietnam opinion data found little evidence of a partisan cleavage, we include variables that capture whether each respondent was a Democrat or a Republican. Particularly on the question of withdrawal, there is strong prior evidence suggesting that many more Democrats came to support withdrawing U.S. forces from Vietnam than Republicans.

We next controlled for two measures of an individual's socioeconomic status, income and education. This is particularly critical if we hope to show that local casualties have an independent effect on support for the war. Respondents with lower socioeconomic status are considerably more likely to live in counties that suffered disproportionately high casualty rates in the war. Without controlling for each individual's income and educational attainment, we cannot discern whether a correlation between a local casualty rate and opinion is a tangible link or merely an artifact of failing to account for the fact that Americans with lower levels of income or educational attainment may simply be less likely to support an aggressive military policy than wealthier, better-educated Americans.[15] After controlling for these factors, however, we can be confident that any effect we observe for local casualty rates exists even after accounting for the socioeconomic backgrounds of those who tend to live in high- and low-casualty regions.

To capture potential differences in support along age and gender lines, we included three additional variables: the first identified whether each respondent was a male; the second controlled for each respondent's age; and the third measured whether or not the respondent was a draft-age male between the ages of eighteen and twenty-nine. In a study of cleavages along gender lines in attitudes toward the use of force, political scientist Richard Eichenberg found that, prior to the 1991 Persian Gulf War, women were considerably less likely to support the use of force than men; however, after the First Gulf War's successful conclusion, the gap closed considerably. By including a gender variable in our model, we can determine whether a differential between the sexes characterized the Vietnam conflict.[16] The age variable allows us to assess whether young Americans were systematically more likely to oppose the war than older Americans. Furthermore, the draft-age male variable singles out those with perhaps the most immediate stake in military policy decisions, which enables us to examine whether their opinions differ from those of other Americans.

An extensive literature has examined the role of race in shaping attitudes toward the Vietnam War.[17] Although in chapter 2 we find no evidence that communities with greater percentages of African Americans suffered greater casualty rates than similar communities with smaller minority populations, many have speculated that because of blacks' heavy losses in the early stages of the war and because of the gradual opposition to the war of many civil rights leaders, including Dr. Martin Luther King Jr., African Americans should be less prone to support government policy in Vietnam than other racial groups.[18] To account for possible racial opinion differences, we included a variable that identified whether each respondent was black.[19]

Finally, we controlled for possible variation along religious lines. Specifically, we accounted for whether or not each respondent identified with Judaism or Catholicism. Political scientists William Lunch and Peter Sperlich found that Jews were on average considerably less supportive of the war than other religious groups.[20] Catholics split over Vietnam. Many Catholic leaders, particularly Cardinal Francis Spellman, vocally rallied in support of the Vietnam War under the banner of anti-Communism. Others, notably Jesuit Priest Daniel Berrigan and his brother Philip, protested Vietnam as part of a Catholic peace movement.[21]

In addition to individual-level demographic characteristics, we also considered the possibility of regional variance in respondents' support for the war. We controlled for this in two ways. First, we included a variable that identified respondents from the southern United States to account for that region's historically strong ties to military institutions and an aggressive military policy. Alternatively, we reestimated all of the models with state fixed effects, which control for all unobserved state-level factors (e.g., state-to-state differences in general attitudes toward war). All of the models were virtually identical in this expanded specification. However, for simplicity's sake, we report the more parsimonious models, which include only the South indicator variable.

RESULTS AND DISCUSSION

Should the United States Have Stayed Out of Vietnam?

We begin by analyzing the factors that governed respondents' overall evaluation of whether the United States was right to have engaged in Vietnam militarily or whether it should have stayed out of the conflict in Indochina. The basic trend in opposition to the war throughout our surveys is summarized in figure 6.1. In both 1964 and 1966, only 31 percent of Americans answered that the United States would have been better served by staying out of the conflict in Vietnam. After the Tet offensive and the widening of the credibility gap between the Johnson administration and the public, a majority of Americans openly regretted the initial decision to intervene. Finally, by 1972 60 percent of Americans disapproved of America's entry into the war, though there was considerable disagreement over the proper course of U.S. involvement in Vietnam looking forward. Because the survey question was binary—respondents either replied that "yes," the United States should have stayed out of the conflict, or "no," the United States was right to have become involved—we use a logistic regression to estimate each explanatory variable's effect on the probability of a respondent's preferring that the United States had stayed out of the war.

Because logistic regression coefficients are difficult to interpret directly, the regression output is reported only in the technical appendix. Instead, figure 6.2 presents a series of first differences that illustrate each variable's impact on the probability of answering that the United States should not have engaged in the Vietnam War. Each bar represents the estimated effect of a shift in the independent variable of interest while holding all other variables constant at their means or medians.[22] The black region represents the change in probability of responding that the United States should have stayed out, given an increase in the explanatory variable from the 25th to the 75th percentile. The gray region represents the additional impact of a shift from the variable's 10th to 90th percentile with all other

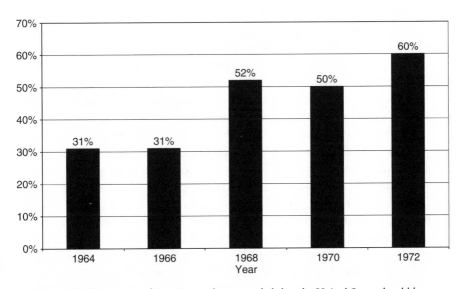

Figure 6.1. Percentage of Americans who responded that the United States should have stayed out of Vietnam, 1964–1972.

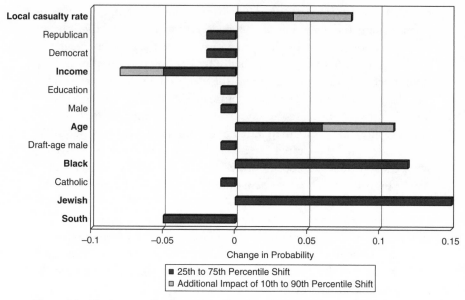

Figure 6.2. The impact of local casualties, demographics, and regional factors on opposition to the Vietnam War, 1964–1972.

Note: Statistically significant effects are indicated with boldface.

factors held constant. Significance levels for each coefficient are reported in the technical appendix.

Most importantly, even after controlling for a host of demographic characteristics for each respondent, both national and local casualty rates were significantly correlated with respondents' support for the decision to intervene in Vietnam. The model is consistent with prior studies asserting that Americans responded to the overall level of casualties when forging their evaluation of the war; yet it also strongly suggests that Americans' views were simultaneously moderated by the casualty rate suffered by their local community in the national struggle in Vietnam.

Because logged cumulative casualties sustained by the United States on the battlefield are so highly correlated with time, the logged casualties variable largely captures the growing opposition to the war over the period. The dramatic increase in cumulative American war dead from roughly 6,000 in 1966 to more than 32,000 by October 1968 may be one of the primary factors explaining the dramatic rise in opposition to the war from 31 percent in 1966 to more than 50 percent just two years later. By 1972, another 20,000 U.S. soldiers had laid down their lives in Southeast Asia, and opposition to the war peaked with 60 percent answering that the United States should have stayed out of the conflict altogether.

This correlation may suggest a causal relationship; however, it may also simply be the result of omitted variable bias.[23] Other major developments in the country at large were unfolding between 1964 and 1968: the radicalization of the civil rights movement, urban riots and unrest, and an economy overheating under the strain of attempting to provide both guns and butter. Because all of these were developing at the same time that Vietnam casualties were increasing, it is difficult to determine whether mounting cumulative casualties were the key factor eroding popular support for the war. As a result, rather than making any causal inference, we note only that the logged casualties variable tracks this downward trend during this period.

However, strongly consistent with our main argument, the results also show that war is not just a national, but also a *local* event. As figure 6.2 illustrates, the experience of a respondent's local community in the war—his or her county's casualty rate—greatly influenced the probability of opposing the conflict. An increase in a respondent's local casualty rate from the 25th to the 75th percentile increased that person's probability of opposing the decision to go to war by 4 percent on average. The effects of local casualties were even larger at the tails of the distribution. Our model suggests that increasing a community's local casualty rate from the 10th to the 90th percentile would make its residents, on average, 8 percent more likely to assert that the United States should have stayed out of Vietnam.

One could argue that such estimates overstate the effect of local casualties because even if wealthier Americans had lived in communities with higher casualty rates, those wealthy individuals would not have adjusted their support for the conflict as readily based on local casualties. According to this logic, wealthy individuals—secure in the knowledge that their sons were still unlikely to die on the front lines because of educational and occupational deferments or assignments to lower-risk military occupations—may be relatively unaffected by local deaths, as such losses would have few direct ramifications for them and their families.

To test the plausibility of this argument, we return to the data and investigate whether there is any difference in how wealthy and poor individuals responded to casualties within their communities.[24] When we estimate separate statistical models for split samples of wealthy and non-wealthy respondents, we find strong evidence that rich and poor Americans responded almost identically to losses within their local communities. Both rich and poor respondents were more likely to oppose the war as their county's casualty rate grew. Furthermore, the size of the effect is substantively the same for individuals in the top quarter of the income distribution as for those in the bottom quarter. Thus, our empirical analysis suggests that wealthier respondents living in communities that suffered high casualty rates were just as responsive to them and therefore more likely to oppose the war as were poorer respondents in high-casualty communities. However, wealthier Americans were less likely to live in high-casualty communities than were poorer Americans.[25] In fact, when reestimating our models separately for Republicans and Democrats, men and women, young people and older people, blacks and whites, and even for members of different religious groups, in each case we find that all groups of Americans responded, on average, in almost the same way to local casualties within their communities. See the technical appendix for a full presentation and discussion of these results.

Putting these findings together, we conclude that, if all Americans had seen the costs of war through the lens of the hardest-hit communities, public opinion would have turned against the war more quickly and more uniformly than it ultimately did. To put such potential changes in perspective, again recall the general trends in support in figure 6.1. Only 8 percent more Americans believed intervening in Vietnam was a mistake in 1972 than they did in 1968. If all Americans had experienced the war as intensely as those that suffered the highest casualty rates, opposition to the war could have approached the 60 percent mark much earlier than it ultimately did in the waning months of the U.S. commitment in 1972. And if this heightened war opposition had forced political leaders to respond by curtailing the war earlier, it would have spared the nation thousands of lives and countless millions of dollars.

Having established a strong relationship between local casualties and support for the Vietnam War, we briefly examine the influence of our demographic control variables. Consistent with Verba et al., we find no evidence of a partisan cleavage in retrospective judgments of the Vietnam War. However, we do observe significant differences along socioeconomic lines: Wealthier Americans were more likely to support the war than poorer Americans.[26] With respect to respondents' gender, despite conventional wisdom both within academia and within popular culture, we find no evidence that men were more militant than women when it came to supporting active containment of Communist expansion in Southeast Asia.[27]

Another surprising result is the strong positive correlation between respondents' age and their opposition to the war. This relationship is particularly shocking when contrasted with the prominent images of young antiwar demonstrators lashing out against the government's Vietnam policies. The images still seared on our collective consciousness are of burning draft cards, Kent State, and college student protests in Washington, D.C., led by a youthful John Kerry, who threw away his service medals to protest an immoral war. Although the observed positive correlation between age and war opposition corresponds with prior research, the disjunction with the conventional wisdom is so great that we pushed further to ensure the relationship was not spurious.[28] We describe these additional rounds of analysis in the technical appendix; however, in each case, the result continues to hold. Younger Americans may well have constituted a larger percentage of those with the most intensely held views against the war, but on average they were less likely to oppose the war than older Americans throughout the period. In a similar vein, the models reveal no evidence that draft-age males were any more likely to oppose the war than other Americans not eligible for the draft.[29]

We do, however, find strong evidence of opinion cleavages along racial lines. Consistent with a number of other studies, first differences from our model show that African Americans were 12 percent more likely, on average, to oppose the war than whites.[30] With respect to religion, after controlling for other demographic factors, we find no significant difference in opinion between Catholics and non-Catholics.[31] However, we find that Jewish Americans were 15 percent more likely to oppose the war, on average, than were other respondents with identical demographic characteristics. Finally, we also find strong support for regional variation in support for the war. As expected, support for military operations in Vietnam was particularly strong—all else being equal, 5 percentage points higher—in the South, a region historically known for its rich military tradition and heritage.[32]

Should the United States Withdraw from Vietnam?

The empirical data show strong relationships between local casualty rates and respondents' retrospective judgments of whether the United States was right to enter the war in Vietnam. To determine whether variance in local casualties also shaped Americans' prospective policy preferences for the war's prosecution, we now turn to our second National Election Studies question, which examines respondents' support for withdrawing U.S. forces from Vietnam. Figure 6.3 summarizes the basic trend from 1964 to 1970. As late as 1966, whereas 30 percent of Americans said that the United States should have stayed out of the Vietnamese conflict, only 11 percent advocated withdrawing U.S. forces. After Tet and the bloody fighting of 1968, this number doubled to 22 percent, and it soared to 37 percent by the midpoint of Richard Nixon's first term in office in 1970.

As in the preceding models, we used a logistic regression to estimate the impact of local casualties, controlling for the regional and demographic characteristics discussed earlier, on a respondent's likelihood of supporting the withdrawal of U.S. troops. Figure 6.4 presents a series of

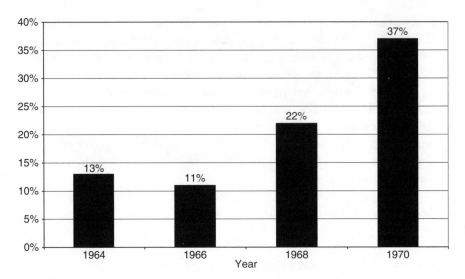

Figure 6.3. Percentage of Americans who favored withdrawal of U.S. forces from Vietnam, 1964–1970.

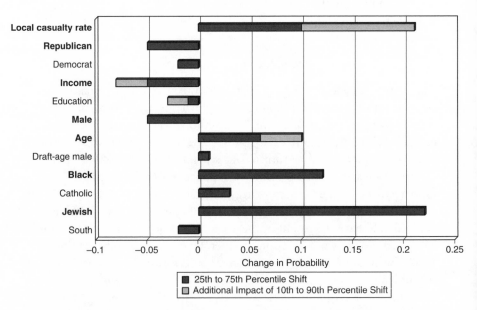

Figure 6.4. The impact of local casualties, demographics, and regional factors on support for withdrawing U.S. forces from Vietnam, 1964–1970.

Note: Statistically significant effects are indicated with boldface.

first differences that illustrate the estimated effect of a shift in each independent variable while holding all other variables constant at their means or medians. The black bars show the estimated effect of an increase in each variable from its 25th to its 75th percentile; the gray bars represent the additional impact obtained by a shift from that variable's 10th to its 90th percentile.

The coefficient for national logged cumulative casualties is again positive and statistically significant. However, because cumulative casualties are so highly correlated with time, it is difficult to assess the variable's independent causal impact on war support. As a result, we do not include this variable in figure 6.4.

More importantly for our argument, even after controlling for cumulative casualties and a host of demographic and regional factors we continue to find a strong, statistically significant relationship between a respondent's local casualty rate and his or her probability of supporting the withdrawal of U.S. troops from Vietnam. A shift in a respondent's local casualty rate from the 25th to the 75th percentile increased that person's probability of supporting withdrawal by 10 percent. Again, the size of the effect is even greater at the upper ends of the distribution. By 1970, 10 percent of the nation's counties had suffered casualty rates exceeding 11 deaths per 10,000 male residents. By contrast, 10 percent of counties in the United States had suffered casualty rates of less than 2.5 deaths per 10,000 male residents. Because of this great disparity in local connection to war casualties, similar respondents from these two different sets of communities had dramatically different views of the war. Our model estimates that a citizen from a county that suffered a casualty rate of 11 per 10,000 male citizens was 21 percent more likely, on average, to support withdrawal than a citizen from a county that had suffered just 2.5 casualties per 10,000 male residents.

Thus, our analysis offers an important corrective to most existing studies of the relationships between casualties and wartime opinion. Consistent with existing theory, our findings offer considerable evidence that the public's policy preferences do co-vary with a war's costs. Yet, this reaction is far from uniform across the country; rather, it is most acute among citizens from communities that suffered higher casualty rates.

With respect to the demographic controls, the dynamics that influenced support for withdrawal are very similar to those that affected respondents' overall evaluation of whether the Vietnam War was worth the cost. Partisan differences are again substantively small, though we find that Republicans were marginally less likely, on average, to support withdrawing U.S. forces from Vietnam than other Americans. The very limited evidence of a partisan divide is particularly striking when contrasted with the dynamics governing opinion on the war in Iraq, which we investigate in the next chapter. Socioeconomic status is again significantly correlated with opinions on ending the war, as wealthier Americans were less likely to support withdrawing U.S. forces from Vietnam than were their less advantaged peers.[33]

Turning to the three potential indicators of respondent self-interest in the war, we again find that men and even draft-age men were no more likely to advocate a withdrawal of U.S. forces from the region than were women or men not of draft age. Also, iconoclastically, we again find that age is positively correlated with opposition to the war. Additional analyses are described in the technical appendix, but the result holds across alternative specifications.

In addition to being more likely to assert that the United States should have stayed out of Vietnam, blacks and Jews were both also more likely to believe the United States should withdraw its forces from Southeast Asia. Finally, the model suggests that Southerners were slightly less likely than other Americans to support withdrawal from Vietnam; however, the relevant coefficient is not statistically significant.[34]

THE ELECTORAL CONSEQUENCES OF LOCAL CASUALTIES

The empirical analyses of the preceding section show a strong relationship between casualties, particularly local casualties, and individual Americans' evaluations of the Vietnam War and their support for ending it. Yet, for these attitudes and opinions to be of political import, they must also shape the electoral pressures brought to bear on elected officials.[35] Policymakers are most likely to respond to shifts in constituent preferences if they perceive an electoral risk from failing to do so.[36]

For many years, the conventional wisdom among political scientists held that, because most citizens knew and cared little about foreign affairs, even major questions of foreign policy were likely to be of little electoral consequence.[37] However, more recent studies of public opinion and foreign policy have challenged this characterization and demonstrated significant linkages between electoral trends and military policy developments.[38] Most of this scholarship has focused on the electoral ramifications of combat casualties for the commander-in-chief.[39] This emphasis is for good reason, as the president is clearly the focal point of military policymaking in the United States and the official most likely to be held accountable for the fate of a military action. Indeed, scholars have long suggested that Congress abdicates its constitutional role in military affairs in part to distance itself from responsibility for military outcomes.[40] Political wrangling over the war in Iraq at the close of the

Bush administration supports such a perspective. For example, when explaining his vote against setting a timetable for withdrawal from Iraq, Mississippi Republican Thad Cochran did not so much defend President Bush's policies as lay the responsibility for fixing them at the president's feet alone. About the proposed timeline that Democrats attached to a key supplemental war appropriations bill, Cochran warned, "We're part of the problem if this doesn't work." Instead, Cochran reminded his colleagues that Iraq was Bush's battle: "Let him [Bush] and the commanders in the field figure out a way to win."[41]

However, a handful of recent studies have suggested that war developments—including local casualty rates—also influence congressional election outcomes.[42] Building on this emerging literature, we now examine whether variance in community casualty rates suffered in Vietnam—which significantly shaped respondents' retrospective judgment of the decision to enter the war and their policy preferences for its future conduct—also influenced their votes in congressional races for the House of Representatives from 1964 to 1972. Evidence of significant differences in congressional voting patterns between high- and low-casualty communities would bolster our claim that the casualty gap had significant consequences in the voting booth during the Vietnam War.

MODELING VOTE CHOICE

To assess the impact of variance in local casualty rates on individuals' votes, we again employ National Election Study data querying more than 4,000 respondents about their preferences in the weeks immediately preceding the 1964–1972 congressional elections. But how should casualties affect the probability of voting Democratic? On the one hand, for much of the period, Vietnam was Lyndon Johnson's war in the same way that Korea belonged to Harry Truman. It began as a Democratic war, tacitly launched by President Kennedy, who inherited the presence of U.S. advisors in Vietnam from President Eisenhower. Kennedy expanded the number of U.S. troops on the ground from 1,000 to 16,000, and President Johnson greatly escalated the war until more than half a million U.S. troops were stationed in Southeast Asia. Moreover, strong Democratic majorities controlled both Houses of Congress throughout the war.

On the other hand, beginning in the late 1960s the Democratic Left spearheaded challenges to the Vietnam War. Arkansas Democrat William Fulbright and Oregon Senator Wayne Morse led the charge against the administration's war policies in the Senate, while Robert Kennedy and Eugene McCarthy ran presidential campaigns fundamentally based on opposition to the war. Nevertheless, at the 1968 Democratic National

Convention in Chicago the party nominated Vice President Hubert Humphrey, who stood by the Johnson administration's conduct of the war and resisted calls for immediately drawing down the American commitment in Vietnam. By 1970 and 1972, however, antiwar sentiment within Democratic ranks had grown considerably, and the contrast between the median Democrat and the stalwart hawks in the Nixon administration was stark.

As a result, while Democrats occupied the Oval Office from 1964 to 1968, we expect them to pay an electoral price for rising casualties, particularly in communities that suffered a disproportionate share of the nation's wartime sacrifice. However, in 1970 and 1972, the conflict had become Nixon's war, particularly its escalation into Laos and Cambodia. In this later period, we expect the effect of casualties on Democratic vote share to be reversed. Casualties should produce a growing willingness to vote against Nixon's Republican allies in Congress, and this incentive should be strongest among citizens who experienced casualties most intensely through the lens of their local community.

Because the dependent variable—intention to vote for the Democratic candidate—is binary, we again employ a logistic regression to assess the electoral ramifications of combat casualties for members of the House of Representatives. To ensure that any correlation between casualties and Democratic voting propensity is not spurious, we include all of the demographic and regional controls included in the earlier models.

RESULTS AND DISCUSSION

The percentage of Americans who expressed their intention to vote for the Democratic House candidate in each election is summarized in figure 6.5. The plot suggests a curvilinear dynamic. Sixty-five percent of Americans declared their intention to vote Democratic in 1964. This produced the very liberal 89th Congress, which rode into office on the coattails of Lyndon Johnson's landslide victory over Barry Goldwater. By 1966, support for the Democrats had fallen back to a more normal 57 percent of the public, and by the next election cycle support for the Democrats had fallen further still. Then in 1970, Democratic fortunes began to rebound, and by 1972 support had almost returned to its 1966 levels.

Because of the changing political dynamics of the late 1960s discussed earlier, we expect the relationships between local casualties and Democratic vote choice to change dramatically. To capture this dynamic, we divided our sample into two periods: The first model assesses the effects of local casualties on the 1964, 1966, and 1968 elections, and the second model

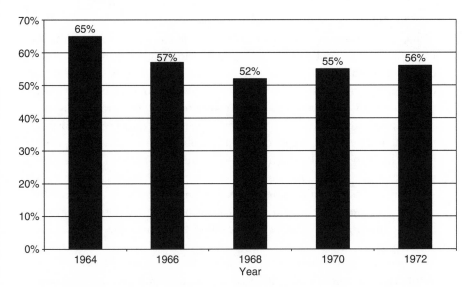

Figure 6.5. Percentage of Americans voting Democratic in U.S. House elections, 1964–1972.

estimates the influence of local casualties on the 1970 and 1972 contests. As in the preceding sections, we again present our results in terms of first differences. Full regression results are reported in the technical appendix.

In the 1964–1968 model, the coefficient for the logged cumulative casualties variable is negative as expected and statistically significant. As the human toll in Vietnam mounted, likely support for Democratic congressional candidates decreased. Again, because this variable is so highly correlated with time, we cannot make any independent causal claims. Rather, we note only that the logged casualties variable tracks the downward trend in Democratic support during the period.

However, even after controlling for this general trend, as well as respondents' partisanship, demographics, and region, the model offers strong evidence that local Vietnam casualties had a significant impact on Americans' intended vote choice. Variance along this dimension is not simply tapping the growing unrest in the country. Rather, within a given year, we see considerable variance in support for Democratic congressional candidates depending on whether a potential voter hails from an area that suffered a large human toll in the war or whether the respondent is from a community less directly affected by the conflict.

Figure 6.6 illustrates the effect of local casualty rates, as well as of the other demographic and regional control variables, on a respondent's probability

of voting Democratic in the 1964–1968 elections.[43] Increasing a respondent's county casualty rate from the 25th to the 75th percentile decreased
the respondent's probability of voting Democratic by 5 percent. The
effects are even greater at the extremes. Our model suggests that a resident of a community at the 90th percentile in terms of local casualty rates
was more than 10 percent less likely to vote for the Democratic congressional candidate in this period than was another individual with identical
political and demographic characteristics from a community at the 10th
percentile of the casualty distribution. The numbers are stark—they suggest that if all Americans had experienced casualty rates as extreme as
those in the hardest-hit counties, there would have been considerably
greater pressure on Democratic lawmakers to reevaluate the U.S. course
in Vietnam, pressure so great that it could have threatened the party's
majority in Congress.

The control variables also largely accord with theoretical expectations.
While local casualties had a significant influence on respondents' voting
calculus, as we would expect, partisanship is the clearest harbinger of
behavior at the ballot box. To preserve the scale of the figure, two variables—whether a respondent was a Democrat or a Republican—were
not included in figure 6.6. Unlike in the models of opinion on the war,

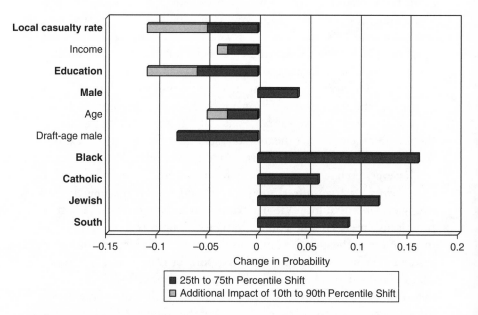

Figure 6.6. The impact of local casualties, demographics, and regional factors on support for Democratic House candidates, 1964–1968.

Note: Statistically significant effects are indicated with boldface.

in which partisanship played no role, party identification was the single most important predictor of a respondent's vote intention. The average Republican respondent had only a 25 percent probability of voting for a Democrat in the last three congressional contests of the 1960s, while the average Democrat voted for the Democratic party's candidate 72 percent of the time.

Socioeconomics also influenced vote choice; income and education are both negatively correlated with Democratic voting, but only the education coefficient is statistically significant.[44] Interestingly, in contrast to the gender gap that emerged in the 1980s, in the 1960s our model suggests that men were slightly more likely to vote Democratic than women.[45] The model also suggests that both older Americans and draft-age males may have been less likely to vote for the Democratic congressional candidate during this period; however, neither coefficient reaches conventional levels of statistical significance.

The observed effects of race and religion both accord with prior research on voting patterns in the 1960s. With President Johnson and the Democratic Congress delivering first the Civil Rights Act of 1964 and then the Voting Rights Act of 1965, blacks were firmly entrenched in the Democratic camp. Similarly, Catholics and Jews were also significantly more likely to toe the party's line at the ballot box. Finally, despite the growing pressure on the party's Southern base, Southern Democratic Congressmen, whose ideological orientation matched their more conservative districts, continued to retain stronger support on average from their partisan rank and file than did Democrats in other parts of the country.

In the 1960s, our analysis reveals that Democratic congressional candidates paid a substantial price at the polls in communities that had suffered high casualty rates in Vietnam. By contrast, the second model presented in the technical appendix demonstrates that by the 1970s a starkly different dynamic had emerged. First differences in figure 6.7 again illustrate the effect of changes in each independent variable on the probability of voting for the Democratic congressional candidate while holding all other variables constant at their means or medians.[46]

The most dramatic difference in the dynamics that influenced individuals' votes for congressional candidates between the 1960s and the early 1970s is the diametrically opposite effect of local casualties on respondents' willingness to vote Democratic. Whereas respondents from high-casualty areas were less likely to vote for Democrats in the 1960s, when the war was Lyndon Johnson's, they were more likely to do so in the 1970s, when the war was Richard Nixon's and congressional Democrats led the drive first to limit and then to end America's military

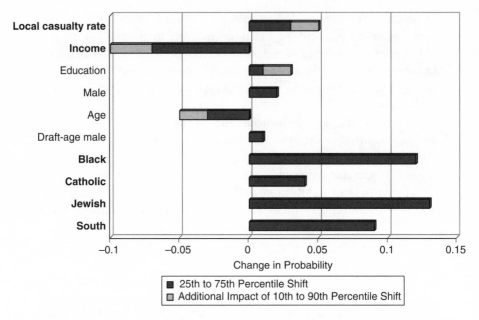

Figure 6.7. The impact of local casualties, demographics, and regional factors on support for Democratic House candidates, 1970–1972.

Note: Statistically significant effects are indicated with boldface.

involvement in Indochina. First differences suggest that an increase in a citizen's local casualty rate from the 25th to the 75th percentile increased that respondent's estimated probability of voting Democratic by 3 percent. Furthermore, at the tails of the distribution, the estimated effects are even larger. For example, a shift in local casualty rates from the 10th to the 90th percentile increased support for the Democratic candidate, on average, by 5 percent.

While the effects of local casualty rates on Democratic vote shares switched after Richard Nixon replaced Lyndon Johnson in the White House, almost all of the partisan, demographic, and regional control variables operate in the same fashion in the 1970s as they did in the 1960s. For a full discussion of these control variables and their effects, we refer readers to the technical appendix.

Thus, in House elections in the 1960s and 1970s, as in the models of opinion on Vietnam, we find evidence that Americans were highly sensitive to local casualties. Local casualties had a powerful effect on individuals' voting behavior as residents of high-casualty communities were significantly more likely first to turn against Democrats when they held power and then to revolt against Republicans when Nixon sat in the Oval Office.

THE CASUALTY GAP AND THE DEMOCRATIC BRAKE
ON MILITARY ADVENTURISM

An extensive literature in international relations argues that one of the most important constraints on a democratic executive's freedom of action in the realm of military affairs is domestic public opinion. Because the public must bear the human costs of war, it is particularly sensitive to combat casualties.[47] Anticipating this, government leaders should be loath to rush into conflict because the costs and even the outcome of war are—as Winston Churchill presciently warned—inscrutable.[48] If democratic leaders do decide to go to war, theory further predicts that they will be very aware of the public's limited tolerance for costs in blood and treasure and will therefore seek to end conflicts expeditiously.[49] According to political scientists Peter Feaver and Christopher Gelpi, this assumption is implicit in virtually all international relations studies that assert differences in conflict behavior between democracies and nondemocracies.[50] In this way, numerous scholars have argued that public opinion serves as a critically important democratic brake on aggressive military policies. As the number of casualties sustained in a military venture mounts, public support for the mission wanes and public pressure on policymakers to change course increases accordingly.

Although this theoretical perspective is conventional academic wisdom, most studies look past the empirical reality that war is not a monolithic event experienced equally by all members of the national community. Rather, some pay its costs most directly with their lives and limbs on the battlefield. And some noncombatants sense its costs more acutely through the lens afforded by their local community's experience with the conflict.

Our analysis of Vietnam War opinion and voting dynamics offers at least partial empirical support for existing theoretical claims about the interactions of casualties, public opinion, and the political pressure brought to bear on policymakers. As the human toll of the Vietnam War mounted, public support for the conflict eroded, and political pressure for ending the costly conflict increased. Yet, the empirical analysis also reveals an oft-overlooked aspect of this democratic brake—that it is far from uniform throughout society.

The existence of a casualty gap critically mediates the patterns of citizen response to the human costs of military conflict. Those who saw the human costs of the Vietnam War most directly through the high casualty rates sustained in their local communities were significantly more likely to oppose the war, advocate its termination, and vote against its political standard-bearers in Washington than were their fellow citizens with identical characteristics from low-casualty communities. Our models suggest that if all Americans had viewed Vietnam through the experience of those communities hardest hit by the conflict, the politics of the era could have unfolded in a dramatically different way. Pressure to end the disastrous conflict in Southeast Asia may have built considerably more quickly and perhaps to an even greater degree than eventually occurred in the early 1970s.

What if a casualty gap had not emerged? If all communities suffered identical casualty rates and all Americans were equally exposed to the costs of war, our analysis suggests that some Americans, who in reality saw disproportionately low casualty rates in their communities, in this counterfactual scenario would be more antiwar than they were before. However, Americans from communities that in reality had witnessed disproportionately high casualty rates would, in this thought experiment, have fewer incentives to oppose the war and its political leaders. As a result, it is possible that the net effect of the casualty gap on the balance of antiwar sentiment in the country was minimal.[51] Indeed, this likely *would* be the case if unequal casualty rates were randomly distributed across the country. In such a scenario, the effects of high and low local casualty rates might simply cancel each other out.

However, the analyses in chapter 2 show that this is decidedly *not* the case. The variance in local casualty rates is not randomly distributed around the country; rather, casualty rates are systematically higher in socioeconomically disadvantaged communities. Once we bring the socio-economic nature of the casualty gap to the fore, its political ramifications become clear. A robust literature in American politics has demonstrated that citizens from low-income, low-education communities are dispro-portionately less engaged in politics than their fellow citizens from socio-economically advantaged communities.[52] Accordingly, the casualty gap concentrates the human costs of war among the very segment of the citizenry that possesses the fewest resources needed to engage government. By contrast, the casualty gap ensures that citizens from socioeconomi-cally advantaged communities, citizens who have the strongest rates of political participation, also have the least direct exposure to the human costs of war. As a result, the pressure brought to bear on political leaders to change course is less than what would have emerged in the absence of a casualty gap. The casualty gap does not eliminate the democratic brake on costly military policies, but it does blunt its force.

Technical Appendix to Chapter 6

The full regression results used to derive the first differences illustrated in figures 6.2, 6.4, 6.6, and 6.7 are presented in the following tables. Table 6A.1 presents the results of a logistic regression that estimates the impact of national cumulative casualties, county casualty rates, and a host of other demographic control variables on respondents' likelihood of believing the United States should not have entered the Vietnam War. Most importantly, the coefficient for a respondent's local casualty rate is positive and statistically significant. The positive coefficient for cumulative casualties suggests that as war costs mounted, the public in general turned against the war. Yet, the effect of casualties on opinion was far from uniform. Respondents from communities hardest hit by the war were considerably more likely to believe that the United States should not have entered the Vietnam War than were their peers.

The control variables largely follow theoretical expectations with the notable exception of age. In stark contrast to popular images of youthful rebellions against the draft and the Vietnam War, the coefficient for age is positive and statistically significant. The first differences illustrated in figure 6.2 show that increasing a respondent's age from the 25th to the 75th percentile increased, on average, that person's probability of asserting that the United States should have stayed out of Vietnam by 6 percent. Even though this finding echoes previous research, we conducted

Table 6A.1. Regression Analyses of the Factors Influencing Opposition to the Vietnam War, 1964–1972

	All	Low Income	High Income
Local casualty rate	0.03***	0.03***	0.04*
	(0.01)	(0.01)	(0.02)
National cumulative casualties	0.21***	0.19***	0.25***
	(0.02)	(0.02	(0.03)
Republican	−0.09	0.00	−0.27*
	(0.08)	(0.10)	(0.15)
Democrat	−0.12	−0.09	−0.18
	(0.08)	(0.09)	(0.14)
Income	−0.11***	−0.17***	0.10
	(0.02)	(0.04)	(0.12)
Education	0.00	−0.02	0.02
	(0.02)	(0.02)	(0.03)
Male	−0.04	0.00	−0.11
	(0.05)	(0.07)	(0.09)
Age (in 10s)	0.10***	0.06***	0.19***
	(0.02)	(0.02)	(0.04)
Draft-age male	−0.04	−0.19	0.30*
	(0.10)	(0.12)	(0.17)
Black	0.49***	0.45***	0.52***
	(0.09)	(0.10)	(0.20)
Catholic	−0.06	−0.06	−0.05
	(0.06)	(0.08)	(0.10)
Jewish	0.64***	0.83***	0.48***
	(0.15)	(0.24)	(0.19)
South	−0.19***	−0.18***	−0.21**
	(0.05)	(0.07)	(0.10)
Constant	−2.23***	−1.70***	−3.85***
	(0.22)	(0.27)	(0.61)
Log-likelihood	−4883.61	−3183.62	−1687.44
Observations	7,415	4,798	2,617

All of the models report robust standard errors; all significance tests are two-tailed. *p < .10, **p < .05, ***p < .01.

several additional rounds of analysis to determine whether the result is sensitive to model specification. We examined various transformations of the age variable to see whether the effect was nonlinear; yet, in each case, the positive correlation between age and war opposition held. We also examined an alternative possibility that the relationship between age and war opposition changed over time. Perhaps older Americans were on average less supportive of the war in its earliest stages, but after

Tet and the great mass protests of the late 1960s and early 1970s, the gap between age groups narrowed. However, the data do not support this alternative theory. Adopting the dictum of the time (i.e., "Never trust anyone over thirty"), we examined the level of war opposition for respondents between the ages of 18 and 30 and compared it with the levels of war opposition among those older than 30 for every survey from 1964 to 1972. In each case, those over 30 expressed substantially higher levels of opposition to the war (between 4 percent and 8 percent higher) than those under 30. While this result is surprising, more important for our purposes is that, regardless of the operationalization of the age variable, we continue to observe strong, statistically significant correlations between a respondent's local casualty rate and the respondent's support for the Vietnam War.[1]

The second two columns of table 6A.1 examine whether local casualties affected rich and poor residents of the same community equally by dividing our sample into two groups based on family income. For both high- and low-income respondents, the local casualty rate coefficient is positive and statistically significant, which indicates that rich and poor responded in the same way to casualties from their local communities.

Table 6A.2 presents a parallel analysis of the forces that influenced respondents' likelihood of supporting the withdrawal of U.S. forces from Vietnam. The NES question asked respondents to choose their preferred policy option from three alternatives: (1) take a stronger stand, even if it means invading North Vietnam; (2) keep our soldiers in Vietnam but try to end the fighting; and (3) pull out entirely. The first column in table 6A.2 presents an ordered logit analysis that examines the impact of local casualty rates, national cumulative casualties, and other control variables on the probability of observing each of the three possible outcomes. Most importantly, the county casualty rate coefficient is positive and statistically significant; as a respondent's local casualty rate increased, so, too, did his or her support for more dovish policies. To ease the substantive interpretation of each variable's effects, we next reparameterized the dependent variable into a binary measure of whether respondents supported withdrawal (option 3) or not. Results from this model are presented in column 2. Again, the coefficient for the local casualties variable is positive and statistically significant. Finally, columns 3 and 4 mirror the analysis in table 6A.1 and estimate an identical model on split samples of high- and low-income respondents. In both groups, the coefficient for local casualty rate remains positive and statistically significant, which indicates that both high- and low-income Americans adjusted their preferred policy options in

Table 6A.2. Regression Analyses of the Factors Influencing Support for Withdrawing U.S. Forces from Vietnam, 1964–1970

	All ordinal	All binary	Low income binary	High income binary
Local casualty rate	0.06***	0.10***	0.10***	0.11***
	(0.02)	(0.02)	(0.02)	(0.03)
National cumulative casualties	0.12***	0.15***	0.14***	0.18***
	(0.02)	(0.03)	(0.04)	(0.06)
Republican	–0.24**	–0.25*	–0.19	–0.35
	(0.11)	(0.13)	(0.16)	(0.23)
Democrat	–0.03	–0.13	–0.15	–0.10
	(0.10)	(0.12)	(0.15)	(0.21)
Income	–0.09***	–0.14***	–0.28***	–0.08
	(0.03)	(0.04)	(0.06)	(0.19)
Education	0.00	–0.02	–0.08**	0.03
	(0.02)	(0.03)	(0.04)	(0.04)
Male	–0.50***	–0.28***	–0.33***	–0.23*
	(0.06)	(0.08)	(0.11)	(0.14)
Age (in 10s)	0.09***	0.12***	0.07**	0.18***
	(0.02)	(0.03)	(0.03)	(0.06)
Draft-age male	–0.05	0.04	–0.08	0.35
	(0.12)	(0.17)	(0.22)	(0.28)
Black	0.74***	0.57***	0.57***	0.39
	(0.10)	(0.12)	(0.14)	(0.30)
Catholic	0.06	0.16	0.09	0.26*
	(0.07)	(0.10)	(0.13)	(0.15)
Jewish	0.79***	0.99***	1.18***	0.83
	(0.17)	(0.20)	(0.31)	(0.27)
South	–0.25***	–0.12	–0.11	–0.17
	(0.07)	(0.09)	(0.11)	(0.16)
Constant	—	–2.91***	–2.10***	–3.91***
		(0.36)	(0.45)	(0.98)
Log-likelihood	–4350.57	–2165.74	–1385.70	–768.39
Observations	4,443	4,443	2,741	1,702

All of the models report robust standard errors; all significance tests are two-tailed. *p < .10, **p < .05, ***p < .01.

the same manner when confronted with the costs of war through the lens of their local community.

Control variables largely followed theoretical expectations. However, we again observe the surprising positive, statistically significant relationship between respondent age and support for withdrawal. First differences suggest that the average 58-year-old was 6 percent more likely to favor withdrawal than the average 31-year-old. Again, contrasting respondents under 30 with those 30 and over reveals that Americans over the age of 30 were between 4 percent and 7 percent more supportive of withdrawing from Vietnam on average than their younger peers in every survey from 1964 through 1970. However, most importantly, our finding for local casualty rates is not conditional on respondent age. Replicating our model for those over 30 and those 30 and under yields statistically significant, positive coefficients for the local casualty variable for both groups.

Finally, table 6A.3 presents the full logistic regression results used to generate our findings on local casualties' effects on congressional elections. While Lyndon Johnson was in the Oval Office from 1964 to 1968, casualties at both the national and local level compelled respondents to vote against the Democratic candidate in U.S. House races. The coefficients for both variables are negative and statistically significant. After Richard Nixon assumed the presidency and the mantle of war leadership, however, casualties appear to have helped Democratic candidates. The coefficient for national cumulative casualties is now positive, though statistically insignificant, while the coefficient for each respondent's county casualty rate is positive and significant. In this later period, respondents from high-casualty communities were significantly more likely to vote Democratic in House races than were their peers from low-casualty communities with identical personal demographic characteristics.

The control variables behaved almost identically in the two time periods. The effects of the control variables in the 1960s model are briefly discussed in the text. As expected, in the 1970s partisanship remained the most significant predictor of voting patterns. Democrats were 60 percent more likely on average to vote for their copartisan candidates for Congress than were Republicans. Again, there is evidence of a socioeconomic divide in voting patterns; however, in the 1970s, the coefficient for income, not education, is negative and statistically significant.[2] In the latter period, we again find positive correlations between males and the probability of voting Democratic and a negative correlation between age and Democratic voting. However, neither result is statistically significant.

Table 6A.3. Regression Analyses of the Factors Influencing Support for Democratic House Candidates, 1964–1972

	1964–1968	1970–1972
Local casualty rate	−0.08**	0.03*
	(0.03)	(0.02)
National cumulative casualties	−0.08**	2.53
	(0.03)	(1.65)
Republican	−1.55***	−1.35***
	(0.19)	(0.19)
Democrat	1.17***	1.47***
	(0.18)	(0.19)
Income	−0.06	−0.19***
	(0.06)	(0.06)
Education	−0.11***	0.03
	(0.03)	(0.04)
Male	0.23**	0.16
	(0.11)	(0.13)
Age (in 10s)	−0.06	−0.06
	(0.04)	(0.04)
Draft-age male	−0.35	0.09
	(0.26)	(0.25)
Black	1.24***	1.06***
	(0.30)	(0.34)
Catholic	0.34***	0.25*
	(0.13)	(0.15)
Jewish	0.82***	1.22***
	(0.33)	(0.48)
South	0.55***	0.70***
	(0.13)	(0.14)
Constant	1.51***	−27.31
	(0.43)	(18.03)
Log-likelihood	−1120.82	−921.25
Observations	2,393	1,928

All of the models report robust standard errors; all significance tests are two-tailed.
*p < .10, **p < .05, ***p < .01.

Finally, the racial, religious, and regional divides observed in the 1960s also characterized voting patterns in the 1970s. Blacks, Jews, Catholics, and Southerners were all consistently more likely to vote Democratic on average than were their peers with otherwise identical political and demographic characteristics.

7

Political Ramifications of the Iraq Casualty Gap

Echoing the Bard's tantalizingly prophetic warning that "what is past is prologue", politicians and media pundits alike have frequently drawn parallels between the wars in Iraq and Vietnam. Emphasizing its length and the nature of the fighting in the Iraqi deserts, opponents of the war in 2006 and 2007 were quick to latch on to the Vietnam-era term *quagmire* to describe the dilemma that confronted U.S. troops in the Middle East as they battled insurgents and strove to prop up a fledgling democratic government.[1] Many supporters of the war and independent analysts alike chafed at the comparison and emphasized fundamental differences between the two situations. However, in August of 2007 President Bush himself evoked the comparison to argue that a precipitous U.S. withdrawal from Iraq would produce bloodshed and chaos similar to that experienced in Indochina in the mid 1970s.[2]

Irrespective of the merits of such comparisons, there are at least two major differences between the wars that raise important questions about whether the casualty gap will continue to influence wartime support and voting behavior in the contemporary period. First and perhaps most obviously, the scale of the Iraq conflict, while larger than any U.S. military engagement since Vietnam, is still considerably smaller than Vietnam in almost every dimension, save cost.[3] Most importantly, while the toll in human life has been devastating, at more than 4,200 dead and tens of

161

thousands more wounded, the numbers are thus far considerably smaller than the relevant tallies from Vietnam. As a result, variance in local Iraq casualty rates simply may not play as important a role in shaping opinion and voting as Vietnam casualty rates did thirty-five years earlier.

A second prominent dimension along which the two conflicts differ is the degree of partisan polarization over war policy. One of the most surprising findings of Sidney Verba and colleagues' original study of Vietnam War opinion was the absence of any identifiable partisan cleavage with regard to the war.[4] Echoing this finding, the analyses of the preceding chapter find little evidence of a strong partisan divide. Rather, members of each partisan subgroup responded to stimuli, including casualties, in similar ways. By contrast, opinion on the war in Iraq plainly falls along partisan fault lines.[5] As political scientist Gary Jacobson has demonstrated, throughout President Bush's tenure in office, Republicans, virtually without exception, remained in lockstep with their party leader with regard to the war. Nothing has shaken the support of the GOP party faithful—not the failure of the president, who proclaimed "mission accomplished," to make it so; the atrocities of Abu Ghraib; the absence of weapons of mass destruction; or even the escalation of violence in 2006, which pushed Iraq to the brink of civil war. Democrats, for their part, contributed to the partisan polarization by giving President Bush lower average approval ratings than they gave Richard Nixon at the peak of the Watergate scandal.[6] This tense political environment of heightened partisanship may produce considerably different dynamics between local casualty rates, public opinion, and electoral choices.

In short, it is not clear that the political implications of the casualty gap are the same in the contemporary political context of the Iraq War as they were in Vietnam. This is particularly important when considering the likely consequences of the casualty gap for future military conflicts. With continued advances in military technology, weaponry, and front-line medical care, future wars may well be more likely to mirror Iraq both in the scale of forces used and in the number of soldiers killed. If these future conflicts are also waged in an environment of intense partisan polarization like that of today, the effects of the casualty gap on Americans' wartime opinions and political behaviors during the war in Iraq may be especially relevant.

Combining individual-level survey data with state and county electoral returns, this chapter empirically investigates whether the relationships between local casualties, public opinion, and voting behavior in Iraq parallel those observed during the Vietnam era. The data reveal that some of these relationships in the contemporary conflict are dramatically different from those observed in Vietnam, while others remain eerily similar. Most importantly, however, we find that Americans' differential exposure to casualties continues to play a significant role in influencing support for the war and for the political leaders charged with directing it. At their core, the results of our analysis of Iraq strongly reaffirm that the casualty gap has critically important political ramifications for American governance. Public opinion turns increasingly against the war when citizens experience the costs of war firsthand through casualties from their local community. Because high-casualty-rate communities historically tend to have lower levels of income and education and their residents are less engaged with politics than their peers from low-casualty-rate communities, the dampening effect of casualties on hawkish military policies is weaker in practice than conventional wisdom suggests.

IRAQ, CASUALTIES, AND PUBLIC OPINION

The war in Iraq has prompted a number of scholars to reexamine the dominant theories that link battle deaths with Americans' support for war. Some emphasize the similarities between opinion dynamics in Iraq and previous conflicts. For example, in their analysis of weekly presidential approval data, political scientists Richard Eichenberg and Richard Stoll found a strong relationship between logged cumulative casualties and support for President Bush in multiple specifications of the approval series.[7]

Others argue that the Iraq data support a more nuanced conclusion than the conventional view that, as casualties mount, popular support steadily declines. For example, Christopher Gelpi, Peter Feaver, and Jason Reifler argue that the effect of combat casualties on Americans' support for the Iraq War is contingent on whether the public perceives that a military venture is succeeding or failing.[8] In the combat phase of the Iraq War, from the first aerial assault of March 19, 2003, through the declaration of mission accomplished that May, increasing logged cumulative casualties were actually positively correlated with changes in support for the president.[9] However, with the launching of the insurgency, mounting U.S. casualties posed a damaging political problem for Bush and were negatively correlated with his job approval. Finally, in the "sovereignty" phase of the operation, after the transfer of power from the United States to a provisional Iraqi government in June 2004, Gelpi, Feaver, and Reifler found that casualties had no effect on the president's approval rating.

Articulating a third point of view, political scientists Erik Voeten and Paul Brewer argue that casualties have indeed shaped some dimensions of popular wartime support, such as the public's assessments of the war's progress. However, on other aspects of war opinion, such as whether invading Iraq was worth the costs, casualties have had little effect. Moreover, Voeten and Brewer conclude that Iraq casualties have only indirectly influenced Americans' political judgments. In a model of presidential approval, casualties had no independent influence; rather, they influenced support for President Bush only indirectly through their influence on the public's beliefs about progress in the war.[10]

While each of these studies demonstrated some linkage between Iraq casualties and popular support for the war, each also treated casualties as a unitary stimulus that affects all Americans equally. Considering the stark casualty gap that has emerged in the distribution of Iraq casualties across the country, we should not expect all Americans to react to casualties to the same extent. Rather, if the same logic holds in Iraq as held in Vietnam, the effects of casualties on political outcomes should be most concentrated on those who have experienced the war's costs most directly.

Rather than examining relationships between cumulative casualties suffered in Iraq and trends in time-series public opinion data, our analysis focuses on how differential exposure to casualties across the country affects support for war. In the preceding chapter, we examined whether the casualty rate suffered by each respondent's county in Vietnam had any impact on that person's war opinions and political judgments. Replicating such an analysis for the war in Iraq poses two difficulties. First, because the scale of the conflicts differs so greatly, the vast majority of census places and even the majority of counties in the United States have actually lost no soldiers in Iraq. As a result, the variance in individuals' experience with the war as measured strictly by their local casualty rate is limited. Second, although public attitudes on the war are constantly polled, we were unable to obtain polling data with the necessary geographic identifiers for each respondent. Absent these, we were unable to match our data on local casualty rates with individual survey respondents in the same way we could with the Vietnam data.

However, we were able to utilize two Gallup surveys from 2006 to examine the considerable variance with which Americans have been exposed to Iraq War casualties. In these surveys, Gallup explicitly asked respondents whether they personally "have any close friends, family members, or coworkers" who were "wounded or killed while serving in Iraq." Ten percent of survey respondents answered in the affirmative. In chapter 5 we discussed how this figure almost certainly exceeds the actual number of Americans who know the name of a soldier killed or wounded in the Iraq War. As a result, we interpret this question as a more general measure of the varying degrees of personal contact that Americans feel with the human costs of the Iraq War. It is important to remember that our statistical analysis of responses to this question showed no evidence that it is a proxy for partisanship. Democrats were no more or less likely to answer yes to this question than were Republicans. Rather, this question genuinely seems to tap respondents' varying exposure to the costs of war. This varying exposure to war costs, in turn, is influenced, at least in part, by the casualty gap. Aside from age, the only statistically significant predictor of a respondent reporting that he or she "knew" a soldier killed or wounded in Iraq was the casualty rate sustained by the respondent's home state. Respondents from states that were in the top quarter of the casualty distribution were twice as likely to report knowing a casualty of war than were those from states in the bottom quarter of the casualty rate distribution.

To assess the effects of greater perceived personal contact with casualties in the Iraq War, the following models explore whether respondents who reported knowing a casualty—almost certainly, in large part, because they came from communities with disproportionately high casualty rates—held different opinions on the war and exhibited different intended voting patterns than similar respondents who did not.

Knowing a Casualty and Feeling Negatively Affected Personally by the War

For Americans who know a soldier who has given his or her life, the costs of war become more personal. However, given the different ways that one may "know" a deceased soldier, an important first step in our analysis is to explore the underlying premise that "knowing" a casualty is related to one's personal connection to the war. The Gallup survey data from March 2006 allow us to do this. In addition to asking respondents whether they knew an Iraq War casualty, this survey also asked: "Has the U.S. involvement in the war against Iraq had a positive or negative effect on you personally, or hasn't it had much effect on you?" In the analyses that follow, we investigate the factors affecting respondents' probability of perceiving that the war had negatively affected them.

At first glance, there is an obvious positive relationship between reporting a personal connection with a casualty and feeling negatively affected by the war. Only 37 percent of respondents who reported not knowing any casualties of the Iraq conflict replied that the war had had a negative effect on them personally. By contrast, 61 percent of those who did report personal contact with a killed or wounded soldier in Iraq perceived negative, personal consequences of the war.[11] However, to control for other factors that distinguish the two groups, we conducted a logistic regression analysis to assess the impact of knowing a casualty on feeling the war's negative effects personally.

Toward this end, we included the political, demographic, and regional control variables used in the models of Vietnam opinion. The models contained indicator variables for whether the respondent identified as a Republican or a Democrat, as well as measures of each respondent's age, gender, race, region, and educational attainment. Finally, we included an additional variable in the model to capture the effects of opposition to the war more broadly: an indicator variable for whether each respondent believed that the Iraq War was a mistake.[12]

The full regression results are reported in this chapter's technical appendix. To ease interpretation of the estimated effects of each variable on the probability that a respondent would report feeling personally affected negatively by the war, we use a series of first differences illustrated in figure 7.1.

Confirming our preliminary peek at the data, even after controlling for a host of demographic factors and basic opinion cleavages, we find unambiguous evidence that Americans who reported knowing a killed or wounded soldier were considerably more likely to say that the Iraq conflict had harmed them personally than were otherwise identical

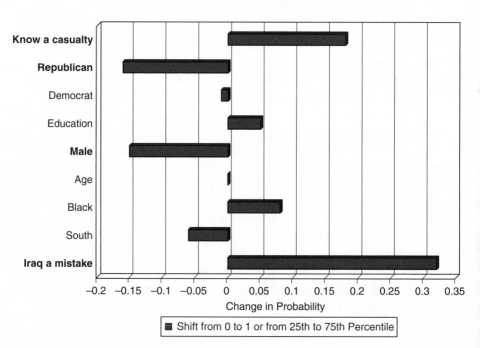

Figure 7.1. The impact of knowing a casualty, demographics, and regional factors on feeling the Iraq War negatively affected one personally.

Note: Statistically significant effects are indicated with boldface.

respondents who did not perceive this personal contact with casualties. Among respondents who believed the Iraq War was a mistake, knowing a casualty increased their probability of answering affirmatively by 18 percent. Among respondents who did not believe the war was a mistake, the effect was even greater, increasing the probability by 23 percent. Thus, there is strong evidence that Americans' contact with Iraq casualties—which is determined in large part by how they experience a war's costs through the lens of their local communities—shapes their view of the war. Respondents who recognize a connection with killed or wounded soldiers are more likely to perceive the war's costs personally than are their peers without this personal contact.

Given the strong evidence of intense partisan cleavages in Iraq War opinion in existing scholarship, we next tested for whether the impact of knowing a casualty was conditional on partisan identification. To do this we separated the sample into three groups, one for respondents of each party affiliation, and reestimated our logistic regression analysis for each set. Results are reported in the technical appendix. In short, we found no evidence that personal connection with a casualty affected the opinions of only Democrats or independents. In each case, we observed a strong positive relationship between personal contact with a killed or wounded soldier and feeling negatively affected by the war. Republicans may have been less likely to believe the war had affected them negatively than other Americans, but they responded to knowing a casualty personally in the same manner as Democratic and independent identifiers.

While partisanship was not a significant factor in this first round of analysis, when we shift the focus away from the question of war's negative personal effects to more explicitly political questions, the effect of knowing a casualty is greatly moderated by individuals' partisan orientations.

Support for Withdrawal

To determine whether perceived personal contact with a casualty also influenced respondents' policy preferences for the war's conduct, we next assess whether respondents who knew a casualty were more likely than other Americans to support quicker withdrawal of U.S. troops from Iraq. In both the March and October 2006 surveys, Gallup presented respondents with a set of four alternatives and asked which plan they most preferred. The possible options were as follows: "Withdraw all troops from Iraq immediately"; "Withdraw all troops by March/October 2007—that is, in twelve months' time"; "Withdraw troops, but take as many years to do this as are needed to turn control over to the Iraqis"; or "Send more troops to Iraq." In the chapter's technical appendix we present ordered logit models that assess the effect of a reported personal connection with a casualty on observing the full range of policy alternatives from immediate withdrawal to escalation. However, to ease interpretation of the effects we transformed this ordinal variable into a binary variable that measures support for withdrawing U.S. forces in Iraq in a timely fashion. This variable was coded 1 if respondents favored immediate withdrawal or withdrawal within the next year and 0 if they favored escalation or staying the course for as long as necessary. Full results for this logistic regression are reported in the technical appendix. Both sets of models, however, yield virtually identical results.

We first estimated a model identical to that employed earlier to explore the effects of knowing a casualty on support for withdrawal. As expected, we found a positive relationship between knowing a soldier killed or wounded in Iraq and greater support for withdrawing U.S. forces from the war zone in a timely fashion. However, the resulting coefficient was statistically insignificant.[13]

To probe further, we next disaggregated the respondent pool by partisan identification and ran separate models for each partisan group. The results were surprising. For Republicans and Democrats, a reported personal connection with a casualty had *no effect whatsoever* on support for withdrawal. For Republicans, the estimated effect was actually negative. Indeed, simply examining support for withdrawal among Republicans broken down by whether respondents reported that they knew a casualty shows that 28 percent of Republicans who did not know someone killed or wounded in Iraq supported withdrawal, while only 22 percent of those who said they did know a casualty supported pulling forces out of the region. Given the small sample sizes, the difference is not statistically significant, but the negative direction of the relationship is suggestive, nonetheless. For Republicans, knowing a wounded or killed soldier may have only strengthened their resolve to keep fighting. This sentiment was on display a year later in the 2007 "These Colors Don't Run" caravan, a national tour sponsored by Move America Forward, a conservative political action committee. With stops in twenty-five cities, the group made its way to Washington, D.C., to show its support for the troops and its opposition to those who would withdraw precipitously from Iraq. Along the way, many who had lost loved ones in Iraq voiced their support. Jan Johnson, who lost her youngest son in the war in 2004, supported the caravan when it came through Georgia. When asked to compare herself to antiwar activist Cindy Sheehan, Johnson said she was trying to "do the opposite" of Sheehan.[14] Our data are consistent with this anecdotal evidence that the pattern of response to Iraq casualties is not straightforward.

By contrast, knowing a casualty had virtually no impact, on average, on Democratic support for withdrawal. By the spring and fall of 2006, most Democrats and Republicans were firmly entrenched in their views on the politically charged question of whether U.S. forces should come home from Iraq. The vast majority of Republicans stood steadfast behind their president and party leaders in Congress and opposed withdrawal, even if they felt a personal connection with a soldier who had been killed or wounded in Iraq. Conversely, almost three-quarters of Democrats supported withdrawing U.S. forces within the next year. Given this high base level of support, a perceived personal connection with a casualty had little effect because almost all Democrats already supported withdrawal regardless of whether they knew someone killed or wounded in the war.

Only among independents, who lacked strong political incentives either to stand by the president or to oppose him and his policies, did we find a strong divergence in opinion between those who reported knowing a casualty and those who did not. Of the 620 independents in our surveys, 13 percent replied that they knew a soldier who had been killed or wounded in the conflict. Of these independents, 67 percent supported reducing the U.S. military commitment in Iraq within the next year. By contrast, among those independents who did not personally know a casualty of the war, support for withdrawal averaged only 53 percent.[15]

Logistic regression allows us to estimate the impact of reported personal experience with war casualties on support for withdrawal among independents after controlling for all of the factors discussed in the preceding model. The effects of each variable on the probability that a respondent supports withdrawal are illustrated through a series of first differences presented in figure 7.2.

The first differences demonstrate that the effect of a sense of personal connection with an Iraq War casualty on support for withdrawal among independents is considerable. Among independents who believed the war was a mistake, knowing a casualty further increased support for withdrawal by 11 percent, from 79 percent to almost 90 percent on average. Among independents who did not judge the war a mistake, the effect was even larger. For this subset, knowing a soldier killed or wounded in the war increased support for withdraw from 39 percent to 55 percent. Whereas personal experience with a casualty had no effect on the policy preferences of Democratic or Republican partisans, it had a strong, unambiguous influence on support for withdrawal among independents.

The critical importance of partisanship in mediating the effect of personal experience with casualties on opinion suggests that the political ramifications of the casualty gap in the context of Iraq may be considerably more complex and contingent than they were in Vietnam. For those who have already made up their mind about Iraq (either to stick it out or

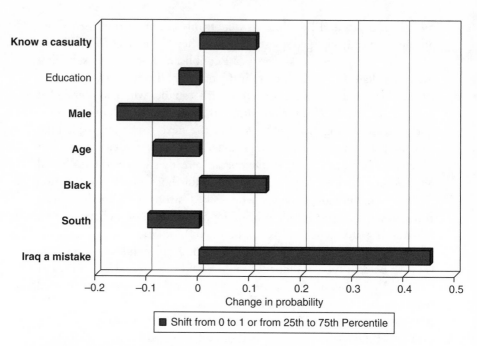

Figure 7.2. The impact of knowing a casualty, demographics, and regional factors on support for withdrawal (independents only).

Note: Statistically significant effects are indicated with boldface.

to withdraw expeditiously), knowing a casualty does not seem to change opinion. However, among the critical set of swing voters who identify with neither of the two increasingly polarized major political parties, personal experience with casualties has a significant effect on public policy preferences.

IRAQ, CASUALTIES, AND ELECTORAL DYNAMICS

Having demonstrated the effects of the casualty gap on public opinion, we now investigate the influence of Iraq casualties on electoral outcomes. The analysis proceeds in two stages. First, we begin again by analyzing individual-level survey data to explore the impact of personal contact with a killed or wounded soldier on vote choice in the 2006 midterm elections. We then supplement this survey analysis with aggregate election return data. If Iraq and its mounting toll hurt Republicans at the polls, their losses should have been most intense in those communities hardest hit by the war. We therefore analyze the correlation between both state and local casualty rates and the change in that state's or county's vote share for the Republican senatorial candidate from 2000 to 2006.

Varying Experience with Casualties and Electoral Choice in 2006

We first examined the effect of reporting a personal connection with a soldier killed or wounded in Iraq on respondents' vote choice. Toward this end, we analyzed a Gallup poll with a nationally representative sample of 1,002 Americans that both contained the contact with a casualty question and also asked respondents about their voting intentions on the eve of the November 2006 election.[16] The model specification is virtually identical to that used previously to study support for withdrawal. In addition to the personal contact with a casualty question, the analysis also controls for each respondent's education, gender, age, race, region, and whether or not the respondent believed the invasion of Iraq was a mistake. One additional control was added—a measure of whether respondents indicated that they would base their vote for Congress primarily on national, state, or local issues. Presumably, with national trends favoring Democrats, respondents who cited national issues as their primary concern would be more likely to vote for the Democratic candidate.

As in our empirical analysis of the factors that influence support for withdrawal from Iraq, we find that the effect of personal contact with a killed or wounded soldier on vote choice is highly conditional on a respondent's partisan identification. For Democrats, direct contact with a killed or wounded soldier had virtually no effect on propensity for voting Democratic. Fully 96 percent of Democrats who did not know a casualty announced their intention to vote Democratic in November, as did 93 percent of those Democrats who reported knowing a casualty, a statistically insignificant difference. Among Republicans, the effect again appears, if anything, to be negative. Eight percent of Republicans who did not know anyone killed or wounded in Iraq said they would vote for the Democratic candidate, while none of the 27 Republicans who knew a casualty said that they would support the opposition party candidate.

However, as in the previous analysis of support for withdrawal, we observed a strong positive correlation among independents between knowing a casualty and voting Democratic. A simple difference in means test reveals that 55 percent of independents who knew a killed or wounded soldier supported the Democratic candidate versus only 44 percent of independents who did not express having personal contact with a casualty, a statistically significant difference.[17] Moreover, even after including all of the control variables in a logistic regression, we continue to find a significant effect for knowing a casualty on support for Democratic House candidates among independent voters. Logistic regression results for all three partisan groups are reported in the technical appendix. First differences in figure 7.3 illustrate the effect of a shift in each variable on

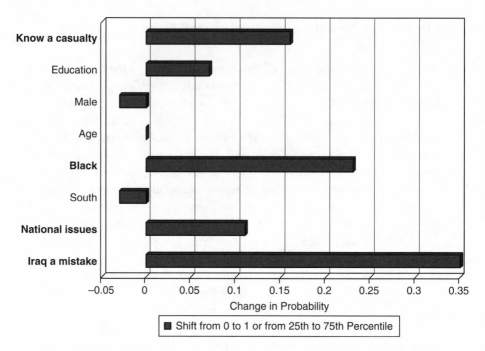

Figure 7.3. The impact of knowing a casualty, demographics, and regional factors on voting Democratic (independents only).

Note: Statistically significant effects are indicated with boldface.

independents' probability of voting Democratic while holding all other factors constant at their mean or median values.

As figure 7.3 shows, personal contact with a deceased or wounded soldier had a strong, significant effect among independents on the probability of voting Democratic. According to the model, independents who felt a personal connection to a casualty of the Iraq conflict were 16 percent more likely to vote for the Democratic candidate, on average, than were their peers. Thus, by affecting Americans' contact with the human costs of the Iraq War, the casualty gap had significant electoral ramifications in the 2006 midterms, particularly among the crucially important swing group of independent voters.

State and Local Casualty Rates and Change in Republican Vote Share

Up to this point we have seen that residents of high-casualty communities are more likely than residents of low-casualty communities, on average, to feel that they know a soldier killed or wounded in Iraq.[18] This personal contact, at least for independents, has significantly influenced

Americans' military policy preferences and voting behavior. Yet, as we discuss in chapter 5, increasing personal contact with casualties is but one mechanism through which the Iraq casualty gap might affect patterns of citizens' opinions and behaviors. Local casualty rates also affect the nature and number of elite cues sent to citizens, as well as the tenor and scope of the local media's coverage of the war. Neither of these mechanisms requires citizens to know the name of a casualty for their opinions and behaviors to be influenced by the death toll sustained in their community. As a result, the survey data we used in the previous section almost certainly fails to capture the full scope of the casualty gap's effects on Americans' opinions and political behaviors. However, by using aggregate-level electoral data we can cast a wider net and attempt to assess the electoral ramifications of the casualty gap even more directly by looking for correlations between a community's casualty rate and its change in vote share for Republican senatorial candidates from 2000 to 2006.

Our analysis proceeds in three stages: The first examines the effects of variance in local casualties on all 2006 senatorial election results at the state level; the second investigates the influence of local casualties on every Senate contest at the county level; and the third focuses narrowly on the casualty gap's impact on the county-level returns for the fourteen Republican incumbents who sought reelection in 2006.[19]

There is considerable evidence that local casualties had a significant negative impact on Republican electoral fortunes in the 2006 Senate races. Looking first at the scatter plot in figure 7.4, we see a strong negative relationship between a state's casualty rate and the Republican senatorial candidate's electoral fortunes.[20] This simple bivariate analysis suggests that an increase in a state's casualty rate of 5 casualties per million residents (approximately one standard deviation) cost the Republican candidate about 5 percentage points at the ballot box.

The negative relationship also appears robust at the county level. Consider the following numbers. By November of 2006, 10 percent of counties had suffered two or more casualties in Iraq since the war began in March 2003. Republican senatorial candidates captured 55 percent of the vote in these counties in 2000. In 2004, a year and a half into the war, President Bush secured 54 percent of the two-party vote in these locales. However, just two years later Republicans won only 48 percent of the vote in Senate contests in these counties. Contrast this precipitous decline with the performance of Republican candidates in the counties that had experienced no casualties in Iraq prior to the election. In these counties, the Republican candidate won 57 percent of the vote in 2000. President Bush won handily in these areas in 2004, garnering 62 percent of the vote. Furthermore, in 2006, Republican candidates continued to do well,

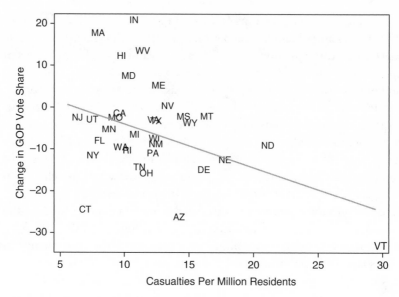

Figure 7.4. Scatter plot of state-level casualty rates and change in GOP vote share in 2006 Senate elections.

earning 55 percent of the two-party vote share. Limiting the analysis to the 993 counties in which fourteen incumbent senators ran for reelection in 2006 also shows a 7 percentage point decrease from their 2000 totals in the counties that had experienced two or more casualties. In counties that experienced no casualties in Iraq, the Republican candidates gained 65 percent of the vote on average in both the 2000 and the 2006 elections. Certainly, something seems afoot.

However, to ensure that the observed Republican losses in high-casualty states and counties are not spurious artifacts of other unobserved factors at play in these areas, we again employ a multiple regression analysis. At both the state and county levels, we model the change in Republican senatorial vote share as a function of local casualties and a number of political, economic, and demographic control variables drawn from prior research. The multivariate analyses employ two operationalizations of a locale's war losses: the raw casualty count and the casualty rate per one million and per 10,000 residents for states and counties respectively.

In addition to casualties, an extensive literature has identified opponent quality and campaign spending as two of the most important predictors of a candidate's electoral fortunes.[21] To account for changes in opponent quality, we coded each Republican's opponent according to the eight-point ordinal scale created by political scientists Don Green and Jonathan Krasno, and we calculated the change in this measure across the two electoral cycles. To control for the influence of campaign expenditures, we include the change in the percentage of total campaign expenditures by the Republican candidate from 2000 to 2006.[22]

In addition to factors specific to the Senate race at hand, scholars have long documented the connections between presidential performance and the success of their copartisans in presidential elections, even in midterm contests.[23] To account for this in the current context, we include a measure of President Bush's share of the two-party vote in each state or county in the 2004 election. Additionally, a number of previous studies have debated the relative impact of economic conditions on congressional election outcomes.[24] To control for economic factors, we include measures, obtained from the Bureau of Labor Statistics, of the change in the state and county unemployment rate during the year preceding the 2006 midterm elections. Voters in areas of increasing unemployment may be more likely to punish Republican candidates in this era of unified Republican control of Congress and the presidency.

Finally, the models also control for two important demographic constituency characteristics that might be correlated with considerable change in Republican electoral fortunes from the peacetime election of 2000 to the wartime 2006 contest: the percentage of residents age 18 to 64 who were serving in the military and the percentage of all residents who were veterans of the armed forces.[25] Conventional wisdom suggests that military communities have largely rallied around the president and his policies; if correct, Republican candidates may have performed better relative to their 2000 baseline in these areas than in otherwise comparable communities. Additionally, an extensive literature at the elite level has examined the different perspectives that veterans bring to questions of military policy; however, expectations for electoral behavior in states or counties with large veteran contingents at the mass level are less clear.[26] It is possible that communities with large contingents of veterans, like those with high percentages of active-duty personnel and their families, rallied around the president and the Republicans in the 2006 midterms; alternatively, residents of such communities may have viewed the war and the administration's military policies through a distinctly different and more critical lens and adjusted their voting behavior accordingly. The empirical analysis will test between these competing hypotheses. Summary statistics for all of the variables are reported in the technical appendix.[27]

State-Level Results

Full regression results for the models of change in GOP vote share at the state level are reported in the technical appendix. To ease the interpretation of the statistical results, table 7.1 presents a series of first differences that illustrate the effect of a shift in each of our independent variables on the change in Republican vote share while holding all other variables constant at their means or medians.

Even after controlling for the political, economic, and demographic factors discussed earlier, our empirical analysis finds the expected negative relationships between a state's casualty tally and rate and the change in Republican vote share. Moreover, consistent with the bivariate relationship

Table 7.1. First Differences Showing the Impact of Each Variable on Change in GOP Vote Share from 2000 to 2006 Senate Elections

Independent Variable	Shift in Variable	Change in GOP Vote Share
STATE LEVEL		
All Senate Races		
Casualty tally	1 standard deviation increase	−1%
Casualty rate	1 standard deviation increase	**−7%**
Opponent quality	1 standard deviation increase	−1%
% GOP spending	1 standard deviation increase	**+4%**
% Bush 2004	1 standard deviation increase	+5%
% Unemployment	1 standard deviation increase	**+3%**
% Military	1 standard deviation increase	**+3%**
% Veterans	1 standard deviation increase	−1%
COUNTY LEVEL		
All Senate Races		
Casualty tally	1 standard deviation increase	**−1%**
Casualty rate	1 standard deviation increase	0%
Opponent quality	1 standard deviation increase	**−5%**
% GOP spending	1 standard deviation increase	0%
% Bush 2004	1 standard deviation increase	**+1%**
% Unemployment	1 standard deviation increase	0%
% Military	1 standard deviation increase	0%
% Veterans	1 standard deviation increase	**−1%**
GOP Incumbents		
Casualty tally	2 standard deviation increase	**−2%**
Casualty rate	2 standard deviation increase	**−1%**
Opponent quality	1 standard deviation increase	**+1%**
% GOP spending	1 standard deviation increase	**+7%**
% Bush 2004	1 standard deviation increase	**+3%**
% Unemployment	1 standard deviation increase	0%
% Military	1 standard deviation increase	**0%**
% Veterans	1 standard deviation increase	**−3%**

Variables in bold are statistically significant, p < .10, two-tailed test. First differences presented in this table are derived from models presented in full in table 7A.5.

illustrated in figure 7.4, the relationship between a state's casualty rate and Republican electoral fortunes is particularly strong and statistically significant. The empirical model suggests that a one standard deviation increase of 4.6 casualties per million residents cost the Republican candidate on average about 7 percentage points at the polls. The size and robustness of this result strongly suggest that variance in state-level casualties significantly influenced Senate electoral dynamics in 2006, despite the Iraq War's relatively small scale.

Turning to the political control variables, most of the relationships are in the expected direction, and many are statistically significant. In both state-level models, strong support for President Bush in 2004 was positively correlated with increases in Republican senatorial vote share, and in the second specification the relationship only narrowly failed to reach conventional levels of statistical significance. Similarly, in both models the change in the opponent quality variable was negative, as expected. Republican candidates tended to lose ground when they faced a tougher opponent in 2006 than in 2000; however, there is considerable uncertainty around the estimates, and the correlations may be spurious. Also consistent with theoretical expectations and prior studies that emphasize the importance of campaign spending, both specifications find a strong link between relative campaign expenditures and the change in Republican vote share. The second state-level model suggests that a one standard deviation increase in the Republican candidate's percentage of the total campaign expenditures produced a 4 percentage point increase on average in GOP vote share from 2000 to 2006.

Economics also appears to have had some influence on Republican electoral fortunes; yet, far from being punished electorally in areas of increasing unemployment as the party in power, the positive coefficients suggest that Republicans actually performed better in these areas on average than they did in the 2000 contests. To explore this relationship further, we reestimated the two state-level models by disaggregating the change in unemployment measure by the incumbent's party affiliation. This additional step reveals that rising state-level unemployment increased Republican vote share only when facing an incumbent Democrat; the coefficients for the effect of changing unemployment on incumbent Republicans' electoral fortunes are negative but statistically insignificant. All other results remain unchanged.

Finally, turning to the military-related demographic characteristics of the states themselves, we find some evidence of states with large active-duty military populations rallying around the Republican Party. In both models, the observed relationship is positive, and in the second specification it is statistically significant. This model suggests that a one standard

deviation increase in the state's active-duty military population resulted
in a 3 percent increase in GOP vote share from the peacetime 2000 contest to the 2006 election. Yet, neither model finds an effect for the size of
a state's veteran population on the change in GOP vote share.

County-Level Results

The next set of models sharpens the scope of the analysis by examining
the influence of the casualty gap on the Republican vote share at the
county level. The dependent variable here is the change in the county-
level vote share from 2000 to 2006 in all 1,856 counties from the thirty-
one states (excluding Vermont and Connecticut, where the independent
candidacies of Bernie Sanders and Joe Lieberman complicate cross-
election comparisons) with senatorial contests. The results at this lower
level of geographic aggregation also strongly suggest that local casualties
influenced Republicans' electoral fates. First differences are presented
in table 7.1.

At the county level, we again find the expected negative correlations
between a locale's casualty rate and the change in vote share for
Republicans. However, at this lower level of aggregation, it is the relationship between the number of Iraq battle deaths and changing electoral fortunes that is statistically significant. It may be that at the county
level the casualty rate is not as important as the simple presence of a
casualty from voters' local communities. After all, a majority of counties as of November 2006 had not suffered a single battle death in Iraq.
As a result, whether one's community had suffered a disproportionate
share of the burden in Iraq in terms of its casualty rate may have been
considerably less important to many voters' calculus than whether they
had experienced the costs of war through the lens of their local community at all.[28] Substantively the size of the relationship between a
county's casualty tally and electoral tides is modest, yet still of political
import: A one standard deviation increase in a county's casualty tally,
on average, cost the Republican candidate approximately 1 percentage
point at the polls.

In both county-level models, the political control variables closely follow theoretical expectations. As expected, we observe a strong negative
and statistically significant relationship between increasing opponent
quality and the change in Republican vote share. A one standard deviation increase in the caliber of the Republican opponent on the Green and
Krasno scale decreased the GOP candidate's vote share by 5 percentage
points. Similarly, the estimated effect for the share of campaign expenditures disbursed by the Republican on GOP electoral fortunes is positive,
though in both specifications it fails to reach conventional levels of statis-

tical significance. Finally, both models suggest that Republican senatorial candidates reaped modest gains over their 2000 showings in counties that strongly supported George W. Bush in the 2004 election.

In the economic realm, the coefficients for change in a county's unemployment rate are negative but statistically insignificant. Again, further analysis suggests that the relationship is contingent on the partisanship of the incumbent senator. Disaggregating the unemployment measure by partisanship shows that rising unemployment bolsters the Republican candidate's fortunes when challenging a sitting Democrat but depresses the GOP vote share when the Republican is the incumbent.

Finally, turning to the two military demographic variables, at the county level there is no evidence of communities with large concentrations of active-duty military personnel rallying behind the Republican Party. However, the models do find a statistically significant, negative relationship between the percentage of veterans in a county and the change in GOP vote share in both specifications. First differences suggest that the Republican candidate fared about 1 percentage point worse in counties with veteran populations one standard deviation above the mean in 2006 than they did in 2000. Considered in conjunction with the state-level analyses, these results suggest that communities with large veteran populations approached the 2006 midterms differently than did those with large active-duty military populations.[29]

Republican Incumbent Races at the County Level

Collectively, the models of election results from all of the states and counties involved in the 2006 elections offer considerable evidence that the experience of voters' state and local communities with regard to the Iraq War influenced their decision calculus in the 2006 midterm elections. However, because these analyses do not differentiate among electoral contests, it is possible that they underestimate the magnitude of local casualties' effects on the Senate races. For example, in the Tennessee Senate race it is not clear that Bob Corker, the former Chattanooga mayor and Republican nominee, should perform worse than the 2000 Republican candidate in counties that experienced higher casualties in Iraq. If anything, Harold Ford, who voted to authorize the war while in the House, might stand to bear the brunt of any voter dissatisfaction on Iraq. Corker acknowledged that mistakes had been made in Iraq and emphasized the need for a change in strategy to get the job done and bring the troops home. Unsaddled by the baggage of voting for the authorization to use force against Iraq and the need to support the president's policies on the Senate floor, there is little reason to expect the effects of Iraq on his candidacy to have been acute.

Taking this into account, we conducted a final set of analyses that focus exclusively on the county-level election results for the fourteen incumbent Republican senators—all but two of whom voted to authorize the war in Iraq—running for reelection in 2006.[30] For this subset of elections, the dependent variable that measures the change in Republican vote share from the previous election is the most clean. Moreover, it is for these senators that our expectations concerning the effects of Iraq casualties on electoral success are most robust.

In this critical test of the electoral import of local casualties, the models find a significant relationship between both the county casualty tally and rate and the change in vote share for the Republican incumbent. Full regression results are presented in the technical appendix. Table 7.1 illustrates the effect of a shift in each independent variable on the change in GOP vote share, while holding all other variables constant at their means or medians. A two standard deviation increase in a county's casualty count cost the Republican incumbent more than 2 percentage points at the polls. Similarly, a two standard deviation increase in the county's casualty rate decreased the Republican incumbent's expected vote share by 1 percentage point from his or her 2000 performance. In terms of the raw numbers, these effects are rather modest; however, a 2–4 percentage point swing could have meant the difference in a number of contests in 2006, particularly in the hotly contested races in Montana, Missouri, Virginia, and Tennessee.

Moreover, the effect of county-level casualty tallies and rates is robust even after controlling for state-level casualty figures. Reestimating the models with both state- and county-level casualty tallies and rates continued to show a strong relationship between county-level casualty measures and the change in GOP vote share.

The control variables, with one exception, again largely accord with theoretical expectations. For this subset of counties, the observed correlation between change in opponent quality and Republican vote share is now actually positive. This anomaly is most likely due to idiosyncratic factors in the smaller number of Senate contests in the restricted sample. For example, the largest change in Republican opponent quality was in Virginia, where George Allen ran against incumbent senator Charles Robb in 2000 and James Webb, who had never held elected office, in 2006. On the Green and Krasno scale, which fails to capture his formidability as a candidate in the 2006 election cycle, Webb scores considerably lower than many candidates running for the Senate. Yet, the other controls follow expectations closely. The greater the change in the share of total campaign expenditures by the Republican, the better the Republican candidate performed. Incumbent GOP senators were most likely to gain ground from their previous election in counties where George W. Bush performed well in the 2004 presidential race. Finally, rising unemployment is negatively correlated with the change in Republican vote share, though the relationship is not statistically significant.

Turning to the military demographics of this subset of counties, we find more evidence of differential voting behavior in areas with high concentrations of active-duty military personnel and veterans. As in the state models, we observe evidence of a small positive relationship between the size of a county's active-duty military population and increased Republican vote shares, and in the first specification it is statistically significant. Yet, as in the model of all county returns, in both specifications we observe a statistically significant negative relationship between the size of a county's veteran population and the change in GOP electoral fortunes. With all appropriate caveats about the dangers of ecological inference, the evidence is at least suggestive that areas with large concentrations of active-duty soldiers and veterans viewed the Iraq war very differently. Counties with large shares of active-duty service members rallied slightly behind the GOP, while counties with strong veteran presences turned against the Republicans.

In sum, the models provide compelling evidence across a wide range of specifications that both state- and county-level Iraq casualties depressed voting for Republican senatorial candidates. The war was indeed a national issue of the greatest import, but its electoral consequences were, at least in part, a function of the distribution of the war's costs across the country.

CONCLUSION

Drawing on multiple data sets at both the aggregate and individual levels, the empirical analyses in this chapter demonstrate that, even with the historically small number of casualties thus far suffered in Iraq, the casualty gap has had considerable ramifications for U.S. politics and policymaking. Independents who reported personal experience with the costs of war were significantly more likely to support withdrawing U.S. forces from Iraq and to vote Democratic in the 2006 midterm elections. Analyses of aggregate election returns also show the political importance of the casualty gap. These results strongly suggest that the United States need not suffer even 5,000 casualties before the public turns against those in power. Rather, even a war with comparatively modest levels of casualties can have a substantial impact on congressional elections, as ruling-party candidates from states and counties that have suffered the heaviest losses bear the brunt of the popular backlash.

These results, in conjunction with those from the Vietnam era discussed in chapter 6, remind us of the very tangible, immediate political consequences of the casualty gap. Consistent with a large literature in political science, we find that Americans *do* respond to combat casualties by lowering their support for military operations and for the political leaders waging them. However, they do not do so *uniformly*. Rather, this backlash is most intense among citizens who have experienced the costs of war most intimately through the lens of their local communities. Beginning with the Korean War, the casualty gap has concentrated these costs disproportionately in socioeconomically disadvantaged communities and insulated many other Americans from direct exposure to the human costs of war. Because residents of socioeconomically disadvantaged communities possess fewer of the resources needed to engage in politics, the casualty gap decreases the political pressure that is brought to bear on military policymakers to change course. If the casualty gap did not exist, swing voters in affluent parts of the country, which exhibit higher levels of political participation, would be more exposed to local casualties. So primed, our analyses suggest that these Americans would be more likely to raise concerns about the costs of America's war efforts and ratchet up the pressure on the nation's political leaders.

We also believe, however, that the casualty gap may have even more fundamental and long-lasting effects. The next chapter provides considerable empirical evidence that the gravest consequences of the casualty gap for American democracy—the political disengagement of large segments of its citizenry—may linger for generations after a war ends.

Technical Appendix to Chapter 7

The full regression results used to derive the first differences presented in figures 7.1, 7.2, and 7.3, as well as in table 7.1, are presented in this appendix. Table 7A.1 presents the full results of a logistic regression that assesses the impact of knowing a soldier killed or wounded in Iraq on the probability that a respondent believed the war had affected him or her personally in a negative way. The dependent variable collapsed responses to the Gallup question into two categories—those who believed the war had affected them negatively versus those who did not. This latter category of respondents answered that the war either had affected them positively (13 percent) or had not had much of an effect on them at all (45 percent).[1] In addition to the personal contact with a killed or wounded soldier measure, the models also included controls for whether each respondent was a Republican or a Democrat, as well as measures of each respondent's age, gender, race, region, and educational attainment.[2] Finally, we also included a measure of whether each respondent viewed the Iraq War as a mistake. Replicating all of the models in table 7A.1 without this variable yields virtually identical results across specifications.

In the model of all respondents, the coefficient for the knowing a killed or wounded solider variable is positive and statistically significant. Moreover, the positive relationship continues to hold even when we disaggregate the sample and estimate separate regressions for independents,

Table 7A.1. Logit Analyses of Factors Influencing Whether the Iraq War Negatively Affected a Respondent Personally

	All	Independents	Republicans	Democrats
Know a casualty	0.98***	1.26**	1.12	0.70
	(0.34)	(0.55)	(0.71)	(0.51)
Education	0.07	0.00	0.10	0.16
	(0.07)	(0.14)	(0.15)	(0.12)
Male	−0.60***	−0.63*	−0.35	−0.73**
	(0.20)	(0.37)	(0.39)	(0.34)
Age	0.00	0.00	0.00	0.01
	(0.01)	(0.01)	(0.01)	(0.01)
Black	0.38	0.11	1.42	0.37
	(0.38)	(0.67)	(1.21)	(0.48)
South	−0.23	−0.12	0.15	−0.43
	(0.22)	(0.40)	(0.40)	(0.35)
Iraq a mistake	1.34***	1.54***	1.18***	1.20***
	(0.24)	(0.45)	(0.41)	(0.47)
Republican	−0.64**	—	—	—
	(0.27)			
Democrat	−0.07	—	—	—
	(0.24)			
Constant	−1.30**	−0.67	−2.55	−2.06
	(0.65)	(1.06)	(1.23)	(1.16)
Log-likelihood	−294.00	−88.38	−86.87	−111.40
Observations	510	147	177	176

All of the models report robust standard errors; all significance tests are two-tailed. $^*p<.10$, $^{**}p<.05$, $^{***}p<.01$.

Republicans, and Democrats. The estimated coefficient is strongest for independents; however, the casualties coefficient remains positive for all three partisan groups and is statistically significant ($p < .10$ on a one-tailed test).

Turning to the control variables, the first important difference between opinion dynamics on the war in Iraq and those that held during the Vietnam era is that, even for this basic, nonpolitical question, we observe the seeds of a partisan cleavage in how Americans view the war. Republican respondents were on average 16 percent less likely to believe that the war in Iraq had negatively affected them personally than were Democrats or independents with identical demographic characteristics. Aside from partisanship, the only other demographic control variable that had a statistically significant effect on feeling a negative personal connection with the war was gender. Consistent with the growing literature on the gender gap in opinion on military action, we find that men were much less likely than women—15 percent on average—to believe the war had negatively affected them directly.[3]

Finally, we see a clear, large divide between those respondents who believed that the war in Iraq was a mistake and those who did not. As we would expect, those that thought the war was a policy blunder of major proportions were considerably more likely to perceive its negative impact personally. Conversely, respondents who still believed the cause of the war to be just were unlikely to feel that the war had negatively impacted their lives.

Table 7A.2 presents the statistical results that generated the first differences presented in figure 7.2.[4] The first column estimates an ordered logit model to assess the impact of personal contact with a casualty on all

Table 7A.2. Ordered Logit and Logit Analyses of Factors Influencing Support for Withdrawing U.S. Forces from Iraq

	All Ordinal	Independents Binary	Republicans Binary	Democrats Binary
Know a casualty	0.29** (0.15)	0.76** (0.32)	−0.07 (0.47)	−0.31 (0.35)
Education	−0.09** (0.04)	−0.09 (0.08)	−0.07 (0.09)	−0.08 (0.08)
Male	−0.44*** (0.10)	−0.85*** (0.22)	−1.00*** (0.24)	−0.23 (0.22)
Age	−0.01*** (0.00)	−0.02*** (0.01)	−0.02* (0.01)	0.00 (0.01)
Black	0.94*** (0.22)	1.51** (0.70)	1.58** (0.68)	0.25 (0.39)
South	−0.20** (0.10)	−0.57*** (0.23)	−0.03 (0.24)	0.08 (0.25)
Iraq a mistake	1.77*** (0.13)	2.04*** (0.23)	1.96*** (0.25)	2.03*** (0.28)
Republican	−0.42*** (0.13)	—	—	—
Democrat	0.41*** (0.13)	—	—	—
Constant	—	1.26* (0.68)	0.12 (0.82)	0.14 (0.77)
Log-likelihood	−1754.11	−250.43	−230.55	−260.54
Observations	1,506	463	486	513

All of the models report robust standard errors; all significance tests are two-tailed. *p<.10, **p<.05, ***p<.01.

respondents' support for withdrawal on a four-point scale: (4) "Withdraw all troops from Iraq immediately"; (3) "Withdraw all troops by October 2007—that is, in twelve months' time"; (2) "Withdraw troops, but take as many years to do this as are needed to turn control over to the Iraqis"; (1) "Send more troops to Iraq." The coefficient for knowing a casualty is positive and statistically significant, which suggests that respondents who knew a soldier who had been killed or wounded in Iraq were more supportive of withdrawing U.S. forces from Iraq than their peers. However, if we disaggregate the data by partisan identification, we find that the effect of knowing casualties is significant only for independents.

To facilitate interpretation of the substantive size of the personal contact effects, we collapsed this ordinal variable into a binary one. Respondents who answered 4 or 3 on the withdrawal scale were coded as supporting withdrawal, while respondents who answered 2 or 1 were coded as opposing withdrawal. In columns 2–4 of table 7A.2, we estimate simple logit models identical in specification to the ordered logit analysis on this binary dependent variable for independent, Republican, and Democratic identifiers.[5] Here, as in the ordered logit analyses discussed earlier, we find that knowing a killed or wounded soldiers had a significant effect on support for withdrawal only among independents. The intense partisan dimension to casualties' influence on wartime opinions in the context of Iraq stands in sharp contrast to the Vietnam analyses we presented in the preceding chapter.

Except for education, all of the control variables had a statistically significant impact on support for withdrawal among independents. In this context, we find evidence of a gender gap; men were on average 15 percent more supportive of continuing and even escalating the war in Iraq than were women. Similarly, age again has a statistically and substantively significant relationship with opinion. However, in contrast to our results from the Vietnam War, in Iraq the relationship is in the expected negative direction. Young Americans, who are bearing the vast majority of the human costs of the war (and who will bear a disproportionate share of its monetary costs since the war is being financed almost exclusively through deficit spending), were considerably more likely to endorse plans to withdraw from Iraq than are older Americans. Consistent with the Vietnam era, African American respondents were consistently more likely to support withdrawal than were whites, while Southerners on average were 10 percent less likely to favor drawing down the U.S. military commitment in Iraq within the next year.

Finally, while not all Americans who believed the Iraq War was a mistake also supported withdrawal—indeed, a subset of Americans adopted former Secretary of State Colin Powell's Pottery Barn "if you break it, you fix it" rule and therefore supported a continued U.S. mission in Iraq, even though they disapproved of the initial decision to intervene—those that considered the war a mistake were also considerably more likely to favor an exit strategy. Such respondents were on average 45 percent more likely to favor ending the war in the next year than were independents who did not believe the war was a mistake.

A third set of analyses that used the Gallup polling data reported in table 7A.3 produced the first differences shown in figure 7.3. Logistic regressions allow us to investigate the effect of personal contact with a casualty on support for the Democratic candidate in the 2006 midterm elections while controlling for an individual's partisanship, education, gender, age, race, region, whether the respondent believed the invasion of Iraq was a mistake, and whether national or local issues were of

Table 7A.3. Logit Analyses of Factors Influencing Probability of Voting Democratic in 2006 Midterm Elections

	All	Independents	Republicans	Democrats
Know a casualty	0.16	0.66**	—	−0.50
	(0.29)	(0.35)		(0.92)
Education	0.09	0.10	0.00	0.20
	(0.07)	(0.09)	(0.21)	(0.20)
Male	−0.01	−0.13	0.49	0.45
	(0.20)	(0.25)	(0.48)	(0.64)
Age	0.00	0.00	−0.01	0.03*
	(0.01)	(0.01)	(0.02)	(0.02)
Black	0.85*	1.13**	—	1.42
	(0.45)	(0.56)		(1.20)
South	−0.28	−0.14	0.17	−1.38**
	(0.22)	(0.27)	(0.51)	(0.57)
National issues	0.36*	0.46*	−0.11	0.42
	(0.20)	(0.26)	(0.50)	(0.58)
Iraq a mistake	1.71***	1.68***	2.41***	0.66
	(0.22)	(0.28)	(0.47)	(0.75)
Republican	−1.63***	—	—	—
	(0.27)			
Democrat	3.36***	—	—	—
	(0.33)			
Constant	−2.24***	−2.29***	−3.38*	0.08
	(0.67)	(0.82)	(1.99)	(1.51)
Log-likelihood	−333.63	−190.69	−64.31	−49.17
Observations	996	316	281	337

All of the models report robust standard errors; all significance tests are two-tailed. *p < .10, **p < .05, ***p < .01.

Table 7A.4. Summary Statistics for Models of Change in GOP Vote Share from 2000 to 2006 Senate Elections

	State Level		County Level	
	Mean	Standard Deviation	Mean	Standard Deviation
Dependent variable				
Change in GOP vote share	–3.85	10.19	–5.54	14.56
Independent variables				
Iraq casualties	61.52	65.93	.85	2.48
Iraq casualty rate[a]	11.34	4.62	.13	.35
Change in opponent quality	.64	2.66	.66	2.88
Change in % GOP spending	.04	12.44	–.47	9.62
% Bush 2004	51.30	8.79	60.46	12.65
Change in unemployment	–.38	.35	–.46	.64
% Military age 18–64	.47	.61	.40	1.99
% Veterans	9.97	1.35	13.66	3.10

[a] Per one million residents at the state level; per ten thousand residents at the county level.

paramount importance in guiding the respondent's vote. Including this measure improves the model's fit; however, excluding it yields virtually identical results. Also, reestimating the models with state fixed effects instead of the South dummy variable yields virtually identical results.

When the model is estimated for all of the respondents, the coefficient for knowing an Iraq War casualty is positive, as expected; however, it fails to reach conventional levels of statistical significance. Estimating separate regressions for the three partisan groups shows that, for independents, personal contact with a casualty had a positive and statistically significant effect on their likelihood of supporting the Democratic congressional candidate. However, the models for Republicans and Democrats offer no evidence of a significant relationship between personal contact and the probability of these respondents voting Democratic in the 2006 midterms.[6]

Among the control variables in the independents model, only three had statistically significant correlations with support for the Democratic candidate. African American independents were more than 20 percent more likely to vote Democratic than were their nonblack peers. Also consistent with expectations, respondents who cited national issues as

Table 7A.5. The Impact of State and County Casualties on the Change in GOP Vote Share from 2000 to 2006 Senate Elections

	State	State	County	County	County: GOP Inc.	County: GOP Inc.
Iraq state casualty count	-0.01 (0.02)	—	—	—	—	—
Iraq state casualty rate	—	-1.46** (.59)	—	—	—	—
Iraq county casualty count	—	—	-0.23* (0.13)	—	-0.41** (0.17)	—
Iraq county casualty rate	—	—	—	-0.06 (0.59)	—	-0.99** (0.47)
Change in opponent quality	-0.69 (0.54)	-0.30 (0.58)	-1.82*** (0.11)	-1.82*** (0.11)	0.19* (0.11)	0.20* (0.11)
Change in % GOP spending	.25 (.18)	.33** (.14)	.03 (.03)	.03 (.03)	.73*** (.06)	.75*** (.06)
% Bush 2004	0.17 (0.32)	0.46 (0.28)	0.11*** (0.02)	0.12*** (0.03)	0.21*** (0.03)	0.23*** (0.03)
Change in unemployment	9.71 (5.94)	10.01* (5.07)	-0.14 (0.48)	-0.16 (0.48)	-0.16 (0.57)	-0.25 (0.57)
% Military	3.06 (3.29)	4.43* (2.24)	-0.13 (0.14)	-0.18 (0.15)	0.21* (0.13)	0.16 (0.11)
% Veterans	-1.09 (1.05)	.28 (1.23)	-0.31*** (0.10)	-0.28*** (0.10)	-0.81*** (0.12)	-0.81*** (0.12)
Constant	1.70 (16.67)	-12.69 (13.70)	-6.38 (2.21)	-7.75 (2.31)	2.53 (2.57)	1.14 (2.57)
Observations	31	31	1,856	1,856	993	993
R^2	.29	.41	.15	.15	.21	.20

All of the models report robust standard errors; all significance tests are two-tailed. * p < .10, ** p < .05, *** p < .01.

trumping state and local concerns in their voting calculus were considerably more likely to support the Democrats. Finally, independents who renounced the invasion of Iraq as a mistake were 35 percent more likely to vote Democratic than independents who did not.

Finally, the OLS regression analyses that we used to create the first differences illustrating the effects of state and local casualties on the change in Republican vote share from the 2000 to 2006 senatorial elections are reported in table 7A.5. After controlling for changes in a number of political variables, each model assesses the effect of local casualties on the change in the Republican candidate's vote share from the 2000 to the 2006 senatorial election.

The first two models investigate the effects of variance in local casualty rates on the change in the GOP's vote share at the state level. The second two models estimate identical analyses at a lower level of aggregation, the county level. The final pair of models reestimates the county-level models for the subset of Republicans who were most vulnerable to paying an electoral price for their support of the Iraq War: incumbents running for reelection. Table 7A.4 reports summary statistics for all of the variables at both the state and county levels used in these analyses.

8

The Casualty Gap and Civic Engagement

By the end of 2008, the sixth year of fighting in Iraq, millions of Americans had little or even no direct personal contact with the human costs of Operation Iraqi Freedom.[1] Even at the community level, exposure to casualties for many was limited. As a result, for many Americans, the war might have been only an abstract international and domestic political battleground with little immediate effect on their individual lives. However, as our analysis repeatedly demonstrates, some Americans have witnessed the war's costs more directly and painfully within their local community. Consider, for example, the residents of Hollidaysburg, Pennsylvania. Hollidaysburg is a small town of 5,500 in Blair County, Pennsylvania, fewer than twenty miles from Altoona. Its median income is approximately 20 percent below the state average, and its median home price in 2005 was a little less than $100,000. Despite its diminutive size, the residents of Hollidaysburg have experienced the costs of war in sharp relief through the deaths of four local servicemen in Iraq. The resulting casualty rate of almost one combat death per 1,000 residents dwarfs that of nearly every other community in the United States.

In the previous chapter, we explored the immediate political ramifications of such inequalities on public opinion and electoral outcomes. Consistent with these statistical results, media reports from Hollidaysburg provide anecdotal evidence that, even in this traditionally conservative

Republican town, the steep local costs of the Iraq War weighed on many and prompted increased calls for a change of course in Iraq.[2] Moreover, there is considerable evidence that these growing pressures also manifested themselves in the electoral arena. While Hollidaysburg's own Bill Shuster was easily reelected, fellow Republican Rick Santorum paid a heavy price in Blair County, dropping 15 percentage points from his previous showing in the 2000 senatorial contest.[3] Indeed, Santorum performed 10 percent worse in Blair County than President Bush did in his 2004 campaign. While the immediate political consequences of this and other unequal losses are considerable, this chapter expands the scope of analysis to examine the enduring influence of the casualty gap on citizens' political and civic engagement long after the last shots are fired.

It is perhaps too early to tell what long-term impact the war will have on Hollidaysburg, or any community with a similar experience, with regard to its residents' future patterns of political and civic engagement. However, past wars may offer important clues as to what the lingering costs of the Iraq War will be for civic life in the United States. The stalemate on the ground and the precipitous decline in public support for both the war and its leaders resemble the political environment of the early 1950s, as the Korean War drew to a close. Moreover, academics and pundits alike often compare the Iraq War to Vietnam. If the Iraq War continues to follow the trajectory of Korea or Vietnam, what might we expect the conflict's long-term impact to be on communities that, because of the casualty gap, suffered a disproportionate share of the human sacrifice on foreign battlefields? How might a community's wartime experience shape its residents' relationships with and attitudes toward the federal government? What consequences might such changes have on patterns of political and civic engagement?

Through a series of empirical analyses of individual-level survey data from the National Election Study and the Social Capital Benchmark Survey, as well as analysis of aggregate electoral turnout data at the county level, this chapter examines the immediate and lasting effects of the considerable variance in communities' wartime experience in Vietnam, Korea, and World War II on their residents' patterns of political engagement and participation. As we might expect, the analysis reveals very different dynamics in the wake of the three conflicts. Across the data sets, statistical models find that respondents from communities that suffered higher casualty rates in Vietnam and Korea reported lower levels of trust in government, interest in politics, and electoral and nonelectoral political participation than respondents with identical demographic characteristics from cities and towns that sustained lower casualty rates in these conflicts. By contrast, respondents from communities that endured the heaviest burdens in World War II were just as politically engaged as their peers, if not more so. However, while the conflicts in Vietnam and Korea may have fundamentally reshaped citizens' relationship with the federal government, our findings suggest that citizens did not let their resentment toward government policies affect all of their participatory activities. More nuanced data from the Social Capital Benchmark Survey reveal that Vietnam casualty rates had no discernible impact on nonpolitical forms of civic engagement such as charitable giving, volunteering, and organizational activity.

These statistical results take on added importance when viewed explicitly through the lens of the socioeconomic casualty gap that emerged in both Korea and Vietnam. When we remember the socioeconomic element of casualty inequality, our analysis in this chapter warns of a highly undemocratic cycle. Society demands the greatest wartime sacrifice from communities that already possess low levels of resources essential to civic life. These costs of war, in turn, further depress the active participation in government of the very groups with the greatest stake in forging the nation's critical military policy decisions.

WAR AND AMERICAN POLITICAL AND CIVIC ENGAGEMENT

Prior research has traced the way in which major conflicts such as the world wars and the American Civil War, have produced both sharp and sustained increases in citizens' political engagement, as well as greater public involvement in a myriad of nongovernmental civic organizations.[4] This literature proposes two distinct mechanisms that spur increased engagement: one in the political sphere, and one in the nonpolitical sphere.

Most analyses of increased engagement in the political realm emphasize the central role of what political scientists call "expressive benefits."[5] Successful wars can increase popular levels of trust in government, feelings of political efficacy, and conceptions of civic duty, all of which motivate citizens to bear the costs of participation.[6] By increasing the expressive benefits citizens derive from engaging in political life, victorious wars augment political participation.

Alternatively, while wars affect political participation by changing the national mood, they are linked to civic engagement writ large through the provision of tangible resources that can be put to use after the war is over. Conflicts that mass mobilize the public sector behind the war effort and forge public-private partnerships have the potential to spur civic voluntarism. They can create new and bolster existing civic organizations by broadly transmitting the civic skills necessary for a robust civil society.[7]

Prior scholarship has thus identified two separate linkages between war and subsequent participatory outcomes: (1) expressive benefits are linked to political engagement, and (2) resource provision is linked to nonpolitical engagement, such as associational life. In the wake of some wars, these mechanisms produce strong increases in political and nonpolitical participation. However, we argue that the consequences of each mechanism for engagement depend on a war's outcome and scale. The effect of a war on expressive benefits is contingent on whether it succeeds or fails, and a conflict's effect on resource provision is contingent on the level of mobilization required to wage it.

Let us look first at variation in the outcome of a war. While a successful war may increase civic pride and trust in government, unsuccessful wars may depress the expressive benefits citizens derive from participating in politics. Because citizens participate only when the expressive benefits they enjoy from participating exceed the costs of doing so, failed wars—far from spurring political activism—should undermine political engagement. Unsuccessful wars can reduce expressive benefits in at least two ways. First, as salient manifestations of failed government policies, they can decrease popular evaluations of governmental performance and competence. Second, a failed military action may undermine levels of popular trust in government. Indeed, scholars have explicitly linked the national experience in Vietnam with decreased levels of trust in national governing institutions.[8] Citizens who are more critical of the federal government's performance and competence and who have lower levels of trust in government should logically derive fewer expressive benefits from actively engaging in politics and therefore should possess fewer incentives to participate than their peers.

Alternatively, the literature on social movements suggests that a costly, unsuccessful war may paradoxically increase political engagement by creating and fostering grassroots movements to end the conflict.[9] Indeed, bloody foreign conflicts seem to be ready catalysts capable of helping many overcome the barriers to movement participation.[10] Combat casualties, combined with changes in political opportunity structure, which they help create, could both increase the incentives to participate and make mobilization more feasible.[11]

However, while wars may initially spur social movements and hence augment participation, such movements are difficult to sustain. In the case of the Vietnam antiwar movement, sociologists Douglas McAdam and Yang Su note that, after a peak in 1969, the movement waned considerably, and "by the time the Paris Peace Accords were signed in January of 1973, the movement was largely moribund."[12] There is considerable uncertainty about what happens to movement participants after the initial movement ends. As sociologist Michael Useem asks, "do they migrate to new protest causes or return to less intensely political lives, perhaps withdrawing from politics altogether?"[13] As a result, while social movements are a potential force countering mechanisms that decrease political engagement, whether they have a long-term positive effect on political activism, particularly once the movements die, is not clear.

We turn next to mobilization and its consequences for spurring nonpolitical participation through the provision of new associational resources. Here, the crucial distinction is that, just as Jocelyn Crowley and Theda Skocpol argue that it was "the *way* the Civil War was fought...[that] served to bolster federated voluntary activities," it is *how* a war directly involves the citizenry that determines whether those citizens will gain new participatory resources.[14] In mass mobilization wars, the involvement of large segments of the public in the war effort on the home front, including many who otherwise would lack the skills and resources normally needed for participation, greatly increases the number of citizens equipped to engage in civic life in the postwar period. Mass mobilization both strengthens engagement in civil society in the aftermath of victorious conflicts and may even increase nonpolitical engagement in the wake of a failed war. Evidence from the associational activities of Southern whites after the Civil War is consistent with this expectation. Skocpol's data from the Civil War era show that, while postwar associationalism increased most dramatically among the "victors" (Northerners and Southern blacks), associational memberships among Southern whites also grew.[15]

In small-scale wars, however, citizens are not mobilized behind the war effort in ways that provide new resources for organizational and associational engagement. Exposure to victory or defeat may affect an individual's political attitudes as described earlier, but this experience alone is not the equivalent of directly organizing, mobilizing, and participating in domestic war efforts. Regardless of the war's ultimate success or failure, if citizens do not experience these concrete activities during the war, the war will have little effect on their subsequent civic life. In short, when citizens do not participate in a war effort, we expect that the war will neither increase nor decrease their nonpolitical civic engagement.

Theoretical Expectations

Applying this theory, with its dual emphasis on the scale of a war and its ultimate outcome, to the U.S. experience in World War II, Korea, and Vietnam yields different predictions for each war's consequences for

Americans' subsequent levels of civic engagement. Because it mass mobilized society and ultimately produced a resounding U.S. victory that bolstered public confidence in government, World War II should have little negative impact on subsequent patterns of citizen engagement despite its ponderous death toll. Instead, as others have argued, the war likely fostered political and civic engagement nationwide.

Vietnam and Korea, however, differed on both dimensions. In contrast to World War II, they both were unsuccessful, low-mobilization wars. Our theory predicts that the ambiguous final results of these wars should lower political engagement. Without the unifying experience of national victory to bolster popular faith in government, the motive force behind earlier surges in postwar political engagement is absent. Indeed, in painting a contrast to World War II, political scientist Robert Putnam explicitly identifies the absence of victory as the factor that prevented a boom in political engagement following U.S. involvement in Korea or Vietnam: "Most Americans in 1945 felt that the war had been a just one and that their terrible collective sacrifice—all those sons and daughters who would not come home—had been in some measure vindicated by victory. This was not a feeling that would be repeated in the 1950s in Korea or in the 1960s in Vietnam."[16] Instead, because exposure to the government's costly failed policies decreased the expressive benefits citizens gain by participating in politics, we expect political engagement to decrease.[17]

Our theory also predicts that because Vietnam and Korea did not mass mobilize society on a war footing, we should see no changes in postwar associational life. Without high levels of direct involvement in the war efforts, the major public-private partnerships between government, business, and labor and civic associations, so prominent in 1917 and 1941, never materialized. As Theda Skocpol has noted, "the aftermath of every previous war in American history brought rising fraternal enrollments, especially among elites, but not the aftermath of the war in Vietnam."[18] If mass mobilization is the engine that leads to postwar associational booms, then there is little reason to expect limited wars to fuel nongovernmental civic engagement.

Thus, our theory predicts that the heavy toll that government military policies in Vietnam and Korea exacted on the public held the potential to depress Americans' levels of political engagement. Moreover, the analyses of each preceding chapter remind us that this toll is not experienced equally by all Americans.[19] Rather, some Americans saw the human costs of war much more acutely than others through the lens of their local communities. Since local casualties are not evenly distributed across the country, the consequences for the relationship between citizen and state after a war should not be equal, either. Rather, Americans from high-casualty communities should be more likely to disengage from the political arena than their fellow citizens from low-casualty communities, who were more insulated from the war's human costs.

If local casualty rates do fundamentally shape the way citizens evaluate their relationship with their government and the expressive benefits they derive from engaging in politics, then the potential consequences of the casualty gap for American society extend far beyond its immediate impact on wartime politics and political outcomes.

THE IMMEDIATE EFFECTS OF VIETNAM ON POLITICAL PARTICIPATION

To examine the ways in which the casualty gap may have lasting consequences for political engagement, we begin with Vietnam. To investigate its immediate ramifications for citizens' levels of political engagement, we first analyze National Election Study (NES) survey results for the ten years following the conflict's conclusion.

The NES affords an opportunity to explore the impact of local casualty rates on respondents' relationship with and attitudes toward the federal government along several dimensions. The first three models examine the effect of their community's experience with the war on respondents' incentives to participate in the political process—their evaluation of the federal government's performance, and trust in the national government. The next set of models explores the influence of local wartime experience on political engagement and participation directly by modeling the effect of local casualty rates on residents' interest in politics writ large and, most importantly, on citizens' propensity to vote.

As in the models in chapter 6, our main explanatory variable of interest is the casualty rate experienced by each respondent's county in the Vietnam War. However, to ensure that any observed relationships between respondents' local casualty rates and patterns of political and civic participation are not spurious, we also controlled for a host of demographic and contextual factors that might correlate with participation.

Building on an extensive literature on the individual-level determinants of civic and political participation, the models include variables for a number of individual-level demographic characteristics known to affect rates of participation.[20] Specifically, following prior analyses by political scientist J. Eric Oliver, the models include measures of each respondent's educational attainment, family income, race, gender, age, marital status, home ownership, length of residence in the community, and partisan affiliation.[21]

In addition to these individual characteristics, the models also include several contextual control variables at the county level. Our results in chapter 2 show unambiguously that poorer, economically depressed communities suffered a disproportionate share of the casualties in Vietnam. Other scholars also argue that communities with greater concentrations of racial minorities suffered high casualty rates. As a result, without suitable controls we cannot be sure that these communities' experience in Vietnam is producing observed correlations or whether other factors unfolding during the period—such as racial unrest, economic shocks, and the failure of Great Society programs—may also have depressed political engagement in precisely the same socioeconomically disadvantaged communities that bore disproportionately large shares of casualties. Accordingly, we control for each county's median income, unemployment rate, and percentage of residents who are not Caucasian.[22]

Finally, because our analysis pools responses from surveys taken in multiple years, the models also include dummy variables for each survey year.[23] All of the models also include state fixed effects. Summary statistics for all of the variables used in both the NES and the Social Capital Benchmark Survey (SCBS) analyses are presented in the technical appendix.

Results

Results from the NES analysis, summarized using a series of first differences in table 8.1, strongly suggest that the local effects of Vietnam significantly dampened citizens' incentives to engage in politics as well as their actual levels of political participation. Specifically, we analyzed the impact of local casualty rates on five measures of respondents' political engagement: (1) their approval of the federal government's performance; (2) their overall level of trust in government; (3) whether they trusted federal, state, or local government the least; (4) their interest in politics; and finally (5), whether they voted in the last election. Models 1, 2, and 4, which have ordinal dependent variables, were estimated by ordered probit analysis; models 3 and 5, which have binary dependent variables, were estimated using probit models. Full results for all of the models are reported in the technical appendix.

Examining respondents' evaluations of the federal government's performance, we find that judgments of the federal government were adversely affected by the casualty rate in a respondent's county. Respondents from counties that suffered disproportionate shares of the national sacrifice in Vietnam gave consistently lower evaluations of the federal government's performance than their peers, even after controlling for a host of demographic factors.

Table 8.1. The Impact of Vietnam Casualty Rates on NES Measures of Political Engagement, 1974–1982

Dependent variable		1 Casualty per 10K	11 Casualties per 10K	Change
Federal government's performance	% in lowest 3 categories	28%	34%	**6%**
Trust federal government	% in lowest 2 categories	70%	73%	3%
Trust federal government least	% yes	59%	74%	**15%**
Interest in politics	% in lowest 2 categories	45%	50%	**5%**
Voted in last election	% yes	68%	62%	**−6%**

Each row presents simulated first differences derived from the statistical models in table 8A.2. The final column presents the change in each dependent variable caused by a shift in a county's Vietnam casualty rate from 1 to 11 casualties per thousand male residents age 18–34 while holding all other variables constant at their means or medians. Statistically significant effects (p < .10, two-tailed test) are in bold.

In a pattern that is repeated across the models, the substantive effect of casualty rates, particularly relative to other traditional explanatory variables, is quite large. The average casualty rate suffered by U.S. counties during the Vietnam War was just under three soldiers killed per thousand men between the ages of 18 and 34 in that county.[24] However, there is considerable variance around that mean. More than 225 counties experienced a casualty rate of one or fewer men killed per thousand, while more than 100 counties suffered rates of more than ten casualties per thousand. Simulations holding all other variables constant at their means or medians show that respondents from counties that suffered death rates of eleven men per thousand were 6 percent more likely to give the federal government's performance one of the lowest three ratings on a nine-point scale than were respondents from counties with a casualty rate of one death per thousand. This shift of ten casualties per thousand represents a three standard deviation increase in the local Vietnam casualty rate. Relative to the influence of other standard control variables, this effect is substantial. For example, the 6 percentage point shift is double the difference between men and women and more than three times that produced by a two standard deviation increase in respondent education.

Perhaps more important, the impact of local Vietnam casualty rates was not limited to respondents' immediate evaluations of the government's performance. If the influence of casualties had stopped there, the lasting consequences of the Vietnam casualty gap for the polity may have been minimal. Both of our models of trust in government strongly suggest, however, that not only did local casualty rates shape Americans' judgments of the government's job performance, but, more fundamentally, they also influenced respondents' trust in national governing institutions. In the first model, which explores the factors that influenced the respondents' overall levels of trust in the federal government, the NES asked respondents (on a four-point scale) how often they trusted their leaders in Washington. Consistent with the hypothesis that respondents will blame the federal government for local wartime deaths, the coefficient for Vietnam casualty rates is negative but narrowly misses conventional levels of statistical significance. However, low trust in the federal government may be a symptom of low levels of trust in government in general. Casualties should have a significant effect on respondents' trust in the federal government, but not necessarily on their feelings toward state and local leaders. Indeed, the results from our model with regard to whether respondents trusted the federal government less than their state or local governments provide strong evidence of a genuine link between the severity of a community's Vietnam War experience and its residents' levels of trust in the national government. Even after controlling for race, gender, education, income, and other individual- and county-level characteristics, this model strongly suggests that local casualty rates had a strong impact on the probability that respondents would have the least faith in the federal government. First differences derived from simulations show that increasing the casualty rate from one per thousand to eleven per thousand, while holding all other variables constant at their means or medians, dramatically increased the probability of having the lowest level of trust in the federal government by more than 15 percent.

A great deal of existing scholarship on social capital and civic and political engagement places a premium on trust and norms of reciprocity both among private citizens and between citizen and state.[25] Consequently, high local casualty rates, at least in part because of the decreased trust in government they yield, may have widespread consequences for levels of political engagement and participation.[26] Indeed, when coupled with decreased approval of the government's performance, lowered levels of trust in government may decrease the expressive benefits citizens stand to reap from engaging in politics and the political process, which in turn should depress their levels of political engagement and participation. The results from our final two models are consistent with this conjecture.

Our fourth model, which explores respondents' interest in politics, confirms expectations that Americans from high-casualty counties emerged from the Vietnam War less engaged in politics than those from low-casualty communities. The relationship is both statistically and substantively significant; simulations suggest that increasing the county casualty rate by ten per thousand raises the probability that a respondent will express one of the two lowest levels of interest in politics by 5 percent. Again, the relative degree of casualties' impact is substantial compared to that of some other key variables that influence political engagement. For example, this estimated effect for casualties equals the 5 percentage point swing caused by a two standard deviation drop in family income. Education, however, remains a much more powerful predictor of respondents' political interest, as the casualty effect is only 40 percent of that produced by a one standard deviation increase in respondent education.

Finally, our model of respondents' voting behavior demonstrates that citizens' differential exposure to the human costs of the Vietnam War also influenced the quintessential act of democratic participation: voting. The probit model yields a strong, negative coefficient for local casualty rates; respondents from high-casualty communities were systematically less likely to vote in national elections in the years immediately following Vietnam than were their peers in lower-casualty areas. It bears repeating that this negative relationship remains robust even after including a host of individual- and county-level controls. Thus, it is not the case that all socioeconomically disadvantaged counties experienced equally lower levels of political engagement in the years immediately following Vietnam; rather, even after accounting for these factors, respondents from high-casualty communities had lower levels of political engagement than their peers with identical personal and community-level demographic characteristics.

Substantively, the estimated size of casualties' effect on voting is substantial. First differences holding all other variables constant at their means or medians suggest that increasing the casualty rate by ten per thousand decreases the probability that a respondent voted by 6 percent, from 68 percent to 62 percent. This change in probability exceeds that produced by a two standard deviation decrease in family income and is slightly more than half that generated by a one standard deviation decrease in respondent education.

Because the NES asked three of these five questions *before* the Vietnam War, as a robustness check we were able to reestimate the analyses with prewar data to insure that residents of these high casualty rate counties were not always less politically engaged than their peers. In each case, the prewar models find no evidence of any significant relationship between county casualty rates and political engagement, and in two of the three models the relevant coefficients are actually positive in the prewar period. We refer readers to the technical appendix for a full presentation and discussion of these results.

Table 8.2. The Impact of Vietnam Casualty Rates on County-Level Presidential Turnout, 1956–1988

	1956	1960	1964	1968	1972	1976	1980	1984	1988
Coefficient	−66	−76	−36	**−153**	**−107**	**−164**	−55	6	−6
P-value	.19	.21	.48	**.01**	**.03**	**.00**	.13	.84	.87
T/O effect	−.5%	−.6%	−.2%	−1.2%	−1.4%	−2.1%	−.7%	0%	0%

This table presents the results of an ordinary least squares regression analysis that assesses the influence of a county's Vietnam casualty rate on its turnout in presidential elections from 1956 to 1988. The bottom row presents the estimated cumulative effect of Vietnam War casualties on turnout. It was generated by first multiplying each county's casualty rate by the relevant coefficient, then summing across counties, and finally dividing this sum by the total number of voters. Statistically significant effects ($p < .10$, two-tailed test) are in bold.

Finally, if the NES results are correct and citizens from high-casualty counties are less likely to vote than their peers from low-casualty communities, then aggregate-level turnout should also decrease in counties that suffered the highest casualty rates in Vietnam. Thus, as a further robustness check we analyzed turnout data from more than three decades of presidential elections from 1956 to 1988. For each presidential contest, we modeled the number of citizens who voted in each county as a function of the number that voted in the previous presidential election, the county's casualty rate in Vietnam, and three county-level contextual controls: each county's unemployment rate, percentage of the population that was nonwhite, and educational attainment. Results from this analysis are presented in table 8.2.

If our theory is correct, then we should see the most significant effects of casualties in the years during and immediately after the Vietnam War. Taken collectively, the new round of analysis provides considerable, if not unconditional support for this theory. We find that the only three statistically significant casualty coefficients are those for the last two war-time elections and for the election immediately following the war's conclusion. Equally important, the magnitude of the estimated relationship between a county's casualty rate and decreased turnout is much greater during the war and in the immediate postwar elections. The average decrease in overall turnout because of declining participation in high-casualty communities during the prewar years was about -0.4 percent per year.[27] In the three wartime elections, the average decrease in turnout generated by declining participation in high-casualty communities was -1.6 percent per year. After 1976, the estimated turnout effect again declined to an average of -0.2 percent per year. As a result, while the evidence suggests that something may have already been afoot depressing turnout in counties that would later suffer high casualty rates in Vietnam before the war, the additional analysis provides strong evidence that turnout in these counties decreased most dramatically in the last two elections of the war and in the first one after its completion.

Often when scholars think of the Vietnam War and its ramifications for the American polity, they concentrate on the war's effect on society as a whole. Yet, the results in this chapter make clear that the lingering ramifications of Vietnam are also spread unevenly across various segments of the nation. Having seen the costs of failed military policies most starkly through the lens of their community, Americans from high-casualty counties were disproportionately likely to disengage from the political process altogether.

THE LINGERING EFFECTS OF VIETNAM ON CIVIC ENGAGEMENT

The National Election Studies analysis unambiguously demonstrates the immediate impact of variance in local communities' Vietnam War experiences on their inhabitants' trust and confidence in government, interest in politics, and patterns of political participation. However, the engagement measures included in the NES are rather limited, and, consequently, the preceding analysis cannot capture the full range of Vietnam's influence on various individuals' political and civic activities. Did the decline in trust, interest in politics, and the general reevaluation of many citizens' relationship with their government wrought by Vietnam affect only voting? Or did the war also dampen other forms of electoral and nonelectoral political participation among citizens from areas that suffered the conflict's human costs disproportionately?

To answer these questions and examine the impact of casualty rates on a wider range of participatory activities, the analysis exploits the rich array of data in the 2000 Social Capital Benchmark Survey. The SCBS is comprised of both a national survey of more than 3,000 individuals from more than 1,100 counties and an intensive sample of more than 26,000 respondents from 41 communities spread across twenty-nine states. Moreover, it measures an extraordinary range of political and nonpolitical participatory activities. The subsequent analyses focus on four broad indices: electoral political participation, nonelectoral political participation, civic organizational participation, and charitable participation. The SCBS Electoral Politics Index comprises two measures of political participation—registering to vote and voting in national elections—a measure of respondents' political interest and two questions that gauge levels of political knowledge. The Nonelectoral Politics Index tracks respondents' participation in a range of political activities from signing a petition to joining a political group to engaging in a rally, march, protest, or boycott.

The SCBS data also allow us to determine whether low-mobilization wars fail to affect significantly levels of nonpolitical civic activity. Because Vietnam did not mass mobilize the country on a war footing, citizens did not gain the types of extra experiences, skills, and resources that fostered greater postwar associational engagement in the wake of previous conflicts. We use two SCBS measures to test our theory. The Organizational Activity Index examines respondents' nonpolitical civic participation, including involvement in civic groups and clubs, serving in leadership capacities within these organizations, and participating in public meetings. Finally, the Charitable Activity Index assesses the scope of respondents' volunteering and financial contributions to a range of religious and secular charitable groups.

For each of these four dependent variables, we estimated an OLS regression model (with state fixed effects and standard errors clustered on county) that is virtually identical in specification to the NES models discussed earlier.[28] In addition to the casualty rate suffered by each county in terms of servicemen killed per thousand men age 18 to 34, the models control for individuals' educational attainment, family income, race, gender, age, marital status, home ownership, and length of residence in the community. To control for community demographics, we again include measures of median family income, the unemployment rate, and the percentage of the community that is not Caucasian. Summary statistics for all of the dependent and independent variables and complete results from the statistical models are presented in the technical appendix.

Results

The SCBS analysis suggests that Vietnam had lingering consequences for political aspects of citizens' civic engagement but not for their participation in nonpolitical activities. The effects of local casualty rates in Vietnam on our four indices of political and civic engagement are summarized in table 8.3.

Consistent with the NES results in table 8.1, which show the immediate negative impact of high Vietnam casualty rates on interest in politics and voting, our electoral participation model finds that, more than twenty years since the last U.S. troops evacuated Saigon, respondents from areas that bore disproportionate shares of the nation's human costs in the Vietnam War remained less interested in politics and less likely to participate in political activities than their fellow citizens from other parts of the country.

Table 8.3. The Impact of Vietnam Casualty Rates on SCBS Measures
of Political and Civic Engagement

	Standard deviation change in index
Electoral Politics Index	**−.08**
Nonelectoral Politics Index	**−.11**
Organizational Activity Index	−.01
Charitable Activity Index	.08

This table presents simulated first differences derived from the statistical models in table 8A.3. The second column presents the change in each dependent variable caused by a shift in a county's Vietnam casualty rate from 1 to 11 casualties per thousand male residents age 18–34 while holding all other variables constant at their means or medians. Statistically significant effects ($p < .10$, two-tailed test) are in bold.

That we continue to see a political participatory gap between high- and low-casualty communities decades after the Vietnam War ended may seem surprising. However, we should not conclude from this result that the conflict is continuing to *actively* depress engagement in these communities twenty years later. Indeed, our county-level turnout analyses suggest that the negative effects of the war were concentrated in the latter stages of the conflict itself and in its immediate aftermath. What our analysis suggests is that a participatory gap emerged in the aftermath of the Vietnam War between residents of high- and low-casualty communities and that subsequent events have not eliminated that gap. Other national forces almost certainly have affected aggregate levels of participation in the intervening years, but they have not eliminated the gap that developed in the late 1960s and early 1970s because they have not raised participation more in high-casualty communities than in low-casualty communities.[29]

As in the NES results, the effect of local casualty rates on political participation is smaller than for other traditional predictors of engagement, though still substantial. For example, the decrease in political participation caused by a three standard deviation increase in a county's casualty rate is more than 60 percent of that produced by a one standard deviation decrease in respondent income and is almost a third of that generated by a one standard deviation decrease in respondent education.

Moreover, the results from our analysis of respondents' nonelectoral participation suggest that the lingering effects of Vietnam were not limited to the electoral realm. Exposure to the costs of the war through the lens of their local community appears to have depressed citizens' willingness to engage government through both direct *and* indirect means. Our analysis shows that respondents from high-casualty areas also were less likely to join political, ethnic, or labor groups, sign petitions, or actively participate in organizations that seek governmental reform than respondents with identical personal and demographic characteristics from areas with less severe experiences in Vietnam. Substantively, the size of casualties' effect on nonelectoral forms of political participation is again large; an increase of ten casualties per thousand in the county decreases nonelectoral participatory activities by the same amount as a one standard deviation decrease in income levels and almost half as much as a one standard deviation decrease in respondent education.

Finally, our models of respondents' political participation in civic organizations and charitable giving expand the scope of analysis to explore whether inequalities in local Vietnam casualty rates also had consequences for nonpolitical forms of participation (table 8.3, rows 3 and 4). Both models suggest they have not. The coefficient for the effect of casualties on civic organizational participation is substantively and statistically insignificant, while the relevant coefficient in the charitable giving model is actually positive, which suggests that residents of high-casualty communities may actually be more active in nongovernmental activities than their peers.

That local casualties did not have a significant negative effect on nonpolitical participation is consistent with our argument; when a war involves low mobilization, it fails to generate the types of participatory resources that citizens can transfer to the nonpolitical realm once the war is over. Put another way, in low mobilization wars citizens do not build as many "human links" among themselves as they do when they share in the nation's high mobilization war efforts.[30] Without these community links the war does not touch nonpolitical civic life, and when the war ends, its effects are restricted to the political realm. However, by reshaping the relations between governors and governed and by depressing the expressive benefits citizens derived from engaging government, exposure to the human costs of failed wartime policies dampened political participation in high-casualty communities.[31]

KOREA, WORLD WAR II, AND PATTERNS OF POLITICAL ENGAGEMENT

While the preceding analyses find strong evidence that exposure to high local casualty rates in the Vietnam War reduced citizens' subsequent levels of political participation, generalizing from these models to speculate on other wars' likely effects on engagement may be complicated by the tumultuous times of the 1960s and 1970s. Racial unrest, the unraveling of the Great Society, Watergate, and economic stagflation all tore at the fabric of American society during the Vietnam era. Of course, for the observed relationship between a county's casualty rate and engagement to be spurious, these other forces must be correlated with a county's casualty rate, independent of community-level economic conditions and racial composition. There is no immediate reason to suggest that this should be so. However, the turbulent times raise the possibility that the casualty gap will not have the same effects on political engagement in less chaotic and poisonous political environments.

An additional question is whether the observed negative relationship between local casualty rates and depressed political engagement characterizes all conflicts or just non-mass-mobilizing, unsuccessful wars. If battle deaths from one's local community inherently depress participation, then we should observe similar dynamics after all major conflicts. However, our theory suggests that exposure to a war's human costs should depress engagement only when it compels citizens to reevaluate negatively their relationship with the government and decrease the expressive benefits they derive from participating in politics. If our theory is correct, then casualties suffered in successful conflicts that enjoy broad-based popular support should not stifle participation. To the extent that they are viewed as patriotic sacrifices in the service of the nation, those casualties may even increase civic pride and participation.

To explore these possibilities, the analysis shifts focus from Vietnam to first the Korean War and then to World War II. Beginning in 1956, the NES reported respondents' home county, and over the next five surveys leading up to the Vietnam conflict the NES asked many of the same questions examined in table 8.1. This affords us an opportunity to determine whether variance in local casualty rates in the Korean War also depressed respondents' levels of trust in government, interest in politics, and propensity to vote. Except for the exclusion of home ownership and length of residence measures, which were not included in these earlier surveys, the model specifications remain identical to those in the Vietnam era.

Results

The effects of Korean casualties on our three measures of political engagement are summarized in table 8.4. Full results for all of the models are presented in the technical appendix. Beginning with an analysis of trust in government, our first model suggests an important difference between the Korean and the Vietnam conflicts. While the estimated relationship between the Korean casualty rate sustained by a respondent's community and his or her trust in government is negative, the coefficient is not statistically significant. Moreover, as the first differences in table 8.4 show,

Table 8.4. The Impact of Korean Casualty Rates on NES Measures of Political Engagement, 1956–1964

Dependent variable		0.5 Casualties per 10K	5.5 Casualties per 10K	Change
Trust in federal government	% in lowest 2 categories	27%	28%	1%
Interest in politics	% in lowest 2 categories	25%	29%	**4%**
Voted in last election	% yes	84%	82%	–2%
Voted in last presidential election	% yes	83%	79%	**–4%**

Each row presents simulated first differences derived from the statistical models in the first four columns of table 8A.4. The final column presents the change in each dependent variable caused by a shift in a county's casualty rate from 0.5 to 5.5 casualties per ten thousand residents while holding all other variables constant at their means or medians. Statistically significant effects ($p < .10$, two-tailed test) are in bold.

the substantive size of the estimated effect is trivial as well. Unlike in the Vietnam models, there is little empirical evidence that respondents from counties that suffered disproportionately large casualty rates in Korea reported lower levels of trust in the national government than their peers from lower-casualty communities.

However, our models of respondents' interest in politics and voting behavior both show strong relationships between local casualty rates and respondents' political engagement, which parallel those observed in the Vietnam-era analysis. We find a strong negative relationship between a respondent's local Korean casualty rate and his or her interest in politics. Moreover, the relationship is substantively important. As in Vietnam, there was considerable variance in the distribution of Korean War casualties across the country. For example, more than 300 counties experienced casualty rates of fewer than 0.5 casualties per 10,000 residents, while more than 100 counties suffered casualty rates exceeding 5.5 battle deaths per 10,000 residents. Simulations reveal that such a shift in a county's casualty rate—a one standard deviation increase—increased the probability that a respondent would report one of the two lowest categories of interest in politics by 4 percent. Relative to other traditional explanatory variables, the size of the effect is considerable; it almost equals that produced by a one standard deviation decrease in respondent income and is roughly half that generated by a one standard deviation drop in respondent education.

In addition to affecting citizens' interest in politics, the experience of a respondent's community in the Korean conflict also appears to have influenced his or her probability of voting in national elections. When we analyze the effect of local Korean War casualties on voting patterns in all five elections in our sample, the estimated relationship is negative as expected, though the regression coefficient fails to reach conventional levels of statistical significance. However, if the Korean casualty gap did influence voting patterns, its impact should be most apparent in presidential elections, which normally mobilize a greater number of less-engaged voters, who are particularly susceptible to pressures simply to stay home. When we narrow our scope to the three presidential election-year surveys in our sample, the estimated negative coefficient for Korean casualties is even larger and is statistically significant. Simulations suggest that an increase of five casualties per 10,000 residents in a county's casualty rate depressed respondents' probability of voting by 4 percent. This decrease almost exactly parallels that caused by a one standard deviation decrease in respondent income and is almost half that produced by a one standard deviation drop in respondent education.

Shifting to the aggregate level again bolsters our confidence that the observed negative effect of local Korean wartime experience on voting is real. Drawing on county turnout data from seven presidential election results from 1940 to 1964, we again modeled each county's vote total in an election year as a function of the county total in the preceding election, its casualty rate in the Korean War, and three county-level controls: measures of its unemployment rate, racial composition, and median educational attainment. Results are summarized in table 8.5.

The aggregate results again suggest that local experience with the human costs of the Korean War decreased turnout in presidential elections.[32] In strong accordance with our theoretical expectations, the

Table 8.5. The Impact of Korean Casualty Rates on County-Level Presidential Turnout, 1940–1964

	1940	1944	1948	1952	1956	1960	1964
Coefficient	−11	−3	−8	**−37**	−2	−13	−9
P-value	.24	.61	.26	**.10**	.75	.37	.43
Turnout effect	−.1%	.0%	−.1%	**−.4%**	.0%	−.1%	.0%

This table presents the results of an ordinary least squares regression analysis that assesses the influence of a county's Korean War casualty rate on its voter turnout in presidential elections from 1940 to 1964. The bottom row presents the estimated cumulative effect of Korean War casualties on turnout. It was generated by first multiplying each county's casualty rate by the relevant coefficient, then summing across counties, and finally dividing this sum by the total number of voters. Statistically significant effects (p < .10, two-tailed test) are in bold.

coefficient for Korean War casualties in 1952, the only presidential election held during the war itself, is by far the largest coefficient for any year, and, indeed, it is the only statistically significant relationship observed across the seven elections. The estimated size of the casualties effect in 1952 is also by far the largest, more than tripling that for any other electoral contest.

Substantively, the overall size of the estimated decrease in turnout due to Korea is modest, particularly in comparison to the large effects for Vietnam. Our analysis suggests that turnout in 1952 decreased by only about half a percentage point as a result of war casualties. However, the estimated effect on turnout of local casualties in high-casualty communities was considerable, and even at the national level, our models suggest that in 1952 the war caused more than a quarter million voters to stay home from the polls.

While our analyses at both the individual and the aggregate level provide strikingly consistent evidence that exposure to high local casualty rates in the Korean and Vietnam wars significantly dampened citizens' subsequent levels of political engagement and participation, the foregoing models leave open the question of whether local casualties always depress political engagement in the hardest-hit communities. To seek additional leverage on this question, we replicated our interest in politics and presidential voting models with an additional covariate—each county's casualty rate in World War II. First differences from these expanded models are presented in table 8.6. Full results are reported in the technical appendix.

Table 8.6. The Impact of Korean and World War II Casualty Rates on NES Measures of Political Engagement, 1956–1964

		Korean casualty change	WWII casualty change
Interest in politics	% in lowest 2 categories	**5%**	−1%
Voted in last presidential election	% yes	**−5%**	4%

Each row presents simulated first differences derived from the statistical models in the final two columns of table 8A.4. The Korean casualty change column shows the estimated effect of a shift from 0.5 to 5.5 casualties per ten thousand county residents while holding all other variables constant at their means or medians. The World War II casualty change column shows the estimated effect of a shift from 15 to 40 casualties per ten thousand county residents while holding all other variables constant at their means or medians. Statistically significant effects (p < .10, two-tailed test) are in bold.

Even when we add the World War II measure to our model of respondents' interest in politics, the coefficient for local Korean War casualty rates remains negative and substantively and statistically significant. Respondents from communities that suffered high casualty rates in the Korean War were considerably more likely to report low levels of interest in politics than their peers from low-casualty communities. Table 8.6 shows that a one standard deviation increase in a community's Korean casualty rate increased its residents' probability of expressing the lowest levels of interest in politics by 5 percent. By contrast, the models offered little evidence that World War II casualties dampened interest in politics, even in counties that suffered the greatest number of casualties in the war. The first differences in table 8.6 report the effect on respondents' interest in politics of moving from a community that suffered fifteen deaths per 10,000 residents in World War II (about 400 counties experienced a casualty rate of this level or lower) to a community that experienced forty deaths per 10,000 residents (about 100 counties suffered a casualty rate this high or higher). This shift had almost no effect on the likelihood of a respondent's being in the lowest two levels of political interest; in fact, all else being equal, it may have even lowered this probability.

The revised model of respondents' voting behavior in presidential elections reveals a similar pattern. While the relationship between Korean casualty rates and voting remains negative and significant, the coefficient for a county's World War II casualty rate is positive and only narrowly misses conventional levels of statistical significance. Respondents from communities that suffered high local casualty rates in Korea were about 5 percent less likely to vote than their peers, while respondents from counties that suffered high casualty rates in World War II may have been even more likely to vote than other respondents with identical demographic characteristics. Consistent with Putnam, Skocpol, Mettler, and others who have documented how World War II provided the impetus behind the long civic generation, our models suggest that respondents from counties that made the greatest human sacrifice in that conflict emerged, if anything, with even greater levels of political engagement than their peers from counties that suffered lower casualty rates.

CONCLUSION

While scholars have long recognized that war has the potential to reshape the relationship between state and society, no consensus has developed as to precisely *how* that relationship will change in the wake of a conflict.[33] Our analysis of Vietnam, Korea, and World War II demonstrates that all wars do not have the same lingering consequences for democratic engagement. War can affect patterns of participation years after a truce or peace is reached, but the direction and magnitude of a war's participatory effects vary with the conduct, perception, and human costs of the conflict.

Perhaps even more importantly, our analysis demonstrates that even a failed war does not, as is so often implicitly assumed, affect all Americans uniformly; rather, its costs and consequences are concentrated in those communities that bear a disproportionate share of the price in blood. Moreover, the political ramifications of the casualty gap do not end once the last gun falls silent. In a 1967 speech titled "The Casualties of the War in Vietnam," the Rev. Dr. Martin Luther King Jr. reminded his audience that the war's repercussions would remain with the nation for years to come: "We are all aware of the nightmarish physical casualties...But the physical casualties of the war in Vietnam are not alone the catastrophes. The casualties of principles and values are equally disastrous and injurious. Indeed, they are ultimately more harmful because they are self-perpetuating."[34]

Our empirical findings echo King's belief that the high costs of war casualties can extend deep into American society and, when the war is unsuccessful, may contribute to a feedback loop further depressing political engagement. The Korean and Vietnam casualty gaps concentrated both wars' human costs among socioeconomically disadvantaged communities. Instead of receiving government services, these communities were asked to bear disproportionate shares of wartime sacrifice. As a result, those communities with the greatest stake in government military policy decisions and the greatest need for government assistance paradoxically became increasingly disengaged from the political process. In this way, the casualty gap may threaten the very fabric of representative democracy.

Technical Appendix to Chapter 8

This appendix presents the full results and additional discussion of all of the analyses used to generate the results in tables 8.1–8.6. Before we present the results, however, a methodological caveat is in order: Attempting to discern the effects of community-level variables on individual behavior poses inherent problems and raises the distinct possibility of selection bias.[1] The selection bias problem is particularly acute for many contextual arguments that assert the importance of factors such as city size, population density, urban design, and socioeconomic segregation because individuals with strong predispositions toward certain patterns of political and civic participation may self-select into specific types of neighborhoods and communities.[2] The prospects for selection bias are considerably less, however, in the context of our analyses. While less civically inclined individuals may logically choose neighborhoods with certain characteristics in terms of size, density, and balance between residential, commercial, and industrial zones, it is unlikely that they would consciously seek out communities that bore disproportionate shares of casualties in Vietnam, Korea, or World War II.

Moreover, in the case of Vietnam, because the NES asked three of the five questions analyzed before the war, the time series affords a unique opportunity to determine whether residents of these high-casualty-rate counties always possessed lower levels of political trust, interest in politics, and participation. After presenting the statistical models used to generate the predicted effects discussed in the chapter, we present two sets of robustness checks, one of which replicates our Vietnam models with pre-war data. These checks greatly improve our confidence that the observed correlations are genuine, not spurious.

Summary statistics for all of the variables included in the NES and SCBS analyses are summarized in table 8A.1.

The models in table 8A.2 assess the impact of local casualty rates in Vietnam on five measures of respondents' political engagement. These models include data from the 1974, 1976, 1978, 1980, and 1982 surveys. All of the data were taken from the NES cumulative data file. Adjusting the time horizon of the years analyzed yields virtually identical results across specifications. In addition to the county-level contextual variables discussed in the text, we also reestimated all of the models with a variety of alternative contextual control variables, many of which are highly correlated, including percentage of residents living in urban areas, population density, median education, and median age. All of the results are virtually identical across specifications. In all but the trust in government model, the coefficient for a respondent's county casualty rate is negative and statistically significant. Both the demographic and contextual control variables also largely accord with theoretical expectations standard in the literature. Most importantly, individual-level education and income are strong predictors of trust and political engagement, while respondents from poor communities with high concentrations of minorities are less politically engaged.[3]

Having established a robust relationship between local casualty rates in Vietnam and political participation in the years immediately following the war, the analysis next examined the effect of Vietnam casualty rates on a broader array of political and civic behaviors from the 2000 Social Capital Benchmark Survey. The specific variable names within the SCBS are ELECPOL2, PROTEST, MACHER, and CHARITY2. Each variable is a continuous index constructed according to the equations outlined in the SCBS codebook. The models are identical in specification to those estimated with the NES data with only a few minor exceptions. The SCBS did not ask individuals for their partisan affiliation; hence, these indicators are not included in the analysis. For the community-level income and percent minority controls, we used the SCBS's measures of mean family income in community and percent nonwhite in community. We also added county-level unemployment from the 2000 census. Since the community sample comprises the vast majority of the observations, the models were also reestimated with community fixed effects and clustered standard errors with virtually identical results. Alternatively, the

Table 8A.1. Summary Statistics for Dependent and Independent Variables, All Models

	Mean	Standard Dev.
National Election Study		
Dependent variables		
Federal government's performance	3.839	1.528
Trust federal government	2.461	.633
Trust federal government least	.471	.499
Interest in politics	2.754	1.060
Voted in last election	.634	.482
Independent variables		
Vietnam casualty rate (per 1K men 18–34)	3.523	3.291
Korea casualty rate (per 10K residents)	2.299	4.976
World War II casualty rate (per 10K residents)	22.934	9.561
Republican	.331	.470
Democrat	.536	.499
Education	3.292	1.760
Income	2.888	1.162
White	.872	.334
Male	.440	.496
Married	.700	.458
Age	45.598	16.862
Own home	.699	.459
Length of residence in community	27.783	28.678
% Nonwhite in county	.110	.111
Median family income in county (in $1,000s)	9.498	2.188
% Unemployed in county	.043	.018
Social Capital Benchmark Survey		
Dependent variables		
Electoral Politics Index	3.058	1.324
Nonelectoral Politics Index	1.125	1.387
Organizational Activity Index	.067	1.038
Charitable Activity Index	5.202	4.305
Independent variables		
Vietnam casualty rate (per 1K men 18–34)	3.523	3.291
Education	3.652	1.840
Income	3.179	2.052
White	.729	.443
Male	.411	.492
Married	.511	.500
Age	44.756	16.703
Own home	.696	.460
Length in community	3.572	1.485
% Nonwhite in community	.282	.155
Mean family income in community (in $10Ks)	3.168	.357
% Unemployed in county	.037	.016

Table 8A.2. Regression Analyses of Relationships between Vietnam Casualty Rates and NES Measures of Political Participation, 1974–1982

	Federal government's performance	Trust federal government	Trust federal government least	Interest in politics	Voted in last election
Vietnam casualty	−.016**	−.007	.040**	−.012***	−.016**
rate	(.007)	(.004)	(.019)	(.004)	(.007)
Republican	.132***	.182***	−.033	.355***	.555***
	(.054)	(.049)	(.099)	(.042)	(.055)
Democrat	.093*	.203***	−.008	.371***	.515***
	(.049)	(.048)	(.093)	(.040)	(.052)
Education	.018	.038***	.013	.221***	.228***
	(.012)	(.010)	(.021)	(.010)	(.012)
Income	−.023	−.013	.020	.069***	.067***
	(.021)	(.016)	(.032)	(.016)	(.018)
White	−.064	.132**	.030	−.013	.028
	(.067)	(.057)	(.082)	(.044)	(.049)
Male	−.104***	.060**	−.057	.289***	.062*
	(.031)	(.027)	(.058)	(.029)	(.036)
Married	−.060	−.021	.015	.072***	.179***
	(.041)	(.037)	(.070)	(.029)	(.044)
Age	−.004***	.000	−.005**	.016***	.018***
	(.001)	(.001)	(.002)	(.001)	(.001)
Own home	.020	−.056	.042	.033	.289***
	(.045)	(.035)	(.067)	(.034)	(.046)
Length of res.	.000	.000	.003**	.000	.004***
in community	(.001)	(.001)	(.002)	(.000)	(.001)
% Nonwhite in	−.380**	−.809***	−1.464***	.116	−.253
county	(.196)	(.166)	(.347)	(.179)	(.254)
Median family	−.025**	.002	−.008	−.017	−.015
income in county	(.011)	(.010)	(.026)	(.012)	(.015)
% Unemployed	−.531	−.249	−4.412	.600	1.246
in county	(1.190)	(1.339)	(2.847)	(1.721)	(2.184)
Constant	—	—	.609	—	−1.478***
			(.394)		(.145)
Log-likelihood	−6689.531	−6319.407	−1517.260	−9188.843	−4615.307
Observations	4,172	7,853	2,334	7,553	8,056

All of the models were estimated with state and year fixed effects. All of the models report robust standard errors clustered on county; all significance tests are two-tailed. *p<.10, **p<.05, ***p<.01.

models were reestimated with just the national sample, which produced similar results. The full results from the OLS analyses with state fixed effects are reported in table 8A.3.

As discussed in the chapter, local Vietnam War casualty rates had a strong, statistically significant effect on respondents' electoral and

Table 8A.3. OLS Regression Analyses of Relationships between Vietnam Casualty Rates and SCBS Indices of Political and Civic Engagement

	Electoral Politics Index	Nonelectoral Politics Index	Organizational Activity Index	Charitable Activity Index
Vietnam casualty	−.011**	−.014**	−.001	.033
rate	(.005)	(.006)	(.004)	(.022)
Education	.205***	.188***	.147***	.609***
	(.006)	(.007)	(.005)	(.020)
Income	.088***	.064***	.057***	.386***
	(.005)	(.005)	(.004)	(.014)
White	.261***	−.147***	−.102***	−.024
	(.036)	(.036)	(.026)	(.090)
Male	.146***	.078***	−.054***	−.587***
	(.015)	(.016)	(.013)	(.051)
Married	.058***	−.097***	−.013	.589***
	(.018)	(.024)	(.014)	(.052)
Age	.025***	−.002**	.002***	.011***
	(.000)	(.001)	(.000)	(.002)
Own home	.186***	.075***	.105***	.680***
	(.021)	(.023)	(.013)	(.065)
Length of residence	.100***	.055***	.048***	.221***
in community	(.006)	(.008)	(.005)	(.021)
% Nonwhite in	.254	.315	−.175*	−.798***
community	(.161)	(.228)	(.095)	(.293)
Mean family income	.036	−.086	−.098***	−.445***
in community	(.062)	(.106)	(.035)	(.127)
% Unemployed in	−1.924***	−1.556	.192	−1.281
county	(.719)	(1.248)	(.527)	(2.022)
Constant	.054	.469	−.517***	1.717***
	(.253)	(.403)	(.144)	(.488)
R²	.35	.11	.12	.19
Observations	25,245	25,251	25,183	25,242

All of the models were estimated with state fixed effects. All of the models report robust standard errors clustered on county; all significance tests are two-tailed. *p < .10, **p < .05, ***p < .01.

nonelectoral political participation but no effect on other nongovernmental forms of engagement. The control variables all largely performed in accordance with expectations from the literature.

To ascertain whether local casualty rates depressed political engagement in the wake of other wars, the models in table 8A.4 examine the effect of Korean and World War II casualty rates on several measures from NES surveys 1956–1964.[4] The models are virtually identical to those in table 8A.2, with two exceptions. First, the casualty-rate measures for Korea and World War II are county casualties per 10,000 inhabitants. Replicating the Vietnam analyses with rates per 10,000 inhabitants yields virtually identical results. Second, the NES did not begin asking the length of residence question until 1968, and the only early surveys that contained the home ownership question were those from 1952 and 1964; hence, both were excluded from the earlier analysis.

Respondents from communities that suffered high casualty rates in the Korean War exhibited less interest in politics and were less likely to vote than their peers from low-casualty communities. The casualty gap in engagement did not emerge in World War II, however. If anything, the empirical results suggest that respondents from high-casualty counties in WWII may have been more engaged than their peers. The personal demographic variables largely accord with standard theoretical expectations. The only anomalous result is the negative and frequently significant coefficient for county median family income and engagement. However, this may be an artifact of having already controlled for income at the individual level.

Finally, to create the regression results reported in the text in tables 8.2 and 8.5 we employed turnout data from ICPSR 13, general election data for the United States, 1950–1990, for the 1956–1988 election analyses, and from ICPSR 8611, electoral data for counties in the United States: presidential and congressional races, 1840–1972, for the 1940–1964 election analyses. For census demographic data we used the county data books included in ICPSR 2896, Historical, Demographic, Economic, and Social Data: The United States, 1790–2000. Because the 1982 county data book does not include median years of school completed, we substituted the percentage of residents at least twenty-five years of age who had completed four or more years of college. Replicating the 1980s models instead with county median education from the 1970 census yields virtually identical results. For the 1956–1968 elections, we used each county's casualty rate as of the 1968 elections as the independent variable of interest. For 1972 and all subsequent elections, we used each county's casualty rate as of the 1972 election as the independent variable.[5]

Table 8A.4. Regression Analyses of Relationships between Korean and WWII Casualty Rates and NES Measures of Political Participation, 1956–1964

	Trust federal government	Interest in politics	Voted in last election	Voted in presidential election	Interest in politics (II)	Voted in presidential election (II)
Korea casualty rate	-.003 (.006)	-.022** (.011)	-.011 (.010)	-.019** (.008)	-.025** (.013)	-.032*** (.011)
World War II casualty rate	—	—	—	—	.002 (.006)	.008 (.005)
Republican	-.002 (.099)	.373*** (.089)	.493*** (.081)	.514*** (.081)	.371*** (.088)	.508*** (.080)
Democrat	.069 (.097)	.260*** (.081)	.570*** (.072)	.534*** (.075)	.259*** (.081)	.529*** (.075)
Education	.037*** (.014)	.157*** (.017)	.160*** (.014)	.165*** (.017)	.156*** (.017)	.165*** (.017)
Income	.042* (.025)	.133*** (.027)	.189*** (.026)	.154*** (.027)	.133*** (.027)	.153*** (.027)
White	-.060 (.114)	.005 (.094)	.280*** (.096)	.293*** (.102)	.004 (.094)	.295*** (.102)
Male	.132*** (.047)	.390*** (.045)	.211*** (.050)	.166*** (.054)	.390*** (.045)	.164*** (.054)
Married	-.091* (.051)	-.013 (.065)	.110* (.057)	.158*** (.060)	-.014 (.065)	.158*** (.060)
Age	-.003** (.002)	.011*** (.002)	.018*** (.002)	.015*** (.002)	.011*** (.002)	.015*** (.002)
% Nonwhite in county	.122 (.554)	.018 (.654)	-.190 (.451)	-.028 (.475)	.040 (.652)	.059 (.489)
Median family income in county	-.054 (.047)	-.103* (.061)	-.158** (.061)	-.163** (.067)	-.098 (.064)	-.142** (.071)
% Unemployed in county	2.673 (2.247)	-.326 (2.674)	-2.881* (1.738)	-2.108 (1.722)	-.342 (2.697)	-2.116 (1.723)
Constant	—	—	-1.699*** (.296)	-1.711*** (.290)	—	-1.866*** (.322)
Log-likelihood	-2415.961	-2848.739	-2812.643	-2078.079	-2848.595	-2076.596
Observations	2,657	2,444	5,651	4,284	2,444	4,284

All of the models were estimated with state and year fixed effects. All of the models report robust standard errors clustered on county; all significance tests are two-tailed. * $p < .10$, ** $p < .05$, *** $p < .01$.

Finally, in addition to dropping counties with missing data, our Korean War casualty analysis also grapples with several potential errors in ICPSR 8611. Calculating the change in total voters from the preceding to the current election reveals a number of very large outliers—alleged changes in turnout of hundreds of thousands of voters during a single electoral cycle within a county. To control for these outliers, we estimated our models by dropping counties whose change in turnout from the preceding to the current election was greater than the 99th percentile and less than the 1st percentile. Using a similar methodology in the Vietnam analysis yields virtually identical results to those presented in table 8.2.

ROBUSTNESS CHECK FOR NES MODELS

All statistical analyses are plagued by the lurking danger of omitted variable bias, and too often there are few even partial solutions. The models in table 8A.2 were reestimated with a variety of additional control variables with similar results; yet, even consistent results across multiple specifications cannot alleviate all of the concerns. Fortunately, in the current context we were able to reestimate three of our five NES models in table 8A.2 with pre–Gulf of Tonkin data from the 1964 NES. The 1964 NES analyses presented in table 8A.5 provide strong support for the contention that residents of counties that suffered high casualty rates in Vietnam began to exhibit lower levels of trust in government and political participation only *after* the war's conclusion. In none of the models is the local casualties coefficient statistically significant, and in two of the models the sign is actually positive. Unless some other unobserved factor common to all of the residents of these counties (aside from minority population, median income, and unemployment, all of which are controlled for in the models) also began influencing respondent behavior precisely in the period after the war's conclusion, the combination of results in tables 8A.2 and 8A.5 provides compelling evidence that individual respondents' local experience with the war greatly influenced their relationship with the federal government and their patterns of political engagement and participation in the years immediately following the U.S. withdrawal.

As a further robustness check, we collapsed both prewar and postwar NES data to perform a difference-in-differences analysis on changes in trust in government, interest in politics, and patterns of voting at the county level. Through this differencing approach we are able to control for unmeasured county-level characteristics that were omitted from the previous analyses and that could potentially be producing a spurious result. The three dependent variables are simply the change in the average

Table 8A.5. Robustness Check for NES Models Using 1964 NES

	Trust federal government	Interest in politics	Voted in last election
Future Vietnam	−.040	.036	.052
casualty rate	(.050)	(.038)	(.042)
Republican	−.152	.574***	.789***
	(.127)	(.112)	(.150)
Democrat	.161	.381***	.691***
	(.127)	(.114)	(.130)
Education	.040*	.198***	.112***
	(.022)	(.024)	(.024)
Income	.036	.130***	.079*
	(.036)	(.035)	(.044)
White	−.168	−.129	−.112
	(.172)	(.132)	(.152)
Male	.118*	.383***	.018
	(.062)	(.066)	(.088)
Married	−.005	−.038	.108
	(.079)	(.083)	(.089)
Age	−.001	.014***	.010***
	(.003)	(.002)	(.002)
Own home	−.099	−.033	.350***
	(.074)	(.077)	(.086)
% Nonwhite in county	−.003	.004	.003
	(.007)	(.008)	(.008)
Median family income in	.000	−.074	−.043
county	(.000)	(.077)	(.087)
% Unemployed in county	2.410	−2.332	−.446
	(2.476)	(3.330)	(2.181)
Constant	—	—	−3.115***
			(.500)
Log-likelihood	−1181.873	−1563.591	−740.868
Observations	1,343	1,359	1,458

All of the models were estimated with state and year fixed effects. All of the models report robust standard errors clustered on county; all significance tests are two-tailed. $^*p<.10$, $^{**}p<.05$, $^{***}p<.01$.

level of trust in government, interest in politics, and voting observed at the county level from the pre-1966 surveys to the five post-Vietnam surveys from 1974 to 1982. The change in each county's casualty rate from 0 in the prewar years to its postwar value is the main independent variable of interest, while the change in all of the other individual-level control variables included in the analysis in table 8A.2, except home ownership and length of residence in the community, are also added as controls. Results from the difference-in-differences analyses are presented in table 8A.6.

Simple summary statistics of the dependent variables show that across all counties, on average, levels of trust in government and voting decreased considerably across the pre- and postwar periods, while overall interest in politics remained virtually unchanged. Yet, the results in table 8A.6 strongly suggest that, along all three dimensions, the decreases in political engagement and participation were most severe in counties that experienced high casualty rates in Vietnam. As in the individual-level models, the estimated effect of a county's casualty rate on its respondents' average level of trust in the federal government is negative, though the resulting coefficient is not statistically significant. However, in both the interest in politics and the voting models, the casualty rate coefficient is negative and statistically significant. A ten casualties per thousand men age 18 to 34 increase in a county's casualty rate decreased its average level of interest in politics by more than 0.70 standard deviations and decreased its average turnout rate by more than 10 percent, a 0.68 standard deviation decrease. Thus, even after differencing out county means to control for unmeasured contextual characteristics, we find considerable evidence that political engagement and participation decreased from the pre-Vietnam years to the postwar era and that these decreases were the sharpest among residents of counties that shouldered a disproportionate share of the burden in the costly war.

ROBUSTNESS CHECK FOR SOCIAL CAPITAL MODELS

While the Social Capital Benchmark Survey provides unique opportunities to explore the influence of local communities' Vietnam War experiences on their residents' behavior across a full range of participatory activities, the very innovativeness of the survey means that we are unable to replicate our models with prewar data as we were with many of the NES models. One additional robustness check, however, is possible. The theoretical logic described earlier suggests that individuals' own experience with the war, as filtered through the community in which they lived at the time, fundamentally reshaped their relationship with government, which affected their willingness to participate accordingly. With more than twenty years having passed since the end of U.S. involvement in Vietnam and the conducting of the SCBS, many individuals may have moved in the interim, and many respondents may have been too young to have had any direct experience with the war. It is certainly possible that even a newcomer to a community may still be affected by that community's wartime experience even if that person did not experience it directly.

Table 8A.6. Robustness Check for NES Models Using Difference-in-Differences Analysis of the Change in County-Level Engagement and Participation

	Trust federal government	Interest in politics	Voted in last election
Vietnam casualty rate	–.023	–.033**	–.013*
	(.022)	(.019)	(.009)
Δ Republican	–.479**	1.439***	.533***
	(.239)	(.379)	(.113)
Δ Democrat	–.379**	1.293***	.422***
	(.213)	(.355)	(.122)
Δ Education	–.056	.130**	.014
	(.048)	(.064)	(.024)
Δ Income	.071	–.097	.031
	(.072)	(.103)	(.063)
Δ White	.207**	.068	–.051
	(.125)	(.259)	(.147)
Δ Male	.243*	.327	.138*
	(.167)	(.271)	(.085)
Δ Married	.080	.224	.120
	(.265)	(.375)	(.120)
Δ Age	.008**	–.013	.009***
	(.004)	(.010)	(.003)
Constant	–.522***	.129*	–.066*
	(.097)	(.088)	(.040)
R^2	.24	.25	.26
Observations	109	110	110

All of the models were estimated with OLS regressions and report robust standard errors clustered on state; all significance tests are one-tailed. $^*p < .10$, $^{**}p < .05$, $^{***}p < .01$.

Neighbors' attitudes and patterns of participation may inexorably influence one's own. However, at the very least we would expect the negative effects of casualty rates on participation to exist at the same (or even higher) levels for long-time residents of high-casualty-rate communities who lived there during or in the immediate aftermath of Vietnam.

As a robustness check, the models in table 8A.7 replicate the two political participation models estimated in table 8A.3, but they divide the respondents into those that had lived in their community for at least twenty years and those who had not. For both long-tenured residents and shorter-tenured residents, higher local casualty rates in Vietnam are strongly correlated with lower levels of electoral and nonelectoral forms of political participation. However, the results in table 8A.7 demonstrate

Table 8A.7. Robustness Check for SCBS Models Disaggregating by Length of Residence

	Electoral Politics Index, 20+ Years	Electoral Politics Index, < 20 Years	Nonelectoral Politics Index, 20+ Years	Nonelectoral Politics Index, < 20 Years
Vietnam casualty	−.014*	−.010*	−.020*	−.013**
rate	(.008)	(.006)	(.011)	(.006)
Education	.183***	.214***	.187***	.187***
	(.008)	(.008)	(.011)	(.009)
Income	.076***	.092***	.062***	.060***
	(.008)	(.006)	(.008)	(.006)
White	.080**	.324***	−.309***	−.087**
	(.039)	(.040)	(.051)	(.038)
Male	.110***	.163***	.107***	.061***
	(.021)	(.019)	(.029)	(.020)
Married	.181***	.000	.036	−.166***
	(.027)	(.022)	(.028)	(.030)
Age	.024***	.025***	−.003***	−.001
	(.001)	(.001)	(.001)	(.001)
Own home	.266***	.145***	.035	.083***
	(.038)	(.023)	(.050)	(.022)
Length of residence	−.045*	.134***	−.067**	.087***
in community	(.028)	(.010)	(.032)	(.014)
% Nonwhite in	.223	.263	.598**	.199
community	(.181)	(.166)	(.309)	(.263)
Mean family income	−.057	.063	−.084	−.099
in community	(.061)	(.067)	(.108)	(.121)
% Unemployed	−2.178**	−1.864***	−.408	−2.195*
in county	(1.013)	(.754)	(1.634)	(1.316)
Constant	1.324***	−.171	1.126***	.466
	(.293)	(.278)	(.420)	(.482)
R^2	.31	.33	.12	.11
Observations	8,633	16,612	8,633	16,618

All of the models were estimated with OLS regressions with state fixed effects. All of the models report robust standard errors clustered on county; all significance tests are two-tailed. *p<.10, **p<.05, ***p<.01.

that the negative effect of casualty rates on political engagement was on average almost 50 percent greater for respondents who had lived in their current communities for more than twenty years than it was among respondents who were more recent arrivals to their communities. While not conclusive proof of a direct causal link between Vietnam and respondents' behavior twenty years later, the larger effects for long-tenured residents are a further observable implication consistent with our theoretical argument.

As a final robustness check, we re-estimated the electoral and non-electoral participation models in Table 8A.7 for a third category of respondents, the 1,650 respondents who moved to their current communities within the last year. While it is certainly plausible that shorter-tenured residents of a high casualty community may also exhibit depressed levels of political participation even if they didn't live in that community during the war because of interactions with neighbors and others through social networks, any indirect effect of a community's war experience should be weakest among the most recent newcomers to a community. Among this subset of the sample, the coefficients for a community's casualty rate are again negative, however neither is statistically significant (p = .66 and p = .18, respectively). Collectively, the SCBS analyses, like the NES and aggregate turnout analyses, strongly support the theoretical contention that the Vietnam War significantly depressed political engagement in the United States and that its effects were most acute for the individuals in communities that experienced the costs of the government's failed war policies most directly.

9

The Future of the Casualty Gap

When he took office on January 20, 2009, President Barack Obama concluded his inaugural address by recalling the words of Thomas Paine: "Let it be told to the future world, that in the depth of winter, when nothing but hope and virtue could survive, that the city and the country, alarmed at one common danger, came forth to meet it."[1] However, President Obama did not quote the sentences immediately before and after this passage. If he had, he would have told the nation: "I call not upon a few, but upon all: not on this state or that state, but on every state...It matters not where you live, or what rank of life you hold, the evil or the blessing will reach you all. The far and the near, the home counties and the back, the rich and the poor, will suffer or rejoice alike."[2]

Paine's 1776 Revolutionary War rallying cry demonstrates that, since the very founding of the country, the American ideal has been one of shared sacrifice in defense of the nation. As we document in this book, however, the reality of military sacrifice has often not accorded with this ideal. In addition, although the casualty gap has characterized all of America's major military conflicts since the 1940s, President Obama's carefully crafted speech suggests that inequality and military sacrifice remain a subject too sensitive to be placed on the national agenda.

Policymakers, scholars, and the media alike have not engaged in sustained dialogue about the casualty gap.[3] The issue of equity in military service has attracted both popular and scholarly attention, but largely lost amid the analysis and debate are questions about inequality and the ultimate sacrifice: death in service to the country. Although rigorous empirical analysis of wartime death has been possible for decades and isolated studies have addressed the topic, the casualty gap has largely failed to emerge on the social science research agenda. Perhaps even more important, the casualty gap is simply not part of our national political dialogue. To borrow a phrase from former Vice President Al Gore, it is an inconvenient truth and one better for both major political parties if left in the shadows.

This concluding chapter argues that we should face up to the casualty gap. Regardless of one's stand on the feasibility or even on the normative desirability of eliminating the gap, there is a need to openly and accurately account for the casualty gap in manpower and strategic calculations. When the costs and benefits of military action are debated, these debates should recognize the casualty gap as a cost—perhaps an unavoidable one—but a real one that should be accounted for, nevertheless.

It is critically important for policymakers and scholars alike to consider the future of the casualty gap and its continued ramifications for American politics and society. Less than a week after President Obama's inauguration, Vice President Joe Biden predicted on national television that, as the military increasingly engages the enemy in Afghanistan, casualties are likely to rise.[4] Indeed, as a result of the Obama administration's escalation of the war in Afghanistan, June and July of 2009 proved to be the costliest two-month period of the nine year war.[5] With a new president and new missions, what should we expect the future of the casualty gap to look like? We answer this question in the first part of this chapter by revisiting our arguments about the forces driving the casualty gaps observed in previous conflicts. Because current military selection and occupational assignment mechanisms are unlikely to change, we believe that the casualty gap will remain with us. We also argue that, due to technological and medical advances in treating battlefield injuries, increasingly a "wounded gap" may become the most salient indicator of inequality in battlefield sacrifice.[6]

Recognizing that the casualty gap is likely to persist, the chapter next considers what, if anything, our national policy response should be. Here, our aim is not to offer a set of bullet-point policy prescriptions. Casualty inequality is too complex to respond with simple answers; indeed, the policy responses that could alleviate the gap may be just as normatively or logically troubling as the gap itself. At first, the dilemma posed by the casualty gap appears to be an intractable one. If policymakers are severely limited in how they can seek to ameliorate (let alone eliminate) the casu-

alty gap, how can we hope to soften some of its most important consequences for American democracy? One promising way in which the
nation might begin to bridge the political divides created by the casualty
gap is to bring the issue of socioeconomic inequality in military sacrifice
to the forefront of political debate. Open engagement of the issue might
reenergize the democratic brake on costly military policies that the casualty gap blunts, and it would ensure that the nation enters into such fate-
ful decisions conscious of the full costs they exact on its citizenry.

In chapters 2 and 3 we documented the existence of a socioeconomic
casualty gap during the Korean, Vietnam, and Iraq wars, in which poorer
and less-educated parts of the country bore a disproportionate share of
the combat casualties. Our simple bivariate analyses showed that the
three lowest income deciles suffered 40 percent more casualties in Korea,
38 percent more in Vietnam, and 65 percent more in Iraq than communities in the top three income deciles.[7] When we examined communities
in terms of their educational attainment, a similar pattern emerged, with
low-education communities bearing a systematically larger share of the
nation's casualties than communities with high levels of educational
attainment in each of these three wars. We confirmed the robustness of
these bivariate results by using multivariate statistical models.

We then posited that two interrelated processes—selection into the
military and occupational assignment within it—produced these community-level gaps by creating a casualty gap at the individual level. We
argued that citizens with fewer *ex ante* skills and educational and occupational opportunities (who also hailed disproportionately from socioeconomically disadvantaged communities) are both more likely, on average,
to find the military an attractive option and, once in the service, to be
assigned to occupations with closer proximity to combat than are their
peers with greater socioeconomic resources. While the necessary data to
prove our hypotheses conclusively are not available, multiple additional
analyses of the extant data suggest that these mechanisms provide the
most plausible explanations for the casualty gaps that we observed.

Looking ahead, what casualty patterns should we expect to see in future
U.S. military conflicts? Our analysis suggests that as long as selection and
military assignment mechanisms remain roughly the same as those operative in the Iraq War, there is little reason to expect the contours of the
casualty gap to change substantially. Neither mechanism is likely to change
significantly in the foreseeable future. Despite concerns about the strain-
ing of contemporary military manpower resources, there is little public
support for making fundamental changes to the current military selection
policies underlying the all-volunteer force. Moreover, our analyses of the
Korean and Vietnam drafts in chapter 3 strongly suggest that even if the

nation reinstituted a draft, it is unlikely that this change alone would eliminate the socioeconomic casualty gap. This is particularly true given both the size of the contemporary military relative to the nation's population and the scale of conflicts likely to be waged in the immediate future, which will almost certainly be considerably smaller than the mass-mobilizing conflict of World War II. Moreover, the military's occupational assignment mechanisms are perhaps even more unlikely to change; if anything, these sorting processes are growing even more rigorous and important with the ever-increasing technological sophistication of the armed forces. For all of these reasons, we believe that the casualty gap promises to remain a tangible feature of future U.S. wars.

What is likely to change, however, is the extent to which a "wounded gap" may become even more salient. Even as the technological sophistication of U.S. military power grows exponentially, in the new terrain of the war on terror, where enemies routinely use crude, but effective weapons such as improvised explosive devices, U.S. soldiers are suffering traumatic, life-altering wounds with startling regularity.[8] As a 2006 CBS News report noted, "A new generation of severely wounded veterans is now emerging among us, their brains battered, their arms and legs blown off. Many would have died in earlier wars but survived in Iraq thanks to better battlefield medicine."[9] Many of these injuries, while no longer fatal, remain life altering. As one of the medical surgeons remarked about the recovery these soldiers can expect, "We can save you, [but] you might not be what you were."[10] The seriousness of the wounds and the high numbers in which they are seen have been so disturbing that, "in a comprehensive Army survey of troop morale across Iraq, taken in September [2003], the unit with the lowest spirits was the one that ran the combat hospitals."[11] Thus, although tremendous advances in medical technology have saved lives in more wartime situations than ever before, it is imperative that we look beyond combat deaths when assessing the human costs of war.[12]

Historical comparisons plainly illustrate the increasing prominence of combat wounds in recent conflicts. For example, the ratio of soldiers killed versus soldiers wounded in Iraq is striking in comparison to earlier conflicts. While the wounded/killed ratio was 1.7 in World War II, 1.9 in Korea, and 2.6 in Vietnam, in Iraq the ratio through December 2008 was 7.3.[13] Thus, when compared with Vietnam and Korea, the ratio of wounded to killed soldiers in Iraq is more than two and a half times larger. When compared to World War II, the ratio in Iraq is more than four times as large.

Given that nonfatal wounds constitute such a large percentage of the human costs of war paid in Iraq, it is important to expand the scope of analysis to investigate possible inequalities in who suffers these nonfatal casualties. Precise data on wounded soldiers are more difficult to obtain than data on fatal casualties, and as a result we were not able to conduct the same sorts of analyses for wounds as we did with deaths in chapters 2 and 3.[14] Ongoing analysis of the available data from Iraq and Korea, however, suggests that in these wars the patterns of wounded soldiers mirror those of deaths: lower-educated and lower-income parts of the country have suffered a disproportionate share of combat wounds.

Furthermore, as the wounded gap increases in prominence, additional research is needed to explore whether the political ramifications of non-fatal American wartime casualties differ from those of fatal casualties. Both fatal and nonfatal casualties are recognized as costs of war in scholarship on casualty sensitivity. However, because the vast majority of empirical analyses focus only on fatalities, new theory is needed to understand how the two distinct conflict events, wounded in action (WIA) versus killed in action (KIA), may well produce different effects on political behavior. Three central differences between wounds and deaths are most salient: (1) lower public visibility, (2) greater frequency, and (3) opportunity for direct mobilization by wounded soldiers.

As the existing political science literature recognizes, the return of a wounded soldier often does not generate the same community response as the return of a deceased soldier. The death of a soldier is typically followed by a well-attended funeral and considerable local media attention.[15] The return of a wounded soldier does not usually trigger the same sort of coverage in local media outlets. Moreover, if the returning soldier's wounds are not physically visible, community members or even family and friends may not know the true extent of the soldier's hardships. This lower visibility could theoretically dampen the likelihood of individual event response, the transmission of elite cues concerning wartime costs, and sustained coverage of the full consequences of war in media outlets. To the extent that the costs paid by wounded soldiers are more removed from the public eye, the behavior of the public and public officials should not be altered.

Cutting against the low visibility expectation, however, is the recognition that, especially in the current Iraq War, WIAs are much more numerous than KIAs. Through December 2008, slightly more than 4,200 U.S. soldiers had been killed in Iraq, while nearly 31,000 had been wounded. Similarly, in Afghanistan 409 Americans had been killed in combat as of December 31, 2008. By contrast, 2,631 Americans had been wounded in action as of that date.[16] It may be the case that even though a death is more visible than many non-fatal wounds, the much larger number of wounded soldiers collectively is just as salient for the political stream.

Finally and critically for the linkage between conflict events and political behavior, wounded soldiers have the ability to directly engage in the political process. Indeed, groups such as Iraq Veterans against the War and Iraq Veterans for Progress have attempted to raise visibility about the needs of wounded Iraq veterans. Interest group activity directly targeted at elites, as well as public campaigns to raise more general awareness, both lead to the expectation that there should be greater sensitivity to WIAs. These competing theoretical expectations make clear the need for more research into the distinction between media, political, and societal recognition of different types of casualties, and their respective consequences for politics and policymaking.

RESPONDING TO THE CASUALTY GAP

Military service is more than just a job, and dying in service to one's country is the highest form of sacrifice that the state can ask of its citizens. As a result, we believe there are strong normative reasons to desire to lessen or even eliminate the socioeconomic casualty and wounded gaps that are likely to emerge in future wars. We also recognize, however, that military and economic realities may make casualty inequalities all but inevitable. The choice allowed by the all-volunteer force is appealing and thus enjoys strong, widespread support among the American people. Moreover, even if the nation returned to a military draft, this change in selection mechanisms alone would be unlikely to eliminate inequalities in current conditions. Similarly, occupational assignment procedures within the military—the second major mechanism posited to produce the casualty gaps described in chapters 2 and 3—are also rational. It could be disastrous to impose policies that deemphasize the logical allocation of rank and roles within the military based on individuals' skill sets in an effort to decrease inequality in sacrifice.[17]

What, then, can policymakers do? We argue that the best and most feasible policy response to the casualty gap is to encourage an open discussion of how the burden of wartime sacrifice, especially the highest sacrifice, is borne differently across the country. Talking about the casualty gap not only raises awareness but also may produce tangible changes in policy outcomes. The results of our experiments demonstrate the undeniable importance of an open and reasoned discussion of the existence and the consequences of the casualty gap. Increased salience and even basic knowledge of the casualty gap in the national political consciousness may raise the political pressure brought to bear on political leaders who pursue costly military conflicts. Ultimately, we argue, this is the most fundamental and appropriate policy response to the casualty gap: Do not engage in war unless the nation is truly ready to accept all of its multifaceted costs.

The idea that poorer segments of the country bear a disproportionate share of the nation's sacrifice on the battlefield is antithetical to American democratic norms. Given this fundamental conflict, it is little wonder that most discussions of the casualty gap are often submerged and kept far from the mainstream of political debate. We hope that this book will serve as a catalyst for academics, politicians, and the general public alike to engage in debate about inequality and war casualties.[18]

Yet, more work remains to be done. We sketch out here several specific directions for future research that might foster this nascent discussion and better inform our understanding of the casualty gap and the pathways by which it affects society. First, research should be carried out on the "wounded gap." As we have already discussed, there are reasons to believe that a wounded gap might have very different political and social ramifications from those produced by inequalities in combat deaths. New data collection and analysis are essential to answering such questions and understanding more completely the effects of the human costs of war, broadly defined, on the polity. Moreover, future research on the wounded gap should also focus on its consequences for veterans' health care. For instance, do patterns of inequality exist in the levels of care that wounded veterans receive? How does institutional context, especially insurance and legal rules that govern provisions for veterans' health care, affect the type of care that returning soldiers receive? How are psychiatric wounds recognized as compared to other types of wounds? Answering questions such as these will require more cooperation from the Department of Defense in releasing accurate data related to wounded soldiers, as well as more collaboration between researchers in political science, health policy, law, and economics. However, additional research along these lines is critically important to help craft effective policy responses to the long-term costs of the wounded gap, which, given the historical trajectory, promises to be increasingly important in future military campaigns.

Second, more work is needed to further define and explore the precise mechanisms through which casualties affect political behavior and public opinion. In chapter 5 we introduced two pathways through which the casualty gap can affect opinion and behavior. The first one posits that, when citizens are made aware of the casualty gap, they will become less supportive of military endeavors, both retrospectively and prospectively. The experimental analyses of chapter 4 strongly supported this hypothesis. However, it is likely that *how* citizens are made aware of the gap will also affect their response.[19] For example, how do various methods of presenting citizens with information concerning the nature and extent of the casualty gap affect its impact on their political judgments and policy preferences? Similarly, how does the effect of simple informative cues about the nature of the casualty gap change when it is presented by partisan actors, military sources, or outside interest groups? Future experiments that modify the content of the casualty gap message or the source of the messenger can address these and similar questions directly.

The second pathway through which the casualty gap can affect opinion and behavior rests on the effects of local casualties. We argue that citizens from high-casualty communities are more likely, on average, to feel a sense of personal contact with the deceased, to receive greater local media coverage of war deaths and costs more generally, and to hear more local elites speaking out about the war. However, many important questions remain about how these mechanisms operate in practice. For instance, what *types* of media coverage are most likely to spur opinion or behavioral change? How do individuals respond when seeing a photo of a grieving widow versus simply reading a name on a page? How do political elites factor casualties into their decision-making processes when crafting the public positions they take on major questions of military policies? And once issued, how does an elite cue about the war and its costs interact with the identity of the sender to determine its influence on public opinion?

Given the key role of the mass media in each of these mechanisms, answering such questions will require a closer examination of military policy for allowing media coverage of casualties. Even when granted access, however, it is not clear how much emphasis the media will give to the reporting of war casualties. In fact, within two years of the initial invasion Iraq casualties had fallen so far from the public view that in 2005 the group Operation Truth began an "Honor the Fallen" campaign. In the words of Iraq veteran and Operation Truth executive director Paul Rieckhoff, "Casualties in Iraq and Afghanistan were major news at the outset of the war, and those who died were given proper respect, but two years later, the mounting human cost is no longer a priority in America's newsrooms."[20] As more time elapses, the names of the fallen in Iraq and Afghanistan have slipped even further from the public eye.

Renewed attention should also be paid to the effects of the military's policy regarding coverage of coffins returning to Dover Air Force Base. While the media may be granted more access to Dover by the Obama administration, further empirical examination is needed to learn whether the change in policy has actually resulted in stories and photos of soldiers' deaths achieving greater prominence in major news outlets. One thing is certain: Despite considerable discussion of the policy reversal, neither side of the debate used the opportunity to ask important questions about the inequality aspects of these deaths. A combination of additional qualitative, quantitative, and experimental research could greatly enhance our understanding of media coverage and of the mechanisms that link differential local casualty rates, media coverage, and the observed cleavages in Americans' opinions and political behaviors.

Each of these promising lines of future research will improve our understanding of how wartime casualties are distributed across the nation, the forces that produce these casualty gaps, and their ultimate effects on politics and policymaking. Continuing to confront these empirical realities directly is critically important; it forces us to reassess our ideals about military participation and sacrifice, evaluate them against the data, and adjust our military policy preferences and judgments accordingly.[21]

FACING UP TO THE CASUALTY GAP

By bringing the casualty gap to the forefront of public debate on military affairs and openly discussing its consequences for the polity, policymakers and the public at large will more fully comprehend war's human costs. Facing up to the truth of casualty inequality may be difficult, but willfully avoiding it is not an acceptable long-term solution. Any debate over future war making that fails to recognize the casualty gap is incomplete.

If we recognize the inequity before us in the distribution of American lives lost in combat, we are forced to reflect, like Ben Franklin did two centuries ago, on the inevitable consequences of recruiting young men and women to serve in exchange for economic rewards:

> The question then will amount to this: whether it be just in a community, that the richer part should compel the poorer to fight in defence of them and their properties, for such wages as they think fit to allow, and punish them if they refuse. Our author tells us that it is "legal." I have not law enough to dispute his authorities, but I cannot persuade myself that it is equitable.[22]

Modern military manpower policies are a far cry from the eighteenth-century British practice of impressment, against which Franklin railed. However, the result is, to a certain extent, the same: socioeconomic inequality in military sacrifice in service to the nation. This inequality is itself a cost of war that must be acknowledged and accounted for just as assiduously as the number of lives lost or dollars spent.

Notes

Preface

1. Quoted in Williams (1998, 195).
2. Geary (1991).
3. Bob Herbert, "Blood Runs Red, Not Blue," *New York Times* (August 18, 2005).

Chapter 1

1. Military leaders have also encouraged this paramount focus on a war's human costs. For example, Army Chief of Staff George C. Marshall remembers how during World War II: "I was very careful to send Mr. Roosevelt every few days a statement of our casualties. I tried to keep before him all the time the casualty results because you get hardened to these things and you have to be very careful to keep them always in the forefront of your mind." Quoted in Pogue (1973, 316).

2. Our argument that the human costs of war cannot simply be measured in terms of the number of casualties echoes recent work by historian Drew Gilpin Faust. In her study of the national response to the Civil War, Faust (2008, xii) notes: "The impact and meaning of the war's death toll went beyond the sheer numbers who died." However, Faust emphasizes not the uneven distribution of these deaths but how they challenged Americans' dominant social norms and belief structures: "Death's significance for the Civil War generation arose as well from its violation

of prevailing assumptions about life's proper end—about who should die, when and where, and under what circumstances."

3. Following the standard practice in political science (e.g., Gelpi, Feaver, and Reifler 2005/2006), unless otherwise noted, throughout this book we use the term *casualty* to denote deaths. Although the military uses the term to refer to both killed and wounded soldiers, in popular dialogue when we speak of casualties, we are almost always referring to soldiers killed in a foreign theater. Moreover, because the Department of Defense has not released comprehensive data on wounded soldiers for all of the wars under examination, our analysis can consider only soldiers killed in wartime. In chapter 9 we discuss the need for more analysis of inequities related to non-fatal wounds.

4. Some media listings, such as the *Washington Post*'s Faces of the Fallen website, have two casualties listed for Charleston. However, both the Department of Defense listings and the *Associated Press* report that Lance Corporal Jonathan Gadsden lived in Jamestown, South Carolina, approximately thirty miles north of Charleston. The median family income in this small town of ninety-seven was only $13,542 per year, less than one-third the state average. All of the figures are taken from the 2000 census.

5. Because the number of casualties suffered in Afghanistan as of December 2008 was less than one fifth of even the number sustained in Iraq, we consciously excluded it from our analysis. For the same reason, we also did not include other post World War II military conflicts such as the 1991 Persian Gulf War and 1999 Kosovo war. The very small casualty totals in these wars all but precluded a similar analysis. However, we return to the issue of Afghanistan in the concluding chapter when we speculate about the future of the casualty gap and its consequences for American politics.

6. Thucydides (1982 [431 B.C.], 2.44–6).

7. George Washington (1783), "Sentiments on a Peace Establishment," reprinted in Weigley (1969). For a review see Richards (1995).

8. Tocqueville (1990 [1840], chapter 23). This demand for shared sacrifice is also captured in political scientist Samuel Huntingon's (1957, 157) description of the dominant liberal perspective on the military and its place in American society: "Military defense is, like suffrage, the responsibility of every citizen. It cannot be delegated to a small exclusive group."

9. We review these literatures in considerably greater depth in future chapters. For the effect of casualties on presidential approval, see Mueller (1973); Kernell (1978); Hibbs, Rivers, and Vasilatos (1982); Brody (1991); Brace and Hinckley (1992); Larson (1996); Kull and Destler (1999); Gartner and Segura (1998); Baum and Kernell (2001); Klarevas (2002); Erikson, MacKuen, and Stimson (2002), Eichenberg (2005); Gelpi, Feaver, and Reifler (2006); Eichenberg and Stoll (2006); and Kriner (2006). On public opinion more generally, see Burk (1999), Jentleson (2002), Boettcher and Cobb (2006), Voeten and Brewer (2006), and Berinsky (2007). On the electoral consequences of casualties see Aldrich (1977), Cotton (1986), Hibbs (2000), Bartels and Zaller (2001), Carson et al. (2004), Karol and Miguel (2007), Kriner and Shen (2007), and Grose and Oppenheimer (2007). And

on the importance of casualties and their anticipation on states' conflict behavior, see Kant (1983 [1795]), Morgan and Campbell (1991), Bueno de Mesquita and Lalman (1992), Morgan and Schwebach (1992), Maoz and Russett (1993), Russett (1993), Bueno de Mesquita and Siverson (1995), Ray (1995), Bueno de Mesquita et al. (1999, 2003), and Russett and Oneal (2001).

10. A few recent studies have broken free from this mold and have analyzed the effects of local casualties on citizens' opinions and behaviors. However, while these studies implicitly recognize that not all communities experience casualties equally, none of them has explicitly considered the impact of the inequality that underlies this variance. See Gartner, Segura, and Wilkening (1997); Gartner and Segura (2000); Gartner, Segura, and Barratt (2004); Karol and Miguel (2007); Kriner and Shen (2007); and Grose and Oppenheimer (2007).

11. While a small number of recent studies have begun to recognize that war costs are not distributed equally across society, they do not explore the correlation between casualty variance and socioeconomic inequality. Although they do not go further, both Gartner and Segura (2000) and Karol and Miguel (2007) recognize this possibility. Indeed, in their analysis of casualties' influence on the 2004 presidential election, Karol and Miguel explicitly acknowledge that likely correlations between community socioeconomics and casualty rates pose a methodological challenge. However, no existing study explicitly considers in detail the political ramifications of socioeconomic inequalities in the distribution of casualties across society.

12. For full details about the question wording and research design, we refer readers to chapter 4 and its accompanying appendix.

13. See, for example, Schaefer and Allen (1944); Mayer and Hoult (1955); Zeitlin, Lutterman, and Russell (1973); Berney and Leigh (1974); Willis (1975); Badillo and Curry (1976); Foust and Botts (1991); Barnett, Stanley, and Shore (1992); Mazur (1995); Wilson (1995); Moskos and Butler (1996); Gifford (2005); and Preston and Buzzell (2006). For a more thorough review of this literature, we encourage readers to see the online appendix that accompanies chapter 2. The relative paucity of scholarship on casualty inequalities stands in stark contrast to the myriad of analyses of the question "Who serves when not all serve?" See, for example, Berryman (1988); National Research Council (2003). The parallel question "Who dies when not all die?" has garnered comparatively little systematic analysis from the academic community. "Who Serves When Not All Serve?" was the subtitle of the 1967 Marshall Report. We discuss the Marshall Report, as well as additional studies of military service, in the online appendix. See also United States National Advisory Commission on Selective Service (1967).

14. Bishop (2003). The *American-Statesman* revisited the issue of casualty inequality in 2005 when it discussed a study by Robert Wood Johnson health policy analyst Brian Gifford, who analyzed racial disparities in casualty rates. Gifford found that Hispanics had suffered casualty rates higher than their proportion in the military (at least in the preinsurgency stage of the fighting); however, the proportion of

Hispanic casualties was still smaller than their percentage of the total military-age population (Castillo and Bishop [2005]). Bill Bishop, "Iraq War Dead: A Sacrifice of Small Towns," *Austin American-Statesman* (October 23, 2003), A1. Juan Castillo and Bill Bishop. "War Costly for Texas Hispanics," *Austin American-Statesman* (February 27, 2005), A1.

15. Other examples include Siegel (2003), Thomas (2003), Conetta (2004), Gast (2004), Cohen (2007), and Milbank (2008). Noam Cohen, "Watching the War and Acknowledging the Dead," *New York Times* (April 16, 2007). Dana Milbank, "What the Family Would Let You See, the Pentagon Obstructs," *Washington Post* (April 24, 2008), A03.

16. Bishop (2003).

17. Appy (1993).

18. Roth-Douquet and Schaeffer (2006,10).

19. Kerry later apologized: "I sincerely regret that my words were misinterpreted to wrongly imply anything negative about those in uniform, and I personally apologize to any service member, family member, or American who was offended." http://www.washingtonpost.com/wp-dyn/content/article/2006/11/01/AR9780195390964.html.

20. Baker and VandeHei (2006). Peter Baker and Jim VandeHei, "Kerry Offers Apology to Troops," *Washington Post* (November 2, 2006), A01.

21. "Bush on Kerry Remark: U.S. Troops Are 'Plenty Smart,'" (November 1, 2006); http://www.cnn.com/2006/POLITICS/10/31/kerry.mccain/.

22. Vagts (1945b).

23. Vagts (1945a, 256) uses the term "politics of casualties" to describe this phenomenon.

24. Vagts (1945a, 258–259).

25. See Schultz (1998, 1999, 2001); for signaling arguments more generally, see Cowhey (1993) and Martin (1993).

26. Though, to be sure, the Pentagon has been challenged on its release of casualty data. Historian Steven Casey (2008) reports that in Korea the press charged the Pentagon with not being forthcoming about true U.S. casualty figures.

27. U.S. Senate Committee on Military Affairs (1918).

28. While many observers have pointed to America's alleged "casualty phobia" as a distinctly post-Vietnam phenomenon, understanding the causes of casualties and reducing casualty totals have been major focal points of U.S. military strategists at least since America's experience in World War I (Huelfer 2003). This strategy became known as meeting the "Dover test" after two speeches by General Hugh Shelton in 1999 and 2000. See General Hugh Shelton, speech at Harvard University, Jan. 19, 2000. The demands of implementing this doctrine of casualty minimization give U.S. Defense Department officials additional incentive to minimize casualty coverage in the media. Many academics, led by Peter Feaver and Christopher Gelpi (2004), have questioned the accuracy of this widely held assumption and have argued that the American public—in certain circumstances—is considerably *less* casualty phobic than routinely believed. See also Kull and Destler (1999); Huelfer (2003).

29. Letter to President Bush on Dec. 7, 2005, signed by Rep. John Conyers Jr., Rep. Sam Farr, Rep. Raul M. Grijalva, Rep. Carolyn Maloney, Rep. Betty McCollum, Rep. Jim McDermott, and Rep. Jan Schakowsky.

30. Milbank (2003). In 2006 a similar debate emerged in Canada when the Canadian government restricted some aspects of media coverage of fallen soldiers returned from Afghanistan. See "Soldiers in Firing Line Approve of Media Ban: Arrival of Dead in Canada, 'Should Be Family and Private Moment,'" *Montreal Gazette* (Apr. 26, 2006), A4. Dana Milbank, "Curtains Ordered for Media Coverage of Returning Coffins," *Washington Post* (October 21, 2003), A23.

31. *New York Times/CBS* Poll (December 2003). Stevenson and Elder (2004). Richard W. Stevenson and Janet Elder, "Support for War Is Down Sharply, Poll Concludes," *New York Times* (April 29, 2004).

32. "The Photos You Weren't Supposed to See (and Do You Really Need to See Them?)," *Atlanta Journal-Constitution* (Apr. 25, 2004), 3E. Similar tensions simmered even outside the political arena. Comments from a forum in the *Atlanta Journal-Constitution* revealed the contours of the split. Some felt the media should be present at the ceremonies. Jane Bright, whose son died in July 2003, commented that "We need to stop hiding the deaths of our young; we need to be open about their deaths." Veteran White House correspondent Helen Thomas (2003) wrote that, although she understood that "the photos would be disturbing to anyone and—if the war goes on much longer—politically damaging to the president," she believed that "the families of the fallen Americans should not have to grieve alone. We can only share by knowing." The *San-Antonio Express News*, too, expressed its opposition to the policy of not allowing photos of the returning coffins: "Americans must not be spared the reality of the high cost of this—or any other—war." The privacy concern, however, resonated with others. Brigadier General Mark Kimmitt said that "I certainly know for myself that I would not want one of my loved ones to be a public spectacle before I'd had that first opportunity to grieve in person" (*San Antonio Express-News* (Oct. 28, 2003), editorial, 6B). Helen Thomas, "Only by Knowing Can We Share Grief for Soldiers," *Houston Chronicle* (November 2, 2003), 3.

33. Secretary of Defense Robert Gates, Feb. 26, 2009. http://www.defenselink.mil/transcripts/transcript.aspx?transcriptid=4361.

34. We refer readers to our online appendix for more information on casualty inequality before World War II.

35. John F. Kennedy. "Commencement Address at Yale University," *Public Papers of the President*, June 11, 1962.

Chapter 2

1. Roberts (2007).

2. Estimates for Beaver Falls and national averages are based on data from the 2000 U.S. census Summary File 3.

3. DeLauter (2006). Lori DeLauter, "Family, Vets Say Goodbye," *Beaver County Times* (October 3, 2006).

4. Lipset (1996).

5. For example, those who have seen Michael Moore's *Fahrenheit 9/11* will remember the scene that features military recruiters. The narrative starts with this exhortation from Moore: "With the war not going as planned and the military in need of many more troops, where would they find the new recruits?...They would find them all across America in the places that had been destroyed by the economy. Places where one of the only jobs available was to join the army. Places like my hometown of Flint, Michigan....Look at the neighborhood I live in. Most of them [i.e., the homes] are abandoned. You know, I mean, that's not right. You wanna talk about terrorism? Come right here, President Bush, right here. Come right here." Conversely, in the early 1990s the late conservative commentator William F. Buckley seized upon the nuanced conclusions of a study by three MIT economists (Barnett, Stanley and Shore 1992) on the socioeconomic demographics of Vietnam War casualties to proclaim that "Vietnam was indeed an all-American effort, and one that, some of us contend, will one day take its place in the annals of national nobility: a witness to America's disposition to endure special sacrifices in discharge of its heavy international responsibility" (Buckley 1992, 62). William F. Buckley, "Poor Man's War?" *National Review* (December 14, 1992), 62.

6. Schaefer and Allen (1944, 168).

7. For studies that report evidence of a socioeconomic casualty gap, see Mayer and Hoult (1955), Zeitlin, Lutterman, and Russell (1973), Foust and Botts (1991), and Preston and Buzzell (2006). For studies with more mixed results, see Willis (1975), Badillo and Curry (1976), Barnett, Stanley, and Shore (1992), and Mazur (1995). For studies that find little evidence of a socioeconomic or racial casualty gap, see Schaefer and Allen (1944), Moskos and Butler (1996), and Gifford (2005). Even more analyses have examined the related, if distinct, question of whether socioeconomic inequalities exist in military service more generally. Investigations of a class bias in military service have also yielded strikingly inconsistent findings. For a more comprehensive discussion of these existing literatures, we refer readers to the online appendix that accompanies this chapter.

8. Wilson (1995, 464). Modell and Hagerty (1991) reach a similar conclusion.

9. Moskos and Butler's (1996) study of race and the military and Willis's (1975) inquiry into both Vietnam and World War II state-level casualty rates are exceptions which examine multiple conflicts simultaneously. Furthermore, Willis (1975, 559) explicitly recognizes that his study omits a parallel analysis of Korea: "If we find differences in social backgrounds of World War II and Vietnam War casualties we can probably assume that the same differences existed between World War II and Korean War casualties."

10. We define "significant" differences as those that reach conventional thresholds in statistical tests. In other words, significant differences in casualty rates are those that our data suggest are very unlikely to have been produced by random chance alone. Casualty gaps could potentially fall along almost any dimension (for example, we could examine whether communities with greater amounts of annual rain

fall suffer higher casualty rates). We define "salient" dimensions as those that frequently appear in academic and political debates.

11. For a description of the 1970 census data available at the place level, we refer readers to the technical appendix.

12. As Barnett, Stanley, and Shore (1992) and others recognize, the hometown of record may not necessarily be the place in which the deceased soldier was living immediately prior to entering the military. Specifically, Barnett, Stanley, and Shore discuss the probability that many soldiers from very small locales listed the nearest larger community as their home of record. As such, very small communities may be underrepresented in any place-level casualty counts. As far as we have been able to ascertain, we believe that the listed hometown of record is indeed a very good indicator of actual hometown. When we endeavored to locate the actual preenlistment home addresses for a sample of Iraq War casualties (a process discussed and described later in the chapter in more detail), we discovered a few instances of soldiers from small, rural communities who had listed a larger, neighboring community as their DOD home of record. However, we observed few major differences in the socioeconomic status of the listed vs. the actual communities. Thus, even if Barnett, Stanley, and Shore are right, while this may introduce some noise into our data, it is unlikely to alter any of our major findings about the nature of socioeconomic casualty gaps at the place level. If anything, however, it suggests that any evidence we find for an urban-rural casualty gap in later wars (in which rural areas perhaps pay a larger share of the human costs of war) may underestimate the true strength of this relationship. This potential problem also poses fewer difficulties for our county-level analyses as both the "actual" and the listed hometowns are likely to be in the same county. An additional concern is that some soldiers may have listed their military base address prior to deploying, as opposed to their hometown prior to entering military service. Here we can take advantage of census place classifications in our Iraq analysis. The 2000 census data allow us to eliminate from our analysis the eighty-nine places classified as M2 ("an installation" or part of an installation of the U.S. Department of Defense). Thus, the small number of soldiers who listed a military base as their "hometown" are excluded from analysis, further alleviating concerns that the listed hometown is not a good reflection of where in the country that soldier comes from. Finally, it is possible that the DOD's hometown-of-record information is simply mistaken. Utilizing independent address-search tools, we attempted to verify pre-service addresses for a random sample of soldiers who have died in Iraq. Our independent analysis suggests that the DOD is accurate more than 95 percent of the time and that there is no systematic variation in the address errors. Rerunning our models with and without the corrections does not change our substantive findings.

13. It should be noted that in Iraq there have been both female and male deaths. The number of female deaths, however, is only 2.4 percent of the overall total as of December 2008 (http://siadapp.dmdc.osd.mil/personnel/CASUALTY/castop.

htm). Replicating our analyses with casualty rates per 10,000 male and female residents yields virtually identical results.

14. This is the nonweighted average. Weighting by county population, the average is a little more than five casualties per 10,000 male residents.

15. We also utilized other income measures such as per-capita income, as well as other education measures such as median years of schooling. The results are substantively the same using these alternative measures.

16. For ease of discussion in the text, throughout the book we use interchangeably the phrase number of residents who have "completed four or more years of college" with the number of residents "with a college degree." In 1940, 1950, and 1970 the census data files we use provide a measure of the number of citizens who had completed four years of college, and in 2000 our data file has a measure of the number of citizens with a college degree. One of the most important changes in American society from the 1940s to the current period is the dramatic increase in the percentage of adults with a college education. Accordingly, we also re-estimated our analyses using the percentage of residents with a high school diploma as our measure of educational attainment. In this alternative specification, we observe the same inverse correlations linking community education levels and local casualty rates in Korea and Vietnam.

17. We also reestimated our World War II models with each county's median income from the 1950 census (which correlates very highly with its median rent from the 1940 census, r = .84). This alternative specification also shows the striking finding of a positive correlation between a county's income level and its casualty rate in World War II.

18. Zavis (2009). Alexandra Zavis, "With jobs harder to find, work gets easier for Army recruiters," *Los Angeles Times* (August 11, 2009), A1.

19. Government Accountability Office (2006b, 4).

20. See Willis (1975).

21. For example, see Jake C. Miller (1979, 2000). For a historical look at the issue, see Reddick (1949).

22. Grove (1966). Gene Grove, "The Army and the Negro," *New York Times Magazine* (July 24, 1966), 4–5, 48–52.

23. King (1968a, 23), cited in Jake C. Miller (2000).

24. See, for example, Guzman (1969), Baskir and Strauss (1978), Goff and Sanders (1982), Holm (1996), and Westheider (1999). For an overview of this literature, see Gartner and Segura (2000).

25. Moskos and Butler (1996, 9).

26. Gifford (2005, 220).

27. A comparable variable for Hispanic population was included in a supplemental Iraq model.

28. Flynn (1993, 64–65).

29. William O'Hare, senior visiting fellow at the University of New Hampshire's Carsey Institute. Quoted in Roberts (2007).

30. Ibid. See also O'Hare and Bishop (2006).

31. See discussion in chapter 3 on multiple motivations for enlisting.

32. See McCormick and Wittkopf (1990) and Wittkopf (1990). The correlation, however, is of course far from perfect. Moreover, particularly in the post–Cold War era the parties may be more divided in terms of their views of the scenarios in which the use of military force is justified. Democrats are more likely, on average, to support the use of force for peacekeeping and humanitarian missions, while Republicans are more likely to view the use of force from a more strictly realpolitik lens.

33. See, for instance, Mueller (1973), Brody (1991), and Gartner and Segura (1998).

34. For our county-level models we use county-level presidential returns. In the Iraq place-level models, where place-level presidential returns data is not available, we employed (in separate models) county-level and state-level partisanship measures.

35. During both the Korean and the Vietnam wars, partisan control of the White House changed in the latter stages of the conflicts. To account for this, we reestimated our Korea models separately for each year to see whether the model results were different in the Truman and Eisenhower presidencies. We used the same procedure for our Vietnam models to look for differences between the Johnson and Nixon administrations. In none of these additional specifications did we find evidence of a casualty gap along partisan lines.

36. U.S. Department of Defense (2006, 2–24).

37. As CNA Corporation analysts Donald Cymrot and Michael Hansen (2004, 131) have noted, "the historical mission of the military, with its focus on war fighting and its resulting reliance on youth and vigor, has supported and encouraged this relatively junior force."

38. We use this age group from the 1940 census because young men between 15 and 19 years of age in 1940 were either at or about to be at prime draft age as draft calls grew in size after 1940. This is consistent with Barnett, Stanley, and Shore's (1992, 859) use of 15-year-olds as an "imperfect surrogate" for the number of military-age males in a community. Using other measures of youth population do not affect the substantive findings reported in the chapter.

39. Because we weight by county population and because county population varies dramatically, the actual number of county units in each decile is not the same.

40. We temper this interpretation of the data with the following caveat: the Iraq inequality figures were calculated using place-level data, while the figures for preceding wars were calculated at the county level. It is possible that if comprehensive place-level data existed for previous wars, we might see larger gaps at the place level.

41. For World War II, Korea, and Vietnam, this analysis is at the county level. For Iraq, it is at the place level. Because the number of casualties in the Iraq War is so small comparatively, we used a slightly different coding scheme for high- and low-casualty communities. High-casualty communities include the 563 census places that have suffered casualty rates higher than 8.16 casualties per 10,000 male residents. This represents the top 25 percent of all communities that suffered at least 1 casualty in the Iraq War. The low-casualty communities in Iraq are

the census places that have not yet suffered a casualty in Iraq—more than 90 percent of the total.

42. Since 1940 county income data were not available in our data sets, we utilize 1950 income as a close proxy in figure 2.6. To create 2000 constant dollar income figures, we used the inflation calculator tool of the U.S. Bureau of Labor Statistics: http://data.bls.gov/cgi-bin/cpicalc.pl.

43. Replicating our map with college data yields a very similar picture with a clear inverse relationship to county casualty rates. Indeed, the two education measures correlate at $r > .80$.

44. Due to concerns about collinearity between our measures of income and education (which are highly and significantly correlated), we ran separate models, one with median family income and a second with the percentage of residents who had completed four or more years of college. The other explanatory variables appear in both models and have very similar coefficients in both models. We report complete models in the technical appendix, but in table 2.1, for the variables that have significant relationships to casualties and appear in both models (unemployment, race, rural, and age), we report the largest estimated effect from the two models.

45. When we employ a $p < .10$ two-tailed test, 0 is outside the 90 percent confidence interval, which means that there is a 5 percent or less chance that the real relationship, given our data, is below this confidence interval (i.e., 0 or less/greater) and a 5 percent chance that it is even further from 0 in the direction of our coefficient than the interval suggests.

46. As shown in the technical appendix, replicating the analysis for Vietnam casualties at the place level also finds strong evidence of a significant community income casualty gap. The estimated magnitude of the gap from the place-level models is larger than that observed from the county-level models, though it is still smaller than the comparable gap for Korea at the county level.

47. The lack of a strong, significant relationship between community unemployment and casualty rates in Vietnam and Iraq was surprising. However, this null finding may be due in part to the greater instability inherent in local unemployment data (particularly at the place level). The snapshot measure of local economic conditions provided by census unemployment data simply may not be sensitive enough to investigate fully the relationships between local labor market conditions and casualty rates. It may also be the case that our unemployment measures, which capture the percentage of all residents fourteen and older that are unemployed, are not sensitive enough to unemployment in the age bracket most likely to be targeted by recruiters. Further research is needed to investigate these potential relationships more fully.

48. See, for example, Appy (1993).

49. Halbfinger and Holmes (2003). David M. Halbfinger and Steven A. Holmes, "Military Mirrors Working-class America," *New York Times* (March 30, 2003).

50. In alternative specifications for the Iraq War, we also considered the relationship between casualty rates and the percentage of Latinos. Even when including this additional explanatory variable, we found a similar, inverse relationship between

the percentage of African Americans and casualty rates and no evidence that communities with greater proportions of Latino residents had higher per-capita casualty rates.

51. Binkin and Eitelberg (1982, 76), quoting from Johnson (1968). Thomas A. Johnson, "The U.S. Negro in Vietnam," *New York Times* (April 29, 1968).

52. This year-by-year analysis is consistent with other studies (e.g., Appy 1993) asserting that the percentage of black casualties also changed dramatically in this time. Reexamining our data provides modest support for this contention. Before 1967, the percentage of black casualties was 15.5 percent; from 1967 to the Paris peace accords, the figure is 12 percent, a modest but not overwhelming difference. According to the 1970 census, African Americans composed approximately 11 percent of the U.S. population during this period.

53. Block groups in our analysis average about 1,100 residents in size (the smallest 5 percent have fewer than 500 residents, and the largest 5 percent, more than 3,000 residents).

54. Individual searches were carried out at http://www.peoplefinders.com/. PeopleFinders searches through a large number of public-records databases in order to provide a list of addresses for a given name and city. If a search returned more than one address, we used additional information from published sources to attempt to identify the soldier's address immediately prior to entering the service. When a single, exact address match could not be made and instead we were faced with several plausible addresses, we conducted separate analyses with each of the addresses. Finally, for individuals with multiple addresses in a city, we also averaged across all known addresses to construct block group income and educational attainment measures. Regardless of which method was employed, the substantive results were virtually identical.

55. A parallel comparison of income levels, presented in the online appendix, reveals a similar trend.

56. Figure 2.9 presents the median percentage of residents with a college degree for all block groups that suffered Iraq War casualties in each city. Thus, half of all casualties from that city came from block groups with an even smaller percentage of their residents' having completed college, and half came from block groups with larger percentages of residents having completed college. Using the average percentage of residents completing college for all block groups with casualties yields substantively identical results.

Technical Appendix to Chapter 2

1. We also ran models using casualty counts as dependent variables and controlling for county or place population as an independent variable. While there were inconsistencies across model specifications, the patterns largely mirror those reported in tables 2A.3 and 2A.4. The inconsistencies across specification are likely due to the fact that population and casualty counts are very highly correlated; hence, multicollinearity is a very real problem in the count models. Because

complete, individual-level data on wounded soldiers are unavailable for several of the conflicts, we limit ourselves to examining soldiers killed in action. To keep our focus on those soldiers killed in the theater of war, we limited our casualty counts to those soldiers who died between June 1950 (as North Korean forces invaded South Korea on June 24, 1950) and July 1953 (as the Military Armistice Agreement was signed on July 27, 1953). For Vietnam, we limited our casualty counts to those soldiers who died between August 2, 1964 (when the U.S.S. *Maddox* was first attacked in the Gulf of Tonkin), and March 29, 1973 (when the last U.S. combat soldiers left Vietnam under the Paris Peace Accords).

2. For World War II, we used the World War II Honor List of Dead and Missing Army and Army Air Forces Personnel. See http://www.archives.gov/research/arc/ ww2/army-casualties/. The vast majority of casualties come from this army and air force datafile. The data on Korea and Vietnam deaths and casualties come from databases archived by the U.S. National Archives as part of its Access to Archival Databases (AAD) system. All of the data were downloaded (first in the summer of 2005 and subsequently in early 2009 after minor file updates) from the AAD website: http://www.archives.gov/aad/. For Korea, we utilized the "Records of Military Personnel Who Died as a Result of Hostilities during the Korean War, ca. 1977–11/1979." The database was created by the Department of Defense, Directorate for Information Operations and Reports, Manpower Management Information Division. For Vietnam, we used the "Records with Unit Information on Military Personnel Who Died during the Vietnam War, Created ca. 1983– 12/18/2005, Documenting the Period 6/8/1956–10/10/2003" (COFFELT file) and the "Records of Deceased, Wounded, Ill, or Injured Army Personnel, Including Dependents and Civilian Employees, 1/1/1961–12/1981." The first database is maintained by the Department of Defense, Washington Headquarters Services, Directorate for Information Operations and Reports, Statistical Information Analysis Division. The second database was created by the Adjutant General's Office.

3. Data online at http://siadapp.dmdc.osd.mil/personnel/CASUALTY/castop.htm.

4. The COFFELT database, which tracks Vietnam casualties, provides home state and city, not county (which is the lowest geographical unit for which complete 1970 census data are available) information for each casualty. Aggregating from the city to the county level generally posed few problems, as we were able to assign counties based on cross-referenced census data. For some, additional steps were necessary. For single cities such as New York City, which span two or more counties in a single state, we followed two methods. The first method, which we used in all of the statistical analyses in this book, evenly divided such casualties for each city among all of the counties it spanned. The second method assigned each casualty to each county spanned by the city under the premise that deaths from a city that spans multiple counties could affect residents of all of the counties involved. The results across specifications for both our analyses here and those in chapters 6 and 8 are virtually identical regardless of which casualty rate operationalization is used. For towns such as Bethlehem, Pennsylvania, for which there is more than one city of the same name in a single state, we also used two methods. First, we dropped all such casualties and ran our models. We then ran alternative models in which we randomly assigned each

casualty to one of the towns. The two methods yielded nearly identical results. To construct casualty rates throughout the book, we employed the first method.

5. The U.S. Census Bureau defines a "place" as "a concentration of population either legally bounded as an incorporated place or identified as a census designated place (CDP), including comunidades and zonas urbanas in Puerto Rico." See http://www.census.gov/geo/www/psapage.html. The U.S. Census Bureau notes that "Incorporated places have legal descriptions of borough (except in Alaska and New York), city, town (except in New England, New York, and Wisconsin) or village." The bureau further distinguishes between "four major 'groups' that differentiate between populated places, other geopolitical and census units, institutional facilities, and terminated entries. Some subclasses relate an entry to a class different from its own, which is useful because a number of entries serve in more than one capacity." Because "some sub-classes identify entries in different classes that are coextensive," we use the major group: Class-C, incorporated places.

6. We also estimated alternative models using other values (e.g., number of males age 18 to 34) as the denominator. The results were nearly identical, as there were very high correlations among all of the alternative population denominator variables.

7. For the 1940, 1950, and 1970 census data, we utilized data files prepared by Michael Haines (2004) and published by the Interuniversity Consortium for Political and Social Research (ICPSR). For the 2000 census data, we downloaded raw summary file 3 (sf3) files from the census bureau website and built our own custom place-level database.

8. For analysis of the Vietnam conflict, using 1960 census data instead of 1970 census data does not significantly affect the substantive results.

9. Median rent is the same measure that Schaefer and Allen (1944) used. Median rent correlates with 1950 median income, r = .84. Alternative models were run using average and median values of owner-occupied dwellings. Because median and average values of owner-occupied dwellings correlate at r = 0.8 (p < .001) with median rent, the results were substantively the same.

10. County-level returns for the 1940 and 1948 elections were obtained from the U.S. Historical Election Returns, 1824–1968 (ICPSR 0001) data file. Returns for the 1964 election were obtained from the general election data for the United States, 1950–1990 (ICPSR 0013).

11. The U.S. Census Bureau identifies four census regions: Northeast, Midwest, South, and West. The South region includes Delaware, Washington, D.C., Florida, Georgia, Maryland, North Carolina, South Carolina, Virginia, West Virginia, Alabama, Kentucky, Mississippi, Tennessee, Arkansas, Louisiana, Oklahoma, and Texas. See http://www.census.gov/geo/www/geo_defn.html.

12. In models that included county-level partisanship measures, the counties from Alaska were dropped because Alaska reports its election returns by election district rather than county.

13. We avoid including both education and income measures in the same regression due to problems of multicollinearity. The two variables are very highly correlated at the county and place levels; thus, following standard practice in many economic analyses, we choose to run separate models.

14. See White (1980).

15. For a general description of the 1970 place-level census data, see ICPSR 9694. We obtained 1970 census place-level data from State of the Cities Data System, which is maintained by HUD. http://socds.huduser.org/Census/Census_Home .htm.

Chapter 3

1. Hays (1967, 34).
2. For instance, John McGrath of the U.S. Army's Combat Studies Institute estimates that the percentage of army soldiers in combat units was 19 percent in World War II but a little more than 7 percent in Korea and Vietnam. See McGrath (2007, table B-4). As the scale of the conflicts decreased, so, too, did the demand for combat troops, which had important ramifications for selection mechanisms.
3. See, for example, Berryman (1988), National Research Council (2003), Altman and Fechter (1967), Bicksler, Gilroy, and Warner (2004), Chambers (1975), Janowitz (1960), Moskos (1970), Karsten (1982), Flynn (1993), and Kindsvatter (2003).
4. Griffith (1982), Moskos and Wood (1988); Segal (1989, 2000); Karsten (1982), National Research Council (2003), Woodruff, Kelty, and Segal (2006), and Grandstaff (1996).
5. Moskos (1977, 2001) and Moskos and Wood (1988).
6. Moskos (1988, 16–17). See also Moskos (1977).
7. In the three decades since Moskos introduced his typology, scholars have proposed numerous adaptations and refinements of the theoretical framework. For example, Segal (1986) suggests that, rather than defining a continuum with purely occupational and purely institutional poles, each may constitute a separate dimension. In this framework, individuals could embrace both conceptualizations of military service simultaneously. We reference Moskos's conceptualization not as the final word on the matter but as a useful, basic framework within which to think about the multiple incentives that underlie the decision to enlist.
8. As an example of recent work within this line of scholarship, a study by Woodruff, Kelty, and Segal (2006) suggests that institutional incentives are particularly important for the 30 percent of new recruits who are "high-propensity" youth (i.e., those that had long planned on joining the military). By contrast, among the 70 percent of recruits who had not thought seriously about enlisting while in high school, occupational and economic incentives were particularly important.
9. The size of the military recruiting budget also had a strong impact on recruiting trends (Asch and Orvis 1994). Among others, see also Altman and Fechter (1967), Brown (1985), and Warner and Asch (2001).
10. McMichael (2008). William McMichael, "DoD: Poor Civilian Job Prospects Help Services Reach Goals," *Army Times* (December 30, 2008).
11. For example, in their analysis of military volunteerism from 1973 to 1978, sociologists Morris Janowitz and Charles Moskos (1979, 194, 195) found that college-educated men, who enjoyed great advantages in the civilian labor market,

were significantly underrepresented in the armed forces. While almost 30 percent of the military-age male population had some college education in 1977, only 5 percent of new army enlistees did. In 1964, more than 17 percent of young men drafted into the service had some college education.

12. Karsten (1982, 3). This is not to say that the relative importance of economic incentives has not changed over time. For example, surveying the history of twentieth-century manpower policy, Moskos (2000) identifies three eras—the modern (1900–1945), the late modern (1945–1990), and the postmodern (1990–present)—and he argues that throughout these periods the military has become increasingly viewed through an occupational rather than through an institutional lens. If correct, this trend could also contribute to the emergence of the socioeconomic casualty gaps we observed in the Korean and Vietnam wars and the widening of these gaps in the Iraq War.

13. As Major General Dennis Cavin (2004, 132) reminds us, even "the all-volunteer force is really an *all-recruited* volunteer force." Moreover, there is variation in the effectiveness of recruiting offices.

14. Griffith (1982, 33, 87, 31, 135).

15. Grandstaff (1996, 306, 311).

16. http://www.goarmy.com/benefits/money_bonuses.jsp#Enlistment. See also Kosiak (2008).

17. http://www.goarmy.com/benefits/total_compensation.jsp#chart. Military sociologist David Segal has similarly observed that "in the era of the all-volunteer force, the military entered the labor market as an employer of first-term enlisted personnel," and "the military competed with other employers primarily on a wage basis" (1989, 3). See also, for example, Larry DeBoer and Brorsen (1989). It should also be noted that the military can affect the distribution of income and wealth in local labor markets. Booth's (2000) statistical analysis finds that, when the military has a greater presence in the local labor market, that market will see greater inequalities between male and female unemployment rates but reduced racial inequalities for males.

18. Congressional Budget Office (2007, 3). Depending on definitions, the figure for Vietnam may vary. Here, we use Flynn's statement that draftees account for about 40 percent of total accessions in enlisted personnel (1993, 171). On other metrics the percentage of the armed forces consisting of volunteers in Vietnam was even higher. However, the percentage of the army in Vietnam made up of draftees in 1968–1970 hovered around the 40 percent mark (see Shafer 1990). We recognize that many volunteers were responding to a new incentive structure introduced by the draft. For instance, "a 1964 survey indicated that 40 percent of all volunteers were draft motivated, and this figure went up to over 50 percent after 1965" (Flynn 1993, 171). However, the differences between Vietnam and Korea on the one hand and World War II on the other are nonetheless stark.

19. For comprehensive overviews of the literature on the AVF see Rostker (2006), Bicksler, Gilroy, and Warner (2004), and the Congressional Budget Office (2007). The best data on individual soldier demographics come from a series of annual

reports from the Department of Defense itself. Following the creation of the AVF, the Senate Committee on Armed Services (Report 93-884, May 1974) mandated annual reports on the social composition of the armed forces. The annual reports are made available online at http://www.defenselink.mil/prhome/. Since the mid-1990s, the reports have provided not only statistical summaries of applicants for enlistment, enlisted and officer accessions, and the enlisted and officer forces but also comparisons with the civil population. The reports draw on data from the Bureau of Labor Statistics and the census to carry out these comparisons.

20. Through a Freedom of Information Act request, we obtained the number of new recruits per ZIP code for the years 1973 through 2006.

21. Annual recruiting figures are calculated according to the fiscal year. When we refer to the number of recruits for a given year we, too, are referring to the fiscal, not calendar, year.

22. Analyses of the recruits data by the Department of Defense (2007) and the National Priorities Project (2007) similarly find disparities between high- and low-income communities. According to the DOD's analysis, in FY 2006 the poorest communities with median incomes of less than $25,000 a year were slightly underrepresented in the army's ranks. Whereas 2.2 percent of the army came from such communities, 2.6 percent of the report's civilian comparison group did. However, lower- and middle-class communities with incomes between $25,000 and $50,000 were overrepresented in the military (58.7 percent of new recruits came from such communities versus 53 percent of the civilian comparison group). Also, at the upper levels of the income distribution, the military reported considerable underrepresentation. Focusing on enlistment data from the army, the National Priorities Project (NPP) analysts also find that the poorest and the wealthiest communities have contributed a disproportionately small share of military recruits, while lower-middle class families have contributed a disproportionately large share. However, competing findings also have been published. In an analysis of FY 2003–2005 recruits for all service branches conducted for the Heritage Foundation, Tim Kane (2006) argues that, if anything, middle- and upper-middle-class communities are providing a disproportionately large share of military recruits. Contra the conventional wisdom, Kane's analysis finds that poor communities with median incomes of less than $35,000 a year were underrepresented in the armed forces during this period, while lower-middle-, middle-, and upper-middle-class communities with median family incomes that range between $35,000 and $80,000 a year were overrepresented.

23. Burns (2007). It may be the case that this particular drop was due in part to the $20,000 "quick ship" bonus made available to those recruits who left for basic training before the end of September, 2007. Robert Burns, "Army Has Record Low Level of Recruits," *Associated Press* (October 31, 2007).

24. However, this change in policy comes late relative to the date of death for the vast majority of the Iraq casualties we analyze. Further, although the new cohorts of recruits will be allowed to include up to 4 percent of Category IV individuals, the overall military average (based on many previous years under a lower Category IV cap) will remain quite low.

25. High-quality recruits are defined as high school graduates whose Armed Forces Qualifying Test (AFQT) scores (these scores are computed from the ASVAB) placed them in categories I through IIIA (i.e., at or above the fiftieth percentile, Office of the Secretary of Defense, Personnel, and Readiness 2006, table D-9, http://www.defenselink.mil/prhome/PopRep_FY06/).

26. Another metric on which we can see evidence of considerable change is the decreasing percentage of recruits who are high school graduates, particularly in the army. DOD records show that whereas 86 percent of new army recruits had graduated high school in 2003, by 2006 less than 73 perent had done so, against 81 percent of 18 to 24 year old civilians. Office of the Secretary of Defense, Personnel and Readiness. 2006. "2006 Population Representation in the Military Services." Appendix D, Table D-7. http://www.defenselink.mil/prhome/PopRep_FY06/. Again, the decline was steepest amongst army recruits. By contrast, for the armed forces as a whole, the decrease in high school graduates from 2003 to 2006 was 91 percent to 87 percent. Kane's figure (2006) of 98 percent likely includes recruits who have earned their GED or other high school diploma equivalency. However, the data clearly shows that a high school diploma is the best predictor of recruit success. Whereas 80% of recruits with a high school diploma successfully complete their training and initial service requirement, only 60 percent of those with a GED or other equivalency do so. The comparison figure for recruits with no high school diploma or GED is 50%. Congressional Budget Office. 2007. "The All Volunteer Military: Issues and Performance." Pub. No. 2960, p. 13. http://www.cbo.gov/doc.cfm?index=8313.

27. Preston and Buzzell (2006). This point is also made by historian George Flynn (1993, 194), who notes that "the deciding factor in casualty rates was not draft equity but how a soldier fulfilled his military obligation."

28. When evaluating the ratio of combat to noncombat troops in a theater of war, the military refers to a "tooth-to-tail ratio" (T3R): the ratio of combat soldiers (the tooth) to noncombat soldiers (the tail). The T3R varies across operations and across divisions within a given operation. This estimate for Korea includes both the 276,581 soldiers deployed to South Korea and the "78,079 logistical troops (and their headquarters elements) in Japan" (McGrath 2007, 26).

29. Ginzberg (1959, 42–48).

30. Janowitz (1965, 57).

31. http://officialasvab.com/history_rec.htm.

32. Army Regulation 601-210, 50.

33. Hogan describes the process of aptitude-based sorting thus: "Recruits are assigned to particular military occupations based on their aptitudes...the needs of the military service, and their preferences. In general, those who score the highest in the various aptitude dimensions will be offered training and assignments in those specialties that are most demanding in those dimensions" (Hogan 2004, 31).

34. Kindsvatter (2003, 260), citing Roger W. Little, "Buddy Relations and Combat Performance," in Janowitz (1964).

35. Flynn (1993, 126).

36. Unfortunately, we do not have comparable data from World War II.

37. We constructed the infantry casualty rate by dividing the number of casualties from army and marine infantry units by the number of males in the community and then multiplying by 10,000 to arrive at a casualty rate per 10,000 males. The noninfantry casualty rate is therefore the number of casualties not from these infantry units, similarly expressed as a rate per 10,000 males. We constructed the enlisted casualty rate by identifying all of the casualties from enlisted pay grades. Our officer casualty rate excludes warrant officers. Including them does not change the substantive findings we present.

38. Scholars have long analyzed the divide between officer and enlisted ranks. Tocqueville remarked in *Democracy in America* that, although the desires of those in lower ranks is great, "it is easy to see, that of all armies in the world, those in which advancement must be slowest in time of peace are the armies of democratic countries. As the number of commissions is naturally limited, whilst the number of competitors is almost unlimited, and as the strict law of equality is over all alike, none can make rapid progress—many can make no progress at all" (Tocqueville 1990 [1840], chapter 22). More recently, Kindsvatter's (2003, 56) study of the American soldier finds that "the soldier got his first taste of the army's caste system during his initial training" upon discovering that "a wide gap still remained between their rights and privileges and those of the officer corps." Historian Lee Kennett has labeled this gap between officers and enlisted personnel "institutionalized inequality," and it has implications for the casualty gap because larger numbers of enlisted soldiers find themselves in the highest-risk assignments (Kennett 1987, 83).

39. Again, our home-of-record data list each casualty's community *prior to entering* military service. Furthermore, in our analysis of more than 400 casualties in the Iraq War, we were able to confirm that in more than 95 percent of the cases, the military home-of-record data did indeed correctly list the soldier's community before entering the military. Thus, on average, officer casualties do not come from home-of-record communities that are wealthier than enlisted communities because their higher military pay allows them to live in communities with higher median incomes.

40. The law specifically provided for deferments for some public officials and for those whom "the President authorized for the 'maintenance of the public health, safety, or interest.'" However, according to a 2007 report by the Congressional Budget Office (2007) on the history of military manpower policy, draft deferments in World War II were considerably more limited than in World War I and earlier wars.

41. However, none of the relevant coefficients in the multivariate models were statistically significant.

42. Mirroring this argument, historian Lee Kennett (1987, 23) has concluded that "the Army was the nation itself, an authentic slice of American society with all its many layers. Given the amount of manpower mobilized, it was probably necessary that the Army be that way."

43. See Ginzberg (1959, 36) and Flynn (1993, 32). In his analysis of the World War II draft, Chambers (1975, 32) echoed this assessment: "The heaviest

conscription rates fell upon the children of the upper blue collar and lower white collar workers," not among the poorest segments of the population. In a similar vein, prior studies of recruiting records between the world wars show that the military consciously avoided recruiting from the lowest stratum of society, many of whom failed to meet various screening requirements because of health or educational reasons (Griffith 1982, 89). Thus recruiting, in addition to the draft, may help explain the lower than average casualty rates in the poorest counties in World War II.

44. National politicians and local draft boards alike also felt considerable political pressure to combat the appearance of draft inequities. For example, draft officials made big news out of the induction of William McChesney Martin, president of the New York Stock Exchange, who "exchanged his salary of $4,000 a month for a private's pay of $21 a month." A *New York Times* editorial expressed the popular expectation that the draft would make "no distinction between men of different social ranks or economic status." See Flynn (1993, 27).

45. http://www.sss.gov/induct.htm.

46. Kindsvatter (2003, 393).

47. Selective Service Act of 1948, PL 80-759. http://www.law.cornell.edu/uscode/html/uscode50a/usc_sec_50a_00000451-000-.html.

48. Kindsvatter (2003, 259).

49. Janowitz (1965, 55–56).

50. Flynn (1993, 160). See also Gerhardt (1971, 309–319).

51. Bureau of the Census, *Historical Statistics of the United States, Colonial Times to 1970*, part 2 (September 1975), 1143.

52. Army data from Janowitz and Moskos (1979, 193, 195).

53. Flynn (1993, 190).

54. In "1973 only about 50,000 registrants were being drafted and in July of that year the statute was allowed to lapse" (Calabresi and Bobbitt 1978, 165). For a more thorough discussion of the lottery and its operation, see Flynn (1993, 245–249) and Gerhardt (1971, 319–347).

55. Card and Lemieux (2001, 98). However, many deferments did not serve to exacerbate the casualty gap. For instance, "of the roughly 13 million men deferred as of June 30, 1971, one-half did not meet the [mental and physical] entry standards," and only 1.3 million had student deferments" (Angrist 1991, 588).

56. This is consistent with other studies of the same period. Flynn (1993, 5) summarizes this transformation: "As mobilization after World War II in the United States reached fewer people, the drafted population became less representative of the population as a whole." The result, according to Naval Health Research Center analyst Anne Hoiberg (1980, 219), was that: "the socioeconomic status of the enlisted force shifted from a fairly proportionate representation of all strata in World War II to an enlisted military consisting predominantly of the lower and working classes in Vietnam and the all-volunteer force."

57. Similarly, from 1977 to 1980, only 62.5 percent of army recruits and 71.2 percent of recruits from the military as a whole had a high school diploma, compared with 78.9 percent of their civilian peers (Office of the Secretary of Defense, Personnel,

and Readiness 2006, tables D-7, D-9, http://www.defenselink.mil/prhome/PopRep_FY06/). High school graduation rates for 18 to 24-year-old civilians were not available in the military report prior to 1977. From 1975 to 1977, the percentage of volunteers who did not hold a high school diploma was even higher than among volunteers in 1964. See Janowitz and Moskos (1979, 195).

58. For recent figures, see Office of the Secretary of Defense, Personnel, and Readiness (2006, table D-7. http://www.defenselink.mil/prhome/PopRep_FY06/).

59. For example, surveys conducted for the Senate Armed Services Committee of family income for new recruits in 1975 in the early years of the AVF showed that more than half of all recruits, 53.2 percent, came from communities with incomes of less than $10,000, compared with only 31.8 percent of the civilian population (Janowitz and Moskos 1979, 198). Our own analyses of recruiting data obtained by FOIA request for 1973–1998 also show significant socio-economic disparities.

60. *Rostker, Director of Selective Service, v. Goldberg et al.* (1981), 453 U.S. 57 at 76. Emphasis added. The Court also quoted Senator Roger Jepsen (R-IA): "The shortage would be in the combat arms. That is why you have drafts." The purpose of the draft—to produce combat troops specifically and not manpower more generally—was so clear that the Supreme Court ruled that "the courts are not free to make their own judgment on the question." In the words of the Court, "the purpose of registration . . . was to prepare for a draft of combat troops."

61. Flynn (1993, 171). Edwards's (2006, 145) analysis of the Korean War tells a similar story: "By late 1951, it was a different kind of war, and a different kind of soldier was fighting it. . . . Those who first manned the battle stations—the old timers, the retreads, the first of the reserves recalled—were now mostly gone." Draftees took their places.

62. Flynn (1993, 171).

63. Kindsvatter (2003, 154).

64. Draftees may have had greater risk for additional reasons. Units that consist of primarily inexperienced soldiers might also have higher risks because "green troops with inexperienced leaders made costly mistakes" (ibid., 71). Kindsvatter cites the World War II recollections of Lt. George Wilson on sending new recruits into combat: "It would be suicidal to take those men into battle" (Wilson 1987, 214, in Kindsvatter 2003, 72). In addition, more fighting led to increased battle fatigue. In Vietnam, sometimes battle fatigue meant ignoring the small details and raising the risks of death.

65. To be sure, there was sorting even among draftees. Analyzing data from a 1964 survey by the National Opinion Research Center, Charles Moskos found that 41.2 percent of prelottery draftees with less than a high school diploma were in combat arms, compared to only 15.5 percent of draftees with some college education. While these disparities between draftees muted the leveling effect of the draft, the data still suggest that, without the draft, the front lines would have seen fewer high-education soldiers (and presumably fewer soldiers from high-education places).

66. To reiterate, some highly skilled recruits are identified by military testing and assigned to very dangerous occupations or missions that require the application of all of their aptitude and skill. It is only *on average* that recruits with lower skills are more likely to be assigned to occupations with greater exposure to combat.

Technical Appendix to Chapter 3

1. Because of the significantly larger number of women serving in the contemporary armed forces, we measured enlistment rates per 10,000 residents. Replicating the model with the enlistment rate per 10,000 males yields substantively identical results. Alternatively, estimating separate regressions for each ZIP code's enlistment rate in each year yields statistically significant negative coefficients for median income and the percentage of residents with a college degree in each model.

2. ZIP code level data were cleaned and prepared for analysis from raw census data files downloaded from ftp://ftp.census.gov/census_2000/datasets/. Summary file 1 and summary file 3 data files were utilized.

3. All of the variables, except GOP presidential vote share, were measured at the ZIP code level. We measure GOP presidential vote share at the county level. To include the county level measure of percent voting for Bush in 2000, we had to match ZIP code tabulation areas with counties. To do this we utilized equivalency files developed by the Missouri Census Data Center (MCDC). The MCDC estimates that approximately 10% of ZIP code tabulation areas span across multiple counties. The results presented in the table exclude these ZIP codes. As a robustness check, we re-ran our models with and without the county-level partisanship variable. The substantive results of the models are not sensitive to the inclusion of the partisanship measure. For a more complete discussion of the ZIP code geographical unit, see http://mcdc2.missouri.edu/webrepts/geography/ZIP.resources.html.

4. ZIP code level recruit data was utilized to estimate counts of recruits by place. Due to the complexities of overlapping boundaries, this does not provide a precise count of recruits by place. Nevertheless, the variable serves as an excellent approximation of the level of military enlistment in each place.

5. To create these separate casualty rates for each war, we rely on occupational and rank data for each soldier in the individual-level casualty files described in chapter 2. From this information, we see that infantry casualties constituted 51 percent of all casualties in Korea, 42 percent in Vietnam, and 59 percent in Iraq. Ninety percent of all casualties were from enlisted ranks in Korea versus 88 percent in Vietnam and 92 percent in Iraq.

Chapter 4

1. Newman (2000).
2. Posner (2003, 28). Richard A. Posner, "An Army of the Willing," *New Republic* 228 (May 19, 2003), 27–29.
3. Moskos and Woods (1988).
4. Form DD 4, page 2 (October 2007).

5. Sparrow (2002, 275).

6. To be sure, the casualty gap is at times brought into the public eye by the media or public officials. Local media outlets have often explored the social background of their deceased soldiers. For instance, a series of articles by the *Austin American-Statesman* has raised alarm that poor, rural communities may be bearing a disproportionately large share of the casualty burden in the Iraq War. However, serious, sustained discussions of casualty inequalities and their consequences are largely absent from our political discourse.

7. Klarevas (2002, 417). For other studies that assert the critical importance of public opinion in driving military policymaking, see Gelb (1972), Hurwitz and Peffley (1987), Sobel (1993, 2001), Foyle (1999), Holsti (2004), Baum (2004), and Larson and Savych (2005). These literatures echo the views of many chief military policymakers themselves; for example, both the Weinberger and the Powell doctrines stress the critical importance of strong popular support for military actions to succeed. Other literatures, particularly game theoretic analyses in international relations, implicitly acknowledge the critical importance of public opinion in their focus on the threat of removal at the ballot box; see Bueno de Mesquita and Lalman (1992), Bueno de Mesquita and Siverson (1995), and Bueno de Mesquita et al. (1999, 2003).

8. For example, see Page, Shapiro, and Dempsey (1987, 23) and Gelpi, Feaver and Reifler (2009, 2).

9. Gartner (2008b, 99).

10. Aldrich et al. (2006, 481).

11. We discuss strands of this literature again in chapter 6. Among others, see Mueller (1973, 1994), Larson (1996), and Gartner and Segura (1998). Most recently in the context of the war in Iraq, see Boettcher and Cobb (2006), Eichenberg (2005), Eichenberg and Stoll (2006), Gelpi, Feaver, and Reifler (2006). Gelpi, Reifler, and Feaver (2007), and Voeten and Brewer (2006). For a recent overview of the wartime opinion literature, see Aldrich et al. (2006).

12. Jentleson (1992), Jentleson and Britton (1998), Russett and Nincic (1976), and Kohut and Toth (1995). Still others argue that whether the military action is a unilateral or a multilateral intervention is key to determining public support. See Kull (1995) and Kull and Ramsay (1994).

13. In a similar vein, Russett (1990–1991, 518) has shown that public support for the 1983 invasion of Grenada was higher when the mission's objectives were framed in terms of protecting Americans on the island instead of overthrowing a Marxist government.

14. Gartner and Segura (1998). See also Gartner (2008a).

15. Feaver and Gelpi (2004) and Gelpi, Feaver, and Reifler (2006, 2009). See also Kull and Ramsay (2001) and Eichenberg (2005). For contrasting perspectives, see Berinsky and Druckman (2007) and Klarevas, Gelpi and Reifler (2006).

16. See Brody (1991), Zaller (1992), Larson (1996), and Berinsky (2007).

17. Several studies, which we discuss in detail in the next two chapters, have examined the influence of geographic variance in local casualty rates on wartime support. However, no prior study has examined the consequences for opinion

formation of whether or not this distribution is more heavily weighted toward socioeconomically disadvantaged communities.

18. Russett (1990, 46).

19. Similarly, political science scholars have long recognized individuals' fluidity of opinion in an extensive literature that examines the ability of elites, the media, and other actors to prime the public to weigh some dimensions of an issue more than others while forming their policy preferences and political attitudes (Miller and Krosnick [1996, 2000], Iyengar and Kinder [1987]). Individuals express their preferences in light of the situation created for them. In our survey, we prime respondents to think about the existence of a socioeconomic casualty gap when forming their wartime judgments and policy preferences.

20. This survey, conducted from September 27–30, 2007, had 1,003 respondents drawn from across the continental U.S.

21. Our decile-level analysis in chapter 2 demonstrates that counties from the poorest three deciles have suffered approximately 1.5 times as many casualties as counties from the wealthiest three deciles. However, to simplify the language and eliminate any potential confusion, we opted for "nearly twice as many" to describe the casualty gap in the experimental manipulation.

22. Gallup Poll, September 14–16, 2007, USGALLUP.091907 R09.

23. T-tests reveal that the difference in means between the inequality treatment and the control groups is statistically significant, p < .10.

24. This initial prompt follows Feaver and Gelpi (2004). The casualty figure for Korea is an approximation of the number of total deaths, both in-theater and nontheater. Since each respondent was given the same information, using this total death figure (rather than the in-theater figure of approximately 36,000) does not affect the results of the experiment.

25. Feaver and Gelpi (2004) discuss the inherent difficulty in using such questions to measure casualty tolerance, and they pay particular attention to problems with using the word "acceptable" to describe casualties. For many, this word may trigger intense emotions; indeed, in various studies, including ours, casualty sensitivity questions routinely have the largest number of respondents who refuse to answer. Nevertheless, we followed Feaver and Gelpi's lead since alternative phrasings to "acceptable" introduce potential problems as well. In more recent work, Gelpi, Feaver, and Reifler (2009) have developed a new method of measuring casualty sensitivity. Rather than asking respondents to state a number of acceptable casualties, the authors asked each respondent whether he or she would be willing to support a given use of force if it produced no casualties. If the respondent said yes, they then asked a follow-up question about whether the respondent would continue to support the mission if it suffered X number of casualties (up to 50,000). While such an approach may afford advantages, for both logistical and financial reasons we adapted their earlier approach for our CARAVAN survey.

26. An additional result of note from this experiment is the general low level of public willingness to accept American casualties in a military strike against Iran. In their pre-Iraq War study, Feaver and Gelpi (2004) found that that the public was not

instinctively casualty phobic and unwilling to tolerate any U.S. casualties, particularly when the hypothetical military mission was justified on realpolitik/national interest grounds. By contrast, after four long years of war in Iraq, Americans in our survey showed little taste for another military conflict in the Middle East, even to protect our position in Iraq and to prevent Iran from acquiring weapons of mass destruction. The median response to our question was actually 0, though the mean was considerably higher at almost 25,000 casualties. This was driven by a number of outliers who replied that they would accept more than 500,000 casualties, the highest permissible response in our survey, to achieve U.S. objectives against Iran. Accordingly, in table 4.2 we examine the differences between inequality treatment and control groups in terms of the mean response and in terms of the number of casualties acceptable to respondents at the 75th percentile.

27. T-tests reveal that the difference in means between the inequality treatment and the control groups is statistically significant, $p < .10$.

28. This question was last asked as part of the General Social Survey by the University of Chicago's National Opinion Research Center in the summer of 2006, when 15 percent of Americans favored a return to the draft. More than a year and another 1,000 casualties in Iraq later, 21 percent of Americans in our survey replied that they supported abandoning the all-volunteer force.

29. T-tests reveal that the difference in means between the inequality and the shared sacrifice treatment groups is statistically significant, $p < .05$.

30. This survey, which produced a sample of 1,003 respondents from the continental U.S., was conducted from March 26–29, 2009.

31. In the first survey, we consciously adopted Feaver and Gelpi's (2004) wording and so used the in-theater and nontheater casualty total for Korea. In this second experiment, we used only the in-theater casualty total, as those are the casualties examined in the analyses of chapter 2.

32. See ibid., 108–109. The six categories of the number of casualties a respondent would accept are as follows: 0; 1–50; 51–500; 501–5,000; 5,001–50,000; and more than 50,000.

33. The online materials provide more details of the historical context of the casualty gap.

34. See chapter 6 of Cohen (1985) for discussion of egalitarian ideology and military service in the United States.

Technical Appendix to Chapter 4

1. Feaver and Gelpi (2004).

2. The figures in table 4.4 were calculated using survey weights.

3. An additional difference between the two surveys is the number of respondents who refused to answer the casualty sensitivity question. In September of 2007, 37 percent of respondents refused to answer this question; this percentage was by far the highest of any of our questions on the survey and is similar to the 30 percent refusal rate experienced by Feaver and Gelpi (2004, 110). By contrast, only 14 percent of respondents refused to answer the question in the March 2009 survey.

4. See, for example, Jentleson (1992), Jentleson and Britton (1998), and Feaver and Gelpi (2004).

Chapter 5

1. Maxwell (2008). Trevor Maxwell, "Tears Flow at South Portland High School over Third War Death," *Portland Press Herald* (May 28, 2008).
2. Brandon (1984, 49).
3. "Town Mourns Fallen Marines." *Newshour with Jim Lehrer* (Aug. 9, 2005). http://www.pbs.org/newshour/bb/military/july-dec05/ohio_8-09.html. In her recent study of Americans' responses to Civil War death, Faust (2008, 205) offers several similar examples of the ripple effects of personal contact with local casualties. Faust notes that Emily Dickinson, whose poetry captures the horrors of the conflict, "understood loss, for citizens of her tight-knit Massachusetts town had already been claimed by war." In letters, Dickinson acknowledged that "the loss of friends to death that struck 'sharp and early' had created in her 'a brittle love—of more alarm, than peace.'"
4. Sledge (2005).
5. Feaver and Gelpi (2004).
6. See, among others, Mueller (1973), Kernell (1978), Hibbs, Rivers, and Vasilatos (1982), Brace and Hinckley (1992), MacKuen, Erikson, and Stimson (1992), Clarke and Stewart (1994), Larson (1996), Gartner and Segura (1998), Baum and Kernell (2001), Kriner (2006), Gelpi, Feaver, and Reifler (2005/2006), Eichenberg (2005), Eichenberg and Stoll (2006), and Voeten and Brewer (2006). For a critique of this literature, see Burk (1999).
7. See Gartner, Segura, and Wilkening (1997), Gartner and Segura (2000, 2008), Carson et. al. (2001), Gartner, Segura, and Barratt (2004), Karol and Miguel (2007), Grose and Oppenheimer (2007), and Kriner and Shen (2007).
8. Berinsky (2007). See also Boettcher and Cobb (2006) and Cobb (2007).
9. Feaver and Gelpi (2004, 106).
10. See Sledge (2005) for a discussion of the historical development of the treatment of fatal casualties. Each service branch maintains its own policies regarding casualty assistance following a soldier's death:

The services have their own ways of handling this duty. In the Marine Corps, the officer—called a casualty assistance calls officer, or CACO—who knocks on a family's door is the same one who will guide them from notification to interment, and often beyond. The Army prefers to separate the tasks, so that those who deliver the shock are replaced by fresh faces. The division of labor is reflected in the jargon—the Army distinguishes between casualty notification officers and casualty assistance officers. (Burkin 2007).

See also Air Force Instruction 36-3002, Casualty Services; Marine Administrative Message 352/07, Casualty Procedures in Support of OEF/OIF Deployments; and Army Regulation 600-8-1, Army Casualty Program. Christian Burkin, "Causalty Officers Bear Heavy Burden One Door at a Time," *The Record* (July 8, 2007).

11. After a congressionally mandated review in 2006 by the Government Accountability Office, a number of steps were taken to improve these services for survivors of service members who die while on active duty. Notifications are made quickly. The air force currently estimates that 93 percent of next of kin are "notified within 4 hours of a confirmed casualty determination as required by Air Force instruction." See Government Accountability Office (2006a), as well as "Policies and Procedures regarding the Notification of Next of Kin of Wounded and Deceased Service Members," Statement of Maj. Gen. Anthony F. Przybyslawski, commander, Air Force Personnel Center, U.S. Air Force, to the U.S. House of Representatives Committee on Armed Services, June 27, 2007.

12. Burke (2007). Garance Burke, "Hundreds Mourn at Funeral for Soldier Slain in Iraq," *Oakland Tribune* (September 1, 2007).

13. Ibid.

14. Preusch and Sullivan (2006). Matthew Preusch and Julie Sullivan, "For Residents of Madras, Pain Replaces Hope Felt for Soldier Thomas Tucker," *Oregonian* (June 21, 2006).

15. Cary Rousseau, "Camden Soldier Remembered as Hero, Caring Student," *Associated Press* (August 3, 2003).

16. Kelsey (2005). Mark Kelsey, "Palmer Pays Respect to Fallen Son," *Mat-su Valley Frontiersman* (September 18, 2005).

17. See Moody (2006). For Moody's calculator see http://www.soc.duke.edu/~jmoody77/Hydra/scaleupcalc.htm. For family estimates, we use Moody's estimate of 49 for the size of an extended family. For the calculation of the number of people who may know a casualty through broader social networks, we draw on recent survey research that suggests that the average American mutually knows the names of 290 other people (Bernard et al. 2001). Adjusting this figure can significantly raise or lower estimates of casualty contact accordingly. Following Moody, we also used 280,000,000 for the U.S. population. Personal contact may be extended further still through the use of the Internet to spread the word about a soldier's death. A number of sites track deaths (American, coalition, Iraqi, and civilian) in the Iraq War. The Iraq Coalition Casualty Count Web site (http://icasualties.org) averages more than one million hits a week and frequently serves as a source for journalists (Cohen 2007). See, for example, the Iraq Coalition Casualty Count; Iraq War Heroes (http://IraqWarHeroes.org); Fallen Heroes Memorial (http://www.fallenheroesmemorial.com/); Iraq Page (http://www.pigstye.net/iraq/); Military Time's Honor the Fallen (http://www.militarycity.com/valor/honor.html); and the *Washington Post*'s Faces of the Fallen (http://projects.washingtonpost.com/fallen/). These sites do more than simply list the names of soldiers. By providing photos, personal information, and links to local newspaper articles and obituaries, they create a virtual space for the community to remember and revisit their fallen heroes.

18. These calculations are based on Iraq casualty data through the day prior to each survey.

19. Brody (1991), Zaller (1992, 1994a), Larson (1996), and Berinsky (2007).

20. For an examination of this hypothesis in a comparative context, see Koch and Gartner (2005).

21. Dreyfus (2006). Robert Dreyfus, "The Three Conversions of Walter Jones," *Mother Jones* (January/February, 2006).

22. Senator Robert Casey, July 11, 2007, press release, http://casey.senate.gov/record.cfm?id=278612.

23. Kriner and Howell (n.d.).

24. Frank H. Murkowski, "Gov. Statement on the Death of Sgt. Arcala," http://www.iraqwarheroes.com/arcala.htm, Sept. 14, 2005, no. 05–151.

25. "Soldier from Pocatello, ID, Killed by Iraq Roadside Bomb," *Associated Press State and Local Wire* (May 9, 2007).

26. Gilliam and Iyengar (2000).

27. Gartner (2004).

28. Howell and Pevehouse (2007).

29. Brandon (1984, 66).

30. Kay Stephens, "Local Soldier Killed in Iraq," *Altoona Mirror* (Aug. 23, 2007).

31. Cory Giger, "The Beat Goes On: Curve Fall Apart in Ninth Inning," *Altoona Mirror* (Aug. 25, 2007).

32. Jessica VanderKolk, "From Panic to Proactive," *Altoona Mirror* (Oct. 1, 2007). The wires similarly reported some details of the crash that killed Spc. Hook and disseminated them widely. However, the most extensive coverage of his death was that produced in his local community. The New Jersey *Star Ledger* also ran an article following Hook's death and noted that Hook frequently spent the summer in Little Egg Harbor with his father and stepmother. "Soldier With Ties to NJ Killed in Iraq Copter Crash," *Star-Ledger* (August 23, 2007).

33. Mac Banks, "Fort Mill's Own," *Fort Mill Times* (Nov. 13, 2003).

34. Mac Banks, "Neff Laid to Rest with Full Honors," *Fort Mill Times* (Nov. 20, 2003).

35. Iyengar and Kinder (1987), Kinder and Sanders (1996), and Nicholson and Howard (2003). On the limits of framing see Druckman (2001).

36. Iyengar and Kinder (1987), Krosnick and Brannon (1993), Iyengar and Simon (1993), and Miller and Krosnick (2000).

Technical Appendix to Chapter 5

1. Because the analysis pools data from both the March and October 2006 Gallup surveys, the model in table 5A.1 was also replicated including a dummy variable identifying the second survey. Results were virtually identical to those presented here.

2. Based on its overall tenor, coders were also asked to make a summary judgment about whether a speech was critical of the administration. Replicating the analyses in this appendix using this alternative coding scheme yields virtually identical results.

3. To identify leaders, we followed the designations in the *Congressional Quarterly Staff Directory*. We coded the following as foreign policy committees: House Armed Services/National Security; House International Relations; House

Intelligence; House Homeland Security; Senate Armed Services; Senate Foreign Relations; Senate Homeland Security and Governmental Affairs; Senate Intelligence.

4. The only exception is for the "Republican leader" first difference.

Chapter 6

1. Brandon (1984, 50, 53).

2. A growing literature in international relations argues that domestic constraints at the ballot box can explain differential conflict behaviors of democracies and non-democracies. See Bueno de Mesquita, et al. (1999, 2003). Political leaders anticipate the reaction of the electorate to various policy options, and they adapt their policy choices accordingly. If the casualty gap alters or even blunts the strength of this electoral check, as we discuss in the chapter's conclusion, then it can have significant consequences for the conduct of U.S. military policy.

3. Certainly, there were contemporary studies of opinion in the Korean War (e.g., Belknap and Campbell 1951; Suchman, Goldsen, and Williams 1953). Also, scholarship by Adam Berinsky (2007, 2009) is now beginning to rediscover the wealth of Gallup survey information from the World War II era, which yields a fascinating look at opinion dynamics in the 1930s and 1940s.

4. Verba et al. (1967).

5. Armor et al. (1967), Hahn (1970), Quinley (1970), Rosenberg, Verba, and Converse (1970), Modigliani (1972), Jennings and Markus (1977), Lau, Brown, and Sears (1978), and Lunch and Sperlich (1979).

6. Mueller (1973).

7. Larson (1996).

8. Gartner and Segura (1998). For experimental evidence that supports this argument, see Gartner (2008a).

9. Gartner, Segura, and Wilkening (1997).

10. In a follow-up study, Gartner and Segura (2000) examine the potentially mediating role of race in casualty response. Interestingly, they find that whites respond to local black casualties in the same way that they respond to local white casualties and largely vice versa.

11. The correlation coefficient is $r = .35$.

12. For the construction of both national and local casualty measures, we used the number of casualties suffered up until the last day of the month preceding the NES pre-election survey in presidential election years. In midterm election years, when there was no pre-election survey, we used the number of casualties suffered up until the last day of the month preceding the postelection survey.

13. Including logged cumulative casualties also helps alleviate concerns about temporal independence as it tracks the gradual decline in all respondents' probability of supporting the war from survey to survey. Indeed, this measure and a simple year variable are correlated $r = .90$.

14. County-level census data allow the construction of multiple alternative operationalizations of a county's casualty rate: per 10,000 males, per 10,000 males 24

and under, and per 10,000 males 34 and under. Just as all statistical results from our casualty gap analyses in chapter 2 were virtually identical regardless of which operationalization is used, so here, too, our choice of operationalization does not substantively alter any reported results.

15. In their broad study of public attitudes over a fifty-year period, Page and Shapiro (1992) found that better-educated Americans are more supportive of an internationalist foreign policy than their peers with lower levels of formal education.

16. Eichenberg (2003). For more on the gender gap, see Conover and Sapiro (1993) and Brandes (1994).

17. Verba et al. (1967), Guzman (1969), Lunch and Sperlich (1979), and Gartner and Segura (2000).

18. Foust and Botts (1991) and Appy (1993).

19. Gartner, Segura, and Wilkening (1997) also include dummy variables for Asians and Hispanics. Some scholars have suggested that Hispanics bore disproportionately high casualty rates in Vietnam and that their opinion could differ accordingly (Ornelas and Gonzalez 1971). However, in the NES studies (as opposed to Gartner and Segura's California data), these groups constitute less than one-half of 1 percent of the total sample. Including dummy variables for these groups yields virtually identical results.

20. Lunch and Sperlich (1979).

21. See Cooney (1984) and Moon (2003, 2008).

22. All of the first differences in this chapter are calculated for Democratic respondents, as they were the modal partisan category in the surveys. All first differences for the opinion models were also estimated by setting the logged cumulative casualties variable to the 1972 level and by using the local casualty rate percentiles in 1972.

23. Indeed, as Gartner and Segura (1998), Berinsky (2007), and others have noted, because logged cumulative casualties are so highly correlated with time, it is virtually impossible to distinguish their independent causal effect on trends in wartime support. Time itself (or any other variable highly correlated with time) could be causing the observed relationship. For a similar point in the context of presidential approval, see Kernell (1978). Because of these recognized difficulties in determining the independent effect of logged cumulative casualties, we do not graphically represent them in the figures. Local casualty rates, by contrast, vary significantly across the country at any given moment; as a result, we do not face similar inferential barriers when assessing relationships between local casualties and individual-level opinions.

24. Our approach is similar to that taken by Scott Gartner and Gary Segura (2000), who addressed a similar question with regard to race. By differentiating local casualties by race, Gartner and Segura examined whether whites responded only to white casualties and largely ignored black casualties and vice versa for African Americans. Indeed, some in the popular press have suggested white indifference to allegedly disproportionate black suffering as an important reason for continued support for the war among whites even in the face of its mounting costs. Gartner and Segura found no evidence of a differential between white Americans' responses to casualties sustained by white and black soldiers.

25. Yet, income does have an independent effect on wartime support, even after controlling for casualties. Thus, even if the casualty gap disappeared, a substantial opinion cleavage would continue to exist between rich and poor Americans.

26. When both income and education measures are included in the model, the coefficient for education is statistically insignificant. However, if we estimate a separate regression that excludes family income, the coefficient for education is also negative and statistically significant.

27. In fact, in all of our surveys pooled together, men and women differed by only 2 percent in the proportion that supported or opposed U.S. involvement in Vietnam.

28. For a similar result, see Lunch and Sperlich (1979). For a discussion of the differences in opinion between activists and non-activists with regards to the Vietnam War, see Verba and Brody (1970).

29. This result is consistent with prior research that suggests very limited relationships between measures of self-interest and attitudes toward the Vietnam War in general. See Lau, Brown, and Sears (1978).

30. Scholars have proposed a number of theories to explain the greater levels of war opposition in the African American community—from arguments that blacks bore a disproportionate share of the burden in Vietnam (or perceived that they did), to others that point to blacks' lower levels of trust in government more generally, to others that emphasize the role of vocal opposition by elites within the black community. See: Robinson and Jacobsen (1968), Hahn (1970), Helmer (1974), and Lunch and Sperlich (1979). Here, we remain agnostic. However, we find strong evidence confirming that blacks systematically differed from whites in how they viewed and responded to the war.

31. This lack of an effect, on average, may be due to the split between Catholics protesting in the name of peace and Catholics supporting the war as a front in the struggle against communism.

32. Model specifications with fixed effects for each state show a similar pattern: Respondents from Southern states were consistently the most supportive of the war when all other factors were held constant.

33. As in the preceding analysis, reestimating a model without the highly collinear income variable yields a negative and significant coefficient for respondent education.

34. In the ordered logit analysis of the original ordinal version of the dependent variable, the South coefficient is negative and statistically significant, $p < .01$.

35. For international relations studies that emphasize the critical importance of electoral dynamics in driving decisions regarding the use of forces, see Bueno de Mesquita and Lalman (1992), Bueno de Mesquita and Siverson (1995), Bueno de Mesquita et al. (1999, 2003).

36. In the last decade, a number of major works in political science have bemoaned the loss of democratic responsiveness among U.S. public officials. Allan Monroe's (1998) comprehensive study of the correlation between government action and public policy preferences in more than five hundred policy issues revealed that responsiveness to the public will was considerably lower from 1980 to 1993 than it was from 1960 to 1979. Similarly, by tracking the concordance between

government policies and popular preferences on social issues over time, Lawrence Jacobs and Robert Shapiro (2000) cogently argue that governmental responsiveness to centrist opinion has declined dramatically since the 1970s. Given this decrease in responsiveness, a strong electoral connection is imperative if variance in local casualty rates caused by the casualty gap is to have significant ramifications for policy.

37. For the public's lack of information in foreign affairs, see Lippman (1922), Almond (1960), Campbell et al. (1960), and Converse (1964). Accordingly, most studies have found low levels of political responsiveness to Americans' foreign policy preferences. For example, forty years ago, political scientists Warren Miller and Donald Stokes (1963) found little evidence that constituents' preferences in matters of foreign policy had any tangible influence on congressional behavior. In a more recent example, Richard Sobel's (1998) careful study of elite debate, media coverage, and public opinion with regard to military intervention in Bosnia revealed considerable discrepancies between policy debates in Washington and in the newsroom and average public opinion on Main Street, USA.

38. With respect to public opinion, recent studies have argued that through a variety of cognitive shortcuts the mass public is able to form cohesive, consistent, even rational beliefs on major questions of foreign affairs. See Page, Shapiro, and Dempsey (1987), Page and Shapiro (1992), Holsti (1992), and Jentleson (1992).

39. Aldrich (1977), Fiorina (1981), Aldrich, Sullivan, and Borgida (1989), Aldrich, Griffin, and Rickershauser (2005), and Gelpi, Reifler, and Feaver (2007). All of these studies have examined the influence of national casualties and war outcomes on presidential electoral results. One study by Karol and Miguel (2007), however, has explored and found evidence for the effect of state casualty rates on presidential electoral outcomes at the state level.

40. Wildavsky (1966), Peterson (1994), Meernik (1995), Gowa (1998), and Moore and Lanoue (2003).

41. Murray and Weisman (2007). Shaliagh Murray and Jonathan Weisman, "Republicans Soften Stance on Pullout Language," *Washington Post* (March 27, 2007), A4.

42. Research into Civil War voting patterns by Jamie Carson and his colleagues (2001) found significant correlations between district-level casualties and voting patterns in the House midterm elections of 1862–1863. Jumping forward more than a century, Gartner, Segura, and Barratt (2004) discovered that state-level casualty rates continued to influence both candidate positioning and, ultimately, popular voting in Vietnam-era senatorial elections. In this section, we build on these prior studies in two ways. First, we shift the focus of analysis from the Senate to the House of Representatives to determine whether the impact of Vietnam battle deaths is limited to just presidential and senatorial election contests in the modern era or whether they had political ramifications for all federally elected officials in contemporary contests. Second, we shift the level of analysis from the aggregate to the individual level. Rather than examining correlations between local casualty rates and raw voting returns at the state or district level, we

again examine the impact of the casualty rate of an individual respondent's local county on the likelihood that the respondent will vote Democratic or Republican in the upcoming congressional election.

43. All of the first differences were estimated for Democratic respondents. All of the first differences for the 1964–1968 models were also estimated by setting the logged cumulative casualties variable to its 1968 level and by using the local casualty rate percentiles in 1968.

44. Replicating the analysis without the education measure yields a statistically significant, negative coefficient for family income.

45. Gilens (1988) and Kaufman and Petrocik (1999).

46. All of the first differences were estimated for Democratic respondents. All of the first differences for the 1970–1972 models were also estimated by setting the logged cumulative casualties variable to its 1972 level and by using the local casualty rate percentiles in 1972.

47. Russett (1993), Ray (1995), Luttwak (1996), and Gartner and Segura (1998).

48. Morgan and Campbell (1991), Morgan and Schwebach (1992), Maoz and Russett (1993), and Russett and Oneal (2001).

49. Reiter and Stam (2002).

50. Feaver and Gelpi (2004, 100) summarize this logic: "Implicit in the argument that democracies behave differently with regard to the use of force is the belief that democracies are sensitive to public opinion and public opinion is sensitive to the human costs of war." While Feaver and Gelpi question the conventional belief in the uniform and extreme casualty sensitivity of the American public, they nonetheless argue that "this assumption is the rarely specified and rarely discussed core causal mechanism behind the so-called democratic peace." Not all democratic peace theories rely so explicitly on casualties. Some emphasize the importance of shared norms of conduct among democratic nations and maintain that these account for democracies' unwillingness to fight one another (e.g., Maoz and Russett 1993, Dixon 1994). In his eighteenth-century theoretical treatise, Immanuel Kant (1983 [1795]) stressed the importance of wartime financial costs. Still others emphasize the greater average levels of trade between democratic dyads (e.g., Oneal and Russett 1997, Mansfield and Pevehouse 2003). Nevertheless, the assumption that the public responds negatively to casualties and that this brings political pressure to bear on military policymakers is widespread. Thus, our finding that this response to casualties is moderated by variance in casualty rates across the country has wide-ranging implications.

51. For the net change to be zero, the effects of local casualty rates on opinion would have to be linear. Our models have implicitly assumed this. However, there are strong reasons to suspect that this may not be the case. For example, increasing the number of casualties in a community from 0 to 5 may cause a significantly greater increase in antiwar sentiment than an increase from 25 to 30 casualties. If so, then the increase in antiwar sentiment caused by communities previously insulated from casualties being exposed to the mean casualty rate may well exceed the decrease in antiwar sentiment caused by communities that previously suffered

high casualty rates now experiencing the lower mean casualty rate. Moving beyond the traditional focus on logged cumulative casualties to examine further nonlinearities in the relationship between casualties—both local and national—and public opinion is ripe ground for future research.

52. See, among others, Verba, Schlozman, and Brady (1995) and Oliver (2000).

Technical Appendix to Chapter 6

1. Indeed, replicating the model in column 1 of table 6A.1 separately for Americans over thirty and thirty and under yields a strong, statistically significant, positive coefficient for local casualty rates for both groups.

2. However, replicating separate models for income and education yields statistically significant negative coefficients for each.

Chapter 7

1. For example, in July of 2006, U.S. Marine veteran and Democratic senatorial candidate in Virginia Jim Webb, who had been decorated for his service in Vietnam, openly evoked the comparison to Vietnam and called Iraq a quagmire on the campaign trail (Jeff Schapiro, "Webb Rips Bush over Iraq Policy," *Richmond Times Dispatch* [July 2, 2006]). Also in July 2006, Nebraska Senator Chuck Hagel called the war in Iraq "an absolute replay of Vietnam" (Jake Thompson, "Hagel's Iraq-Vietnam Parallel Draws Mixed Reactions in D.C.," *Omaha World-Herald* [July 30, 2006]). For an academic comparison of the two, see Campbell (2007).

2. George W. Bush, "Remarks at the Veterans of Foreign Wars Convention in Kansas City, Missouri," *Public Papers of the President*, Aug. 22, 2007.

3. In December 2008 the National Priorities Project estimated that the cost of the Iraq War had already exceeded $590 billion. http://www.nationalpriorities.org/costofwar_home. According to the Congressional Research Service (RL32090), the cost of the Vietnam War in 2006 dollars was approximately $640 billion. If measured in terms of percentage of gross domestic product (GDP), however, the costs of Vietnam still dwarf those of Iraq.

4. Verba et al. (1967)

5. For trends in increasing partisan polarization more generally, see McCarty, Poole, and Rosenthal (2006).

6. Jacobson (2006).

7. Eichenberg and Stoll (2006). See also Mueller (2005).

8. Gelpi, Feaver, and Reifler (2005/2006). Experimental research by Boettcher and Cobb (2006) suggests that the way in which the media and elites frame casualties also influences their impact on public opinion and support for war.

9. Eichenberg (2005) found a similar dynamic in his analysis of opinion polls before and during the fighting in Iraq. Before the invasion, polls showed that an average of 61 percent of Americans supported military action, and during the fighting, an average of 72 percent supported the decision to use force. After the declaration of

mission accomplished, support fell to 51 percent, lower than the prewar level, as casualties rose.

10. Voeten and Brewer (2006).

11. This difference in means is statistically significant, $p < .001$, two-tailed test.

12. The only other variables included in the Vietnam models but not included here are the indicators for draft-age males, Jews, and Catholics. In the era of the all-volunteer force, we have less theoretical reason to believe that 18–29-year-old males should take distinctly different opinions on questions of war. The religious indicators could not be included because Gallup did not collect demographic data on respondents' religious affiliations.

13. In the ordinal model, however, the coefficient is significant: $p < .05$, two-tailed test.

14. Ron Martz, "Vets' Military Families Join Support Troops Rally," *Atlanta Journal Constitution* (Mar. 15, 2007).

15. Despite the small sample sizes, t-tests reveal that this difference in means is statistically significant, $p < .01$, two-tailed test.

16. The poll was taken from October 20–22, 2006. We limit our analysis here to the October poll because its proximity to election day should make it a much better indicator of what happened on November 7 than a comparable survey adminis-tered in March. However, pooling the results for both polls yields very similar results.

17. This difference in means is statistically significant, $p < .10$, two-tailed test.

18. This section is adapted from Kriner and Shen (2007).

19. In the forthcoming statistical models, we include all of the states with senatorial contests except for Connecticut and Vermont. Because these contests were com-plicated by strong, indeed favored, third-party candidates, they were excluded from the analysis. In Connecticut, political newcomer Ned Lamont ran against incumbent Joe Lieberman to protest Senator Lieberman's support for the Iraq war. Although Lamont won the primary, Lieberman successfully ran as an inde-pendent and held his Senate seat by garnering 50 percent of the vote to Lamont's 40 percent. Vermont presents a more difficult case because independent candi-date Bernie Sanders won the Democratic primary but declined the nomination. Sanders defeated his Republican rival, Richard Tarrant, for the seat vacated by independent Senator James Jeffords by securing 65 percent of the vote. To check the robustness of our results, we conducted additional analyses that included these states, which yielded virtually identical results across specifications. In a similar vein, Indiana was an outlier as it was the only race not contested in 2006 by both major parties. Excluding Indiana from the analysis also yields virtually identical results across specifications.

20. The bivariate relationship is statistically significant, $p < .05$, two-tailed test.

21. For opponent quality, see Squire (1992), Green and Krasno (1988, 1992) and Jacobson (2004). For campaign spending, see Jacobson (1978, 1985, 1990), Abramowitz (1988, 1989) and Gerber (1998). An additional political factor that may have influenced the change in GOP vote share is any change in the incumbency status of the Republican candidate from the 2000 to the 2006

campaign. All of the models were reestimated with two dummy variables that indicate whether the GOP candidate went from being a challenger (either facing an incumbent or vying for an open seat) to an incumbent from 2000 to 2006 or vice versa. All of our results remain virtually identical in this expanded specification. These augmented models show the expected negative relationship between a shift from incumbent to challenger status and GOP vote share at both the state and county levels. A complementary shift from challenger to incumbent status, however, had no effect at the state level and, contra expectations, a negative correlation with the change in GOP vote share at the county level. The relationship is almost certainly spurious. Only three states involved a Republican challenger from 2000 (2002 for James Talent) running in 2006 as an incumbent—Virginia, Nevada, and Missouri. In the Virginia race, George Allen lost to James Webb; in Nevada, John Ensign handily beat Jack Carter, but not by the same margins as he trounced his Democratic opponent, who lacked a presidential name, in 2000; and the Missouri races were decided by razor-thin margins in 2000, 2002, and 2006. A confluence of national trends and idiosyncratic factors, not any change in incumbency status, determined the results of these three elections.

22. Green and Krasno (1988). Because Green and Krasno's scale was designed to measure challenger quality, it required one minor modification. If the Republican candidate faced an incumbent senator, we coded the opponent quality score at its maximum value of 8. Prior studies have adopted varied operationalizations of relative campaign spending. To control for several outliers in Republican-opponent spending, in this model we took the log of both major candidates' expenditures as reported to the Federal Elections Commission and calculated the percentage of this total spent by the Republican. All of our results are robust across other operationalizations, such as the change in the percentage of unlogged total expenditures spent by the Republican candidate and the change in the ratio of Republican to Democratic spending. Following Jacobson, Green and Krasno and others, we recoded the handful of missing expenditure data points as $1,000. All of these were minor, dark-horse candidates with little in the way of a formal campaign apparatus.

23. Abramowitz and Segal (1986), Campbell and Sumners (1990), Campbell (1991), Atkeson and Partin (1995), and Carsey and Wright (1998).

24. See, among others, Jacobson and Kernell (1981), Alesina and Rosenthal (1989), and Lewis-Beck and Rice (1992); see Squire (1995) for a review.

25. These demographic controls were constructed from data obtained from the U.S. Census Bureau's summary files (sf3) for the 2000 Census.

26. On the civil-military gap, see, among others, Huntington (1957), Betts (1991), Feaver and Kohn (2001), and Feaver and Gelpi (2004).

27. Casualty figures, particularly at the county level, exhibited considerable variance. For example, at the county level the standard deviation for casualty rates per ten thousand residents was three times the mean value, and a small number of outlying counties, mostly in very sparsely populated areas, had casualty rates of more than fifty times the mean value. To mitigate these extreme outliers, all of the

models at both the state and county levels were replicated by using logged tallies and logged casualty rates. In almost every specification, the observed relationships between casualties and the change in Republican vote share were even stronger when we used the logged measures.

28. Alternatively, as discussed earlier, the considerable variance in county-level casualty rates, particularly the presence of low-population outlier communities that had suffered one or two casualties, may be skewing the results when we assume a linear relationship. To account for this, we reestimated the model by using the logged casualty rate. In this specification, the relevant coefficient is negative, as expected, and statistically significant, $p < .10$ on a one-tailed test. While far from conclusive evidence, the logged casualty rate specification is at least suggestive of a relationship between county casualty rates and a change in the Republican vote share in every Senate contest. Nevertheless, the number of casualties incurred by a county appears to be the strongest correlate of changing GOP electoral fortunes at the county level.

29. The two are positively correlated, though the correlation is not especially high ($r = .16$).

30. Senator Lincoln Chaffee voted against the authorization, and Senator James Talent of Missouri, who defeated incumbent Senator Jean Carnahan in a special election in 2002, did not hold his seat at the time of the authorization vote. Replicating this final set of models at the county level (without Rhode Island and Missouri) yields even stronger results for both casualties measures.

Technical Appendix to Chapter 7

1. Difference in means tests reveal that respondents who had personal contact with casualties were no more or less likely to respond that the war had affected them positively than were those who did not have personal contact with casualties.

2. Because the self-reported income measure was missing for a number of respondents, we exclude it from the models reported in table 7A.1; we are confident that education will pick up any differences along socioeconomic lines. Estimating models with the income variable yields virtually identical results for all of the models reported in the chapter.

3. Conover and Sapiro (1993) and Nincic and Nincic (2002).

4. Because the withdrawal models pool data from both the March and October 2006 Gallup surveys, all models in Table 7A.2 were also replicated including a dummy variable identifying the second survey. Results were virtually identical to those presented here.

5. As discussed in the text, when we reestimated the logit analysis on all of the respondents, the casualties coefficient was positive but not statistically significant.

6. Among Republicans, being black ($N = 2$) and knowing a casualty ($N = 27$) both perfectly predicted failure (i.e., not voting Democratic). Therefore, these variables and observations are dropped from the models.

Chapter 8

1. This chapter is adapted from Kriner and Shen (2009).

2. The residents of Hollidaysburg were far from the vanguard of Americans demanding a withdrawal of U.S. forces from Iraq; however, reports suggest that by 2006 there was considerably more dissent and unease than in parallel rural Republican communities in Pennsylvania without the strong local connection to the war's costs in blood. Indeed, Congressman and Hollidaysburg resident Bill Shuster estimated before the 2006 election that unease concerning the war could cost him up to 8 points at the polls. See Stephen Braun, "War Wears on Small Town's Spirit," *Los Angeles Times* (Oct. 30, 2006).

3. The figure is the change in the percentage of the two-party vote that Santorum received from 2000 to 2006. This represents an approximately 0.5 standard deviation increase over the mean loss for Santorum in the state.

4. Skocpol (1999); Putnam (2000); Skocpol, Ganz, and Munson (2000); Mettler (2002); and Skocpol et al. (2002).

5. See, among others, Downs (1957), Riker and Ordeshook (1968) and Fiorina (1976).

6. Putnam (1993, 2000) and Verba, Schlozman, and Brady (1995).

7. Stein and Russett (1980) and Skocpol et al. (2002).

8. Miller (1974), Citrin (1974), Nye (1997), and Sparrow (2002).

9. Useem (1973) and Fendrich (2003).

10. McAdam and Paulsen (1993).

11. Tarrow (1994).

12. McAdam and Su (2002, 699).

13. Useem (1973, 25).

14. Crowley and Skocpol (2001, 815); italics in original.

15. See Skocpol et. al. 2002 (147–150). Southern whites experienced a sharp decline in associational memberships during the war itself, but such memberships declined among northern whites as well. See also Kage's (2005) analysis of post–World War II Japan.

16. Putnam (2000, 272).

17. In a similar vein, Sparrow's (2002, 274) analysis of the changing relationship between state and society after Vietnam argues that not only did the Vietnam War fail to spur increased engagement, but it was also an important contributor to "the growing reluctance of Americans to participate in or assist the government."

18. Skocpol (1999, 483).

19. Another study that rejects the conventional treatment of war as a monolithic variable that affects all Americans equally is Crowley and Skocpol's (2001) analysis, which operationalizes the "effects of the Civil War" as "percent in Union armies" and "pension dollars per pensioner."

20. Verba and Nie (1972), Wolfinger and Rosenstone (1980), Rosenstone and Hansen (1993), and Verba et al. (1995).

21. Oliver (2000).

22. We have also reestimated all of the models with a variety of alternative contextual control variables, many of which are highly correlated, including percentage of residents living in urban areas, population density, median education, and median age. All of the results are virtually identical across specifications.

23. Beck, Katz, and Tucker (1998).

24. More than 90 percent of all Vietnam casualties were men between 18 and 34 years of age. Reestimating the models with casualty rates calculated in terms of casualties per 1,000 males age 18 to 24 or per 1,000 total inhabitants yields very similar results across specifications in both the NES and the SCBS analyses.

25. Coleman (1990), Putnam (1993, 2000), Fukuyama (1995), Levi (1996), and Hetherington (1998).

26. However, other scholars have found little evidence of a significant causal effect for levels of trust on political participation: See Teixeira (1992), Rosenstone and Hansen (1993), and Brehm and Rahn (1997).

27. These figures represent the estimated number of voters who stayed away from the polls as a result of local casualty rates (generated by multiplying each county's casualty rate by the relevant coefficient and summing across counties) as a percentage of the total number of Americans who voted in that election.

28. For more specifics on the SCBS models, we refer readers to the discussion in the technical appendix.

29. To illustrate this dynamic, consider two hypothetical counties that both exhibited 55 percent turnout rates in the 1964 election. The first county experienced high casualties in Vietnam, and by 1976 its turnout rate had decreased to 50 percent. The second county did not suffer high casualties in Vietnam, and its turnout rate in 1976 remained at 55 percent. If turnout in these counties remains unchanged, subsequent year-by-year models, such as those in table 8.2, would show null results for the casualties variable. By contrast, an individual-level analysis in a future year would still show that, *ceteris paribus*, a respondent from the high-casualty county is less likely to vote on average than a respondent from the low-casualty county. The turnout gap between these counties is not increasing, but it does persist. This finding of a persistent gap in political engagement between citizens of communities that suffered high and low casualty rates in Vietnam is not unique. Indeed, in its duration it parallels research by Putnam (2000, 272), which suggests that Vietnam veterans, unlike veterans of previous wars, experienced greater isolation and social alienation for decades after the war's conclusion.

30. Crowley and Skocpol (2001, 818).

31. The SCBS also contains a measure of trust in the federal government. Replicating the trust in government model in column 2 of table 8A.2 with SCBS data also yields a strong, negative, statistically significant correlation between local casualty rates and trust.

32. Surprisingly, the coefficient for a county's casualty rate in Korea is negative throughout the years surveyed, even before the war. The consistent negative relationship suggests that turnout may have been declining, albeit very slightly, in communities that would suffer high casualty rates in Korea even before the conflict began. Yet, as in the Vietnam analyses, none of the prewar casualties

coefficients are statistically significant, and they are all much smaller in magnitude than the coefficient in the wartime 1952 election.

33. For studies that identify war as a principal agent of major social and institutional change, see Sparrow (1997), Kryder (2000), Buzzanco (1999), Skocpol (1992), Katznelson and Shefter (2002), and Mayhew (2005).

34. King, Martin Luther, Jr. "The Casualties of the War in Vietnam," Speech given February 25, 1967. Transcript online at the Martin Luther King, Jr., Research & Education Institute. http://mlk-kpp01.stanford.edu/kingweb/publications/speeches/unpub/670225-001_The_Casualties_of_the_War_in_Vietnam.htm

Technical Appendix to Chapter 8

1. Achen and Shively (1995) and Sampson, Morenoff, and Gannon-Rowley (2002).

2. See, for example, Oliver (1999, 2000, 2001, 2003), Kohn (2004), Humphries (2001), and Williamson (2002).

3. The results in both tables 8A.2 and 8A.4 are for unweighted NES data. As a robustness check, all of the models were reestimated both by using survey weights and by simply including the weights on the right-hand side of the regression equation with virtually identical results across specifications.

4. The Korea casualty data were obtained from the "Records on Korean War Dead and Wounded Army Casualties, 1950–1970," maintained by the U.S. National Archives. We included in our Korea casualty count soldiers listed as follows: died nonbattle; declared dead (missing in action or captured); died as result of being gassed in action; died as result of missile wound received in action; died as result of nonmissile wound received in action; died as result of radiation received in action; and died of other injuries received in action. The World War II casualty data were obtained at the county level from the "World War II Honor List of Dead and Missing Army and Army Air Forces Personnel," maintained by the U.S. National Archives.

5. Fewer than one hundred U.S. soldiers died between the 1972 elections and the withdrawal of U.S. combat troops from Vietnam in March of 1973.

Chapter 9

1. Barack Obama Inaugural Address, Jan. 20, 2009. http://www.whitehouse.gov/blog/inaugural-address/.

2. The quote is from Thomas Paine's "Common Sense, #1 Crisis." It appeared in the *Philadelphia Journal* in December 1776, and George Washington had it read to his troops at Valley Forge to boost their morale. The full quote reads:

Quitting this class of men, I turn with the warm ardor of a friend to those who have nobly stood, and are yet determined to stand the matter out: I call not upon a few, but upon all: not on this state or that state, but on every state: up and help us; lay your shoulders to the wheel; better have too much force than too little, when so great an object is at stake. Let it be told to the future world, that in the depth of winter, when nothing but hope and virtue could survive, that the city and the country, alarmed at one common danger, came forth to meet and to repulse it. Say not that thousands are gone, turn out your tens of thousands; throw not the burden of the day upon Providence, but "show your faith by your works," that God may bless you. It matters not where you live, or what rank of life you hold, the evil or the blessing will reach you all. The far and the near, the home counties and the back, the rich and the poor, will suffer or rejoice alike. The heart that feels not now is dead; the blood of his children will curse his cowardice, who shrinks back at a time when a little might have saved the whole, and made them happy. I love the man that can smile in trouble, that can gather strength from distress, and grow brave by reflection. 'Tis the business of little minds to shrink; but he whose heart is firm, and whose conscience approves his conduct, will pursue his principles unto death.

Online at http://www.ushistory.org/PAINE/crisis/index.htm.

3. Certainly some in the popular press have raised the issue. For example, a 2003 *New York Times* article (Elizabeth Becker, "The Struggle for Iraq: The Soldiers," Nov. 2, 2003, p. 12) offered this observation: "It is a different war in a different era, fought by a different American Army. Yet the emerging profile of the soldiers, sailors, pilots and other service members dying in Iraq bears a surprising similarity to those who lost their lives in the Vietnam War." The article, however, rests only on some comparisons that it admits are "inexact." Academics are quoted, but no empirical studies are cited. Similarly, in 2006, *USA Today* ran a story titled "Sacrifice: War's Burden Falls on the few." http://blogs.usatoday.com/oped/2006/12/post_49.html.

4. Vice President Joe Biden, *Face the Nation*, Jan. 25, 2009. http://www.cbsnews.com/stories/2009/01/25/ftn/main4752148.shtml.

5. According to the Department of Defense, 70 American soldiers were killed in Afghanistan in June and July of 2009; 490 American soldiers were wounded during this period, which is again by far the most of any two month period during the war. http://siadapp.dmdc.osd.mil/personnel/CASUALTY/oefmonth.pdf.

6. Although we do not have the requisite data from all four wars to directly investigate the claim, it is almost certain that a wounded gap has always accompanied a casualty gap. Based on the wounded data we do have available, the same socioeconomic disparities in casualty rates across the country are present in wounded rates as well.

7. As we report in chapter 2, in Korea, Vietnam, and Iraq, the three lowest income deciles took on 35 percent, 36 percent, and 38 percent of the casualties, respectively. At the same time, in these wars the top three deciles by income suffered only 25 percent, 26 percent, and 23 percent of the casualties, respectively.

8. Karl Vick, "The Lasting Wounds of War," *Washington Post* (Apr. 27, 2004), A01.

9. *CBS News*, "The Wounds of War," Feb. 12, 2006.

10. Surgeon and Lt. Col. Robert Carroll, quoted in Vick (2004).

11. Vick (2004).

12. In addition to the costs of physical wounds, the costs of returning soldiers' psychiatric injuries must also be taken into account. Public health scholars, amongst others, have led the way in trying to bring mental health concerns to public attention. See, e.g. Friedman (2004, 2005, 2006), Hoge, et al. (2006), Pols and Oak (2007), and Seal, et al. (2007).

13. Ratios were calculated using data from the Department of Defense statistical report "Principal Wars in Which the United States Participated: U.S. Military Personnel Serving and Casualties." http://siadapp.dmdc.osd.mil/personnel/CASUALTY/WCPRINCIPAL.pdf. The Korean War ratio utilized the figure of 54,246 for worldwide military deaths.

14. In the context of Operation Iraqi Freedom, critics of the Bush administration have long called for the release of complete and accurate data on America's wounded soldiers. On September 8, 2004, Ralph Nader wrote his second letter to President Bush, in which he requested the full release of the data on those wounded in Iraq. In that letter, Nader called for "information on fatalities, the injured, the sick, and the mentally afflicted, both in combat and non-combat activities in the Iraq War and occupation" in order to show more clearly the "fuller price paid by our sons and daughters in Iraq to the parents, friends, relatives and their fellow Americans." Full release of the number of wounded soldiers, as well as some demographic information about the types of soldiers being wounded, would help the nation better understand the full costs of our current military campaigns. Ralph Nader, letter to President Bush, Sept, 8, 2004. Available online at http://web.archive.org/web/ 20060324011505/http://www.votenader.com/media_press/index.php?cid=188.

15. Gartner (2008b, 99).

16. For Iraq War data, see http://siadapp.dmdc.osd.mil/personnel/CASUALTY/oif-total-by-month.pdf. For Afghanistan data, see http://siadapp.dmdc.osd.mil/personnel/CASUALTY/oefmonth.pdf.

17. Indeed, the experiences of Britain and other European nations in World War I led them to pioneer the use of modern occupational assignment techniques. In his comprehensive study of World War II manpower policies, Ginzberg (1959) laments the United States' failure to follow suit until late in the war, and he meticulously details the costs of early, unsophisticated occupational assignment procedures.

18. Indeed, the issue of inequality and military sacrifice may find its way into our cultural conscience through popular channels. Discussing the title of the last episode of The Sopranos, "Made in America," the show's creator David Chase revealed that the episode "was about the war in Iraq—it was made in America, and as you saw in the show, Tony and Carmela just didn't want their son to go, and they could afford to see that their son didn't go. Like some of our leaders." If the issue can make its way on to The Sopranos, it can surely be raised in serious discussion of the country's military affairs. See: David Chase Interview. *GQ Magazine*. December 2007.

19. Research by psychologist Philip Tetlock (2003) on sacred-secular tradeoffs suggests that when a choice is made to seem tragic rather than taboo, individuals are

more accepting of it. If the casualty gap is framed as an unfortunate byproduct of efficient military manpower policies and market forces, public reactions to it could be starkly different.

20. Operation Truth press release, "Iraq Veterans Call for More Prominent Casualty Reporting in American Newspapers," (Oct. 25, 2005); http://www.freepress.net/release/101.

21. To be sure, there remain many additional research questions worthy of investigation. For instance, throughout this book we treat military manpower policies as an outcome of societal inequality. In chapter 3 we argue that inequality in educational and occupational opportunities shape both the processes by which some young men and women enter military service while others do not and the mechanisms through which new recruits are assigned to positions within the service. From this perspective, inequality in military sacrifice is largely a function of underlying inequality in society as a whole. There is an emerging body of research, however, that examines the extent to which military spending may contribute to economic inequality. Economist John Abell, for instance, studying the period since Vietnam, finds that greater military spending is related to higher levels of income inequality. This relationship holds even after controlling for macroeconomic factors such as taxes, economic growth, interest rates, inflation, and non-military spending. Two economists at the University of Texas, Hamid Ali and James Galbraith, found a similar result when looking at variation in 160 countries from 1987 to 1997. Controlling for a host of confounding factors, they find that higher per-capita military spending is positively and significantly related to income inequality. If future research confirms these linkages and can establish the mechanisms that underlie them, then it would suggest a cyclical effect. Rather than simply reflecting underlying societal inequality, the military may be both a product and a creator of it. See Abell (1994), Ali and Galbraith (2003), Graeff and Mehlkop (2006), and Kick, Davis, and Kentor (2006).

22. Franklin (1810, 228).

References

Abell, John D. 1994. "Military Spending and Income Inequality." *Journal of Peace Research* 31: 35–43.

Abramowitz, Alan. 1988. "Explaining Senate Election Outcomes." *American Political Science Review* 82: 385–403.

———. 1989. "Campaign Spending in U.S. Senate Elections." *Legislative Studies Quarterly* 14: 487–507.

——— and Jeffrey Segal. 1986. "Determinants of the Outcomes of U.S. Senate Elections." *Journal of Politics* 48: 433–439.

Achen, Christopher, and W. Phillips Shively. 1995. *Cross-level Inference*. Chicago: University of Chicago Press.

Aldrich, John. 1977. "Electoral Choice in 1972: A Test of Some Theorems of the Spatial Model of Electoral Competition." *Journal of Mathematical Sociology* 5: 215–237.

———, Christopher Gelpi, Peter Feaver, Jason Reifler, and Kristin Sharp. 2006. "Foreign Policy and the Electoral Connection." *Annual Review of Political Science* 9: 477–502.

Aldrich, John, J. D. Griffin, and Jill Rickershauser. 2005. "The Presidency and the Campaign: Campaigns and Voter Priorities in the 2004 Election." In *The Presidency and the Political System*, ed. Michael Nelson. Washington, D.C.: CQ Press. 219–234.

Aldrich, John, John Sullivan, and Eugene Borgida. 1989. "Foreign Affairs and Issue Voting: Do Presidential Candidates 'Waltz' before a Blind Audience?" *American Political Science Review* 83: 123–141.

Alesina, Alberto, and Howard Rosenthal. 1989. "Partisan Cycles in Congressional Elections and the Macroeconomy." *American Political Science Review* 83: 373–398.

Ali, Hamid E., and James Galbraith. 2003. "Military Expenditures and Inequality: Empirical Evidence from Global Data." University of Texas at Austin Working Paper no. 24. October 10.

Almond, Gabriel. 1960. *The American People and Foreign Policy*. New York: Praeger.

Altman, Stuart, and Alan Fechter. 1967. "The Supply of Military Personnel in the Absence of a Draft." *American Economic Review* 57: 19–31.

Angrist, Joshua D. 1991. "The Draft Lottery and Voluntary Enlistment in the Vietnam Era." *Journal of the American Statistical Association* 86: 584–595.

Appy, Christian. 1993. *Working-class War*. Chapel Hill: University of North Carolina Press.

Armor, David J., Joseph B. Giacquinta, R. Gordon McIntosh, and Diana E. H. Russell. 1967. "Professors' Attitudes toward the Vietnam War." *Public Opinion Quarterly* 31: 159–175.

Asch, Beth, and James Hosek. 2004. "Looking to the Future: What Does Transformation Mean for Military Manpower and Personnel Policy?" In *The All-volunteer Force: Thirty Years of Service*, eds. Barbara Bicksler, Curtis Gilroy, and John T. Warner. Washington, D.C.: Brassey's. 257–296.

—— and Bruce Orvis. 1994. *Recent Recruiting Trends and Their Implications: Preliminary Analysis and Recommendations*. Santa Monica: RAND.

Atkeson, Lonna, and Randall Partin. 1995. "Economic and Referendum Voting: A Comparison of Gubernatorial and Senatorial Elections." *American Political Science Review* 89: 99–107.

Badillo, Gilbert, and G. David Curry. 1976. "The Social Incidence of Vietnam Casualties." *Armed Forces and Society* 2: 397–406.

Barnett, Arnold, Timothy Stanley, and Michael Shore. 1992. "America's Vietnam Casualties: Victims of a Class War?" *Operations Research* 40: 856–866.

Bartels, Larry, and John Zaller. 2001. "Presidential Vote Models: A Recount." *PS: Political Science and Politics* 34: 9–20.

Baskir, Lawrence, and William Strauss. 1978. *Chance and Circumstance*. New York: Knopf.

Baum, Matthew. 2004. "How Public Opinion Constrains the Use of Force: The Case of Operation Restore Hope." *Presidential Studies Quarterly* 34: 187–226.

—— and Samuel Kernell. 2001. "Economic Class and Popular Support for Franklin Roosevelt in War and Peace." *Public Opinion Quarterly* 65: 198–229.

Beck, Nathaniel, Jonathan Katz, and Richard Tucker. 1998. "Taking Time Seriously: Time-series-cross-section Analysis with a Binary Dependent Variable." *American Journal of Political Science* 42: 1260–1288.

Belknap, George, and Angus Campbell. 1951. "Political Party Identification and Attitudes toward Foreign Policy." *Public Opinion Quarterly* 15: 601–623.

Berinsky, Adam. 2007. "Assuming the Costs of War: Events, Elites, and American Public Support for Military Conflict." *Journal of Politics* 69: 975–997.

——. 2009. *America at War: Public Opinion during Wartime, from World War II to Iraq*. Chicago: University of Chicago Press.

—— and James N. Druckman. 2007. "Public Opinion Research and Support for the Iraq War." *Public Opinion Quarterly* 71(1): 126–141.

Bernard, H. Russell, Peter D. Killworth, Eugene C. Johnsen, Gene A. Shelley, and Christopher McCarty. 2001. "Estimating the Ripple Effect of a Disaster." *Connections* 24: 30–34.

Berney, Robert E., and Duane E. Leigh. 1974. "The Socioeconomic Distribution of American Casualties in the Indochina War: Implications for Tax Equity." *Public Finance Quarterly* 2: 223–235.

Berryman, Sue E. 1988. *Who Serves? The Persistent Myth of the Underclass Army*. Boulder: Westview.

Betts, Richard. 1991. *Soldiers, Statesmen, and Cold War Crises*. New York: Columbia University Press.

Bicksler, Barbara A., Curtis L. Gilroy, and John T. Warner, eds. 2004. *The All-volunteer Force: Thirty Years of Service*. Washington, D.C.: Brassey's.

Binkin, Martin, and Mark J. Eitelberg. 1982. *Blacks and the Military*. Washington, D.C.: Brookings Institution Press.

Binkin, Martin, and John D. Johnston. 1973. *All-volunteer Armed Forces: Progress, Problems, and Prospects*. Brookings Institution Report. Washington, D.C.: U.S. Government Printing Office.

Boettcher, William, and Michael Cobb. 2006. "Echoes of Vietnam? Casualty Framing and Public Perceptions of Success and Failure in Iraq." *Journal of Conflict Resolution* 50: 831–854.

Booth, Bradford. 2000. "The Impact of Military Presence in Local Labor Markets on Unemployment Rates, Individual Earnings, and Returns to Education." PhD diss., University of Maryland–College Park, Department of Sociology.

Brace, Paul, and Barbara Hinckley. 1992. *Follow the Leader*. New York: Basic Books.

Brandes, Lisa. 1994. "Public Opinion, International Security Policy, and Gender: The United States and Great Britain since 1945." PhD diss., Yale University, Department of Political Science.

Brandon, Heather. 1984. *Casualties: Death in Vietnam, Anguish and Survival in America*. New York: St. Martin's.

Brehm, John, and Wendy Rahn. 1997. "Individual-level Evidence for the Causes and Consequences of Social Capital." *American Journal of Political Science* 41: 999–1023.

Brody, Richard. 1991. *Assessing the President: The Media, Elite Opinion, and Public Support*. Palo Alto: Stanford University Press.

Brown, Charles. 1985. "Military Enlistments: What Can We Learn from Geographic Variation?" *American Economic Review* 75: 228–234.

Bueno de Mesquita, Bruce, and David Lalman. 1992. *War and Reason: Domestic and International Imperatives*. New Haven: Yale University Press.

———, James Morrow, Randolph Siverson, and Alastair Smith. 1999. "An Institutional Explanation of the Democratic Peace." *American Political Science Review* 93: 791–807.

———. 2003. *The Logic of Political Survival*. New York: Cambridge University Press.

———, Bruce, and Randolph Siverson. 1995. "War and the Survival of Political Leaders: A Comparative Study of Regime Types and Political Accountability." *American Political Science Review* 89: 841–855.

Burk, James. 1999. "Public Support for Peacekeeping in Lebanon and Somalia: Assessing the Casualties Hypothesis." *Political Science Quarterly* 114: 53–78.

Buzzanco, Robert. 1999. *Vietnam and the Transformation of American Life.* Oxford: Blackwell.

Calabresi, Guido, and Philip Bobbitt. 1978. *Tragic Choices.* New York: Norton.

Campbell, Angus, Philip Converse, Warren Miller, and Donald Stokes 1960. *The American Voter.* New York: Wiley.

Campbell, James. 1991. "The Presidential Surge and Its Midterm Decline, 1868–1988." *Journal of Politics* 53: 477–487.

——— and Joe Sumners. 1990. "Presidential Coattails in Senate Elections." *American Political Science Review* 84: 513–524.

Campbell, Kenneth. 2007. *A Tale of Two Quagmires: Iraq, Vietnam, and the Hard Lessons of War.* Boulder: Paradigm.

Capdevilla, Luc, and Daniele Voldman. 2006. *War Dead: Western Societies and the Casualties of War.* Edinburgh: Edinburgh University Press.

Card, David, and Thomas Lemieux. 2001. "Going to College to Avoid the Draft: The Unintended Legacy of the Vietnam War." *American Economic Review* 91: 97–102.

Carsey, Thomas, and Gerald Wright. 1998. "State and National Factors in Gubernatorial and Senatorial Elections." *American Journal of Political Science* 42: 994–1002.

Carson, Jamie, Jeffery Jenkins, David Rohde, and Mark Souva. 2001. "The Impact of National Tides and District-level Effects on Electoral Outcomes: The U.S. Congressional Elections of 1862–63." *American Journal of Political Science* 45: 887–898.

Casey, Steven. 2008. *Selling the Korean War: Propaganda, Politics, and Public Opinion in the United States, 1950–1953.* New York: Oxford University Press.

Cavin, Dennis. 2004. "Commentary." In *The All-volunteer Force: Thirty Years of Service,* eds. Barbara Bicksler, Curtis Gilroy, and John T. Warner. Washington, D.C.: Brassey's.

Chambers, John. 1975. *Draftees or Volunteers: A Documentary History of the Debate over Military Conscription in the United States.* New York: Garland.

Citrin, Jack. 1974. "Comment: The Political Relevance of Trust in Government." *American Political Science Review* 68: 973–988.

Clarke, Harold, and Marianne Stewart. 1994. "Prospections, Retrospections, and Rationality: The 'Bankers' Model of Presidential Approval Reconsidered." *American Journal of Political Science* 38: 1104–1123.

Cobb, Michael. 2007. "Dispelling Casualty Myths: Citizens' Knowledge and News Media's Coverage about Casualties." Paper presented at the annual meeting of the Midwest Political Science Association, Chicago.

Cohen, Eliot. 1985. *Citizens and Soldiers: The Dilemmas of Military Service.* Ithaca: Cornell University Press.

Coleman, James. 1990. *Foundations of Social Theory.* Cambridge, Mass.: Harvard University Press.

Conetta, Carl. 2004. "Disappearing the Dead: Iraq, Afghanistan, and the Idea of a 'New Warfare.'" Project on Defense Alternatives Research Monograph no. 9. February 18. http://www.comw.org/pda/0402rm9.html.

Congressional Budget Office. 1999. *What Does the Military "Pay Gap" Mean?* Washington, D.C.: Congress of the United States.

———. 2007. "The All-volunteer Military: Issues and Performance." Pub. no. 2960, July. http://www.cbo.gov/doc.cfm?index=8313.

Conover, Pamela Johnston, and Virginia Sapiro. 1993. "Gender, Feminist Consciousness, and War." *American Journal of Political Science* 37: 1079–1099.

Converse, Phillip. 1964. "The Nature of Belief Systems in Mass Publics." In *Ideology and Discontent*, ed. David Apter. New York: Free Press. 206–261.

Cooney, Patrick. 1984. "Journalists in Uniform: Military Public Affairs during the Grenadan Operation." Master's thesis, University of Kansas–Lawrence, Department of Journalism.

Cotton, Timothy. 1986. "War and American Democracy: Electoral Costs of the Last Five Wars." *Journal of Conflict Resolution* 30: 616–635.

Cowhey, Peter. 1993. "Domestic Institutions and the Credibility of International Commitments: Japan and the United States." *International Organization* 47: 299–326.

Crowley, Jocelyn Elise, and Theda Skocpol. 2001. "The Rush to Organize: Explaining Associational Formation in the United States, 1860s–1920s." *American Journal of Political Science* 45: 813–829.

Cymrot, Donald, and Michael Hansen. 2004. "Overhauling Enlisted Careers and Compensation." In *Filling the Ranks: Transforming the U.S. Military Personnel System*, ed. Cindy Williams. Cambridge, Mass.: MIT Press. 119–144.

Danzig, Richard. 1999. "The Big Three: Our Greatest Security Risks and How to Address Them." Syracuse University, Maxwell School of Citizenship and Public Affairs.

DeBoer, Larry, and B. Wade Brorsen. 1989. "The Demand for and Supply of Military Labor." *Southern Economic Journal* 55: 853–869.

Dixon, William. 1994. "Democracy and the Peaceful Settlement of International Conflict." *American Political Science Review* 88: 14–32.

Downs, Anthony. 1957. *An Economic Theory of Democracy*. New York: Harper and Row.

Druckman, James. 2001. The Implications of Framing Effects for Citizen Competence. *Political Behavior* 23: 225–256.

Edwards, Paul M. 2006. *The Korean War*. Westport, Conn.: Greenwood Press.

Eichenberg, Richard. 2003. "Gender Differences in Public Attitudes Toward the Use of Force by the United States, 1990–2003." *International Security* 28(1): 110–141.

Eichenberg, Richard. 2005. "Victory Has Many Friends: U.S. Public Opinion and the Use of Military Force 1981–2005." *International Security* 30: 140–178.

——— and Richard Stoll. 2006. "War President: The Approval Ratings of George W. Bush," with Matthew Lebo. *Journal of Conflict Resolution* 50: 783–808.

Erikson, Robert, Michael MacKuen, and James Stimson. 2002. *The Macro Polity*. New York: Cambridge University Press.

Faust, Drew Gilpin. 2008. *This Republic of Suffering: Death and the American Civil War*. New York: Knopf.

Feaver, Peter, and Christopher Gelpi. 2004. *Choosing Your Battles: American Civil-military Relations and the Use of Force*. Princeton: Princeton University Press.

——— and Richard Kohn, eds. 2001. *Soldiers and Civilians: The Civil-military Gap and American National Security*. Cambridge, Mass.: MIT Press.

Fendrich, James. 2003. "The Forgotten Movement: The Vietnam Anti-war Movement." *Sociological Inquiry* 73: 338–358.

Fiorina, Morris. 1976. "The Voting Decision: Instrumental and Expressive Aspects." *Journal of Politics* 38: 390–415.

———. 1981. *Retrospective Voting in American National Elections*. New Haven: Yale University Press.

Flynn, George Q. 1993. *The Draft: 1940–1973*. Lawrence: University of Kansas Press.

Foust, Brady, and Howard Botts. 1991. "Age, Ethnicity, and Class in the Vietnam War: Evidence from the Casualty File." *Vietnam Generation* 3: 22–31.

Foyle, Douglas. 1999. *Counting the Public In: Presidents, Public Opinion, and Foreign Policy*. New York: Columbia University Press.

Franklin, Benjamin. 1810. *Works of the Late Doctor Benjamin Franklin: Consisting of Memoirs of his Early Life, Written by Himself, Together with a Collection of his Essay, Humorous, Moral and Literary, Chiefly in the Manner of the Spectator*. Easton, Md.: Henry W. Gibbs.

Friedman, Matthew J. 2004. "Acknowledging the psychiatric cost of war." *New England Journal of Medicine* 351: 75–77.

———. 2005. "Veterans' mental health in the wake of war." *New England Journal of Medicine* 352: 1287–1290.

———. 2006. "Posttraumatic Stress Disorder Among Military Returnees From Afghanistan and Iraq." *American Journal of Psychiatry* 163: 586–593.

Fukuyama, Francis. 1995. *Trust: The Social Virtues and the Creation of Prosperity*. New York: Free Press.

Gartner, Scott Sigmund. 2004. "Making the International Local: The Terrorist Attack on the USS *Cole*, Local Casualties, and Media Coverage." *Political Communication* 21: 139–159.

———. 2008a. "The Multiple Effects of Casualties on Popular Support for War: An Experimental Approach." *American Political Science Review* 102: 95–106.

———. 2008b. "Secondary Casualty Information: Uncertainty, Female Casualties, and Wartime Support." *Conflict Management and Peace Science* 25: 98–111.

——— and Gary Segura. 1998. "War, Casualties, and Public Opinion." *Journal of Conflict Resolution* 42: 278–320.

———. 2000. "Race, Opinion, and Casualties in the Vietnam War." *Journal of Politics* 62: 115–146.

———. 2008. "All Politics Are Still Local: The Iraq War and the 2006 Midterm Elections." *PS: Political Science and Politics* 41: 95–100.

——— and Bethany Barratt. 2004. "War Casualties, Policy Positions, and the Fate of Legislators." *Political Research Quarterly* 53: 467–477.

———. Gary M. Segura, and Michael Wilkening. 1997. "All Politics Are Local: Local Losses and Individual Attitudes toward the Vietnam War." *Journal of Conflict Resolution* 41: 669–694.

Gast, Kelly. 2004. "The Political Manipulation of War Images." Typescript. University of Delaware.

Geary, James. 1991. *We Need Men: The Union Draft in the Civil War*. DeKalb: Northern Illinois University Press.

Gelb, Leslie. "The Essential Domino: American Politics and Vietnam." *Foreign Affairs* 50: 459–475.

Gelpi, Christopher, Peter D. Feaver, and Jason Reifler. 2005/2006. "Success Matters: Casualty Sensitivity and the War in Iraq." *International Security* 30: 7–46.

———. 2009. *Paying the Human Costs of War: American Public Opinion and Casualties in Military Conflicts*. Princeton: Princeton University Press.

———, Jason Reifler, and Peter Feaver. 2007. "Iraq the Vote: Retrospective and Prospective Policy Judgments on Candidate Choice and Casualty Tolerance." *Political Behavior* 29: 151–174.

Gerber, Alan. 1998. "Estimating the Effects of Campaign Spending on Senate Election Outcomes Using Instrumental Variables." *American Political Science Review* 92: 401–411.

Gerhardt, James. 1971. *The Draft and Public Policy: Issues in Military Manpower Procurement, 1945–1970*. Columbus: Ohio State University Press.

Gifford, Brian. 2005. "Combat Casualties and Race: What Can We Learn from the 2003–2004 Iraq Conflict?" *Armed Forces and Society* 31: 201–225.

Gillens, Martin. 1988. "Gender and Support for Reagan: A Comprehensive Model of Presidential Approval." *American Journal of Political Science* 32: 19–49.

Gilliam, Franklin, and Shanto Iyengar. 2000. "Prime Suspects: The Influence of Local Television News on the Viewing Public." *American Journal of Political Science* 44: 560–573.

Ginzberg, Eli. 1959. *The Ineffective Soldier: Lessons for Management and the Nation*. New York: Columbia University Press.

Goff, Stanley, and Robert Sanders, with Clark Smith. 1982. *Brothers: Black Soldiers in the Nam*. Novato, Calif.: Presidio.

Goodwin, Robert C. 1951. "Manpower Problems in Defense Production." *Annals of the American Academy of Political and Social Science* 278: 137–146.

Gowa, Joanne. 1998. "Politics at the Water's Edge: Parties, Voters, and the Use of Force Abroad." *International Organization* 52: 307–324.

Graeff, Peter, and Guido Mehlkop. 2006. "Excavating a Force That Drives Income Inequality: Rethinking and Analyzing the Link between Military Participation Ratio and Inequality." *Journal of Political and Military Sociology* 34: 257–280.

Grandstaff, Mark. 1996. "Making the Military American: Advertising, Reform, and the Demise of an Antistanding Military Tradition, 1945–1955." *Journal of Military History* 60: 299–323.

Green, Don, and Jonathan Krasno. 1988. "Salvation for the Spendthrift Incumbent: Reestimating the Effects of Campaign Spending in House Elections." *American Journal of Political Science* 32: 884–907.

———. 1990. "Rebuttal to Jacobson's 'New Evidence for Old Arguments.'" *American Journal of Political Science* 34: 363–372.

Griffith, Robert. 1982. *Men Wanted for the U.S. Army: America's Experience with an All-volunteer Army between the World Wars*. Westport, Conn.: Greenwood.

Grose, Christian, and Bruce Oppenheimer. 2007. "The Iraq War, Partisanship, and Candidate Attributes: Explaining Variation in Partisan Swing in the 2006 U.S. House Elections." *Legislative Studies Quarterly* 32: 531–557.

Guzman, Ralph. 1969. "Mexican-American Casualties in Vietnam." PhD diss., University of California–Santa Cruz, Dept. of Political Science.

Hahn, Harlan. 1970. "Correlates of Public Sentiments about War: Local Referenda on the Vietnam Issue." *American Political Science Review* 64: 1186–1198.

Hays, Samuel H. 1967. "Military Conscription in a Democratic Society." *Army Magazine* (February): 31–41. Reprinted in Chambers (1975, 505–515).

Helmer, John. 1974. *Bringing the War Home: The American Soldier in Vietnam and After.* New York: Free Press.

Hetherington, Marc. 1998. "The Political Relevance of Political Trust." *American Political Science Review* 92: 791–808.

Hibbs, Douglas, Jr. 2000. "Bread and Peace Voting in U.S. Presidential Elections." *Public Choice* 104: 149–180.

———, Douglas Rivers, and Nicholas Vasilatos. 1982. "The Dynamics of Political Support for American Presidents among Occupational and Partisan Groups." *American Journal of Political Science* 26: 312–332.

Hogan, Paul. 2004. "Overview of the Current Personnel and Compensation System." In *Filling the Ranks: Transforming the U.S. Military Personnel System*, ed. Cindy Williams. Cambridge, Mass.: MIT Press. 29–54.

Hoge, Charles W., Jennifer L. Auchterlonie, and Charles S. Milliken. 2006. "Mental health problems, use of mental health services, and attrition from military service after returning from deployment to Iraq or Afghanistan." *Journal of the American Medical Association* 295: 1023–1032.

Hoiberg, Anne. 1980. "Military Staying Power." In *Combat Effectiveness: Cohesion, Stress, and the Volunteer Military*, ed. Sam Sarkesian, Beverly Hills: Sage. 212–243.

Holm, Tom. 1996. *Strong Hearts, Wounded Souls: Native American Veterans of the Vietnam War.* Austin: University of Texas Press.

Holsti, Ole. 1992. "Public Opinion and Foreign Policy: Challenges the Almond-Lippman Consensus." *International Studies Quarterly* 36: 439–466.

———. 2004. *Public Opinion and American Foreign Policy*. Ann Arbor: University of Michigan Press.

Howell, William, and Douglas Kriner. 2007. "Bending so as Not to Break: What the Bush Presidency Reveals about Unilateral Action." In *The Polarized Presidency of George W. Bush*, eds. George Edwards and Desmond King. New York: Oxford University Press. 96–144.

——— and Jon Pevehouse. 2005. "Presidents, Congress, and the Use of Force." *International Organization* 59: 209–232.

———. 2007. *While Dangers Gather: Congressional Checks on Presidential War Powers.* Princeton: Princeton University Press.

Huelfer, Evan Andrew. 2003. *The "Casualty Issue" in American Military Practice: The Impact of World War I.* Westport, Conn.: Praeger.

Humphries, Stan. 2001. "Who's Afraid of the Big, Bad Firm? The Impact of Economic Scale on Political Participation." *American Journal of Political Science* 45: 678–699.

Huntingon, Samuel. 1957. *The Soldier and the State: The Theory and Politics of Civil-military Relations.* Cambridge, Mass.: Harvard University Press.

Hurwitz, John, and Mark Peffley. 1987. "The Means and Ends of Foreign Policy as Determinants of Presidential Support." *American Journal of Political Science* 2: 236–258.

Iyengar, Shanto, and Donald Kinder. 1987. *News That Matters: Television and American Public Opinion*. Chicago: University of Chicago Press.

Iyengar, Shanto, and Adam Simon. 1993. "News Coverage of the Gulf Crisis and Public Opinion." *Communication Research* 20: 365–383.

Jacobs, Lawrence, and Robert Shapiro. 2000. *Politicians Don't Pander: Political Manipulation and the Loss of Democratic Responsiveness*. Chicago: University of Chicago Press.

Jacobson, Gary. 1978. "The Effects of Campaign Spending in Congressional Elections." *American Political Science Review* 72: 769–783.

———. 1985. "Money and Votes Reconsidered: Congressional Elections, 1972–1982." *Public Choice* 47: 7–62.

———. 1990. "The Effects of Campaign Spending in House Elections: New Evidence for Old Arguments." *American Journal of Political Science* 34: 334–362.

———. 2004. *Politics of Congressional Elections*. New York: Pearson Longman.

———. 2006. *A Divider, Not a Uniter: George W. Bush and the American People*. New York: Longman.

——— and Samuel Kernell. 1981. *Strategy and Choice in Congressional Elections*. New Haven: Yale University Press.

Janowitz, Morris. 1960. *The Professional Soldier: A Social and Political Portrait*. Glencoe, Ill.: Free Press.

———, ed. 1964. *The New Military: Changing Patterns of Organization*. New York: Sage Foundation.

———. 1965. *Sociology and the Military Establishment*. In collaboration with Roger Little. New York: Sage Foundation.

——— and Charles C. Moskos Jr. 1979. "Five Years of the All-volunteer Force: 1973–1978." *Armed Forces and Society* 5(2): 171–218.

Jennings, M. Kent, and Gregory Markus. 1977. "The Effect of Military Service on Political Attitudes: A Panel Study." *American Political Science Review* 71: 131–147.

Jentleson, Bruce. 1992. "The Pretty Prudent Public: Post Post-Vietnam American Opinion on the Use of Military Force." *International Studies Quarterly* 36: 49–74.

——— 2002. "Use of Force Dilemmas: Policy and Politics." In *Eagle Rules? Foreign Policy and American Primacy in the Twenty-first Century*, ed. Robert J. Lieber. Upper Saddle River, N.J.: Prentice Hall. 266–281.

———. and Rebecca Britton. 1998. "Still Pretty Prudent: Post–Cold War American Public Opinion on the Use of Military Force." *Journal of Conflict Resolution* 42: 395–417.

Kage, Rieko. 2005. "Defeat and Reconstruction: Explaining the Rise of Civic Engagement in the Wake of Wars." PhD diss., Harvard University, Department of Government.

Kane, Tim. 2006. "Who Are the Recruits? The Demographic Characteristics of Military Enlistment, 2003–2005." CDA06–09. Washington, D.C.: Heritage Foundation.

Kant, Immanuel. 1983 [1795]. *Perpetual Peace and Other Essays*, trans. Ted Humphrey. Indianapolis: Hackett.

Karol, David, and Edward Miguel. 2007. "The Electoral Cost of War: Iraq Casualties and the 2004 U.S. Presidential Election." *Journal of Politics* 69: 633–648.

Karsten, Peter. 1982. "Consent and the American Soldier: Theory versus Reality." *Parameters* 12: 42–49.

Katznelson, Ira, and Martin Shefter. 2002. *Shaped by War and Trade: International Influences on American Political Development*. Princeton: Princeton University Press.

Kaufmann, Karen, and John Petrocik. 1999. "The Changing Politics of American Men: Understanding the Source of the Gender Gap." *American Journal of Political Science* 43: 864–887.

Kennett, Lee. 1987. *G.I.: The American Soldier in World War II*. New York: Scribner.

Kernell, Samuel. 1978. "Explaining Presidential Popularity." *American Political Science Review* 72: 506–522.

Kick, Edward, Byron Davis, and Jeffrey Kentor. 2006. "A Cross-national Analysis of Militarization and Inequality." *Journal of Political and Military Sociology* 34: 319–338.

Kinder, Donald, and Lynn Sanders. 1996. *Divided by Color: Racial Politics and Democratic Ideals*. Chicago: University of Chicago Press.

Kindsvatter, Peter. 2003. *American Soldiers: Ground Combat in the World Wars, Korea, and Vietnam*. Lawrence: University of Kansas Press.

King, Martin Luther, Jr. 1968a. "The Casualties of the War in Vietnam." In *Speeches by the Reverend Doctor Martin Luther King, Jr. about the War in Vietnam*. Annandale, Va.: Turnpike.

———. 1968b. *The Trumpet of Conscience*. New York: Harper and Row.

Kittinger, Robert. 2007. "Web 2.0: Social Behavior of Internet Users." Typescript. http://www.auburnmedia.com/pdf/kittinger_web_2.0.pdf.

Klarevas, Louis. 2002. "The 'Essential Domino' of Military Operations: American Public Opinion and the Use of Force." *International Studies Perspectives* 3: 417–437.

———, Christopher Gelpi, and Jason Reifler. 2006. "Correspondence: Casualties, Polls, and the Iraq War." *International Security* 31: 186–198.

Koch, Michael, and Scott Sigmund Gartner. 2005. "Casualties and Constituencies: Democratic Accountability, Electoral Institutions, and Costly Conflicts." *Journal of Conflict Resolution* 49: 874–894.

Kohn, Margaret. 2004. *Brave New Neighborhoods: The Privatization of Public Space*. New York: Routledge.

Kohut, Andrew, and Robert Toth. 1995. "Intervention in the Post–Cold War World: A Public Perspective." In *Managing Conflict in the Post–Cold War World: The Role of Intervention*. Aspen: Aspen Institute.

Kosiak, Steven. 2008. *Analysis of the FY 2009 Defense Budget Request*. Washington, D.C.: Center for Strategic and Budgetary Assessments.

Kriner, Douglas L. 2006. "Examining Variance in Presidential Approval: The Case of FDR in World War II." *Public Opinion Quarterly* 70: 23–47.

———, and Francis X. Shen. 2007. "Iraq Casualties and the 2006 Senate Elections." *Legislative Studies Quarterly* 32: 507–530.

———. 2009. "Limited War and American Political Engagement." *Journal of Politics* 71: 1514–1529.

———, and William G. Howell. n.d. *Congressional Leadership of War Opinion: Conditional influence and the risk of "backlash."* Typescript, Boston University.

Krosnick, John, and Laura Brannon. 1993. "The Impact of the Gulf War on the Ingredients of Presidential Evaluations: Multidimensional Effects of Political Involvement." *American Political Science Review* 87: 963–975.

Kryder, Daniel. 2000. *Divided Arsenal: Race and the American State during World War II*. New York: Cambridge University Press.

Kull, Steven. 1995. "What the Public Knows That Washington Doesn't." *Foreign Policy* 101: 102–115.

——— and I. M. Destler. 1999. *Misreading the Public: The Myth of a New Isolationism*. Washington, D.C.: Brookings Institution Press.

——— and Clay Ramsay. 1994. *U.S. Public Attitudes on U.S. Involvement in Bosnia*. College Park: Program on International Policy Attitudes, University of Maryland.

———. 2001. "The Myth of the Reactive Public: American Public Attitudes on Military Fatalities in the Post–Cold War Period." In *Public Opinion and the International Use of Force*, eds. Phillip Everts and Pierangelo Isneria. London: Routledge, 205–228.

Larson, Eric. 1996. *Casualties and Consensus: The Historical Role of Casualties in Domestic Support for U.S. Military Operations*. Santa Monica: RAND.

——— and Bogdan Savych. 2005. *American Public Support for U.S. Military Interventions from Mogadishu to Baghdad*. Santa Monica: RAND.

Lau, Richard, Thad Brown, and David Sears. 1978. "Self-interest and Civilians' Attitudes toward the Vietnam War." *Public Opinion Quarterly* 42: 464–483.

Laurence, Janice H. 2004. "The All-volunteer Force: A Historical Perspective." Santa Monica: RAND.

Levi, Margaret. 1996. "The Institution of Conscription." *Social Science History* 20: 133–167.

Lewis-Beck, Michael, and Tom Rice. 1992. *Forecasting Elections*. Washington, D.C.: CQ Press.

Lippmann, Walter. 1922. *Public Opinion*. New York: Macmillan.

Lipset, Seymour Martin. 1996. *American Exceptionalism: A Double-edged Sword*. New York: Norton.

Lunch, William, and Peter Sperlich. 1979. "American Public Opinion and the War in Vietnam." *Western Political Quarterly* 32: 21–44.

Luttwak, Eric. 1996. "A Post-heroic Military Policy." *Foreign Affairs* 75: 33–44.

MacKuen, Michael B., Robert S. Erikson, and James A. Stimson. 1992. "Peasants or Bankers? The American Electorate and the U.S. Economy." *American Political Science Review* 86: 597–611.

Mansfield, Edward, and Jon Pevehouse. 2003. "Trade Blocs, Trade Flows, and International Conflict." *International Organization* 54: 775–808.

Maoz, Zeev, and Bruce Russett. 1993. "Normative and Structural Causes of Democratic Peace, 1946–1986." *American Political Science Review* 87: 624–638.

Martin, Lisa. 1993. "Credibility, Costs, and Institutions: Cooperation on Economic Sanctions." *World Politics* 45: 406–432.

Mayer, Albert J., and Thomas Ford Hoult. 1955. "Social Stratification and Combat Survival." *Social Forces* 34: 155–159.

Mayhew, David. 2005. "Wars and American Politics." *Perspectives on Politics* 3: 473–493.

Mazur, Allan. 1995. "Was Vietnam a Class War?" *Armed Forces and Society* 21: 455–459.

Mazur, Diane H. 2003. "Why Progressives Lost the War When They Lost the Draft." 32 *Hofstra Law Review* 553: 563–564.

McAdam, Doug, and Ronnelle Paulsen. 1993. "Specifying the Relationship between Social Ties and Activism." *American Journal of Sociology* 99: 640–667.

McAdam, Doug, and Yang Su. 2002. "The War at Home: Antiwar Protests and Congressional Voting, 1965 to 1973." *American Sociological Review* 67: 696–721.

McCarty, Nolan, Keith T. Poole, and Howard Rosenthal. 2006. *Polarized America: The Dance of Ideology and Unequal Riches*. Cambridge, Mass.: MIT Press.

McCormick, James, and Eugene Witkopf. 1990. "Bipartisanship, Partisanship, and Ideology in Congressional-executive Foreign Policy Relations, 1947–1988." *Journal of Politics* 52: 1077–1100.

McGrath, John J. 2007. *The Other End of the Spear: The Tooth-to-Tail Ratio (T3R) in Modern Military Operations*. The Long War Series Occasional Paper 23. Fort Leavenworth, Kans.: Combat Studies Institute Press.

Meernik, James. 1995. "Congress, the President, and the Commitment of the U.S. Military." *Legislative Studies Quarterly* 20: 377–392.

Mettler, Suzanne. 2002. "Bringing the State Back in to Civic Engagement: Policy Feedback: Effects of the GI Bill for World War II Veterans." *American Political Science Review* 96: 351–365.

Miller, Arthur H. 1974. "Political Issues and Trust in Government: 1964–1970." *American Political Science Review* 68: 951–972.

Miller, Jake C. 1979. *The Black Presence in American Foreign Affairs*. Washington, D.C.: University Press of America.

———. 2000. "African American Males in Foreign Affairs." *Annals of the American Academy of Political and Social Science* 569: 29–41.

Miller, Joanne, and Jon Krosnick. 1996. "News Media Impact on the Ingredients of Presidential Evaluations: A Program of Research on the Priming Hypothesis." In *Political Persuasion and Attitude Change*, eds. Dianna Mutz, Paul Sniderman, and Richard Brody. Ann Arbor: University of Michigan Press. 79–100.

———. 2000. "News Media Impact on the Ingredients of Presidential Evaluations: Politically Knowledgeable Citizens Are Guided by a Trusted Source." *American Journal of Political Science* 44: 301–315.

Miller, Warren, and Donald Stokes. 1963. "Constituency Influence in Congress." *American Political Science Review* 57: 45–56.

Modell, John, and Timothy Hagerty. 1991. "The Social Impact of War." *Annual Review of Sociology* 17: 205–224.

Modigliani, Andre. 1972. "Hawks and Doves, Isolationism, and Political Distrust: An Analysis of Public Opinion on Military Policy." *American Political Science Review* 66: 960–978.

Monroe, Alan. 1998. "Public Opinion and Public Policy, 1980–1993." *Public Opinion Quarterly* 62: 6–28.

Moody, James. 2006. "Fighting a Hydra: A Note on the Network Embeddedness of the War on Terror." *Structure and Dynamics: eJournal of Anthropological and Related Sciences* 1, Article 9. http://escholarship.org/uc/item/7x3881bs.

Moon, Penelope Adams. 2003. "'Peace on Earth-Peace in Vietnam': The Catholic Peace Fellowship and Antiwar Witness, 1964–1976." *Journal of Social History* 36: 1033–1057.

————. 2008. "Loyal Sons and Daughters of God? American Catholics Debate Catholic Antiwar Protest." *Peace & Change* 33: 1–30.

Moore, Will, and David Lanoue. 2003. "Domestic Politics and U.S. Foreign Policy: A Study of Cold War Conflict Behavior." *Journal of Politics* 65: 376–396.

Morgan, T. Clifton, and Sally Campbell. 1991. "Domestic Structure, Decisional Constraints, and War." *Journal of Conflict Resolution* 35: 187–211.

Morgan, T. Clifton, and Valerie L. Schwebach. 1992. "Take Two Democracies and Call Me in the Morning: A Prescription for Peace?" *International Interactions* 17: 305–320.

Moskos, Charles C. 1970. *The American Enlisted Man: The Rank and File in Today's Military.* New York: Russell Sage Foundation.

————. 1977. "From Institution to Occupation." *Armed Forces and Society* 4: 41–50.

————. 2000. "Toward a Postmodern Military: The United States as a Paradigm." In *The Postmodern Military,* eds. Charles C. Moskos, John Allen Williams, and David R. Segal. New York: Oxford University Press. 14–31.

————. 2001. What Ails the All-volunteer Force: An Institutional Perspective. *Parameters: US Army War College* 31: 29–47.

———— and John Sibley Butler. 1996. *All That We Can Be: Black Leadership and Racial Integration the Army Way.* New York: Basic Books.

———— and Frank R. Wood, eds. 1988. *The Military: More than Just a Job?* Washington, D.C.: Pergamon-Brassey's.

Mueller, John. 1973. *War, Presidents, and Public Opinion.* New York: Wiley.

————. 1994. *Policy and Opinion in the Gulf War.* Chicago: University of Chicago Press.

————. 2005. "The Iraq Syndrome." *Foreign Affairs* 84(6): 44–54.

National Research Council. 2003. *Attitudes, Aptitudes, and Aspirations of American Youth: Implications for Military Recruitment.* Washington, D.C.: National Academies Press.

Newman, Katherine S. 2000. *No Shame in My Game: The Working Poor in the Inner City.* New York: Vintage.

Nicholson, Stephen, and Robert Howard. 2003. "Framing Support for the Supreme Court in the Aftermath of *Bush v. Gore.*" *Journal of Politics* 65: 676–695.

Nincic, Miroslav, and Dianna Nincic. 2002. "Race, Gender, and War." *Journal of Peace Research* 39: 547–568.

Nye, Joseph S. 1997. "Introduction: The Decline of Confidence in Government." In *Why People Don't Trust Government,* eds. J. S. Nye Jr., P. D. Zelikow, and D. C. King Cambridge, Mass.: Harvard University Press. 1–18.

Office of the Secretary of Defense. 2006. "*2006 Population Representation in the Military Services.*" Washington, D.C.: Author.

O'Hare, William, and Bill Bishop. 2006. "U.S. Rural Soldiers Account for a Disproportionately High Share of Casualties in Iraq and Afghanistan." Carsey Institute Fact Sheet. http://www.carseyinstitute.unh.edu/publications/FS_ruralsoldiers_06.pdf.

Oliver, J. Eric. 1999. "The Effects of Metropolitan Economic Segregation on Local Civic Participation." *American Journal of Political Science* 43: 186–212.

————. 2000. "City Size and Civic Involvement in Metropolitan America." *American Political Science Review* 94: 361–373.

———. 2001. *Democracy in Suburbia*. Princeton: Princeton University Press.

———. 2003. "Mental Life and the Metropolis in Suburban America." *Urban Affairs Review* 39: 228–253.

Oneal, John, and Bruce Russett. 1997. "The Classical Liberals Were Right: Democracy, Interdependence, and Conflict, 1950–1985." *International Studies Quarterly* 41: 267–294.

Ornelas, Charles, and Michael Gonzalez. 1971. "The Chicano and the War: An Opinion Survey in Santa Barbara." *Journal of Chicano Studies* 2: 23–35.

Page, Benjamin, and Robert Shapiro. 1992. *The Rational Public: Fifty Years of Trends in Americans' Policy Preferences*. Chicago: University of Chicago Press.

——— and Glenn Dempsey. 1987. "What Moves Public Opinion?" *American Political Science Review* 81: 23–44.

Peterson, Paul E., ed. 1994. *The President, Congress, and the Making of U.S. Foreign Policy*. Norman: University of Oklahoma Press.

Pogue, Forrest C. 1973. *George C. Marshall: Organizer of Victory 1943–1945*, 2d ed. New York: Viking Adult.

Pols, Hans, and Stephanie Oak. 2007. "War & Military Mental Health: The US Psychiatric Response in the 20th Century." *American Journal of Public Health* 97: 2132–2142.

Preston, Samuel, and Emily Buzzell. 2006. "Mortality of American Troops in Iraq." Population Studies Council Working Paper Series PSC 06–01.

Putnam, Robert. 1993. *Making Democracy Work: Civic Traditions in Modern Italy*. Princeton: Princeton University Press.

———. 2000. *Bowling Alone: The Collapse and Revival of American Community*. New York: Simon and Schuster.

Quinley, Harold. 1970. "The Protestant Clergy and the War in Vietnam." *Public Opinion Quarterly* 34: 43–52.

Ray, James Lee. 1995. *Democracy and International Conflict: An Evaluation of the Democratic Peace Proposition*. Columbia: University of South Carolina Press.

Reddick, L. D. 1949. "The Negro Policy of the United States Army, 1775–1945." *Journal of Negro History* 34: 9–29.

Reiter, Dan, and Allan Stam. 2002. *Democracies at War*. Princeton: Princeton University Press.

Richards, Carl. 1995. *The Founders and the Classics*. Cambridge, Mass.: Harvard University Press.

Riker, William, and Peter Ordeshook. 1968. "A Theory of the Calculus of Voting." *American Political Science Review* 62: 25–42.

Roberts, Joel. 2007. "Small Towns Hit Hard by War." *Associated Press* (February 20). http://www.cbsnews.com/stories/2007/02/20/national/main2494309.shtml.

Robinson, John, and Solomon Jacobsen. 1968. "American Public Opinion about Vietnam." *Peace Research Society International Papers* 10: 69.

Rosenberg, Milton, Sidney Verba, and Philip Converse. 1970. *Vietnam and the Silent Majority: The Dove's Guide*. New York: Harper and Row.

Rosenstone, Steven, and John Mark Hansen. 1993. *Mobilization, Participation, and Democracy in America*. New York: Macmillan.

Rostker, Bernard. 2006. *I Want YOU: The Evolution of the All-volunteer Force*. Santa Monica: RAND.

Roth-Douquet, Kathy, and Frank Schaeffer. 2006. *AWOL: The Unexcused Absence of America's Upper Classes from Military Service—and How It Hurts Our Country*. New York: Harper Collins.

Russett, Bruce. 1990. *Controlling the Sword: The Democratic Governance of National Security*. Cambridge, Mass.: Harvard University Press.

———. 1990–1991. "Doves, Hawks, and U.S. Public Opinion." *Political Science Quarterly* 105: 515–538.

———. 1993. *Grasping the Democratic Peace*. Princeton: Princeton University Press.

——— and Miroslav Nincic. 1976. "American Opinion on the Use of Military Force Abroad." *Political Science Quarterly* 91: 411–431.

——— and John Oneal. 2001. *Triangulating Peace: Democracy, Interdependence, and International Organizations*. New York: Norton.

Sampson, Robert, Jeffrey Morenoff, and Thomas Gannon-Rowley. 2002. "Assessing 'Neighborhood Effects': Social Processes and New Directions in Research." *Annual Review of Sociology* 28: 443–478.

Sandel, Michael. 2000. "What Money Can't Buy: The Moral Limits of Markets." In *Tanner Lectures on Human Values 21*, ed. Grethe Peterson. Salt Lake City: University of Utah Press. 89–122.

Schaefer, Janet, and Marjorie Allen. 1944. "Class and Regional Selection in Fatal Casualties in the First 18–23 Months of World War II." *Social Forces* 23: 165–169.

Schultz, Kenneth. 1998. "Domestic Opposition and Signaling in International Crises." *American Political Science Review* 92: 829–844.

———. 1999. "Do Democratic Institutions Constrain or Inform? Contrasting Two Institutional Perspectives on Democracy and War." *International Organization* 53: 233–266.

———. 2001. *Democracy and Coercive Diplomacy*. New York: Cambridge University Press.

Seal, Karen H., Daniel Bertenthal, Christian R. Miner, Saunak Sen, and Charles Marmar. "Bringing the war back home: mental disorders among 103,788 US veterans returning from Iraq and Afghanistan seen at Department of Veteran Affairs facilities." *Archives of Internal Medicine* 167: 476–482.

Segal, David R. 1986. "Measuring the Institutional/Occupational Change Thesis." *Armed Forces and Society* 1: 351–376.

———. 1989. *Recruiting for Uncle Sam: Citizenship and Military Manpower Policy*. Lawrence: University Press of Kansas.

———. 2000. "Stratification and Labor Market Dynamics in the American Military." In *The Oxford Companion to Military History*, ed. John Whiteclay Chambers. New York: Oxford University Press. 695–697.

——— and Mady Wechsler Segal. 2004. "America's Military Population." *Population Bulletin* 59. Washington, D.C.: Population Reference Bureau.

Shafer, Michael D. 1990. "The Vietnam-Era Draft: Who went, who didn't, and why it matters." In *The Legacy: The Vietnam War in the American Imagination*, ed. D. Michael Shafter. Boston: Beacon Press. 57–79.

Siegel, Pascale Combelles. 2003. "Is U.S. Casualty Reporting Suffering from Double Standards?" Washington, D.C.: Foreign Policy in Focus (April 15).

Skocpol, Theda. 1992. *Protecting Soldiers and Mothers: The Political Origins of Social Policy in the United States.* Cambridge, Mass.: Harvard University Press.

———. 1999. "How Americans Became Civic." In *Civic Engagement in American Democracy*, eds. Theda Skocpol and Morris Fiorina. Washington, D.C.: Brookings Institution Press. 27–80.

———, Marshall Ganz, and Ziad Munson. 2000. "Nation of Organizers: The Institutional Origins of Civic Voluntarism in the US." *American Political Science Review* 94: 527–546.

———, Ziad Munson, Andrew Karch, and Bayliss Camp. 2002. "Patriotic Partnerships: Why Great Wars Nourished American Civic Voluntarism." In *Shaped by War and Trade: International Influences on American Political Development*, eds. Ira Katznelson and Martin Shefter. Princeton: Princeton University Press. 134–180.

Sledge, Michael. 2005. *Soldier Dead: How We Recover, Identify, Bury, and Honor Our Military Fallen.* New York: Columbia University Press.

Sobel, Richard. 1993. *Public Opinion in U.S. Foreign Policy: The Controversy over Contra Aid.* Lanham, Md.: Rowan Littlefield.

———. 1998. "Portraying American Public Opinion toward the Bosnia Crisis." *Harvard International Journal of Press/Politics* 3: 16–33.

———. 2001. *The Impact of Public Opinion on U.S. Foreign Policy since Vietnam: Constraining the Colossus.* New York: Oxford University Press.

Sparrow, Bartholomew. 1997. *From the Outside In: World War II and the American State.* Princeton: Princeton University Press.

———. 2002. "Limited Wars and the Attenuation of the State: Soldiers, Money, and Political Communication in World War II, Korea, and Vietnam." In *Shaped by War and Trade: International Influences on American Political Development*, eds. Ira Katznelson and Martin Shefter. Princeton: Princeton University Press. 267–300.

Squire, Peverill. 1992. "Challenger Quality and Voting Behavior in Senate Elections." *Legislative Studies Quarterly* 17: 247–263.

———. 1995. "Candidates, Money, and Voters: Assessing the State of Congressional Elections Research." *Political Research Quarterly* 48: 891–917.

Steel, Robert. 2004. "The All-volunteer Force: An Employer's Perspective." In *The All-volunteer Force: Thirty Years of Service*, eds. Barbara Bicksler, Curtis Gilroy, and John T. Warner. Washington, D.C.: Brassey's. 169–190.

Stein, Arthur, and Bruce Russett. 1980. "Evaluating War: Outcomes and Consequences." In *Handbook of Political Conflict: Theory and Research*, ed. T. R. Gurr. New York: Macmillan. 399–424.

Strawn, Thomas. 2004. "The War for Talent in the Private Sector." In *Filling the Ranks: Transforming the U.S. Military Personnel System*, ed. Cindy Williams. Cambridge, Mass.: MIT Press. 69–92.

Suchman, Edward, Rose Goldsen, and Robin M. Williams Jr. 1953. "Attitudes toward the Korean War." *Public Opinion Quarterly* 17: 171–184.

Tarrow, Sidney. 1994. *Power in Movement: Social Movements and Contentious Politics.* New York: Cambridge University Press.

Teixeira, Ruy. 1992. *The Disappearing American Voter*. Washington, D.C.: Brookings Institution Press.

Tetlock, Philip E. 2003. "Thinking the unthinkable: sacred values and taboo cognitions." *Trends in Cognitive Sciences* 7: 320–324.

Thucydides. 1982 [431 B.C.]. *History of the Peloponnesian War*, trans. Richard Crawley. New York: Modern Library.

Tocqueville, Alexis de. 1990 [1840]. *Democracy in America*, trans. Henry Reeve. New York: Vintage.

U.S. Government Accountability Office. 2006a. *Military Personnel: DOD Needs an Oversight Framework and Standards to Improve Management of Its Casualty Assistance Program*. GAO-06-1010. Washington, D.C.: Author.

———. 2006b. *Military Recruiting: DOD and Services Need Better Data to Enhance Visibility over Recruiter Irregularities*. GAO-06-846. Washington, D.C.: Author.

U.S. National Advisory Commission on Selective Service. 1967. *In Pursuit of Equity: Who Serves When Not All Serve?* Washington, D.C.: U.S. Government Printing Office.

U.S. Senate Committee on Military Affairs. 1918. "The Delay in the Publication of Casualty Lists of the American Expeditionary Forces of the Army." December 3. Washington, D.C.: Government Printing Office.

Useem, Michael. 1973. *Conscription, Protest, and Social Conflict: The Life and Death of a Draft Resistance Movement*. New York: Wiley.

Vagts, Alfred. 1945a. "Battle and Other Combatant Casualties in the Second World War, I." *Journal of Politics* 7: 256–294.

———. 1945b. "Battle and Other Combatant Casualties in the Second World War, II." *Journal of Politics* 7: 411–438.

Verba, Sidney, and Richard A. Brody. 1970. "Participation, Policy Preferences, and the War in Vietnam." *Public Opinion Quarterly* 34: 325–332.

———, Edwin Parker, Norman Nie, Nelson Polsby, Paul Ekman, and Gordon Black. 1967. "Public Opinion and the War in Vietnam." *American Political Science Review* 61: 317–333.

——— and Norman Nie. 1972. *Participation in America*. New York: Harper and Row.

——— Kay Lehman Schlozman, and Henry Brady. 1995. *Voice and Equality: Civic Voluntarism in American Politics*. Cambridge, Mass.: Harvard University Press.

——— and Norman Nie. 1993. "Citizen Activity: Who Participates? What Do They Say?" *American Political Science Review* 87: 303–318.

Voeten, Erik, and Paul Brewer. 2006. "Public Opinion, the War in Iraq, and Presidential Accountability." *Journal of Conflict Resolution* 50: 809–830.

Warner, John, and Beth Asch. 2001. "The Record and Prospects of the All-volunteer Military in the United States." *Journal of Economic Perspectives* 15: 169–192.

Weigley, Russell F. 1969. *The American Military: Readings in the History of the Military in American Society*. Reading, Mass.: Addison-Wesley.

Westheider, James E. 1999. *Fighting on Two Fronts: African Americans and the Vietnam War*. New York: New York University Press.

White, Halbert. 1980. "A Heteroskedasticity-consistent Covariance Matrix Estimator and a Direct Test for Heteroskedasticity." *Econometrica* 48: 817–838.

Wildavsky, Aaron. 1966. "The Two Presidencies." *Trans-Action* 4: 7–14.

Williams, Cindy, ed. *Filling the Ranks: Transforming the U.S. Military Personnel System.* Cambridge, Mass.: MIT Press.

Williams, David. 1998. *Rich Man's War: Class, Caste, and Confederate Defeat in the Lower Chattahoochee Valley.* Athens: University of Georgia Press.

Williamson, Thad. 2002. "Sprawl, Politics, and Participation: A Preliminary Analysis." *National Civic Review* 91: 235–244.

Willis, John. 1975. "Variations in State Casualty Rates in World War II and the Vietnam War." *Social Problems* 22: 558–568.

Wilson, George. 1987. *If You Survive: From Normandy to the Battle of the Bulge to the End of World War II, One American Officer's Riveting True Story.* New York: Ballantine.

Wilson, Thomas C. 1995. "Vietnam-era Military Service: A Test of the Class-bias Theory." *Armed Forces and Society* 21(3) (Spring): 461–471.

Wittkopf, Eugene. 1990. *Faces of Internationalism: Public Opinion and American Foreign Policy.* Durham: Duke University Press.

Wolfinger, Raymond, and Stephen J. Rosenstone. 1980. *Who Votes?* New Haven: Yale University Press.

Woodruff, Todd, Ryan Kelty, and David R. Segal. 2006. Propensity to Serve and Motivation to Enlist among American Combat Soldiers. *Armed Forces and Society* 32(3): 353–366.

Zaller, John. 1992. *The Nature and Origins of Mass Opinion.* New York: Cambridge University Press.

———. 1994a. "Elite Leadership of Mass Opinion: New Evidence from the Gulf War." In *Taken by Storm: Media, Public Opinion, and U.S. Foreign Policy in the Gulf War,* eds. W. Lance Bennett and David L. Paletz, 186–209. Chicago: University of Chicago Press.

———. 1994b. "Strategic Politicians, Public Opinion, and the Gulf Crisis." In *Taken by Storm: Media, Public Opinion, and U.S. Foreign Policy in the Gulf War,* eds. W. L. Bennett and D. Paletz. Chicago: University of Chicago Press. 250–274.

Zeitlin, M., K. G. Lutterman, and J. W. Russell. 1973. "Death in Vietnam: Class, Poverty, and the Risks of War." *Politics and Society* 3: 313–328.

Index

Page numbers followed by "*f*" and "*t*" refer to figures and tables, respectively.